e-Business

STRATEGIC THINKING AND PRACTICE

second edition

e-Business
STRATEGIC THINKING AND PRACTICE

Brahm Canzer
John Abbott College and McGill University

HOUGHTON MIFFLIN COMPANY
Boston   New York

This book is lovingly dedicated to my late brother, Saul Canzer.

Vice President, Publisher: Charles Hartford
Vice President, Editor-in-Chief: George Hoffman
Associate Editor: Jessica Carlisle
Senior Project Editors: Nancy Blodget, Audrey Bryant
Editorial Assistant: Sean McGann
Senior Composition Buyer: Sarah Ambrose
Senior Art and Design Coordinator: Jill Haber
Manufacturing Coordinator: Renee Ostrowski
Executive Marketing Manager: Steven W. Mikels
Marketing Associate: Lisa Boden

Cover image: © Chad Baker/Getty Images

Printed in the U.S.A.

Library of Congress Control Number: 2004114514

ISBN: 0-618-51988-2

23456789-MP-09 08 07 06 05

brief contents

v

contents

Chapter 6	**Researching and Analyzing Opportunities for Growth 147**

Chapter 7	**Understanding Online Communication and Behavior 175**

Module III Implementing the e-Business Plan 207

preface

As we continue our study of online commercial activity with this second edition of *e-Business: Strategic Thinking and Practice*, the Internet has grown in size to approximately 500 million regular users. Although North America and Europe remain dominant geographic centers of activity, Internet growth is rapidly spreading to all regions of the world, changing the way people and businesses communicate and make decisions. Stock markets, especially the NASDAQ, have partially recovered from the dramatic declines suffered in 2000–2003, and indications are that the next stage in Internet-related economic development is under way.

The Internet has clearly emerged as a powerful global force that is influencing, and sometimes significantly changing, strategic behavior in many organizations. A number of observers, including Harvard Business School professor Michael Porter, suggest that the Internet simply provides a new communications tool that can be used to improve conventional business practices, by, for instance, building closer relationships with customers, suppliers, and employees. Others, however, believe that the Internet has precipitated a radical change in the traditional business paradigm, opening up new opportunities to those who are willing to venture forth. Wherever the truth lies, it is clear that the first wave of Internet activity has been dramatic, creating many e-business successes as well as many failures that we can learn from. This early body of knowledge, which is the focus of this book, can provide important lessons to those concerned with strategic planning and a better understanding of the influences the Internet continues to have on a wide range of social issues today.

Purpose of the Book

e-Business: Strategic Thinking and Practice, Second Edition presents a wide variety of topics important to understanding e-business strategy, including environmental factors that can influence e-business and online behaviors, research methodologies in e-business planning, and important marketing, management, and financial issues relevant to the preparation of an e-business plan. Furthermore, the text takes a strategic planning approach in order to help structure this information so that it can be readily applied to actual business situations and to the preparation of an e-business plan.

The use of websites to market products and organizations, web-enabled customer relationship management and supply chain management software solutions that improve operations and increase efficiencies, and e-commerce ventures that can reach global customers 24/7 are only a few of the popular e-business strategies available to decision-makers. However, for many strategists, e-business is a field characterized by complexity, requiring a map to help sort and simplify this growing body of new vocabulary, concepts, and thinking. Furthermore, an ideal map would also help lead the intrepid travelers to an understanding of how opportunities might be converted into concrete business actions in their own organizations. This text is an attempt to create such a map.

e-Business: Strategic Thinking and Practice, Second Edition presents a comprehensive overview of the fundamental concepts, vocabulary, and strategic thinking taking place in e-business practice today. Furthermore, the text explores these at all three primary organizational levels of the firm—corporate, strategic business unit (SBU), and operational—and within small as well as larger enterprises. By providing a learning environment that illustrates how strategic e-business plans can be developed at any level of the firm, learners are guided toward the objective of preparing their own plan. This might be an independent start-up plan or one that involves the introduction of e-business strategies into an existing business operation. Strategists are assisted in this effort by a variety of text features and supplemental materials, several of which are new to the second edition.

A Comprehensive Case Study: The appendix to the text provides students with a thoroughly updated comprehensive case study of a real community e-business firm that caters to the student populations of individual campuses. After establishing itself in the marketplace, the firm has recently merged with a larger community site looking to expand the services provided to the same target audience. Students are taken through the start-up phase of the firm and left with the open invitation to advise management on what they would do to build on the synergies of the two brands.

Tutorial for Preparing a Case Study Report: The website provides a revised online tutorial to help guide students through a recommended structure and the steps necessary for properly preparing a case study report.

Additional e-Business Case Studies: Because cases studies help bridge the gap between theory and application, the second edition website provides more case studies to further develop student understanding about a variety of e-business problems and opportunities. New cases are added regularly, and all are kept up-to-date to reflect the changing conditions facing various industry decision-makers as they attempt to incorporate e-business thinking into their business practices. Shorter as well as longer comprehensive cases will provide a selection of material to answer the needs of students at all academic levels, including the graduate level.

A Model Business Plan: New to the second edition, the model e-business plan is offered on the student website and provides students with a template that can be used to launch an actual B2B firm. Students are presented with suggestive and guiding questions at the conclusion of the current e-business plan and asked to make revisions to the plan for the future.

Tutorial for Preparing an e-Business Plan: The website provides a revised online tutorial to help guide students through a recommended structure and the steps necessary for properly preparing an e-business plan. Ideas for developing a new business or creating an e-business division as an adjunct to a firm's existing operations are also presented. Students may choose to create their own e-business plan based on one of these suggestions or on one of their own.

e-Business Journal Digest: The monthly digest presents a selection of articles drawn from accessible publications and those websites deemed most worthwhile to keep students informed about the fast-changing e-business environment.

Tutorial for Preparing a Journal Article Report: This new online tutorial guides students through a recommended structure and the steps necessary for properly preparing a report on a journal article.

Research Gateway to e-Business Resources: This portal connects e-business researchers to a variety of online sources of information. Resources are tagged and categorized according to the chapters and topics within each chapter. This value-added benefit provides both students and instructors with a highly versatile and up-to-date source of information with which to conduct research for e-business planning, case studies, and other course work.

Web Appendix: The Internet and Related Technologies: In the second edition, we have updated and transferred the entire Chapter 3 of the first edition to the website. This allows us to expand other e-business strategic planning topics in the textbook while still providing a solid introductory section on the history and development of the Internet in the form of a Web appendix.

Intended Audience

This text is written primarily for learners at the college and undergraduate university levels, where e-business is finding its way into the curriculum as a single-semester marketing or management course, as a stream of several courses comprising a major in e-business, and as a full certificate, diploma, or degree program focusing on e-business decision-making and strategic thinking.

The integration of theoretical content and strategic thinking makes the text ideal for an introductory e-business course and makes it a logical complementary second text if a general (principles) business textbook has been used earlier in a program of study. It will also be of great interest to instructors seeking an alternative small-business management text for e-business entrepreneurs.

Programs at the college and university levels are typically found in these academic areas: business (management and marketing), computer technology, and website development. Business programs tend to focus on strategic thinking about e-business opportunities for established firms, and especially entrepreneurial dot-com start-ups that receive much public attention. Computer technology programs are generally concerned with hardware, networks, and engineering issues. Web development programs (diplomas) are more often found at the college level and as shorter programs (certificates) at both universities and colleges where the focus is on teaching students how to use Web-authoring tools for designing and maintaining websites. These programs often produce entrepreneurs who launch independent small businesses providing services to clients as well as employees of firms responsible for website activity.

An additional target audience for this textbook is businesspeople interested in an academic overview of e-business and strategic approaches to planning for their organizations. The book and website materials provide an excellent foundation and resources for corporate training seminars and online learning programs. Business learners can use the text to develop their organizational e-business plan.

Features of the Book

e-Business: Strategic Thinking and Practice, Second Edition is designed to help learners understand and organize e-business developments to date and to provide a structure that can facilitate the assimilation of new e-business information that appears each day. The newest edition continues to emphasize and promote an analytical and critical approach to understanding strategic decision-making so that learners emerge from their course better prepared to create real plans for their own organizations.

Text Content and Organization

Module I: A Framework for Understanding e-Business   Module I presents a map for exploring e-business and understanding how business activity on the Internet has evolved into what it is today. This framework focuses attention on several important subject areas that help lay the groundwork for strategic business planning, which we examine later in Modules II and III. In Chapter 1 we define and explore the world of e-business and fundamental models and industry participants. We also focus on several examples of e-business strategies in managerial, marketing, and financial situations in order to illustrate how e-business is applied across primary functional areas. In Chapter 2 we take a closer look at the major environmental forces, such as globalization, that affect e-business planning and practices. In Chapter 3 we look at the complex and controversial ethical, legal, and social concerns that have emerged as use of Internet technology and e-business continues to impact societies around the world.

Module II: Strategic Business Planning for the Internet   Module II introduces the strategic business planning process in greater detail. We focus attention on the three key components of strategic planning: research, analysis, and the formulation of an e-business plan. In Chapter 4 we present a structure for organizing and understanding the variety of e-business models and how each model serves to direct the entire organization in its search to generate revenues and create competitive advantage online. In Chapter 5 we examine these activities from the point of view of strategists working at each of the three primary organizational levels of the firm: corporate, division/strategic business unit, and operating/functional levels. In Chapter 6 we detail the research- and information-gathering process, and then in Chapter 7 we explore online communication and user behaviors. The module presents a broad base of understanding about what e-business models and their strategies can help the firm achieve and how they can be incorporated within the existing organization and business plan. Managerial details and implications inherent in any e-business plan are addressed in the third module.

Module III: Implementing the e-Business Plan   In Module III we link the strategic-thinking concepts generated thus far in the e-business planning process with the specific marketing, management, and financial plans of action. These three functional components are universally recognized as the core foundations for any strategic business plan. Therefore, we incorporate them into our study of the design and creation of the complete e-business plan while also examining related issues that affect e-business strategy. Each chapter helps e-business planners answer questions related to each of these core subject areas. The final chapter in this unit brings closure to the entire planning process by looking at how the e-business plan can be integrated into an organization's current structure, and then controlled, measured, and evaluated for future decision-making. The entire chapter focuses on the experiences of a small e-business and the steps they took to implement and control their current plan of action.

Chapter Pedagogy

Each chapter provides a clear and accessible writing style and a variety of pedagogical techniques that facilitate both academic knowledge and students' ability to apply what they have learned. Case study reports, exercises, and especially the research and preparation of an e-business plan as a group or individual course assignment tie theory and practice together for students.

Learning Objectives   Each chapter is organized around a set of Learning Objectives that introduce and structure the content that students are about to study.

Key Glossary Terms   Important terms in each chapter are identified in boldface, and definitions are highlighted in the margin for easy reference.

Inside e-Business   Each chapter-opening vignette focuses on a theme associated with that chapter. Many of these have been either updated or replaced in the second edition. New examples of featured companies include eBay, Google, and Amazon.

Case Study: Return to Inside e-Business   This feature at the end of each chapter provides additional information related to the opening vignette and builds on the content of the chapter. Questions for discussion help generate class debate and offer direction for preparing a case study report.

e-Business Insight   To help highlight and explore important issues, each chapter contains two *e-Business Insight* boxes that focus on relevant topics, many of which have been updated or replaced in the second edition. For example, "Can Socially Undesirable Online Behaviors Be Stopped?" and "Spam Is More Than A Nuisance" are featured in Chapter 3, "Ethical, Legal, and Social Concerns." In the second edition, a question for discussion has been added to each box to encourage classroom discussion and to explicitly connect the box to chapter concepts.

Go to the Web: e-Business Online   New to the second edition, this feature is denoted by a marginal icon and sends students to the website for more information and examples of business models, creating customer value, and more.

Chapter Review   Near the end of each chapter a *Summary* presents the main ideas contained in the chapter in a format that follows the Learning Objectives. To further reinforce what students learned, the Chapter Review includes a set of *Review Questions* that focus on chapter definitions and concepts and a set of *Discussion Questions* designed to encourage students' critical thinking and writing about chapter topics.

Building Skills for Career Success   A feature called *Building Skills for Career Success* appears near the end of every chapter. All exercises in this section provide detailed introductory material along with a student assignment. The five exercises include *Exploring the Internet, Developing Critical Thinking Skills, Building Team Skills, Researching Different Careers,* and *Improving Communication Skills.*

Exploring Useful Websites   Every chapter ends with a feature called *Exploring Useful Websites.* This feature is a comprehensive list of websites that provide information related to the topics discussed in the chapter.

A Fully Integrated Package

The *e-Business: Strategic Thinking and Practice* text is the centerpiece of a package of ancillary materials created to assist instructors and learners. An instructor website and the *Instructor's Resource Manual with Test Bank* contain a variety of tools tied to the text and designed to facilitate instructor-led classes as well as online learning environments. The student website is integrated with the text structure and content, thereby creating an expanded, richer learning environment for students to explore.

Instructor Website

The instructor website contains a variety of content designed to enhance the learning and teaching experience. Instructors will find PowerPoint slides, class lecture outlines, quizzes, and a variety of other resources related to the *Instructor's Resource Manual with Test Bank* content. All content is written and frequently updated by the main text's author.

Student Website

The student website is an extension of the text and is updated on a regular basis. Like the instructor website, all content is written by the main text's author. Additional cases, tutorials for preparing case study reports and e-business plans, and a variety of resources for conducting research and keeping up-to-date are presented in an easy-to-use environment to assist students. The *Go to the Web* marginal icon periodically directs students to the website for valuable information.

Instructor's Resource Manual with Test Bank

The *Instructor's Resource Manual with Test Bank* is written by the main text's author and has been thoroughly updated for the second edition. It features the following items for each chapter: Notes from the Author; Learning Objectives; Brief Chapter Outline; Comprehensive Lecture Outline; Answers to Text Review Questions, Discussion Questions, and Case Study Questions; suggested answers to assigned questions; and ideas about using the *Building Skills for Career Success* exercises. The Test Bank has been revised and updated, and contains a variety of essay, true/false, and multiple-choice questions. Each question is tied to a learning objective and a text page reference. Answers are provided.

HM Testing

This computerized version of the *Test Bank* allows instructors to select, edit, and add questions, and to generate randomly selected questions to produce a test master for easy duplication. Online Testing and Gradebook functions allow instructors to administer tests via their local area network or the World Wide Web, set up classes, record grades from tests or assignments, analyze grades, and produce class and individual statistics. This program can be used on both PCs and Macintosh computers.

Acknowledgments

This text would not have been possible without the considerable contributions of many talented people. I would first like to thank the following reviewers whose suggestions and comments helped shape the final product:

Maryam Alavi
Emory University

David Ambrosini
Cabrillo College

Lloyd W. Bartholome
Utah State University

Brent Beal
Louisiana State University

Joseph Bell
University of Northern Colorado

Tom Bryant
Rutgers University

John R. Bugado
National University

John W. Clarry
College of New Jersey

Wilfred T. Demoranville
Kishwaukee Community College

Wolfgang Grassl
Hillsdale College

Chris Grevenson
DeVry College of Technology

John Hafer
University of Nebraska at Omaha

Kathy Harris
Northwestern Oklahoma State University

John Heinemann
Keller Graduate School

Susan K. Jones
Ferris State University

Keith C. Jones
Lynchburg College

F. Scott Key
Pensacola Junior College

Rob K. Larson
Luther College

Tammy Lee
*Rochester Community and
Technical College*

Roger McMillian
Mineral Area College

Carla Meeske
University of Oregon

Robert Mills
Utah State University

Jim Newton
Baker College

Carolyn Predmore
Manhattan College

Sandra S. Reid
Dallas Baptist University

Linda Salchenberger
Loyola University

Srivatsa Seshadri
University of Nebraska

Nagaraj Sivasubramaniam
Binghamton University

Kenton B. Walker
University of Wyoming

Dennis Williams
Penn College

In addition, I would like to express my gratitude to the Houghton Mifflin team: Editor-in-Chief George Hoffman, Associate Editor Jessica Carlisle, Senior Production Editors Nancy Blodget and Audrey Bryant, and copyeditor Paul Bodine.

Finally, I would like to express my love and gratitude to my wife, Carole; son, Matthew; and daughter, Sarah, whose encouragement and presence made this project possible.

Brahm Canzer

About the Author

Brahm Canzer currently teaches business management courses to John Abbott College students in Montreal. He is also an adjunct lecturer at McGill University's MBA program and Concordia University's undergraduate and graduate programs in e-Marketing. During his teaching career he has also taught undergraduate-level marketing courses at Concordia University and corporate learning programs under the auspices of the University of Toronto. Professor Canzer received his PhD (1995) and MBA (1976) from Concordia University in Montreal. With a strong interest in the use of Internet technology in education, he was among the first pioneers to design and teach MBA courses online for Simon Fraser University. He is a contributing author to several business textbooks and editor of the Canadian edition of the Houghton Mifflin textbook *Business* (Pride, Hughes, Kapoor, Canzer). He has helped create a variety of web-based supplemental learning materials in academic and corporate learning settings. Professor Canzer also provides consulting services to businesses seeking assistance as they explore web-based opportunities and solutions for improving their operations.

A Framework for Understanding e-Business

Module I presents a map for exploring e-business and understanding how business activity on the Internet has evolved into what it is today. This framework focuses your attention on several important subject areas that help lay the groundwork for the strategic business planning that we examine in Modules II and III. First, in Chapter 1, we define and explore the world of e-business and its fundamental models and industry participants. We also focus on several examples of e-business strategies in managerial, marketing, and financial situations to illustrate how these strategies are applied across primary functional areas. In Chapter 2 we take a closer look at the major environmental forces, such as globalization, that affect e-business planning and practices. Finally, in Chapter 3 we look at the complex ethical, legal, and social concerns that have emerged as Internet technology and e-business continue to make an impact on societies around the world.

> **CHAPTER 1**
> Exploring the World
> of e-Business

> **CHAPTER 2**
> Environmental Forces
> Affecting Planning and
> Practice

> **CHAPTER 3**
> Ethical, Legal, and Social
> Concerns

chapter 1

Exploring the World of e-Business

INSIDE
e-business

AOL—Poster-Child of the Dot-Com Bubble?

The history of America Online Inc. (AOL) reflects much of the excitement and disappointment experienced by investors, employees, and analysts who participated in the spectacular first phase of e-business growth and development. Co-founded by Steve Case in 1985, AOL (**www.aol.com**) started out as simply one of many service firms providing customers with a way to connect to the Internet through their telephone line. Remarkably, only fifteen years later, AOL entered the new millennium as the world's leading online service firm, with more than 20 million paying subscribers and a phenomenal revenue growth rate. AOL grew mainly by acquiring smaller firms, which like itself provided Internet connection to subscribers in various regions of the United States. But by merging in 2001 with the world's leading media company, Time Warner Inc. (**www.timewarner.com**), AOL successfully transformed itself into an Internet colossus. With combined revenues of $36 billion, the new firm, AOL Time Warner Inc., was touted as "the world's first media and communications company of the Internet age." However, by the fall of 2003, failure to realize new revenue growth from the $106 billion acquisition of Time Warner Inc. and the dramatic fall in stock value in excess of 60 percent, led to Steve Case's resignation as chairman, a transfer of control to the Time Warner side of management, and the dropping of AOL from the corporate name. The bubble had burst.

The union of AOL and Time Warner illustrates the fast-paced approach to growth and the stock market fever that were common during this first wave of e-business development. Management was able to capitalize on the rapid increase in the firm's stock market value and use it to acquire other businesses that might have been competitors with desirable clients or who offered other resources deemed valuable to strategic plans for growth. For instance, AOL's stock had risen from 50 cents in 1993 to about $50 in 2001 when the merger with Time Warner took

place. By exchanging shares in each other's companies for the newly formed merged AOL Time Warner Inc., managers were able to acquire the resources of each other's firms without using cash. Generally, as long as the newly acquired firm continued to contribute to expected revenue growth, the stock market value of the firm continued to increase. Much of the explanation for the Internet stock market bubble, which inflated values until the bubble began bursting in the spring of 2000, can be understood by investors' willingness to pay for expected growth in companies. As long as the mergers resulted in positive indications of continued growth, investors seemed willing to push stock values ever higher in anticipation of realizing real earnings some day in the future.

Partnerships and mergers can be quicker and less expensive ways for firms to grow. By merging with AOL, Time Warner gained instant access to the huge client list of AOL subscribers—all of which were potential customers of Time Warner content. By merging with Time Warner, AOL enhanced its offerings of Internet content, since it was now able to provide its customers with some of Time Warner's rich variety of entertaining and informative products, such as CNN online news services and journals. By the same token, Time Warner found a partner that could deliver its internationally appealing content to a large existing audience—the audience that AOL had built up through earlier mergers and acquisitions, as well as by introducing its internally developed products and services. For instance, in 1998 AOL acquired ICQ from Israel-based Mirabilis, the world's largest communications community, comprising more than 50 million registered users. ICQ's free access service allows users to locate and chat with individuals and groups online regardless of which Internet service provider they use. More than two-thirds of ICQ registrants live outside the United States, and so AOL's acquisition of ICQ has helped the company open the door to customers worldwide. Given that people living in North America are still the dominant users of the Internet, this strategic merger continues to make sense in the race to enlist customers globally and build brand recognition on the Internet. And given that AOL community chat rooms remain a focus of AOL's strategy, the product continues to be a contributing asset to the firm.[1]

AOL is an example of a firm that can trace its history only as far back as the start of commercial activity on the Internet. Like other well-known e-business firms such as Yahoo! (**www.yahoo.com**), eBay (**www.ebay.com**), and MP3 (**www.mp3.com**), AOL owes its very existence to the Internet. Quite simply, without the Internet, there would be no AOL, Yahoo!, or MP3.

Most firms, on the other hand, have developed or will develop an Internet presence by gradually transferring some of their business activities to the Internet. This was the route taken by Time Warner, which had placed some of its entertainment and information content online well before its merger with AOL. Providing services on the Internet delivers added value to a firm's customers, an important goal for any business. For reasons that we will examine more closely throughout this textbook, many businesses will eventually find themselves seeking opportunities to conduct more of their affairs on the Internet. Given that multiple research sources such as the Computer Industry Almanac Inc. (**www.c-i-a.com/**), the CIA's World Factbook (**www.cia.gov/cia/publications/factbook/**), and Nielsen//NetRatings (**www.nielsen-netratings.com**) suggest that the global Internet population will surpass 1 billion users in 2005 and that major markets in North America and Europe have already reached or are close to passing the 60 percent participation rate, it is clear that the Internet will continue to play an important role in a variety of future business situations.[2]

As illustrated in Figure 1.1, there is a fundamental division between businesses that invented themselves on the Internet, such as AOL, and previously established firms that have transferred only some of their activities to the Internet, such as the Gap (**www.gap.com**). Firms with no history other than the one they have defined on the Internet make their business decisions with a clear focus on the online world. They are not concerned about interfering with other, established business activities. At the other extreme, firms like the Gap are very much concerned about how developing their Internet presence will affect their current retail store sales, costs, customer relations, and so forth.

This chapter examines the development of both types of businesses and provides a structure for understanding how and why the business activities finding their way onto the Internet will change the way businesses function in the future. We also take a closer look at how firms conduct business on the Internet and what growth opportunities may be available to both new and existing firms. But before we explore this new and exciting arena for business competition, let's begin by building a framework that can help us understand how all of this came about.

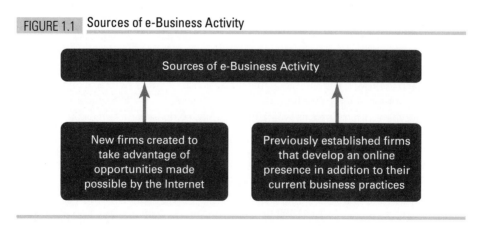

FIGURE 1.1   Sources of e-Business Activity

Defining e-Business

e-business (electronic-business)
The organized effort of individuals to produce and sell, for a profit, products and services that satisfy society's needs through the facilities available on the Internet.

Business can be defined as the organized effort of individuals to produce and sell, for a profit, products and services that satisfy society's needs. In a simple sense, then, **e-business (electronic-business)** can be defined as the organized effort of individuals to produce and sell, for a profit, products and services that satisfy society's needs *through the facilities available on the Internet.* And just as we distinguish between any *individual* business and the general term *business,* which refers to all such efforts within a society, we similarly recognize the *individual* e-business, such as AOL, as well as the general concept of *e-business.* IBM's e-business website (**www.ibm.com/ebusiness/**) defines this concept as the transformation of key business activities through the use of Internet technologies.[3]

It is this transformation of key business activities, such as buying and selling products and services, building better supplier and customer relationships, and improving general business operations, that has stimulated so much excitement about this new and rapidly evolving business environment.

Sometimes people use the term *e-commerce* instead of *e-business.* In a strict sense, *e-business* refers to all business activities conducted on the Internet by an individual firm or industry. In contrast, **e-commerce** is a part of e-business; the term refers only to the activities involved in buying and selling online. These activities may include identifying suppliers, selecting products or services, making purchase commitments, completing financial transactions, and obtaining service.[4]

e-commerce
A part of e-business; the term refers only to the activities involved in buying and selling online, which may include identifying suppliers, selecting products or services, making purchase commitments, completing financial transactions, and obtaining service.

We generally use the term *e-business* because of its broader definition and scope.

Organizing e-Business Resources

Every business must properly organize a variety of *human, material, informational,* and *financial* resources in order to conduct business successfully, as illustrated in Figure 1.2. Many highly specialized forms of these resources are required if the firm is to succeed on the Internet. For example, in the area of human resources, people who can design, create, and maintain websites are only a small segment of the specialists required by businesses that are considering an Internet presence. The material resources required include specialized computers, equipment, software, and high-speed Internet connection lines. Computer programs that track the efficiency of the firm's website operations and that offer insight into customers' interactions with the website are generally among the specialized informational resources required. For firms whose primary emphasis is online, financial resources, the money required to start the firm and allow it to grow, usually reflect greater participation by individual entrepreneurs and venture capitalists, instead of conventional financial sources like banks.

The difficulties and even failure of so many early Internet-based start-up firms during the industrywide downturn in 2000 can best be understood in terms of the reasons why most new businesses fail: *management and financial problems.* In general, the managements of these companies failed to build

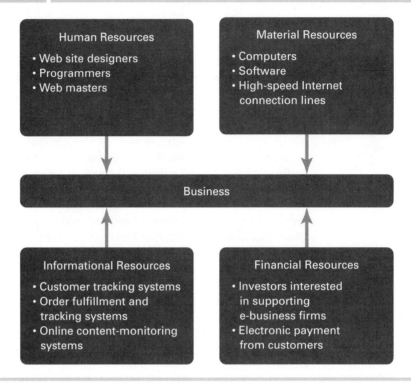

FIGURE 1.2   Combining e-Business Resources

(*Source:* From William M. Pride, Robert J. Hughes, and Jack R. Kapoor, *Business,* Seventh Edition. Copyright © 2002 by Houghton Mifflin Company. Reprinted with permission.)

sufficient continuous revenue flows to keep the company going before their start-up financing was consumed. In some cases, customers failed to materialize in sufficient numbers once the website and the necessary infrastructure to run the e-business were created. Building a website is not that difficult an objective to achieve. Building a web identity and drawing regular users is a far more difficult task.

Of course, the more complicated question is why the management of any particular firm failed to organize the necessary resources and then use them properly to assure the long-term viability of the business. The answer to this question is specific to each organization; however, it is probably safe to say that many of the early enthusiastic entrepreneurs and investors were simply unprepared for what would be required. Information changed quickly and was often unknown. While learning through practical experience, managers made mistakes—and these mistakes were often fatal if the company's financial backers were unwilling to continue funding the business development process. Those firms that have survived the first industry shakeout and others that are now entering the field for the first time can benefit from the knowledge we all have gained by studying past successes and failures.

Satisfying Needs Online

The customer needs that are satisfied by Internet firms may be unique to the Internet environment, or this environment may be an improvement over conventional business practice. For example, AOL provides Internet access, browser services, chat rooms, databases, and exclusive Time Warner entertainment content, among other services, to its customers. Amazon.com gives customers anywhere in the world access to the same virtual store of books, CDs, DVDs, and so forth. And at eBay's global auction site, customers can, for a fee, buy and sell almost anything. Even your college's website satisfies informational needs for people in the area who are interested in courses and educational programs. In each of these examples, customers receive a *value-added* service through the Internet.

Internet users can now access print media, such as newspapers and magazines, and radio and television programming at a time and place that is convenient to them. In addition to offering such a wide selection of content, the Internet provides the opportunity for *interaction*. In other words, communication between the online program and the viewer is an active two-way street. In contrast to the passive position customers occupy vis-à-vis traditional media, Internet customers can respond to Internet programming by requesting more information about a product or by posing specific questions, which may lead to a purchase decision. In any case, the ability to engage the viewer in two-way communication means that e-businesses can have a more involved, and therefore more valuable, viewer. For example, CNN.com (**www.cnn.com**) and other news content sites encourage dialogue among viewers in chat rooms as well as exchanges with the writers of articles posted to the site. Live televised programming such as talk shows includes viewers' questions, which can be sent by e-mail.

The Internet allows customers to specify the content they receive. For example, they can custom-design daily online newspapers and magazines that contain only articles that are of interest to them. Knowing what is of interest to an individual customer allows an Internet firm to direct appropriate, *smart advertising*, to that customer. For example, someone who wants to read articles on the New York Yankees might be a potential customer for products and services related to baseball. Advertising that is likely to be of interest to the viewer has a greater chance of resulting in a sale. For the advertiser, knowing that its advertisements are being intelligently directed to the most likely customers represents a value-added service.

Creating e-Business Profit

Generating profit is both a fundamental goal of business and a measurement of business success. Profits are instrumental in rewarding employees and investors for their skills and efforts. Profits also help pay for the development of the new products that will eventually be needed to replace older and outdated items whose sales are declining. Strategically, firms can increase their profits by either increasing sales revenue or reducing expenses. Internet-based technology provides a wide variety of ways to accomplish both objectives. Although much of this textbook is about developing e-business strategies, let's just examine a few examples in the following sections.

Revenue Growth

Online merchants have the advantage of being able to reach a global customer base twenty-four hours a day, seven days a week. The opportunity to shop on the Internet is virtually unrestricted, as the Internet removes such barriers to retail shopping as limited store operating hours and the inability of some customers to get to a conveniently located outlet. The removal of the barriers that may keep some customers from shopping at conventional retail stores explains the ever-increasing expectations for the sales revenue of e-businesses like Amazon.com (**www.amazon.com**), Barnes & Noble (**www.barnesandnoble.com**), and The Walt Disney Company (**www.disney.com**).

Intelligent informational resource systems are another major factor in generating sales revenue for Internet firms. Such systems store information about each customer's purchases, along with a variety of other information about the buyer's preferences. Using this information, the system can assist the customer in making a purchase decision the next time he or she visits the website. For example, if the customer has bought a Shania Twain or Dave Matthews compact disc in the past, the system might suggest CDs by similar artists.

Interestingly, customers may use a website simply to browse and then delay making the actual purchase until they are in the firm's physical store. For instance, when buying clothing, customers often consider it critical to try on a garment before they purchase it. A site like **Gap.com** thus serves not only online customers but also those who eventually come to Gap stores to finalize their selection. Similarly, **Toyota.com** can provide basic comparative information for shoppers so they are better prepared for their visit to an automobile showroom. Thus, while in certain situations customers may not make a purchase online, the existence of the firm's website and the services it provides may lead to increased sales in the firm's physical store. For example, according to a study by Ipsos-Reid, online traffic analysis from Canada, the United States, Australia, and the United Kingdom supports the value of the Internet as a research tool for new and used car buying, as well as a method for contacting auto manufacturers. The study found that 63 percent of online Canadians reported that they have used the Internet to search online for vehicle prices, features, or other information.[5]

revenue stream
The source of revenue flowing into the firm, such as revenues earned from selling online or selling advertising.

A fundamental concern for online firms is how to select, develop, and nurture sources of revenue. Each source of revenue flowing into the firm is referred to as a **revenue stream**. Since revenue streams provide the dollars needed to operate the firm, developing them is a primary strategic issue for any business. Furthermore, the simple redirection of existing revenue to an online stream is not desirable. For example, shifting revenues received from customers inside a real store to revenues received from those same customers online does not create any real new revenue for the firm. A web-based business may not generate sufficient new revenues to offset the high start-up costs of going online for a long time. Investors examine the probability of the company's reaching the targeted revenue projections in the e-business plan and assess the firm's current and long-term value on the basis of these numbers. This orientation helps to explain why an e-business such as Amazon.com could command high investor confidence in the absence of any real profit during its

toyota.com

(*Source:* Photo © Kevin Necessary)

start-up phase. Investors take a longer-term view of the level of profit that they hope will materialize when a firm like Amazon.com reaches its full potential and settles down to stable revenue streams and expenses.

Typically, e-business revenue streams come from the sale of products and services, from advertising placed on the businesses' webpages, and from subscription fees charged for access to online services and content. For example, AOL's principal revenue streams include subscription fees paid by members who connect to the Internet through local dial-in connections and advertising revenues earned on AOL websites. AOL competes with Microsoft, Yahoo!, Google, and dozens of other major online sites.

Many Internet firms that distribute content, such as magazine and newspaper articles, generate revenue primarily from advertising and from commissions from the sellers of products linked to the site. Online shopping malls may create communities of related vendors of electronic, computer hardware and software, health foods, fashion items, and other products. Sites like Petco.com (**www.petco.com**) and Petsmart.com (**www.petsmart.com**) compete in the large market for pet supplies. WebMD (**www.webmd.com**), the world-renowned Mayo Clinic (**www.mayoclinic.com**), and other health information sites provide information about remedies, disease, and a variety of health-related topics and issues. In many cases, the vendors share online sales revenues with the site owners.

Expense Reduction

Expense reduction is the other major way in which e-business can help increase a firm's profitability. Providing online access to information that customers want can reduce the cost of dealing with customers. For example, most airlines, like American (**www.aa.com**) and Continental (**www.continental.com**) routinely provide updated scheduling and pricing information, as well as promotional material, on their websites. This can reduce the costs of dealing with customers through a call center operated by employees and of mailing brochures, which may be outdated within weeks or easily misplaced by customers. Sprint PCS (**www.sprintpcs.com**) maintains an extensive website where potential customers can learn more about cell phone products and services. Current customers can access personal account information, send e-mail questions to customer service, and purchase additional products or services. With such extensive online services, Sprint PCS probably does not have to maintain as many physical store locations as it would without these services. Table 1.1 provides a summary of some of the major advantages and disadvantages of e-business practices.

TABLE 1.1   Advantages and Disadvantages of e-Business Practices

Advantages	Disadvantages
• Increases productivity for both customers and employees by saving time and money	• Requires specialized knowledge to use
• Allows for communications at a more convenient place and time through e-mail and other software	• User must have Internet access
• Provides access to information anytime, anywhere	• May be perceived as undesirable means of communications compared to direct contact between people
• Can be used to transfer some work to the firm's customers, releasing employees for other tasks	• May result in lost customers or sales if online experience is unsatisfactory
• Allows firms to profitably serve smaller markets	• Online promotional efforts such as e-mail and pop-up advertising may be annoying and possibly counterproductive
• Facilitates online shopping to geographically dispersed customers	
• Inexpensive means to promote the firm and its products to current and potential customers	
• Can provide potential customers with a trial or sample of the product or service	

(*Source:* From William M. Pride, Robert J. Hughes, and Jack R. Kapoor, *Business,* Seventh Edition. Copyright © 2002 by Houghton Mifflin Company. Reprinted with permission.)

A Framework for Understanding e-Business

The Internet was originally conceived as an elaborate military communications network that would allow vital messages to be transmitted in the event of war. Should one element of the network be destroyed, the system was designed to ensure that an alternative route could be found in the remaining network, thus allowing messages to be communicated to decision centers.

Prior to 1994, the National Science Foundation, the agency that funded and regulated the use of the Internet, restricted its use to noncommercial activities, such as e-mail communication among university researchers and the sharing of data. However, as the potential commercial benefits of the Internet became increasingly obvious, a growing number of commercially interested groups demanded that the doors be opened to business activity. At about the same time, new technology emerged that simplified the use of the Internet and allowed the addition of multimedia content. This multimedia environment of audio, visual, and text data came to be known as the **World Wide Web** (or more simply, **the Web**).

World Wide Web (the Web)

The multimedia Internet environment; it may present a blend of audio, visual, and text data to viewers.

The Internet can be envisioned as a large network of computers, connected by cables and satellites, that pass small, standardized packets of electronic data from one station to another until they are delivered to their final destination. In a sense, the Internet is the equivalent of the telephone network, which was first created almost one hundred years ago. However, instead of just voice communication, the Internet can transfer many types of multimedia data around the world at speeds far faster than those of the telephone network. In order to be transferred over the Internet, data need to be **digitized**, which means that they are converted into the type of digital signal that the computers and telecommunications equipment that make up the Internet can understand.

digitized

For data, converted into the type of digital signal that the computers and telecommunications equipment that make up the Internet can understand and transfer.

As illustrated in Figure 1.3, most firms involved in e-business fall more or less into one of three primary groups that are defined by their e-business activities: those that create the telecommunications infrastructure, Internet software producers, and online sellers and content providers. In this section we examine a framework for understanding e-business by looking at these three groups, and then consider global, small business, and internal e-business perspectives.

Telecommunications Infrastructure

Telecommunications hardware and equipment producers, computer hardware manufacturers, and Internet service providers supply the telecommunications infrastructure of the Internet. Cisco Systems (**www.cisco.com**), Nortel Networks (**www.nortelnetworks.com**), and Lucent Technologies (**www.lucent.com**) produce most of the telecommunications equipment and hardware that allow the Internet to work. Companies such as IBM (**www.ibm.com**), Hewlett-Packard (**www.hp.com**), Dell Computer (**www.dell.com**), Sun Microsystems (**www.sun.com**), Apple Computer (**www.apple.com**), and Gateway (**www.gateway.com**) produce many of the computers used by consumers and businesses. Internet service providers (ISPs), which buy their technological capability from the makers of telecommunications hardware, provide

FIGURE 1.3   The Three Primary Groups of e-Business

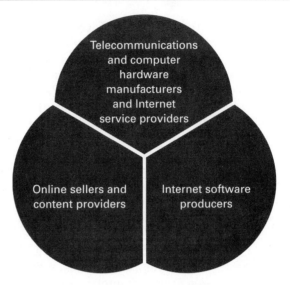

Most firms overlap into more than one area of e-business. (*Source:* From William M. Pride, Robert J. Hughes, and Jack R. Kapoor, *Business,* Seventh Edition. Copyright © 2002 by Houghton Mifflin Company. Reprinted with permission.)

customers with the necessary technology to connect to the Internet through various phone plugs and cables. The last link to the Internet, provided by local telephone and cable television companies, is the shortest, but typically the slowest, in the global electronic network. However, as home users' lines are replaced by faster cable and fiber-optic connections, they will come to enjoy the same speed as businesses in city centers where the telecommunications infrastructure has already been upgraded. AOL is the largest and best-known ISP, but others like EarthLink (**www.earthlink.com**) and MSN (**www.msn.com**) as well as hundreds of smaller ISPs in both urban and rural areas also provide access to the Internet. Furthermore, recent developments involving wireless networks within office buildings and small communities of buildings like college campuses are helping to create a more readily accessible Internet using a variety of communications devices.

Internet Software Producers

Producers of software that provides users with the functional capability to do things on the Internet are the second primary group of e-business firms that have emerged since the start of online commercial activity. Searching the Internet, browsing websites, sending e-mail messages, shopping online, viewing multimedia content, and other online activities all require specialized computer software programs. Browser software is the single most basic product for user interaction on the Internet. Currently, the dominant browser is Microsoft's Internet Explorer,

e-BUSINESS insight

Understanding the Size of the World Wide Web

An extensive and ongoing study by the University of California at Berkeley into information creation, transmission, and storage suggests that not only is the Internet the fastest growing media—but it is doubling in size every year. As of 2002, an estimated 2.5 billion webpages had been created while 7.3 million new ones were being added each day. The average page size is estimated to vary from 10 to 20 kilobytes per page, and so the total amount of information on the Web is estimated to be somewhere from 25 to 50 terabytes of information. (Note: 1 kilobyte equals 1,000 bytes; 1 megabyte equals 1 million bytes; 1 gigabyte equals 1,000 megabytes; 1 terabyte equals 1,000 gigabytes; and 1 exabyte equals 1 billion gigabytes.)

But this only reflects what is euphemistically called the "surface Web" that most people would explore online. The entire Web is actually 400 to 550 times greater than this when the "deep Web" is also included. The deep Web refers to the far larger but relatively unknown specialized databases that are 95 percent publicly accessible online. If we take into account all deep Web components such as Web-connected databases, dynamic pages, intranet sites, and so forth, there are 550 billion Web-connected documents, with an average page size of 14 kilobytes. Two of the largest deep websites—the National Climatic Data Center and NASA databases—contain 585 terabytes of information, which is 7.8 percent of the deep Web. Furthermore, reflecting the concentration of content, sixty of the largest websites contain 750 terabytes of information, which is 10 percent of the deep web.

Question for discussion: Can the Internet ever become too big?[26]

followed a distant second by AOL's Netscape Communicator. Not many years ago, in the short history of the Internet, the rankings for these two browsers were just the opposite, with Netscape the dominant leader. Microsoft's rapid expansion into Internet software and services illustrates the dynamic nature of e-business. However, Microsoft's dominance in the software market also makes it a target of criticism and government legal action. Other software producers claim that Microsoft has an unfair competitive advantage because of the strength of its Windows software and should be broken up into two or more separate companies. Although this scenario seems unlikely, pressure by the U.S. Congress and more recently, the European Community is likely to open the market to greater competition and lead to a greater variety of products, to the benefit of customers. Competition in other online areas is more obvious, as a wide variety of software products are available in such areas as web management, e-commerce, and conferencing from Oracle (**www.oracle.com**), IBM (**www.ibm.com**), Lotus Development (**www.lotus.com**), and Sun Microsystems (**www.sun.com**).

In order to find websites and information on the Internet, msn.com, yahoo.com, google.com, altavista.com, aol.com, lycos.com, netscape.com, and hundreds of lesser known sites provide *search engine software* so users can search the Internet in general or their own sites' data specifically. By entering key words and phrases, users are guided to available online information, which is intelligently ranked according to the individual engine's rules for listing search results. For instance, some engines will list sites according to how often users have selected them after their own searches, the idea being that someone who selected a site after entering the same or similar search criteria is intelligently pointing the ways for others. Not surprisingly, a two-year study by Alexa Research found that the most popular term people search for online is "sex," representing 0.33 percent of all searches.[7]

Today e-mail is considered a standard *communication software* tool for all businesspeople. Whether for internal or external communication, the low costs and benefits derived from implementing e-mail software solutions are well established and make it the easiest Internet-based software solution to rationalize. More advanced and complex communications solutions might include *customer relationship* and *supply chain management software* solutions. Several large firms now sell complete **customer relationship management (CRM)** software solutions that incorporate a variety of means for managing the tasks of communicating with customers and sharing this information with employees in order to create more efficient relationships. The concept behind CRM is to establish a seamless system for handling any and all information that involves customers' interaction with the firm's employees, incorporating everything from website e-commerce services to telephone-based services such as SprintPCS (**www.sprintpcs.com**). And just as CRM software solutions help firms create more efficient relationships with their customers, **supply-chain management (SCM)** software solutions focus on ways to improve communication between the suppliers and users of materials and components. By providing their production requirements and planning information directly to their suppliers, manufacturers can reduce inventories, improve delivery schedules, and reduce costs, which can quickly show up as improved profitability. For example, Dell Computer's **Valuechain.dell.com** virtually eliminates the need for the firm to maintain any inventory, as suppliers are tied directly into Dell's new OptiPlex plant in Round Rock, Texas. Manufacturing schedules and parts orders are revised every two hours. Suppliers must keep an agreed-upon level of inventory for Dell on hand at nearby local warehouses. As a result, 95 percent of Dell's PCs are built and shipped to customers within twelve hours of their orders being entered into the system. OptiPlex has improved productivity 160 percent, increased order velocity 50 percent, and reduced errors in orders by 50 percent.[8]

customer relationship management (CRM)
Software solutions that incorporate a variety of means to manage the tasks of communicating with customers and sharing this information with employees in order to create more efficient relationships.

supply-chain management (SCM)
Software solutions that focus on ways to improve communication between the suppliers and users of materials and components, enabling manufacturers to reduce inventories, improve delivery schedules, reduce costs, and so forth.

Online Sellers and Content Providers

The third primary group of e-business firms consists of all the firms that customers actually interact with on websites. The Internet would still be limited to communication between individuals and among groups of special-interest researchers were it not for the activity of online sellers and content providers. In this area of e-business, we have just begun to see the development of online strategies for reaching out to existing and new customers.

As noted earlier, some e-businesses, such as AOL and eBay, owe their existence to the Internet. They offer products and services that can be found only online. In contrast, other firms—among them the Gap, Nike, and Gear—carry out only some of their business activities on the Internet. They use the Internet simply to provide information and supplement their regular business activities.

Although it is uncertain what content and activities will eventually make their way to the Internet, it is clear that the dominant trend today is the movement of existing business activities to the Internet. Time Warner's decision to merge with AOL is a case in point. By arranging for online distribution of content that was formerly distributed through the technologies of magazines, radio, and television, Time Warner has found new opportunities for revenue growth. Similarly, traditional ways of shopping have been transferred to a virtual environment, where cyberspace retailers can provide more information to customers and exert a greater degree of influence on the customer's decision. The Internet is jammed with shopping, as anyone who has entered the keyword *shop* on a search engine like Yahoo! has discovered.

Businesses that operate exclusively online, such as eBay and Amazon.com, are at one extreme of the e-business spectrum; conventional businesses that have only begun the process of developing an Internet presence are at the other. The pace at which firms adapt their business activities to a business environment that includes the Internet generally depends on the value they perceive to be gained by going online. If the case presented to management is that expenses can be reduced dramatically, revenues can be increased, or new customers in new markets can be reached more cost-effectively, then online strategies will appear more attractive. If, on the other hand, the impact of an online program is less predictable and the benefits are less certain, then decision-makers would be expected to be more cautious and slower to charge ahead into the unknown.

The greatest area for entrepreneurial adventure on the Internet is in the production of some service or content. Anyone with a good idea that might appeal to a globally distributed audience stands a chance of successfully launching an e-business. As the short history of the Internet indicates, we are only at the beginning of developing new and exciting applications that can be delivered online. According to Timothy Draper, an insider in the world of e-business and managing director of Draper Fisher Jurvetson, a West Coast venture capital firm, "The Internet has opened the world up and that means everyone's now going to be part of the world economy."[9]

Global e-Business

All three primary groups of e-business firms are in a race to capture global business revenues that are only just now emerging. Telecommunications firms are competing to build the infrastructure in countries all over the world; in many cases, they are skipping technological stepping-stones. For example, in areas of poor countries where telephone poles have never existed, ground-based wireless systems are now providing instant state-of-the-art communications. In many places, ISPs and software producers like AOL are competing against better-known local firms. And online sellers and content providers see no limits to their ability to penetrate markets anywhere in the world where customers want their products.

The ability to customize content for individual customer needs makes the Internet an adaptable tool for global enterprise. Consider Berlitz's website (**www.berlitz.com**), which allows anyone in the world to jump quickly to a website designed in the viewer's preferred language. By clicking on the appropriate icon, viewers can move forward to a website that was created to meet their needs in one of a wide variety of languages. Once there, the viewer can examine a range of products and services, including multimedia language-learning material, online translation services, and referrals to local Berlitz classroom-based instruction. This global strategy, which reaches out to the world and yet allows for individual viewer customization, is at the heart of e-business strategic thinking.

Despite the enormous potential for growth, generating global success is demanding and complex. Markets are substantially different around the world, reflecting different economic conditions and consumption patterns. Understandably, firms with an established global presence and global experience, like Berlitz, are likely to venture ahead of others that lack such a history.

Research by Nielsen/NetRatings suggests that the estimated 253 million active global Internet users spend an average of 32 minutes online, totalling more than 12 hours each month.[10]

More indicative of Internet usage, however, are the data from Nielsen/NetRatings surveys that show that monthly average use was 25 hours online at home and 75 hours at work—suggesting the importance of the Internet as a work-related tool.[11]

The slowdown in e-business activity that began in 2000 continues to undermine confidence in predictions for growth. However, we can safely say that the long-term view, held by the vast majority of analysts, is that the Internet is now part of a new global communications technology that will continue to expand along with related technologies. The only point that is debated is whether growth rates will return to the levels seen during the early years of commercial activity on the Internet. Although many analysts believe that the first rush of enthusiasm to create an online presence has been exhausted, only a small percentage of the potential global users have yet gone online. Current estimates suggest that perhaps between 400 to 500 million people use the Web on a daily basis. However, according to research by Ipsos-Reid Inc. (**www.ipsos-reid.com**), even among the world's most developed Internet markets, such as the United States, Canada, Sweden, and the Netherlands, about one-third of the people who could use the Internet choose not to do so. In fact, Ipsos-Reid found that only 6 percent of the world's 6 billion people are online, suggesting great opportunities for growth if more people can be persuaded that the benefits are worthwhile. About 40 percent of those surveyed expressed no need for or interest in going online, while 33 percent lacked a computer. As barriers to Internet access are removed and nonusers are persuaded of the utility of the Web, it is clear that greater usage is likely.[12]

Small e-Business

If early experience is any indication of the future, the Internet will continue to be an attractive and powerful strategic tool for small business. According to a report by Access Markets International (AMI) Partners (**www.ami-partners.com**) and *Inc.*

magazine, small-business online activity got off to a very quick start. Research showed that an estimated 400,000 U.S. small businesses sold their products and services on e-business sites in 1998, and that number jumped 50 percent to 600,000 in 1999. During the same period, online transactions and purchases grew more than 1,000 percent, rising from $2 billion to $25 billion, and the actual number of small businesses transacting online increased 55 percent, from 1.8 million to 2.8 million. Interestingly, a significant number of small firms—six out of ten—were reluctant to sell their products online at the time because of security concerns, technology challenges, or the belief that their products were unsuited for online selling.[13]

However, despite these early concerns, online activity continues to grow, as suggested by a recent American Express survey. It reported that 66 percent of small businesses had already implemented the Internet as a tool to help them run their businesses. They used it for making travel plans and purchasing office supplies, equipment, or other business services (tied at 36 percent); conducting industry or market research (34 percent); marketing or advertising (29 percent); networking with other entrepreneurs (24 percent); purchasing goods from wholesalers (22 percent); and managing accounts and making payments (16 percent).[14]

Although the global-scale firms that dominate e-business are well known to many people, the remarkable thing about the Internet is how accessible it is to small businesses. The relatively low cost of going online means that the Internet is open to thousands of small businesses that seek opportunities to grow internationally. In some cases, small firms have found a niche service or product to sell online. Special online shopping malls bring shoppers a wider selection of unique crafts or artistic creations. And many small online magazines, or **e-zines**, as they are often called, have found their special audience through the virtual world of online publishing. In fact, many small publications that began online have gone on to create print versions of their e-zines. In each case, audiences were attracted to a specialized product that could take advantage of lower online delivery costs.

e-zines
Online magazines.

Applying e-Business Strategies to Managerial, Marketing, and Financial Situations

Another way to approach the study of e-business is to focus attention on how operations within each of the three primary functional areas of business—management, marketing, and finance—can be improved by adopting online software and solutions.

Management Activities and Practices

Management activities and practices focus on how best to organize and coordinate the work carried out by employees so basic business objectives like building profitability and maintaining good customer and supplier relationships can be achieved. Moving management activities to the Internet can often improve a firm's internal practices and procedures. For example, allowing a company sales representative to enter a customer's order while he or she is at the customer's place of business can be facilitated through a Web-based order-entry system. The sales representative can verify quantities of available inventory and set a delivery date. Internet-based systems can provide information, improve performance, and generally assist employees in both selling and nonselling situations. However, any change in procedure will normally require employees to invest some time and effort in learning how to use the new system. The question that management must consider, then, is whether the investment is warranted given the benefits that would be derived. Just as managers once weighed the cost of exchanging typewriters for computers and word processing against the benefits that the switch would provide, today they must evaluate the benefits that might follow from adopting any of the available Internet-based solutions relative to the costs that would be incurred.

Marketing Applications and Solutions

Marketing involves a variety of activities that, when done well, add value to the product or service purchased by the customer. The Internet can help provide strategic marketing solutions that reduce customer service and order-entry costs, minimize inventory levels, and provide a variety of valuable information to customers.

A firm's website can provide a wide assortment of opportunities for communicating with customers, investors, suppliers, and other interested public groups. Archived press releases and public relations statements posted online by the firm can serve to inform both internal and external parties. The most important promotional tool that is readily available online is advertising, which can motivate customers to either enter their order online immediately or delay their actual purchase until they are at the firm's retail store.

For most purchase decisions, customers must weigh certain information before making their selection. As a marketing medium, the Internet has advantages over television and radio since customers are able to interact with the multimedia information they receive over the Internet. Advertisements can be linked to other information, thus allowing customers to control their research. For instance, consider a webpage that presents a home entertainment electronics system, complete with home theater and stereo sound systems. By clicking on different areas of the screen, the customer could explore the information found in those highlighted areas.

A successfully designed website can provide a high level of personalized communication between the website sales presentation and the customer. The informed customer should come away empowered and confident of having the necessary information for making the best selection of merchandise. And a satisfied customer will share that experience and sense of control with friends and family and thereby create a ripple effect that will influence other potential customers. Many websites offer their customers a bonus of some sort for referring the site to a friend. Furthermore, customers who have confidence in their purchase are more likely to be loyal and return for other purchases in the future.

Well-designed websites attract targeted customers, create interest in the products presented, and stimulate the desire to explore the purchase decision further. The job of the website designer is to anticipate the customer's behavior and thinking processes. The online experience should simulate the experience that the customer would actually have in the store. Where possible, however, aspects of the real experience that might be counterproductive should be improved upon. For instance, being able to pause, ask questions, and find information at any time and then return to the same point in the presentation is a powerful capability of online marketing design. Offering the customer intelligent and helpful suggestions based on knowledge inferred from the choices that he or she made on the site is another smart marketing feature of good website design. Information about what the customer has bought previously, selected online, or volunteered in profile data can be intelligently used to enhance the online buying experience for customers. This sort of intelligent online marketing and customer relationship management capability is the primary reason for the success of firms like Amazon.com. In fact, this approach to online customer relationship management and web design is often referred to as the Amazon.com business model.

Financial Services and Solutions

Financial applications include all matters involving money, such as online stock market trading, banking services, and the collection of payments for e-commerce transactions. In most applications, online forms facilitate the secure entry and search of financial data from any location connected to the Internet, reducing much of the associated overhead and service costs.

e-BUSINESS insight

Content versus Personal Communications

As the Internet continues to grow, the dichotomy of its purpose—communication versus content—will continue to be a point of interest and study. In spite of the explosive growth of online content available to the public, communications between individuals remains the primary "killer" Internet application. Approximately 610 billion e-mails were transmitted in 2002, whereas 2.1 billion static webpages were created. Measured another way, about 500 times as much e-mail is being produced per year as are webpages.

Furthermore, the growing use of IP telephony, a technology that incorporates voice communications with computer networks, results in savings on toll charges for long distance calls as well as costs associated with assigning a phone number to a device and any subsequent costs. For instance, since the device, an IP phone, or computer station has its own unique address that is recognized by the network each time the device is activated, employees can change offices and simply take their phones with them without needing to inform the network of their new location. Research by Sage Research Inc. suggests that it costs organizations as much as $125 each time to adjust their telephone networks, and 75 percent of decisions to switch to IP telephony is guided by simple cost savings. Cisco Systems Inc, a leading supplier of IP telephony technology, suggests that old telephone systems will rapidly be replaced by IP technologies and integrated with wireless systems to gain further benefits. But the real growth will come as new communications products are developed for use along with IP telephony.

Question for discussion: Do you think personal communications will be more popular in the future than the search and use of webpage content?[15]

The banking and financial services industries were quick to recognize the inherent advantages of using the Internet. Today, online stock trading, banking, and financial services are available to both businesses and the consumer market. Financial institutions such as Netherlands-based ING (**www.ing.com**) can provide customers with direct global access to their accounts, allowing them to make payments, transfer funds between accounts, secure loans, apply for credit, and generate reports. Clients and the financial institutions share the enthusiasm and motivation for using online services because the electronic processing of large numbers of standardized transactions provides increased efficiencies. These systems also provide an added measure of security, since transactions can be handled without human intermediaries and paper documents. Savings in processing charges for the banking industry are huge and contribute directly to the banks' profitability.

Fundamental Models of e-Business

business model

A group of shared or common characteristics, behaviors, and methods of doing business in order to generate profits.

One way to get a better sense of how businesses can adapt to the opportunities made available to them through the Internet is to identify and understand the fundamental nature of e-business models. A **business model** is a group of shared or common characteristics, behaviors, and methods of doing business that enables a firm to generate profits through increasing revenues and reducing costs. For example, large food stores share a basically similar business model when it comes to their selection of merchandise, their organizational structure, their employee job requirements, and often, their financing needs. The models discussed in this section focus attention on the identity of the firm's customers, the users of the Internet activities that are offered, the uniqueness of the online product or service, and the firm's degree of online presence.

Business-to-Business Model

business-to-business (B2B) model

A business model in which firms use the Internet mainly to conduct business with other businesses.

Many e-businesses can be distinguished from others simply by their customer focus. For instance, some firms use the Internet mainly to conduct business with other businesses. These firms are generally referred to as having a **business-to-business (B2B) model.** Currently, the vast majority of e-business is B2B in nature. When firms with a B2B model are examined, two clear types emerge. In the first type, the focus is simply on facilitating sales transactions between businesses. For example, Dell manufactures computers to specifications that customers enter on Dell's website. The vast majority of Dell's online orders are from corporate clients who are well informed about the computer products they need and are looking for fairly priced, high-quality products that will be delivered quickly. Basically, by building only what is ordered, Dell reduces storage and carrying costs and rarely is stuck with unsold older technology. By dealing directly with Dell, customers eliminate the costs associated with wholesalers and retailers, thereby helping to reduce the price they pay for equipment.

A second, more complex type of B2B model involves the relationships between companies and their suppliers, which often are numerous, geographically dispersed, and difficult to manage. Suppliers today commonly use the Web to make bids on the products and services that they wish to offer, learn about the conditions under which business will be conducted, find out which rules and procedures to follow, and so forth. Likewise, firms that are seeking specific items can now ask for bids on their websites and choose suppliers from those that make offers in response through the online system. For example, the online leader in the auto industry, Ford Motor Company, links 30,000 auto-parts suppliers and 6,900 dealers in its network, resulting in an estimated $8.9 billion savings each year from reduced transaction costs, materials, and inventory. This $8.9 billion savings represents about a quarter of the retail selling price for an average new car. This provides Ford with a considerable competitive advantage in the marketplace through its ability to either reduce selling prices or earn higher profits. In addition, Ford expects to earn approximately $3 billion a year from the exchange fees it charges for use of its supplier network.[16]

Similarly, the supplier system at General Motors is expected to eliminate the costs of processing more than 100,000 annual purchase orders, which average $125 each.[17]

Given the magnitude of Ford's cost savings, it is all the more surprising to learn that these savings are derived primarily from the elimination of transaction costs related to manual labor and errors created by the repetitive entry of data. For example, under the old system, Ford might fax an order for parts to a supplier. The supplier would fill out its own order form and send a copy to Ford for confirmation. The data would have to be entered into each company's computer system at each step of the way. However, under the new system, the supplier has access to Ford's inventory of parts and can place bids for parts online. Ford eliminates the labor costs of data entry and much of the order-processing costs by connecting suppliers to the system. Ford's system is an illustrative example of an advanced **electronic data interchange (EDI)**, which uses the Internet to exchange information and thereby avoids the use of printed forms. Before the Internet, EDI systems were much more expensive to set up, since connections between users had to be made directly between exchange members. Furthermore, Internet-based EDI has been a welcome addition to **enterprise resource planning (ERP)**, the back-office accounting software systems that handle order entry, purchasing, invoicing, and inventory control. Today, the Internet facilitates the data exchange process and is a primary reason for the strong growth in B2B activity.

Given the substantial savings from such networks, it is little wonder that many other manufacturers and their suppliers are beginning to use the same kind of system. These systems reduce costs and create a structure that makes it simpler for suppliers to deal with each of the automakers. The suppliers are also able to use the system to bid on work and monitor their participation with the manufacturers. Their activities are integrated with those of their customers. There is less separation between the buyer and the seller, as suppliers become part of the production strategy designed by the companies they serve.

Although managing the dealings between a firm and its suppliers is an established business activity that existed before the Internet came along, it is a focal point of e-business activity for many firms. This is due mostly to the savings and

electronic data interchange (EDI)
An electronic system that allows for the exchange of formatted information as is typically found in such documents as purchase orders and invoices without using printed forms.

enterprise resource planning (ERP)
The back-office accounting software systems that handle order entry, purchasing, invoicing, and inventory control.

improvements that can be gained by changing a firm's existing business processes and practices to better ones that are structured around a website. The result is not only the financial improvement gained by cost savings but also the establishment and control of standard procedures of operation made clearly visible through the firm's website. However, firms that are considering the implementation of e-business strategies often face resistance—both internally from employees and externally from customers and suppliers—to changing what might be long-established and familiar practices.

Business-to-Consumer Model

business-to-consumer (B2C) model
A business model in which firms use the Internet mainly to conduct business with consumers.

In contrast to those firms using a B2B model, firms like Amazon.com and eBay are clearly focused on individual buyers and so are referred to as having a **business-to-consumer (B2C) model.** In a B2C situation, understanding how consumers behave online is critical to the firm's success. Will consumers simply use websites to simplify and speed up comparison shopping and then end up buying at a traditional store? What sorts of products and services are well suited for online consumer shopping, and which ones simply are not good choices at this stage of online development? Although an enormous amount of research has been done to answer these and other questions about consumer shopping behavior in traditional stores, relatively little research on online consumer behavior has been done to date. No doubt, as more and more consumers make use of online environments, an increasing amount of research will help explain how best to meet their needs.

In addition to giving customers round-the-clock global access to their products and services, online B2C firms often make a special effort to build long-term relationships with those customers. The thinking behind this is that customers should be valued not only for the sale at hand but also for their long-term contribution to the firm's profitability. The cost incurred in earning a customer's trust is high, but if a firm gains a loyal customer for life, that customer's repeated purchases will repay the investment many times over. Many financial models that attempt to evaluate the real value of a dot-com business make use of estimates of the long-term value of the current customer base.

The Internet has enhanced firms' ability to build good customer relationships. One factor contributing to this enhanced ability is specialized software that allows sellers to track the decisions customers make as they navigate a website. Using the resulting data on buying preferences and customer profiles, management can make well-informed decisions about how best to serve its customers. This approach can also enhance inventory decisions, buying selections, and decisions in many other managerial areas. In essence, this is Amazon.com's selling approach. By tracking and analyzing customer data, Amazon.com can provide individualized guided service to its customers.

consumer-to-consumer (C2C) model
A business model in which firms facilitate the exchange of data directly between individuals over the Internet using peer-to-peer software.

Consumer-to-Consumer Model

Unlike the B2B and B2C models, which focus on business transactions and communications, the **consumer-to-consumer (C2C) model** involves the increasingly

peer-to-peer (P2P) software
Software that allows individuals to exchange data directly with one another over the Internet without the use of an intermediary central computer.

server
A central computer that distributes requested files to individual users.

popular use of **peer-to-peer (P2P) software** that facilitates the exchange of data directly between individuals over the Internet. The traditional method of distribution of files on the Internet requires an individual to request a copy of a file from a central computer, called a **server** and then receive it. P2P software, however, allows individuals to directly access files—including music and digital images—stored on one another's computers. The opportunity for users to violate copyright law is a concern associated with the use of P2P software. However, P2P software is also a legitimate collaborative tool for employees who need to be able to share data that are distributed among many geographically dispersed individuals. For example, software from NextPage Inc. (**www.nextpage.com**) of Salt Lake City allows clients like the legal firm Baker and McKenzie to share documents that are stored on computers around the world. Attorneys can work together on a project without having to be concerned about the physical location of important files. According to project director Mark Swords, NextPage's software helps the firm move 25 percent faster and improves client relationships.[18]

A broader definition of a C2C model can also include hybrid websites such as eBay, which facilitate exchanges between consumers but also have a commercial dimension. Another example, SnapFish (**www.snapfish.com**), allows customers to display their photographic images online free of charge. Individuals can be granted access to as many images as the customer wants to permit them to see—in effect, the customer can create customized photo albums for friends and relatives online. SnapFish earns revenue by processing film and prints for customers and also generates additional revenue by selling copies of prints to those who are granted access to online views of the images. Customers can also upload digital photographic images for display and then order prints as well.

Taxonomy for the Fundamental Models of e-Business

The list of e-business models continues to grow and has no established taxonomy. Most models are modified versions of traditional business models such as retailing or publishing. The following segment examines several e-business models that have emerged as well as their primary descriptive characteristics. Like most interested parties looking at a business model, we will first focus our attention on the basic question of how the firm earns revenues and then explore the other descriptors related to the model.

brokerage e-business model
An e-business model that encompasses online marketplaces in which buyers and sellers are brought together in an organized environment to facilitate the exchange of goods.

Brokerage e-Business Model

The **brokerage e-business model** encompasses online marketplaces where buyers and sellers are brought together in an organized environment to facilitate the exchange of goods and services. Brokerage firms often specialize in a particular product classification and may even be organized by a major supplier or vendor of these products, as is the case with the auto-parts exchange organized by General Motors and the airline industry supply exchange set up by Air Canada. Though the vast majority of brokerage activity is conducted among businesses, the popular and profitable eBay (**www.ebay.com**) provides both businesses and consumers with access to a communications structure for buying or selling virtually anything.

Advertising e-Business Model

advertising e-business model

An e-business model based on earning revenues in exchange for the display of advertisements on a firm's website.

An **advertising e-business model** is based on earning revenues in exchange for the display of advertisements on a firm's website, in much the same way that other media such as television, radio, newspapers, and magazines earn revenues. Websites like Yahoo! (**www.yahoo.com**) and MSN (**www.msn.com**) depend on high volumes of traffic to generate revenues. Audiences are likely to continue to readily accept distributed online entertainment or information that is sponsored by advertising. They see advertising as the price they have to pay for receiving free content online. But unlike conventional media, where engaging the consumer is often problematic, the Internet provides both the advertiser and the website content provider with the opportunity for unique design and interaction with the targeted audience.

Subscription, Pay-per-View, and Membership e-Business Models

subscription e-business model

An e-business model in which access to a site is controlled by a subscription fee.

pay-per-view e-business model

An e-business model in which access to a site is controlled by a charge to view single items.

membership e-business model

An e-business model in which access to a site is controlled by membership fees.

Website content providers may elect to earn revenues through the use of a **subscription**, **pay-per-view**, or **membership e-business model**, in which access to the site is controlled by a subscription fee, a charge to view single items such as a report, or a membership fee, respectively. Often these sources of revenue are combined with advertising revenue. The subscription model, which is popular with publications and research organizations like Forrester Research, Inc. (**www.forrester.com**), often provides samples of the site's content free of charge and then seeks to induce interested clients to subscribe to the full range of products and services available. A common strategy is to offer a trial subscription for a limited time period and at a substantial price reduction to entice new subscribers.

Distribution Channel Member e-Business Model

distribution channel member e-business model

An e-business model that includes the activities of retailers, wholesalers, and manufacturers conducting business through the Internet.

The **distribution channel member e-business model** includes the activities of retailers, wholesalers, and manufacturers conducting business through the Internet. It is a natural choice for businesses that are currently active at any of these levels in the distribution system of delivering products to end users. Taking product offerings into a global and virtual environment is easier than ever, as e-commerce software that facilitates this is available for relatively small fees from hosting firms that provide everything required to get started. Furthermore, firms can easily scale up if their initial activities produce positive results, as is illustrated by online retailer Amazon.com (**www.amazon.com**). Newcomers to the Internet might wish to place only their top-selling products in an online facility and gradually build up an entire online catalog in tandem with their bricks-and-mortar retail or wholesale operations.

Affiliation e-Business Model

affiliation e-business model

An e-business model that involves payments to website operators for customers who find their way to a company's site and either buy merchandise or services or perform some other action, such as registering and providing certain information.

The affiliation concept is important for website operators to consider for several reasons. The **affiliation e-business model** involves payments to website operators for customers who find their way to a company's site and either buy merchandise or services or perform some other action, such as registering and providing certain information. This model was popularized by Amazon.com (**www.amazon.com**), which, like other operators of affiliate programs, has automated the process of registering and creating an online link to the destination site. Any website operator that wants to earn a share of the revenues from books and other products sold through the Amazon.com website to customers that the website operator sent there simply has to make a few clicks at the Amazon.com registration site. An Amazon.com link will then appear on the affiliate's website. Amazon.com currently pays a 15 percent finder's commission for customers sent its way, which helps to explain why the program is such a success with website operators.

Community e-Business Model

community e-business model

An e-business model built around the idea that a group of online users can be regularly brought together at a commonly used website for commercial purposes.

The **community e-business model** is built around the idea that a group of online users can be regularly brought together at a commonly used website for commercial purposes. The sorts of communities brought together can vary widely and can include people who share an interest like playing bridge or poker, wish to exchange their opinions about politics and public affairs, or wish to find and reestablish contact with old high school friends on websites like Classmates.com (**www.classmates.com**). Communities are the great growth opportunity for any individual or organization that can think of a reason why someone would be interested enough in its site to make the effort to visit it. Online communities such as those set up by educational institutions and religious organizations can be self-supporting as a result of their association with their respective larger organizations and their fee structures for members or donors. These online communities are generally regarded as simply another method for enabling members to communicate with one another and are usually free of any revenue-generating aspect. However, online communities, along with the advertising and shopping services that are unique to their focus, continue to flourish as a niche for small and special-interest groups. For example, Oxygen (**www.oxygen.com**), Oprah Winfrey (**www.oprah.com**), and iVillage (**www.ivillage.com**) have all developed large numbers of regular users by focusing mainly on topics that are of interest to women. Geocities (**www.geocities.com**), the build-your-own-web-site-for-free service provided by Yahoo!, provides an environment for individuals who wish to explore their own creative skills by constructing a website. In all of these communities, advertising, affiliate programs, and online shopping provide the revenues needed to make the communities viable. The success of this model is obviously based on building awareness among interested users and spreading the word. Therefore, most site operators offer incentives such as rewards and prizes to current members who enlist new users.

Infomediary e-Business Model

infomediary e-business model
An e-business model based on the collection and sale of online information.

The **infomediary e-business model** is based on the collection and sale of online information. Obvious infomediaries include research firms such as Forrester Research (**www.forrester.com**) and ComScore (**www.comscore.com**) as well as firms like ClickZ.com (**www.clickz.com**), all of which display articles written by their own reporters as well as from other sources. But in addition to these types of infomediaries, many sites, especially communities, are in a position to analyze their users' online interests and behaviors and then sell the results of this research to other interested parties, such as advertisers. Communities can earn revenues by providing informational services from advertisers to users who accept the offer, usually in the form of e-mail advertisements or announcements of another type. Without a community site that has large numbers of users, no data collection activity is really possible unless the infomediary firm uses other methods to attract online users and motivates them to volunteer information. In some cases, this is done by providing free Internet access or free access to a website and its content in exchange for registration and permission to collect online behavior data, send out e-mail advertisements, and conduct other such activities. Gomez.com (**www.gomez.com**) is an infomediary that pays users for permission to track their movements on the Internet and sell the information to advertisers and other interested parties. Users load a software program that presents intelligent advertisements that Gomez directs to match the user's demographic profile and online behavior.

Portal e-Business Model

portal e-business model
A type of infomediary that earns revenues by drawing users to its site and serving as a gateway or portal to information located elsewhere on the Internet.

horizontal portals
Portals that have a wide general reach into different informational topics.

vertical portals
Portals that have a narrow focus into a particular informational topic.

The **portal e-business model** is a type of infomediary that earns revenues by drawing users to its site and serving as a gateway or portal to information located elsewhere on the Internet. Some portals, such as search engines, have a wide general reach into different informational topics and are referred to as **horizontal portals**, whereas others have a narrow focus on a particular topic and are called **vertical portals**. Both types of portals can earn revenues by selling advertising, providing search services to users who are seeking merchants and products, and charging finder's fees for customers sent to a particular merchant. Portals are websites that serve as entry points to the Internet, providing users with a gateway to other websites. Portals may focus on providing news, entertainment, a search engine service for the Internet, and so forth. Portals such as Microsoft's **www.msn.com** generally allow users to select and customize their view of news, local weather, topics of interest, and other content.

Preparing e-Business Plans

business plan

A document containing detailed descriptions of the fundamental structure of a firm and the activities within it, including sources of revenue, the identity of target customers, pricing, promotion, and other strategies.

e-business plan

A business plan or part of a larger business plan that focuses on a firm's Internet business activities.

Detailed descriptions of the fundamental structure of a firm and the activities within it are organized and presented in the firm's **business plan.** If the firm is an Internet-based business, like Yahoo!, or if we are examining only the part of a firm that includes its Internet business activities, like those of the Walt Disney Company, we can refer to the document as the firm's **e-business plan.** We will use the two terms interchangeably here; however, learners should recognize that the insertion of "e-" before any business term generally implies that there is a connection to the Internet in some fundamental way. So e-marketing implies a focus on marketing activities related to the firm's e-business plan and so forth.

The business plan is the most detailed description of what individuals within the firm are doing and what the business is trying to achieve. It should be revised as conditions and circumstances demand. A fundamental change in market prices or competition should elicit a response from the firm, and a descriptive explanation or rationale for the choices the firm has made should be in the business plan. This allows anyone to understand how and why managers are making their day-to-day decisions in the way they are.

A solid business plan is necessary for serious discussions with anyone who is interested in the firm, including potential partners, investors, lenders, customers, and employees. Obviously, business plans can be edited to suit the circumstances and the reader's needs. A document that is presented to a potential investing partner who is interested in joining the firm is not likely to contain the same information as a document that is presented to the firm's bank manager when the firm is applying for a loan. The needs of the reader are different in each situation, and the document should reflect these needs and cater to them appropriately.

We end this chapter with a brief introduction to the preparation of e-business plans in order to help those learners who wish to get started early conceptualizing and building their e-business projects. A more complete tutorial on preparing an e-business plan is available on the textbook's website. Part of the aim of this textbook is to provide learners with all the necessary tools to build and maintain an e-business plan. The topics covered in this textbook are presented in a manner and a sequence that allow learners to clearly understand them as independent topics but also recognize them as contributions to an e-business plan. The website presents a detailed guide for researching and preparing an e-business plan as well as a link to websites, such as that of the U.S. Small Business Administration (**www.sba.gov/starting/indexbusplans.html**), that elaborate on business plan preparation.

TABLE 1.2   Basic Components of an e-Business Plan

1. *Cover Page:* The cover page should include the title of the document, the name of the firm, the authors of the report, the date, and any other descriptive information that highlights the intended audience and use of the report.

2. *Introduction:* The introduction should provide a basic description of the firm and the purpose of the report.

3. *Executive Summary:* The executive summary is written last and should contain the highlights of the entire report.

4. *Environmental Analysis:* This section of the report should examine all of the relevant external and internal environmental forces discussed in the first module of the text that can affect planning.

5. *e-Business Model:* This section should present a full description of the basic nature of the business and its primary revenue streams.

6. *Marketing:* Here the plan should expand on marketing-related details such as who the targeted customers are, what is known about their behavior, and so forth.

7. *Management and Organizational Issues:* This section should provide details such as who will do what specific work, how the organization's communication system will function, and so forth.

8. *Finance:* This section of the plan will probably have three- to five-year financial projections using pro forma income statements, balance sheets, and statements of cash flows.

9. *Conclusion:* A short conclusion should bring the report to a close. Suggested actions by individuals or a timeline for action before the recommendations within the report are considered outdated might be included here.

10. *Appendix:* The appendix should contain any supplementary information that would be useful to the reader, such as sample questionnaires used to gather research data, documents used to prepare the report, and so forth.

**Go to the Web:
e-Business Online**
For tutorials and more on the topics in this chapter, visit the student website at **http://business.college .hmco.com/students** and select "Canzer e-Business."

For now, however, Table 1.2 presents a brief overview of the key components of an e-business plan that is more suitable at this stage and will serve to structure our exploration of the topic.

Conclusions

This chapter has presented an overview of the fast-paced emerging world of e-business. Several structured approaches have been discussed, including an organizational overview of the firms in the industry that supply products and services, the primary strategic models (B2B, B2C, and C2C) that focus on targeted audiences, and a taxonomy of these primary models. Finally, an overview of how to begin the preparation of an e-business plan has been presented to help learners get started with projects early in their course of study. Throughout the text you will find more e-business references and examples as they apply to different aspects of business. Chapter 2 will take a closer look at the primary environmental forces affecting e-business strategic thinking. The structure presented here will help explain what areas decision-makers need to research and monitor on a continuous basis in order to develop and manage e-business plans properly.

RETURN TO
inside e-business

According to AOL's research, 70 percent of all on-line consumers regularly or occasionally receive their news through the Internet. Thus, investors believed the synergy of the fit between AOL and Time Warner, and the abilities of their managements to capitalize on opportunities were very strong. However, since the merger, both parties have failed to make much progress in their efforts to grow their e-businesses. AOL's exclusive access to Time Warner content gave the company a major competitive advantage over other Internet service providers that lacked access to this content. The merger also heightened the possibility that Time Warner could increase the number of consumers for one or more of its dozens of lifestyle and news magazines, such as *Business 2.0, InStyle, Time, Sports Illustrated, People, Teen People, Golf,* and *Entertainment Weekly.* Other Time Warner products, including music (Atlantic Records, Rhino Records, Warner Brothers Records), cable television (WB, TNT, Cartoon Network, Turner Classic Movies, CNN, HBO), films (Warner Brothers, New Line Cinema), and their accompanying websites provided the firm with great possibilities. Furthermore, the variety of communication products AOL Time Warner offers—such as Internet-based telephone service, e-commerce products, and cross-promotion of a variety of consumer products—still provide many more new opportunities for growth. However, the firm continues to suffer from the loss of AOL dial-up subscribers as they switch to higher-speed broadband service from competing firms. Critics point to AOL's failure to properly prepare for the transfer of their low-tech customers to high-speed services and to the products that could be better distributed using faster connection speeds. By 2003, AOL's dial-up market dominance had fallen to one out of three customers in the U.S. while just one in thirty broadband customers subscribed through AOL.

Because customers can change Internet service providers with relative ease, some have begun to see little difference between firms except with respect to price. Being able to offer its customers Time Warner content allows AOL to avoid competing with other Internet service providers on a price basis alone. This major competitive advantage changes the way the battle for customers will be fought. Internet service providers like AOL need to focus attention not only on price, but on the value-added services they can offer their customers. Whether these services take the form of entertainment content or access to specialized communications and software, customers will find Internet service providers offering a growing selection of services as each seeks to attract and keep customers.

To underscore this awareness, AOL Time Warner announced a renewed effort to focus on delivering content to "tweens," the 8- to 12-year-old kids who, research showed, are the fastest-growing group of Internet users. They prefer being online to watching television, and on average spend over an hour online each day. This puts AOL Time Warner's product called *KOL,* in direct competition with online gaming sites and television channels such as Nickelodeon, Disney, PBS, and the Cartoon Network.

ASSIGNMENT

1. Examine the AOL Time Warner sites (**www.aol .com** and **www.timewarner.com**) and describe the current content offering. How would you improve them? What other special customer groups like "tweens" should the firm consider targeting? What could they do to reach this group, and how could they satisfy their online needs? What package of products and services should the firm offer?

2. Besides lowering prices, what else would you do to help AOL retain dial-up customers?

Chapter Review

1. **Define and explain the meaning of e-business.**

   e-Business, or electronic business, can be defined as the organized effort of individuals to produce and sell, for a profit, products and services that satisfy society's needs through the facilities available on the Internet. The term *e-business* refers to all business activities conducted on the Internet by an individual firm or industry. In contrast, *e-commerce* is a part of e-business; the term refers only to the activities involved in buying and selling online; these include identifying suppliers, selecting products or services, making purchase commitments, completing financial transactions, and obtaining service. e-Business needs highly specialized forms of the human, material, informational, and financial resources that any business requires. New customer needs created by the Internet as well as traditional ones can be satisfied in unique ways by e-business. By using a variety of e-business activities, firms can increase their sales revenues and reduce their expenses in order to increase profits.

2. **Explore a framework for understanding e-business.**

   Most firms involved in e-business fall more or less into one of three primary groups as defined by their e-business activities: those that create the telecommunications infrastructure; Internet software producers, which provide the ability to do things on the Internet; and online sellers and content providers. The Internet would still be limited to communications between individuals and among groups of special-interest researchers were it not for the activity of online sellers and content providers. In this area of e-business, we have just begun to see the development of online strategies for reaching out to existing and new customers. The special characteristics of e-business provide increased opportunities for firms to reach global markets and for small businesses to start up and grow. Another way to approach the study of e-business is to focus attention on how operations within each of the three primary functional areas of business—management, marketing, and finance—can be improved by adopting online software and solutions.

3. **Identify and explain fundamental models of e-business.**

   e-Business models focus attention on the identity of the firm's customers, the users of the Internet activities, the uniqueness of the online product or service, and the firm's degree of online presence. Many e-businesses can be distinguished from others simply by their customer focus. Firms that use the Internet mainly to conduct business with other firms are generally referred to as having a business-to-business, or B2B, model. Currently, the vast majority of e-business is B2B in nature. In contrast to the focus of the B2B model, firms like Amazon.com and eBay are clearly focused on individual buyers and so are referred to as having a business-to-consumer, or B2C, model. Unlike the B2B and B2C models, which focus on business transactions and communications, the consumer-to-consumer, or C2C, model involves the increasingly popular use of peer-to-peer, or P2P, software to facilitate the exchange of data directly between individuals over the Internet.

4. **Examine a taxonomy for e-business models.**
   An online broker brings buyers and sellers together, often specializes in a particular product classification, and may even be organized by a major supplier or vendor of the products. An advertising e-business model is based on earning revenues in exchange for the display of advertisements on the firm's website. Website content providers may elect to earn revenues through subscription fees, charges to view single items such as a report (pay-per-view), or membership fees to gain access to the site. The distribution channel member model includes activities of retailers, wholesalers, and manufacturers conducting business through the Internet. Affiliation programs pay website operators for customers who find their way to a company's site and either buy merchandise or services or perform some other action, such as registering and providing certain information. The community model is built around the idea that a group of online users can be regularly brought together at a commonly used website. Infomediaries sell information such as online customer behavior to advertisers and other interested parties. The portal e-business model is a type of infomediary that earns revenues by drawing users to its site and serving as a gateway or portal to information located elsewhere on the Internet.

5. **Examine the basic components of an e-business plan.**
   The business plan is the most detailed description of what individuals within the firm are doing and what the business is trying to achieve. It should be revised as conditions and circumstances demand. Critical components of the plan include an environmental analysis of forces affecting decision-makers; the firm's e-business model and detailed marketing strategies; management and organizational issues; and financial concerns.

REVIEW QUESTIONS

1. What are the major characteristics that define e-business?
2. How does e-business differ from e-commerce?
3. How do e-businesses generate revenue streams?
4. What roles do telecommunications firms and Internet service providers play in e-business?
5. How do software producers contribute to e-business?
6. What does the term *content providers* mean?
7. Why does e-business represent a global opportunity to reach customers?
8. What are the three fundamental e-business models?
9. What does smart advertising mean?
10. Define each e-business model in the taxonomy.
11. What is a business plan?
12. When should a business plan be prepared?

DISCUSSION QUESTIONS

1. Can advertising provide enough revenue to enable an e-business to succeed in the long run?
2. How can small businesses compete against large-scale e-businesses?
3. What distinguishes the B2B, B2C, and C2C e-business models?
4. Explain why it is worth paying more for *smart advertising.*
5. Why is the advertising e-business model so popular?
6. Why bother creating an e-business plan?

Building Skills for Career Success

EXPLORING THE INTERNET

In order to thrive, all websites need visitors. Without the revenue that comes from firms that buy banner advertising on websites or the subscription fees paid by viewers, firms simply would not have the cash needed to create and maintain a website and to expand their activities. What attracts viewers varies according to their lifestyle, age, gender, and information requirements. Many online communities focus on the interests of a selected target audience. MarthaStewart.com (**www.marthastewart.com**) and iVillage.com (**www.ivillage.com**) are two well-known sites catering mostly to college-educated women who are interested in leisure, parenting, business, nutrition, and the like. However, these are only two sites in a sea of choice.

ASSIGNMENT

1. Identify and describe two or more websites whose content attracts you and keeps you returning on a regular basis.
2. How would you describe the target audience for these sites?
3. What advertisements are typically displayed?

DEVELOPING CRITICAL THINKING SKILLS

Although the variety of products available to online shoppers is growing rapidly, many people are reluctant to make purchases over the Internet. For a variety of reasons, some individuals are uncomfortable with using the Internet for this purpose, while others do so easily and often. The considerations involved in making a business-to-business purchase decision differ from those involved in making a personal purchase. However, the experience of buying office supplies from Staples.com (**www.staples.com**) for a business might influence an individual to visit other online sites to shop for personal items.

ASSIGNMENT

1. Which sorts of products or services do you think would be easy to sell online? What kinds of things do you think would be difficult to purchase online? Explain your thinking.

2. Have you ever purchased anything over the Internet? Explain why you have or have not.
3. Explain how the considerations taken into account in buying office supplies from Staples.com for a business might differ from those involved in making a personal purchase.

BUILDING TEAM SKILLS

An interesting approach taken by Yahoo.com and several other websites is to provide viewers with the tools they need to create a personal webpage or community. Yahoo.com's GeoCities site (**http://geocities.yahoo.com/home/**) provides simple instructions for creating a site and posting your own content, such as articles and photographs. Yahoo! earns money by selling banner advertising, which is visible to viewers of all the different communities that Yahoo! hosts.

ASSIGNMENT

1. Working in a group, examine some of the GeoCities communities and personal webpages. Discuss which sites you think work well and which do not. Explain your reasoning.
2. Develop an idea for your own site and sketch out how you would like to see the site appear on the Internet. You may use ideas that look good on other people's personal pages.
3. Who is your target audience, and why do you think they will want to visit the site?

RESEARCHING DIFFERENT CAREERS

The Internet offers a wide assortment of career opportunities in business as well as in Internet-related technologies. As firms seek opportunities online, new e-businesses are springing up every day. In many cases, these firms want people who have a fresh outlook on how e-businesses can succeed, and they prefer individuals without preconceived notions of how to proceed. Website managers, designers, creative artists, and content specialists are a few of the positions available. Many large online job sites, such as Monster.com (**www.monster.com**), can help you find out about employment and the special skills required for jobs.

ASSIGNMENT

1. Summarize the positions that appear to be in high demand in e-business.
2. What are some of the special skills required to fill these jobs?
3. What salaries and benefits are typically associated with these positions?
4. Which job seems most appealing to you personally? Why?

IMPROVING COMMUNICATION SKILLS

Describing websites in summary form can be difficult because of the mix of information they involve. A useful exercise is to create a table, which can serve not only as an organizational tool for the information but also as a means of quick comparison.

ASSIGNMENT

1. Create a table that will compare ten websites you have visited. Place the title of one type of information at the head of each column. For example, you might start with the firm's name in the first column, the type of product it sells online in the second column, and so forth.
2. Enter short descriptive data in each column.
3. Write a descriptive summary of the table you have prepared, identifying a few of the outstanding characteristics listed in the data.

Exploring Useful Websites

These websites provide information related to the topics discussed in the chapter. You can learn more by visiting them online and examining their current data.

1. AOL Time Warner (**www.timewarner.com**) is the world's largest online service and media company. AOL (**www.aol.com**), EarthLink (**www.earthlink.com**), and MSN (**www.msn.com**) are three major ISPs.

2. IBM's e-business website, **www.ibm.com/ebusiness/**, contains strategic e-business information, case studies, white papers on emerging issues, and information on software and hardware.

3. Amazon.com (**www.amazon.com**) is considered the largest retailer that sells exclusively online and is responsible for developing many of the strategies that are now considered standard for all online vendors.

4. Barnes & Noble (**www.barnesandnoble.com**) is a major competitor of Amazon.com that has transferred some of its business to the Internet to complement its bricks-and-mortar stores.

5. The Walt Disney Company (**www.disney.com**), which also owns the ABC television network, is a major media corporation that uses the Internet to develop new products and to help promote well-established ones like the Disney characters and Disneyland.

6. Petco.com (**www.petco.com**) and Petsmart.com (**www.petsmart.com**) sell pet supplies online.

7. WebMD (**www.webmd.com**) and the Mayo Clinic (**www.mayoclinic.com**) provide information about remedies, disease, and a variety of health-related topics and issues.

8. Sprint PCS (**www.sprintpcs.com**) is a telecommunications service firm that maintains an extensive website where customers can learn about products, access personal account information, send e-mail questions to customer service, and purchase additional products or services.

9. Lucent Technologies (**www.lucent.com**), Cisco Systems (**www.cisco.com**), and Nortel Networks (**www.nortelnetworks.com**) produce most of the tele-communications hardware that allows the Internet to work. Companies such as IBM (**www.ibm.com**), Hewlett-Packard (**www.hp.com**), Dell Computer (**www.dell.com**), Sun Microsystems (**www.sun.com**), Apple Computer (**www.apple.com**), and Gateway (**www.gateway.com**) produce many of the computers used by consumers and businesses. Microsoft (**www.microsoft.com**) and Oracle (**www.oracle.com**) provide software. Lotus Notes (**www.lotus.com**) software allows databases to be shared over the Internet.

10. Berlitz's website, **www.berlitz.com**, allows anyone in the world to jump quickly to a website designed in the viewer's preferred language.

11. NextPage (**www.nextpage.com**) P2P software makes possible collaboration and the sharing of documents anywhere in the world.

12. SnapFish (**www.snapfish.com**) allows customers to display their photographic images online free of charge and earns revenues by selling film processing and print copies of photos to those allowed to view them.

13. Monster.com (**www.monster.com**) is the largest online recruiting firm.

14. Forrester Research, Inc. (**www.forrester.com**), Ipsos-Reid Inc. (**www.ipsos-reid.com**), Nielsen/NetRatings (**www.nielsen-netratings.com**), Jupiter Media Metrix (**www.mediametrix.com**), ComScore (**www.comscore.com**), Computer Industry Almanac Inc (**www.c-i-a.com/**), the CIA's World Factbook (**www.cia.gov/cia/publications/factbook/**), and ClickZ (**www.clickz.com**) are good sources of online statistics and usage behavior.

15. Online stock trading is provided by many brokerage firms, including Charles Schwab (**www.schwab.com**), TD Waterhouse Group (**www.tdwaterhouse.com**), Ameritrade (**www.ameritrade.com**), and E-Trade Group (**www.etrade.com**).

16. iVillage (**www.ivillage.com**) is an online community for women, and Classmates (**www.classmates.com**) brings former schoolmates together. GeoCities (**www.geocities.com**) is a portal to a huge selection of online communities and allows users to create websites free of charge.

17. Gomez.com (**www.gomez.com**) is an infomediary that pays users for permission to track their movements on the Internet and sell the information to advertisers and other interested parties.

18. The Small Business Administration (**www.sba.gov/starting/indexbusplans.html**) is one of many websites that provides detailed guidelines for preparing a business plan.

web appendix

The Internet and Related Technologies

LEARNING OBJECTIVES	WEB APPENDIX OUTLINE
1. Explore the early history of the Internet and the World Wide Web.	*Inside e-Business: Wireless Internet Access—The Next "Big Thing"*
2. Examine the primary components of the Internet's infrastructure: computers, devices, and related technologies.	**The Early History of the Internet and the World Wide Web** Packet Switching—The Technological Basis of the Internet IP Addresses and the Universal Resource Locator Code Early Internet Software Applications The Beginning of the World Wide Web
3. Understand the specialized software used to create and manage websites and web-based content.	**The Internet Infrastructure and Related Technologies** The Five Primary Internet Infrastructure Components Computer Technology and the Internet Hand–Held Devices and Other Telecommunication Devices
	Website and Related Software Computer Programming Languages for Creating Webpage Content Webpage Authoring/Editing Software Convergence of Technologies

To access this appendix, go to **http://college.hmco.com/business/students/** and select "Canzer/e-Business 2e" from the drop-down menu.

chapter 2

Environmental Forces Affecting Planning and Practice

LEARNING OBJECTIVES

1. Explore the major environmental forces that can affect e-business planning and practice.

2. Examine the primary external environmental forces that can affect e-business planning and practice.

3. Examine the primary internal environmental forces that can affect e-business planning and practice.

INSIDE
e-business

Global Entertainment Industry Responds to Change

According to the Recording Industry Association of America (**www.riaa.com**), worldwide sales of music fell from $40 billion in 2000 to $32 billion in 2002. Much of that dramatic decline was attributed to the increasing popularity of illegal downloading and file-sharing made popular by the growing use of peer-to-peer (P2P) software like KaZaA (**www.kazaa.com**) and the first version of the "grandfather" of file-sharing software, Napster (**www.napster.com**). The rapid and dramatic drop in sales jolted industry participants who responded in several ways to the perceived threatening changes taking place in their business environment and their long-standing business model.

A controversial reaction was to launch lawsuits against individuals as well as firms that the industry charged with piracy. But a more pragmatic decision was the move to online distribution of music and the reduction of compact disc (CD) prices in stores. Strategically, several online retail sites emerged to offer legal copies of music for sale. Among them were Apple Computer Inc.'s i-Tunes Music Store (**www.apple.com/itunes/**); Roxio Inc.'s PressPlay, which the Santa Clara, California software firm bought from Sony Corp. and Vivendi Universal SA in 2003 and is now marketed under the acquired Napster brand (**www.napster.com**); RealNetworks Inc.'s Rhapsody (**www.real.com**); and MusicNet (**www.musicnet.com**), which is supported by AOL Time Warner, Bertelsmann AG, and EMI Group. Most sites selected the subscription or pay-per-play e-business model, which allowed customers to download content for use on MP3 players and self-created CDs. Vendors' plans required subscribers to register and pay fees that allowed various combinations of music retrieval.

In response to falling European sales attributed to file-sharing websites like Limewire (**www.limewire.com**) and iMesh (**www.imesh.com**), British-based retailer Virgin Megastore (**www.virgin.com**) launched an online pay-per-play plan that offered new single releases at about 60 pence or about US$1 *before* they became available on CDs in stores. In addition to this new approach to distribution and cost reduction for packaging singles, Virgin's response to competition from file-sharing sites offered customers what they called a legal alternative to file-sharing at the cheapest prices in Europe. Virgin is among several other retailers and technology firms, including Microsoft and Tiscali (**www.tiscali.com**), who are licensed to resell more than 200,000 songs from British technology firm OnDemandDistribution OD2 (**www.od2.com**). OD2, in turn, has licensing agreements with the five major music labels to resell digital downloads on the Internet. Virgin's pricing is estimated to be 20 percent cheaper than its main competitors, Microsoft and Tiscali. Thus, the European music industry has responded with actions that it hopes will stem the tide of falling revenues, estimated at 26 percent by the British Phonographic Industry in 2003.

In the $12 billion American music market, retail giant Wal-Mart (**www.walmart.com**) accounts for approximately 14 percent of sales. Its decision to sell music files through its website reflects Wal-Mart's acceptance of alternative channels to avoid lost sales. Given that Jupiter Researcher Inc. suggests that online music sales will grow from $100 million in 2004 to $700 million in 2008, the stakes are significant for producers and distributors alike. In the battle for online sales, brand recognition will benefit firms like Wal-Mart and Virgin as current and new customers migrate to online purchasing.

According to a 2003 study by Forrester Research of Cambridge, Massachusetts, 20 percent of Americans over the age of twelve download music over the Internet, and by 2008, downloads are expected to represent one in three sales. Furthermore, Forrester estimated that about one-third of all Internet users will be employing P2P computing services to exchange and store personal data. P2P computing software allows anyone with a computer that is connected to the Internet to share material directly with anyone else, without going through a central computer server. This material can include music, photographs, images, movies, and other content files that they have created themselves or acquired in some other way.

Undoubtedly, many users attracted by P2P content distribution are drawn by the capacity to retrieve copies of recorded music and other multimedia free of charge. Critics of P2P software argue that firms like KaZaA violate copyright law and prevent artists who produce entertainment content from controlling the legitimate sale and distribution of their products. Others see the entertainment industries as entering a new era in which the Internet will forever transform distribution and sales promotion, causing the industry giants to redesign their established business models.[1]

Although P2P Internet software products present potentially great new ways of approaching business thinking, a very real problem arises for the entertainment industry when an unauthorized copy of a song is illegally posted for free distribution. The recording companies argue that when this happens, they and the artists lose revenue from customers who would otherwise buy the CD. However, research appears to suggest that although this may be true for some customers, the net result is a greater amount of purchasing overall. This fact suggests that perhaps potential customers use the P2P software to sample music before deciding to purchase it, so that it stimulates buying in much the same way as the free play of music on radio and television does. Perhaps P2P users simply regard the software as a radiolike distribution of free music. If the Internet and P2P computing service firms are in fact catalysts for an old-economy industry like the entertainment industry, then perhaps it is possible to both increase sales and offer the consumer the opportunity to explore content without purchasing it first.

In fact, the entertainment industry had similar concerns in the early 1980s when another new technology, videotape, first entered the consumer market. Today, the industry realizes that videotape simply opened up a new source of revenue: the sale and rental of films and television programming. Ways of exploiting P2P computing services are being explored, and strategic alliances between media groups suggest that the industry will have to recognize the need to change its business planning and work with the Internet, rather than trying to fight it.[2]

The entertainment industry closely monitors the continuous changes taking place in the e-business environment so it can respond properly with new strategies in a timely fashion. Improving business strategies with the help of the Internet is but one example of strategic thinking in response to technological, economic, and other forces at work today. Developing new plans to better serve customers and compete in the marketplace begins with an understanding of the changes that are taking place both outside and within the business organization.

Chapter 2 will take a closer look at the primary environmental forces that can influence e-business strategic planning. We will present a simplified but comprehensive model of these forces to help you research and develop e-business plans, analyze case studies, and complete other activities presented later in the text. Although a variety of forces are always at work at any moment, we will examine those that can be considered more critical to managers who are involved in the strategic planning process. We will start with an overview of the model and then examine each force individually.

The Environmental Forces Affecting Planning and Practice

external environmental forces

Those factors affecting e-business strategic planning that originate from outside the organization proper and are unlikely to be controllable by business decision-makers; they include globalization, sociocultural, demographic, economic, competitive, intermediary and supplier, technological, and political and legal forces.

Although the environmental business forces at work today are complex, often overlapping, and interrelated, it is useful to think of them as falling into two broadly defined categories. **External environmental forces** are those factors affecting e-business strategic planning that originate from outside the organization proper. External environmental forces are unlikely to be controllable by business decision-makers. Instead, planners and strategists will generally react to these forces, attempting to shield the organization from any undue negative effects and seek ways to exploit positive ones. For example, a large firm's decision to reduce its prices is generally recognized as a strategic action that a competing firm's business manager must respond to in some manner but that is outside of his or her direct control. Thus, when Virgin Megastores decides to reduce the prices of its latest music CDs other competitors must respond in some way to offset that decision and protect their market share. However, Virgin's decision to cut its prices is beyond the direct control of its competitors; they can only respond to it.

The primary external environmental forces that we will explore include globalization, sociocultural, demographic, economic, competitive, intermediary and supplier, technological, and political and legal forces. As a group, these forces present management with a list of areas to regularly survey and monitor for changes and developing trends. As we will see later in this chapter, management's research and intelligence-gathering efforts must begin with an understanding that is based on information continuously gathered from the external environment.

internal environmental forces

Those factors that are closely associated with the organizational functions and activities taking place within the firm, including the firm's management and organizational structure, human resources, information and knowledge, and finance.

In contrast, **internal environmental forces** are those factors that are closely associated with the organizational functions and activities taking place within the firm. These forces emerge from a variety of internal interacting forces, including the firm's management and organizational structure, human resources, information and knowledge, and finance. Internal environmental forces can have a significant impact on e-business strategic planning and should be continuously monitored so managers can incorporate into their planning any changes that are taking place, as well as the influences from external environmental forces. For example, existing shortages of skilled employees needed for specialized project work can undermine the firm's ability to sell its services to clients. However, management might consider that a particular project or client justifies the effort required to recruit the needed staff from another country or to pay premium salaries. Unlike the external environmental forces affecting the firm, internal forces such as this one are more likely to be under the direct control of management. In this case, management can either go out and hire the needed staff or can choose to pass over a prospective project.

Understanding this multidisciplinary framework and the forces that are at work can help decision-makers develop a better appreciation of both the opportunities and the many challenges facing the firm. As we will see later in the text, developing new e-business plans and revising existing plans begins with intelligence gathering that focuses on these forces in the e-business environment.

External Environmental Forces

Among the external environmental forces that influence e-business decision-making and predictions for future development, perhaps none is more complex or sensitive than globalization. Globalization is related closely with many of the other external forces as well as with internal environmental forces. As such, it is appropriate that we begin our examination of the primary sources of influence and their connection to e-business thinking here (see Figure 2.1).

Globalization Forces

globalization forces
The forces drawing the people of the world together to live under universally shared standards of culture, communication, technologies, and economics.

Globalization is currently the focus of a great deal of discussion and debate, and with good reason. From many people's point of view, **globalization forces** are inevitably drawing the people of the world together to live under universally shared standards of culture, communication, technologies, and economics, and they see this as positive. To others, globalization forces represent a threat to individual national cultures, identities, languages, and sovereignty that have managed to survive until today but may not survive the growing pressures created by the process of globalization in the future.

FIGURE 2.1   External Environmental Forces

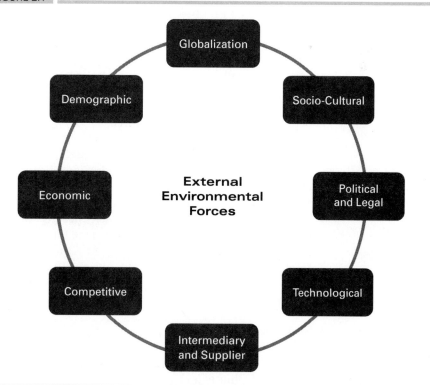

To those who see globalization as a positive force for change, the most important factor is their belief that globalization provides the best foundation for the global creation and distribution of wealth. They believe it to be the best system for creating the greatest amount of wealth because of the efficiencies inherent in standardizing global business practices. They consider it to be the best system for creating products quickly and efficiently and then distributing that newly created wealth to those who contributed to its creation.

Globalization obviously did not originate with the Internet. Historians trace the patterns of globalization back two thousand years to the days of the Roman Empire, when trade routes, common currency, and political control by Rome spread the Roman way of life across much of Europe and Asia. Today, however, globalization is highly associated with the growth of the Internet, which helped speed the delivery of new ideas, information, and communications technologies, thus changing the geopolitical boundaries of the world the way the Roman military did in its day. The Internet exemplifies globalization—for whether a person or a machine is in North America, Europe, Africa, or Asia, the Internet demands conformity to its standards and protocols. Computers, fax machines, and wireless devices like cellular telephones that wish to connect to and play a part in the global communications network must comply, or they simply will not function.

As a result of the Internet, workers in third-world economic zones are able to join forces with the first world on a more equal footing. Today, it is not uncommon to find software engineers in India doing programming for American-based firms that are selling products to German customers. Along with this collaboration by workers in the production of globally distributed products comes the transfer of common business practices and the necessary capital investments to provide the infrastructure for communications equipment. Jobs that previously would not have been available to engineers in India because of geography, trade barriers, and other restrictive factors are now made accessible because the Internet creates a virtual workplace, allowing individuals anywhere to be part of a global network of production and marketing efforts.

Among the economic spinoffs that benefit the local economy is an accelerated leap forward that results when the knowledge and skills gained from multinational corporations are applied to the production of other products that also can be channeled to markets through the same global network. For example, local Indian firms that provide software programming services are more likely to channel their products and services to global markets because of their association with firms that are already doing business through the Internet. Furthermore, the risk of losing skilled knowledge workers such as software engineers, who in the past might have left third-world countries to advance their careers and personal financial success in first-world economies, is reduced now that these workers are better able to find opportunities closer to home.

Success Stories

Let's look more closely at some examples of globalization success stories and individual firms' trends toward expanding e-business activities. Call centers that provide telephone- and computer-based customer information and services are now a booming business in India, thousands of miles away from where most of the customers they serve live—in North America and Europe. General Electric and British Airways are only two of the many firms that have invested heavily in Indian information technology centers located in cities like Bangalore and Hyderabad. The reasons for this are India's recently installed and reliable high-capacity telephone lines in most major centers, which make calls to India sound as clear as local calls, and its large base of low-cost English-speaking employees. Call-center employees are even trained to assume American identities and speaking styles in order to artificially create the perception that the customer is in fact dealing with a local customer service representative who may just live nearby in, say, Chicago.

In addition to customer service representatives in low-cost call centers, who earn about $1,600 to $2,100 annually, higher-paid Indian professionals such as accountants, software engineers, developers, website designers, and animators are increasingly joining the global information technology industry's back office. According to a report by Boston-based McKinsey & Company, by 2008 India's involvement in the global information technology industry will generate 800,000 new jobs and contribute $17 billion to the economy. Today, more than 2.8 million people work in India's information technology sector, and firms like Infosys Technologies—the first Indian software firm to be listed on NASDAQ—Wipro, Customer Asset, and Bangalore Labs have already established or have made plans to establish offices in the United States so as to be closer to their clients. A senior India-based technology executive accurately described the effect of globalization when he said, "We see ourselves as a next-generation company that is neither Indian nor American."

A New World Order?

According to proponents of globalization like author and *New York Times* columnist Thomas L. Friedman, the global free marketplace demands minimal interference by governments in the form of taxation and regulations, American-style capitalism and free movement of capital investments, and the establishment of democratically elected governments, courts, and institutions. Friedman's thesis is that globalization represents the emergence of something of a new world order that will eventually find its way to all corners of the globe. He argues that globalization is a self-directed movement guided by principles of democracy, technology, and free-market capitalism. Friedman warns that no one and no country controls globalization and that even the United States is subject to its rules. He believes that individuals and nations will have no choice but to dismantle the barriers between them if they are going to be players in this new emerging global business club. In short, either nations and individuals will conform to internationally accepted standards of business and political behavior or the other club members will exclude them from membership. If there is a club that favors globalization, it might be the World Trade Organization (WTO; **www.wto.org**). See the Developing Critical Thinking Skills exercise at the end of this chapter for more information.

According to Friedman, as globalization expands, the political, legal, and cultural barriers that tend to divide people are going to become less clear. Eventually, the only differences that will remain will be some degree of local language and culture. This is one of the reasons there is so much antiglobalization protest around the world. The acceptance by globalization supporters of the loss of individual sovereignty, culture, and, most importantly, the ability of governments to control activities of all sorts within their borders is incomprehensible to opponents to globalization. Opponents argue that they are not against free trade, but rather against the terms of free trade, which they believe give the majority of benefits to multinational corporations with little regard for the local culture, the natural environment, and the poor. They believe that individuals will lose whatever ability they may have to handle local concerns through labor laws, unions, and contracts, as these might be overruled by global trade tribunals. Instead of their own national courts and elected governments, they argue, cases will be decided by unelected trade bureaucrats who, they believe, will be motivated to promote the expansion of globalization and favor its proponents rather than local interests.

Critics of the globalization movement, such as MIT economist Paul R. Krugman and the English philosopher John Gray, view globalization with much concern. Both of these critics question the very premise that globalization is in fact the political and economic panacea that its supporters see it to be. Regardless of which position you take with regard to globalization, it will remain a force to contend with for the foreseeable future and one that will play an important role as e-business strategies and the influence of the Internet spread around the world.[3]

e-BUSINESS insight

Globalization Forces Change in Silicon Valley

Silicon Valley, the heartland of the high-technology industry, is geographically centered around the San Francisco area. It is facing a growing threat to its importance as a center of activity as globalization forces continue to encourage decentralization and redistribution of work around the world.

According to Forrester Research Inc., offshore outsourcing could mean more than 3.3 million lost U.S. jobs and $136 billion in lost wages in the next ten years, with three-quarters of those jobs going to centers in India. Savings can reach more than 50 percent since Indian salaries for skilled university graduate employees are about 25 percent of those in North America according to Mark Kobayashi-Hillary, author of *Outsourcing to India*. As a result, Microsoft, Hewlett-Packard, British Airways, Ford Motor Company, IBM, and Lufthansa are among the firms operating in the south-central Indian city of Bangalore.

Andy Grove, chairman of Intel Corp., suggests that many of the 200,000 jobs lost during the 2000–2003 recession will not return to Silicon Valley firms and that the number of software and tech service jobs in India could surpass those in the U.S. by 2010 as working relationships between globally operating firms become more common.

Question for discussion: How can Silicon Valley firms respond to these job losses as lower-cost centers develop around the world?[4]

Sociocultural Forces

Perhaps the broadest and most complex component of the external environment is the relevant social and cultural influences on the individual Internet user. The more managers know about the **sociocultural forces** that can influence their customers, suppliers, and employees, the more accurately they will be able to design appropriate e-business strategies. But what limits or boundaries should be placed on so broad a study? Providing sociocultural descriptions for all groups of people around the world would be impractical for this textbook. Instead, e-business strategists are advised to research and study the local sociocultural factors that are important to their firms' specific e-business planning requirements. Since the majority of the users of this book are likely to be interested in North American e-business plans and, as we have already suggested, globalization effectively transmits shared American values, we will discuss a short list of some basic North American cultural values that are likely to be among the forces at work.

sociocultural forces
The forces that can influence the socially and culturally defined characteristics of a firm's customers, suppliers, and employees.

Achievement and Success

People are motivated to achieve socially and culturally honored goals. Our culture celebrates the achievements of those who overcome obstacles and adversities. We admire the drive, discipline, and talent associated with achieving excellence in life. Winning may not be the only thing, but it counts for a lot in our view of life as a competition among products, firms, and people. We willingly trade up from one computer or software version to another because trading up reflects our view that the newer version is a better product and will succeed in some area where earlier versions had poorer performance. Customers will be drawn to firms that present images of success and especially to those that promise to make customers successful if they use their products and services. In short, firms that look like winners in the race will attract customers.

The culture of achievement and success is often an integral component in the marketing of Internet technology. Advertisements portray successful firms that are using the Internet and outperforming their competitors, who are slow to realize the value of initiating online strategies for success. Virtually every website vendor of Internet solutions, such as IBM or Microsoft, provides corporate and individual profiles of successful adoptions of their Internet strategic solutions, such as customer relationship management (CRM) or e-commerce. The message communicated is that the Internet represents success: If you want to be successful like these people, get the same solutions they have adopted for their firms.

Besides selling the idea of businesses' success and achievement, these vendors also portray individuals as enjoying more success in their personal lives when they adopt Internet-provided solutions. Financial planning, investing online, home decorating, and even cooking nutritious meals for your family are only a few common Internet lifestyle activities in which Internet-based information is said to promote successful personal behaviors. The popular image of the Internet user these vendors portray is that of a successful high achiever who became successful because of what she learned through the Internet and what she can do with the Internet as a technological tool.

Freedom and Individualism

Our culture embraces the concept of individual liberty and concurrently suggests that others should not attempt to interfere with that right. This makes it difficult for governments, corporations, or other people to impose restrictions or behavioral demands in areas that are basically viewed as belonging in the realm of individual choice and freedom. Hence, passing legislation to ban the distribution or sale of certain content on the Internet might be viewed as a challenge to personal liberty. For instance, peer-to-peer (P2P) software programs like KaZaA (**www.kazaa.com**) are designed to bypass the centralized controlled distribution of material over the Internet. The belief of those who share content over the Internet is that once an item has been produced and released, it is fair game for distribution by whomever wishes to pass it along to others who, in turn, have chosen to receive it. Even the unauthorized distribution of copyrighted material is considered a part of the free-exchange culture of the Internet and so should not be regulated by governments.

The argument that is often heard from people who wish to see the Internet left alone by governments and corporate interests is that it is sort of a freedom frontier where no one should attempt to control the exchange processes among users. The proponents of this view argue that there is a fair trade-off between the benefits and costs associated with providing a high degree of unregulated Internet use. Although there are some negative aspects to this lack of regulation, such as the illegal distribution of copyrighted material, the Internet also has done more than anyone could have imagined to spread ideas about freedom, democracy, and individual rights to parts of the world that would not have otherwise known about these cultural gifts.

Finally, the Internet is built around the idea of individualism. Individuals can often choose to select only the sort of information that they want to view when visiting a website rather than accept the default generic version for all viewers. So, for example, a viewer of MSN from upstate New York and another from southern California can select different weather and news displays that match their local geography and interests. Likewise, online music distributors like Napster (**www.napster.com**) now allow individuals to buy single songs rather than an entire CD if they so choose.

Efficiency, Progress, and Technology

Our culture embraces the idea that when a better way to do something is found, then a change is natural and represents human progress. We tend to believe that technological discoveries and inventions will solve current problems. Nowhere is this more evident than in the rapid acceptance of Internet-based solutions for both work and personal problems. For example, the widespread use of e-mail and other personal messaging systems represented a clear improvement over the regular postal service or courier delivery firms for facilitating communication. Internet messaging is instant and virtually free after the initial costs of connection to a service provider. Both factors have helped make Internet messaging a huge success, with rapid adoption by even the most technologically challenged users.

The continuously evolving nature of social behaviors—especially behaviors that are related to the virtual worlds created on the Internet—is among the key environmental forces influencing e-business strategic planning and decision-making.

Knowing about how people in general behave in social situations as well as their cultural characteristics provides the foundation for understanding how they are likely to behave on the Internet. Any business strategy will require an understanding of the target group of customers, and any management strategy will require an understanding of the firm's employees.

Demographic Forces

demographic forces
Descriptive population characteristics such as age, gender, race, ethnicity, marital status, parental status, income, and educational level.

Demographic forces involve descriptive population characteristics such as age, gender, race, ethnicity, marital status, parental status, income, and educational level. In addition to its use in describing groups in the general population, demographic categorization is also a tool that provides a high degree of predictability for current and future behavior. For instance, if research shows that large numbers of married women with young children in preschool are users of iVillage.com's (**www.ivillage.com**) informational services about child care, then iVillage will be better able to predict the potential size of the total iVillage.com market if it researches the demographic characteristics of this group. These data might come from government or private sources, but the result will be a better sense of the scale of the site's user base, the sorts of products that users might buy online, and so forth.

In order to begin any e-business strategic plan, it is critical to define and then continuously monitor the changing patterns of behavior of the demographic group that has been identified. Let's look at some current information about different demographic groups and their online behaviors.

According to Forrester Research Inc. (**www.forrester.com**), up until the late 1990s the fundamental demographic characteristics of people online were pretty simple: Internet use was limited to technologically knowledgeable and career-oriented middle-aged white males—not surprisingly, the same group that started up the Internet. As a result, the online activities, products, and services provided by e-business to serve the online marketplace were pretty much limited to the interests of this group of users. There was little in the way of commercial activity as we know it today until the demographics of the Internet changed. Regardless of which came first, the products and services or the entry of new demographic groups, research today clearly shows a changing pattern of demographics emerging online, one that is beginning to reflect the same demographic portrait as the overall population of North America.

A recent Nielsen/NetRatings (**www.nielsen-netratings.com**) survey reported that the average users of the Internet were changing from younger to older, richer to poorer, and white to those of color. The survey indicated that the fastest-growing group of Internet users was over 55 years old, with working-class incomes and matching tastes. Those who were cruising online were as likely to be found cruising the aisles at their local Wal-Mart. As cheaper, more widely available, and easy-to-use connection services to the Internet like AOL continue to penetrate, the market continues to grow. According to research by Jupiter Media Metrix (**www.mediametrix.com**), by 2006 there will be about 210 million online users in the United States, or about 71 percent of the population, up from the current level of about 182 million, or 59 percent of the population.[5]

A survey by Harris Interactive Inc. shows that Internet usage by women has caught up to and surpassed that of men, growing 900 percent in six years. Similarly, whereas technology news used to be the most popular subject for information online, now it's the weather. Research also shows that the group that spends the most time surfing from home is urban, working-class African Americans, who use the Internet mostly to chat online, send e-mail, and visit entertainment and sweepstakes sites. Single African Americans residing in the South spend 12.6 hours online each month, 26 percent more than the overall American average. Other groups of heavy Internet at-home users mostly live in the South and have lower incomes, modest educations, and blue-collar jobs. An interesting consistency emerges from the research: It suggests that a user's income is strongly associated with the length of time he or she spends online—the lower the income, the more time spent online.

The Nielsen/NetRatings survey also found that experience and efficiency are beginning to have an effect on online usage and behavior. For instance, the average number of websites that a user visited each month dropped in a year from fifteen to ten, but users are now examining more pages at these ten sites, spending an average of 50 seconds on a page. This suggests that familiarity and loyalty are forming; users are shifting from surfing to checking in at their favorite sites. And although the Internet is clearly breaking down the barriers between socioeconomic groups, the research suggests that the online behaviors of different socioeconomic groups are quite different. Those on the upper end of the scale are using the Internet as a convenient tool for gathering information for big-ticket purchases, and those on the lower end are using it as an alternative to television where they can chat, play games, and enter sweepstakes.

According to research by the Pew Internet & American Life Project, men and women use the Internet equally to do banking, send instant messages, and download music. However, men tend to use the Internet more to buy stocks, get news, compare products, buy products, bid at auctions, and visit government websites, and women are more likely to send e-mail, play games, collect coupons, and get information on health, jobs, and religion. Furthermore, a Media Metrix Inc. (**www.mediametrix.com**) study of teenagers found that boys are much more likely to download software and play games online, whereas girls are more interested in reading online magazines, doing homework, and staying in touch with their friends online.

The continuing research into the demographics of those people who use the Internet and what they actually do while they are connected is helping to build a clearer understanding of the Internet's basic social and cultural nature. This in turn contributes to the development of e-business strategies for serving markets.[6]

Economic Forces

The forces at play in the economy can have a major impact on individual and industrywide decision-making. Employment and income levels, interest rates and inflation, foreign exchange values of currencies, individual corporate growth as measured by annual percentage increases in earnings, and overall general economic growth as measured by gross domestic product (GDP) are only a few of the economic forces that should be of interest to strategic e-business planners. We will now briefly examine the basic concepts associated with each of these potential sources of influence on planning.

Employment and Income Levels

The percentage of the workforce that is gainfully employed and the amount of money people earn are strong indicators of their ability to spend on all sorts of products and services. When employment and incomes are rising, it is likely that more spending will find its way to the cash drawers of both firms in the local economy and global firms that are involved with the Internet. To put it simply, people without money cannot be customers. The ability of any individual or firm to spend money on Internet products and services is tied to the ability of that individual or firm to generate income. For example, as employment levels and incomes rise for the technology workers in India that are paid more than the average, their spending would be expected to increase. Some of this economic growth will eventually result in additional spending by the Indian firms they work for to supplement their original necessary infrastructure of computers, fiber-optic cables, and satellite dishes.

Interest Rates and Inflation

The interest rates charged to borrowers for short- or long-term bank loans, bonds, and other lending instruments are a cost to a business for their temporary use of someone else's money. If the cost of borrowing money increases, it follows that some projects that might have been worthwhile and profitable when interest rates were lower may no longer be so. As a result, small increases in interest rates can precipitate a slowdown in economic activity as a variety of projects are shelved. For example, the telecommunications industry slowdown that began in 2000 affected the drive to install Internet solutions around the world by firms like Cisco Systems, Lucent, and Nortel Networks. It was largely caused by several consecutive rounds of interest-rate increases by the U.S. Federal Reserve, the central banking authority responsible for setting monetary policy for the United States. As a result of the reduction in sales growth, thousands of employees around the world were laid off, further slowing global economic activity.

inflation
A general rise in prices or fall in the buying power of a currency.

Interest rates are directly related to the level of inflation in an economy. **Inflation** can be defined as a general rise in prices or a fall in the buying power of a currency. Interest rates are generally 2 to 3 percent above whatever the inflation rate happens to be. So if the central bank borrowing rate—rate at which the Federal Reserve lends to its member banks—is 5 percent, then inflation is probably running at about 2 to 3 percentage points below that. The rates for all other forms of lending, from credit cards to leases on computers by consumers, are set taking into consideration the anticipated rate of inflation for the duration of the loan. In this way, lenders are compensated for the loss of buying power that they experience while their money is temporarily being used by a borrower who will be paying back the loan in a currency that will have less buying power than when it was borrowed.

Explanations for the causes of inflation, why it is a bad thing for an economy, and how central banks attempt to deal with it are beyond the scope of this textbook. However, it can be said that inflation forces people and businesses to change their spending priorities and thereby generally causes a loss of business activity for some firms and less growth for most others. For example, if inflation has caused rent and employees expenses to rise, a business may have to cut back on plans to install a website and e-business solutions because it lacks internal sources of funds to pay for the effort. An individual who was planning to buy a powerful laptop computer may, if the price of the computer or of other goods and services rises too much, choose instead to buy a less powerful machine, which generally means an older model. As a result, sales of newer models slow down, and the logical negative effects on the manufacturers and distributors follows. The slowdown in sales partly explains the merger of Compaq Computer with Hewlett-Packard in 2002. (The merger resulted in a more productive organization that was judged a success after pre-merger quarterly losses for the two firms of $372 million were replaced by profits in 2003.)[7]

Foreign Exchange Values

Like inflation and interest rates within a country, the foreign exchange value of one country's currency in terms of another country's currency is an important economic factor, especially for e-business. In general terms, a rise in a currency's foreign exchange value means that the holders of that currency have gained buying power for purchasing foreign-made products and services. Since e-businesses buy many of these from North American–based suppliers like IBM, Microsoft, Nortel Networks, Cisco Systems, and Sun Microsystems, the purchasing ability of these firms' foreign customers is directly related to the buying power of their currency. In short, a strong U.S. dollar may make imports inexpensive for Americans, but it simultaneously means potentially fewer sales in foreign markets, where customers must trade their currencies for dollars to pay for purchases from U.S. firms. Part of the drop in telecommunications business activity that began in 2000 was also attributed to the strong U.S. dollar, especially against the weaker currencies in Europe and Asia.

Individual Corporate and Overall Economic Growth

It is important for e-business strategic planners to monitor the growth of individual corporations as well as overall general economic growth, as both can have an impact on important areas of decision-making. For example, firms like Yahoo! that earn a major portion of their revenues from advertisements placed on their websites can often be harbingers of things to come—both good and bad. By looking at these firms, decision-makers can gain some idea of what is happening in the industry and the implications of that for their planning. The large drop in online advertising revenues at Yahoo! and other firms that began in 2000 was an early indication that the so-called dot-com firms were running out of cash for advertising campaigns on the Internet. All of the websites that wanted to build a customer base of users were looking to online advertising (along with traditional print and television advertising for those that could afford it) as a logical way to reach Internet users. When sales revenues at many of these websites failed to provide satisfactory returns on the total investments that had been made, the dot-com bubble burst and corporate stock market values collapsed. Many, like Yahoo!, fell dramatically by 70 to 80 percent in value, while others went bankrupt. The message for planners is that by watching the reported developments at other industry players, like Yahoo!, they can better understand what is likely to be happening to their firm now or what might happen in the near future if a trend is developing. Most observers look at the trend in a firm's percentage growth of earnings (or the lack of it), which in turn is based on changes to both revenues and expenses.

During the summer of 2003, the business press began publishing articles suggesting that dramatic improvements in revenue and stock values were underway at Yahoo!. Yahoo's improvements in revenue growth reflected a successful attempt to diversify from its online advertising base into nonadvertising products and services, such as high-speed and dial-up Internet access and online dating and job search websites. By the summer of 2003, Yahoo's registered users numbered more than 116 million, up from 83 million the year before. More significantly, fee-paying users increased to 3.5 million from 2.9 million, suggesting that Yahoo learned that new opportunities could be realized by developing new products and services.[8]

Similarly, it is worthwhile to pay close attention to the overall growth in economic activity as measured by changes in GDP in order to understand the impact that economic conditions will likely have on a firm's strategic planning. A healthy, noninflationary expanding economy grows at a rate of about 3 to 4 percent annually. Growth that occurs faster than this is generally associated with potential inflation and subsequent interest-rate increases. A slowdown in the overall economy will generally lead to an eventual slowdown in e-business earnings—if not concurrently, then shortly thereafter. By late 2003, the stock markets seemed to suggest that the slowdown that started in 2000 was indeed over and that a new phase of sustainable growth was emerging. Particularly, Asian markets were improving, and business sentiment was more upbeat than in earlier years, leading to renewed optimism about increased revenue opportunities. For example, by the summer of 2004, the Japanese economy was growing at a healthy annual rate of 3.2 percent and its stock market was up 45 percent over the previous year—its best economic performance since 1996.[9]

Competitive Forces

The competitive forces that are at work in the external environment relate mostly to the direct competition between firms that offer similar or substitute products and services. In terms of e-business, there are giants in all three primary industry sectors, but there are also many smaller firms that seek niche markets in the globally expanding marketplace for products and services. Generally speaking, the barriers to entry in many areas of e-business are relatively low, and partnering opportunities are increasingly being used to leverage the advantages offered when smaller and larger firms find ways to work together.

Competition also exists between the providers of e-business solutions and the providers of alternative solutions from competing industries. For example, an e-business provider of access to e-mail communication services is not just in competition with other e-mail providers. E-mail service providers are also in competition with alternative services available from the U.S. Postal Service, couriers, telephone voice communication services, and even personal travel service firms that provide face-to-face communication between participants. The convenience, cost, and

e-BUSINESS
insight

Technological Change Creates Opportunities As Well As Threats

According to the Photo Marketing Association International of Jackson, Michigan, digital camera sales surpassed regular camera sales for the first time in 2003 with 31 percent of American households owning a digital camera. Although rapid growth of digital cameras sales only began in 1998, they were expected to exceed 12 million units, about half of all cameras sold, as buyers switch to the new technology. Because digital photography allows individuals to discard unwanted images, select and alter images before making their own prints, or send them over the Internet, digital photography is expected to continue to increase in popularity, providing opportunities for firms that can capitalize on the trend. For example, cell phone users have added built-in digital cameras that allow them to communicate visually, which provides phone companies with greater revenues and phone manufacturers with a new product feature to sell.

However, other firms, like Eastman Kodak Company (**www.kodak.com**), that depend heavily on traditional camera technologies for sales of products and processing services have been devastated. Kodak's chief executive, Dan Carp, suggests that digital influences will likely continue to erode traditional sales revenues by 8 to 10 percent annually, and as a result, Kodak will continue to restructure, laying off 6,000 more employees in 2003 while its stock value falls to its lowest values in 20 years. This is in spite of Kodak's relative successes at joining in the digital photography market. The competitive advantages that Kodak's business model enjoyed in the older technology marketplace have not transferred to the new-technology environment sufficiently to compensate for the lost revenues.

Question for discussion: What can old-technology dependent firms like Kodak do to respond to the new-technology challenges of digital imaging?[10]

time-saving advantages of e-mail over alternative choices generally mean that it will be used unless there are mitigating issues. For example, suppose either the sender or the receiver does not have access to e-mail services. In this case, the next logical competitive choice will likely be selected. It is important for e-business strategic thinkers to recognize the range of alternative competitors they are facing and the particular issues, such as access to technology, relevant to the user's decision set.

Intermediary and Supplier Forces

Intermediary and supplier forces refer to the behaviors of wholesalers, online brokerages, and auctions from which buyers and sellers are able to efficiently conduct exchanges and secure a supply of needed materials. A firm like Dell Computer relies on a supplier network in order to locate, purchase, and deliver the components that it uses to manufacture high-quality computer hardware at competitive prices.

Along with the broader network of suppliers that provide needed materials, a firm must closely watch for changes that might affect the prices it pays for parts and the way its competitors are responding to the same environmental circumstances.

For example, is a new supplier attracting attention because of its better service or lower prices? New intermediaries are emerging every day as large vendors and financial institutions look for ways to participate in the huge volume of transactions conducted through the Internet. All decision-makers need to monitor their continuously changing supply chain in order to know when circumstances suggest it might be advantageous to switch to alternative sources of supply.

Technological Forces

Technological forces refer to the influence that the complex hardware and software used in e-business has on planning. Examples of the influence of technological change on e-business thinking are presented throughout this text, and the companion website presents a descriptive overview of the Internet and related technologies. In addition to decisions about what technology to buy, whether it is better to lease or to own, and what new technological breakthroughs will affect current planning, e-business managers must weigh countless decisions that relate in some manner to technological forces. The following example illustrates the influence that technology can have on e-business strategic planning for both buyers and sellers of products and services.

hosting
Providing hardware and software services to clients who connect to their files over the Internet.

Consider a firm's decision to use hosting services provided by a firm like IBM as a means of dealing with the rapidly changing forces of technology. **Hosting** refers to providing hardware and software services to clients who connect to their files over the Internet. For example, rather than trying to keep up with quickly outdated e-commerce computer servers, software, and security systems, many businesses prefer to have their e-commerce activities hosted by a firm that specializes in this field. This eliminates the need to hire experts to manage the site and keep them trained and informed of constantly changing technology. Hosting also generally means less chance of downtime, since the host usually provides multiple backup operations should one part of its network experience technical problems. A firm that opts for hosting also will not have to be concerned with customers overloading its Internet connection or its computer servers. This is particularly important to firms that expect large volumes of traffic on their site.

Technology also provides a bridge that can simplify transactions with customers in a global economy. For example, Internet software technology can provide customer-selected webpages and menus in a preferred language, links to international online credit card services that allow anyone with a card to make a purchase and assure payments to vendors, and search agents that can be used to assist buyers looking for suppliers.

Political and Legal Forces

Political and legal forces refer to activities related to governments and government agencies. In general, governments and the courts treat e-business activity as an extension of the regular activities carried out by the non-e-business part of a firm. Therefore, in a general sense, a firm located in California is expected to function according to the laws of that state, regardless of the fact that its activities may be partly or entirely carried out over the Internet. In short, if it is illegal to do something in the state of California, then it is illegal for a firm located in California to do it anywhere.

In our discussion of globalization earlier in this chapter, we discussed the forces that are promoting the emergence of global standards for government and courts to serve as a condition for firms investing in any country. As globalization expands, it was argued, these standards will also migrate to places that wish to participate in the global economy. In the meantime, however, standards are far from the rule. There are places in the world where businesspeople need to watch out, where the rule of law means something quite different from the conventional North American and European model. In our economy, disputes are generally settled through negotiation between parties who have signed contractual agreements that stipulate their positions and outline their rights in a business arrangement. If negotiations fail, one or both parties can take the matter to the courts, where judgment is rendered according to interpretation of business laws. Clearly, this is not universally true throughout the world today, and businesses need to be concerned with who their business partners are as the Internet opens possibilities for both large and small firms around the world. The history of Napster illustrates the point. After legal action from the music industry, U.S. courts ordered the California-based Napster to cease operations in 2001 because it could not prevent the illegal distribution of copyright content. Although the Napster brand re-emerged in 2003 as a legal file-purchasing website, other firms such as KaZaA continue illegal and questionable operations off shore and out of reach of U.S. legal authorities. KaZaA's parent company, Sharman Networks, is based in the South Pacific tax haven of Vanuatu.[11]

Internal Environmental Forces

Managers may tend to focus their attention on researching the external environmental sources of influence on the firm, thereby seeking opportunities and threats to current planning and operations. However, they must also recognize the internal environment of the organization itself as a force to be reckoned with. Some managers may incorrectly assume that the internal environmental forces are already known to planners and therefore do not require any study. However, unless careful attention is also paid to the forces originating from within the internal environment, it is highly unlikely that whatever planning does emerge will be optimal for the firm (see Figure 2.2).

Management and Organizational Structure Forces

A firm's management and organizational structure forces include those related to theories about leadership and motivation of employees, the organizational culture, communications styles, and operations of the business. Together, these forces form a descriptive definition of the nature and character of the organization; that is to say, they define just who and what the firm is. For example, the more liberal-thinking and flexible of the information technology firms, the dot-coms, have been celebrated in countless journal articles as places where work environments are

FIGURE 2.2   Internal Environmental Forces

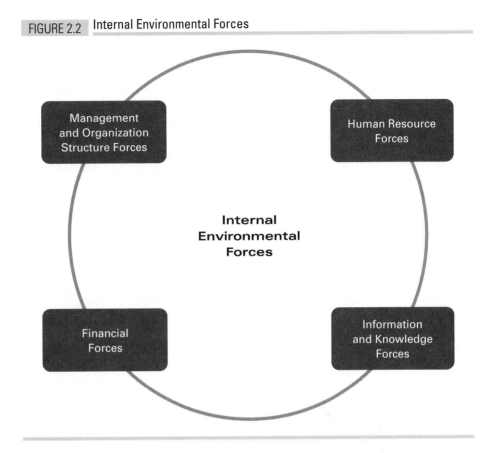

radically different from the traditional North American model. Executive leaders often attempt to motivate staff by using a coaching and team-style approach in the workspace and may be indistinguishable from the lower-level employees they work alongside. Commonplace are offices without walls or conventional barriers to emphasize a culture of equality among all staff members. A dress code that generally allows staff to dress in whatever way they feel most comfortable and policies that allow people to work whatever hours they want from whatever location (office or home) are also hallmarks of the new management and organizational structure of today's information technology firm.

If there is a new managerial culture emerging in business, it is more likely to emerge from the countercultural organizational environments of the information technology industry. This is particularly true in areas such as website design, where work production requires creative energy and is often spontaneous rather than metered out as it would be in producing automobiles on an assembly line. This is not to suggest that all managerial structures encourage or even permit radically loose organizational environments. The assembly line that puts together Dell Computer's products does not operate very differently from the assembly lines at

Ford Motor Company. However, even in these positions the atmosphere is generally reported to be more relaxed, team-oriented, and sociable.

Because the information technology industry is relatively new and enjoys low barriers to entry, many firms were started and are still led by the same principal personalities. Examples of some better-known industry leaders in this category include Bill Gates of Microsoft, Larry Ellison of Oracle, Michael Dell of Dell Computer, Thomas Siebel of Siebel Systems, and Steve Case of AOL. In each case, they established a managerial style that reflected their personal vision as the founders of these firms. How they conceptualized their company and their relationships with people inside and outside the organization is still very much reflected in the leadership and managerial structures currently in place at these firms. Although industry giants like IBM are not led by the same people who started the firm, each of them has a unique corporate culture that has an equivalently influential effect on its strategic planning.

Human Resource Forces

Closely related to the internal forces associated with management and organizational structure are the forces connected to the firm's human resources. Human resource forces include issues related to employees: the work they are assigned to do, how new employees are recruited, development and advancement strategies within the organization, and even how the firm maintains employee expertise through training and promotions. When competitive job markets make it difficult to find, hire, and keep skilled and knowledgeable employees, planning strategies need to reflect these conditions and the effect they may have on the workplace. Besides offering hiring bonuses, stock options, and very relaxed working conditions, firms may also seek additional means of attracting desirable personnel. For example, providing day care and health club facilities on the company work site are not unusual at many firms today.

Planners need to recognize the impact that human resources can have on operations. For example, a belief among employees that their personal career is stalled if they are not promoted every two years can be problematic in terms of the individual's performance and overall corporate operations. If corporate growth has not provided for a level of internal mobility and advancement that meets employee expectations, then the firm may lose valuable people who might be difficult to replace. Furthermore, replacing these people will certainly require time and money and reduce current levels of operating efficiency. The problem faced by most information technology firms is how to provide their employees with fair opportunities for career growth that are competitive with those offered by other technology firms in e-business. A firm's success or failure in responding to this challenge will determine not only the human resources available to operate the business but also the overall long-term performance of the entire organization.

Information and Knowledge Forces

Information and knowledge forces include employee skills, availability of information, and the general level of employee knowledge. These can have considerable influence on the ability of the firm's human resources to perform the work they are expected to do. Information and knowledge should be thought of as the tools that employees need in order to do their jobs. Providing poor information services or information that is difficult to understand or locate obviously weakens the potential performance of the employee.

Besides training employees so they have specialized knowledge about the firm, its customers, its suppliers, its products, and other important things, the information technology industry faces more rapid obsolescence of information than most industries do. The firm's human resources effort must incorporate regular training of employees so they can maintain their expertise in a variety of areas. To answer this need, an entire training industry specializing only in software and hardware for the information technology worker provides regularly scheduled seminars for employees. For example, Siebel Systems provides dozens of courses globally on the use of its products and services through Siebel University. Courses are available through Siebel's website, **www.siebel.com**, as well as through instructor-led classroom sessions. Clients can receive certification after completing prescribed courses for specific Siebel knowledge areas. This training model is fundamentally the same for Microsoft, IBM, Lotus Development, and many other information technology firms.

Access to training is especially important once a firm has decided to acquire a particular software or hardware product solution. It is certain that the current version of the software will be revised and eventually replaced. When that day arrives, the firm must also be ready with employees who have been trained to move with the changeover to newer technologies. This issue is such a problem for many firms that they decide to continue using older software rather than scrap it for a more up-to-date technology. **Legacy software** is a term that refers to the older and very dated programs that a firm is still using, sometimes in conjunction with recent software additions. Legacy programs may simply be so familiar to so many employees that the task of training everyone who would need to be trained to work with a new program is considered too costly. Furthermore, the chance of failing to switch over to the newer software successfully may be considered too great a risk to take. Sometimes, adopting a new software solution is considered only when the old solution can no longer satisfy the firm's needs or support is unavailable from its creators.

legacy software
Older and sometimes very dated programs that a firm is still using, sometimes in conjunction with recent software additions.

Financial Forces

Financial forces include any money-related influences on e-business planning. A firm's financial conditions, structure, and other related issues play an important role in determining the available range of strategic planning possibilities. For example, just as managerial and human resources conditions set limits, so too does the amount of funding available, whether it is in the form of a loan or equity, come from external sources or from investors who are also playing a managerial or planning role in the firm. We will examine financial topics in greater detail throughout this text but particularly in Chapter 10, where we will explore investing and financial topics.

Go to the Web:
e-Business Online
For tutorials and more on the topics in this chapter, visit the student website at **http://business.college .hmco.com/students** and select "Canzer e-Business."

Conclusions

In this chapter, we explored a model that helps managers organize both the external and internal forces that can influence e-business strategic planning. By remaining current on the changing conditions of factors external to the firm as well as those within the organization, managers are better able to develop and control the planning process. This structure provides a template for the **Environmental Analysis** component of the **e-business plan.** A more detailed tutorial on the preparation of the **Environmental Analysis** component and the rest of the e-business plan is available on the textbook's website.

In the web appendix at the end of Chapter 1, we will examine the technology of the Internet and the various products, services, and related technologies that make e-business possible.

RETURN TO
inside e-business

CASE STUDY

The music industry is dominated by five global firms: the Universal Music Group, BMG (Bertelsmann), Sony, the EMI group, and the Warner Music Group. (Note: In November 2003, Time Warner sold off Warner Music for $2.6 billion to a group led by Edgar Bronfman Jr. and in the summer of 2004, Sony and BMG were still seeking legal approval of their proposed union from European regulatory bodies.) Collectively, these firms managed to exercise a considerable amount of control over distribution and pricing of their product until Internet file-sharing software emerged. The mergers and alliances among these players suggests their recognition that the industry must find new strategies to combat the competitive changes taking place.

P2P technology exemplifies the Internet's *democratization* of business because it gives greater power to small businesses and individuals. For example, artists who choose to record a song and make it available on the Internet through P2P software see this technology as an additional strategic tool to help promote the sale of their CDs and attendance at concerts. Unknown performers can use P2P software to generate a following and build public awareness. Instead of relying on the recording industry to launch their careers, struggling performers, animators, and writers can take control of their own product in the hope of being discovered by larger globally distributed audiences. The challenge to many businesses, especially those in the media and entertainment industries, is to develop new strategies that take advantage of emerging technologies like P2P software and the distribution power of the Internet.

Whether delivered from a traditional centralized server or through a P2P network the distribution of entertainment content is changing dramatically, as is the way the industry's artists and businesses will compete in the future. In short, we are witnessing a major transformation in the business plans of all industry competitors because of this new strategic tool. The Internet offers any firm the potential to create a competitive advantage so it can better serve its customers and grow. Like all ways of creating competitive advantage, this means adding a perceived value-added service or product for customers that is better than that offered by other competitors. This might mean providing more convenient methods of shopping for music, the ability to create a customized CD of only the music the customer desires, information about the artist to enhance the purchase experience, or simply a lower price.

ASSIGNMENT

1. What other strategies could be used to create a greater competitive advantage for an entertainment company operating on the Internet?

2. How do you think consumers will respond to the growing establishment of fee-based plans for the distribution of entertainment files?

3. Do you think that eventually every major website will provide P2P software for its users, just as online chat software and e-mail are now made available?

Chapter Review

SUMMARY

ACE Self-Test
For a quick self-test of the content in this chapter, visit the student website at **http://business.college .hmco.com/students**. Select "Canzer e-Business."

1. **Explore the major environmental forces that can affect e-business planning and practice.**

   Although the environmental forces that are at work are complex, often overlapping, and interrelated, it is useful to think of them as belonging to two broadly defined categories. *External environmental forces* are those factors affecting e-business strategic planning that originate from outside the organization. External environmental forces are unlikely to be controllable by business decision-makers. Instead, planners and strategists must generally react to these forces and attempt to shield the organization from any undue negative effects and seek ways to exploit positive ones. The primary external environmental forces include globalization, sociocultural, demographic, economic, competitive, intermediary and supplier, technological, and political and legal forces. In contrast, *internal environmental forces* are those that are closely associated with the organizational functions and activities taking place within the firm. These forces emerge from a variety of internal interacting forces, including the firm's management and organizational structure, human resources, information and knowledge, and finance.

2. **Examine the primary external environmental forces that can affect e-business planning and practice.**

   From many people's point of view, *globalization* is an inevitable force drawing the people of the world together to live under universally shared standards of culture, communication, technologies, and economics. To others, it represents a threat to individual national cultures, identities, languages, and sovereignty that have managed to survive until today but that may not be able to survive the growing pressures created by the process of globalization in the future. Principal North American *sociocultural* values include achievement and success, freedom and individualism, efficiency, progress, and technology. The more managers know about the socially and culturally defined characteristics of their customers, suppliers, and employees, the more accurately they will be able to design appropriate e-business strategies. *Demographic* characteristics refer to population descriptors such as age, gender, race, ethnicity, marital status, parental status, income, and educational level. Besides describing groups in the general population, demographic categorization is also a tool that provides a high degree of predictability for current and future behavior. *Economic forces* include employment and income levels, interest rates and inflation, foreign exchange values, and individual corporate and overall economic growth. The *competitive forces* at work in the external environment relate mostly to the direct competition between firms that offer similar or substitute products and services. *Technology* is a large and critical part of e-business strategic thinking. Finally, *governments* and the courts treat e-business activity as an extension of the regular activities carried out by the non-e-business part of the firm.

3. **Examine the primary internal environmental forces that can affect e-business planning and practice.**

   Internal environmental forces can have a significant impact on e-business strategic planning. A variety of issues and concerns emerge from the firm's *management and organizational structure,* including those related to leadership and motivation, the organization' culture, communications, and operations. Closely related to the internal forces associated with management and organizational structure are those connected to the firm's *human resources.* These include the employees who have been hired, the work they are assigned to do, how new employees are recruited, development and advancement strategies within the organization, and even how the firm maintains employee expertise through training and promotions. The sort of *information and knowledge* available to employees operating within the organization will substantially influence their ability to perform the work they are expected to do. Information and knowledge should be thought of as the tools that employees need in order to do their job. And finally, *financial* conditions, structure, and other related issues play an important role in determining the range of strategic planning possibilities available.

REVIEW QUESTIONS

1. What is globalization?
2. How is the Internet related to globalization?
3. What are the primary sociocultural characteristics that describe the North American population?
4. What are the primary demographic characteristics that describe the North American population?
5. Describe the current North American Internet user in demographic terms.
6. Name one economic factor that affects strategic planning. Describe how it does this.
7. Describe how intermediaries and suppliers affect strategic planning.
8. How do governments influence Internet use? How might they?

1. Discuss the advantages and disadvantages of globalization.
2. Are the benefits that accompany globalization worth the risks?
3. Why do you suppose the demographic characteristics of Internet users appear to reflect those of the population as a whole?
4. How can management and organizational structure forces influence strategic e-business planning?

**Building
Skills
for Career
Success**

EXPLORING THE INTERNET

Shari Steele of the Electronic Frontier Foundation (EFF, **www.eff.org**) says, "copyright law is out of step with the views of the American public and the reality of music distribution online." The EFF has launched a campaign called "Let the Music Play" that suggests that licensing fees paid by manufacturers of MP3s and CD-ROMs could help solve the problem of making fair payments to artists and copyright owners while also allowing for file-sharing as well. This comes in response to the Recording Industry Association of America's (RIAA, **www.riaa.com**) announcement that it will file thousands of lawsuits against individuals who use peer-to-peer (P2P) software like KaZaA (**www.kazaa.com**), Grokster (**www.grokster.com**) and Morpheus (**www.morpheus.com**). Furthermore, Representatives John Conyers Jr., a Michigan Democrat, and Howard Berman, a California Democrat, have introduced the "Author, Consumer, and Computer Owner Protection and Security Act of 2003" (ACCOPS Act), which would make the unauthorized uploading of a single copy of a file a felony offense.

ASSIGNMENT

1. Describe how each of these websites is currently responding to the file-sharing issue?
2. What affect do you think the threat of legal action against individuals has had on individual decisions to download music files?

DEVELOPING CRITICAL THINKING SKILLS

The WTO is perhaps the most widely recognized and visible representative voice of the growing movement favoring greater global trade. Established in 1995 after the Uruguay round of trade negations, the WTO replaced the General Agreement on Trade and Tariffs (GATT), which was born in 1945 out of the need to reconstruct trading relations among countries in the chaotic aftermath of World War II. The WTO's 140 members include most of the world's industrialized nations. Its mandate is to facilitate expanding trade relations among member countries and settle any trade disputes that might develop. As such, the WTO is the primary target of protest by the movement against greater globalization, especially at regular WTO meetings, which are held in various cities around the world. The WTO website, located at **www.wto.org**, is an excellent source of information about many of the issues and arguments favoring and opposing globalization and expanding trade.

ASSIGNMENT

1. Describe the information found at the WTO website that is related to technology and the Internet.
2. After viewing the information presented on the website, what is your opinion about the benefits of growth in information technology trade?

BUILDING TEAM SKILLS

Learning how to build an understanding about some topic as a member of a group is an important skill, especially in the information technology field. Productive business meetings typically have clear objectives, such as establishing what the members of a strategic planning team believe is true about the external and internal forces that affect the firm and its customers.

ASSIGNMENT

Working in a group, select a business or industry that all of you are somewhat familiar with, such as a sports team. Using the structure established in this chapter for exploring forces that may influence the e-business strategic planning for your selection, establish a description of those forces that is acceptable to all, or at least most of, your team members. Start by determining how one team member views the degree to which the current forces of globalization are acting on your selection. Build your group's understanding by allowing each member to add his or her opinion. Have someone take notes, and then prepare a final summation of the team's position. Then move on to the next environmental force until the list has been completed.

RESEARCHING DIFFERENT CAREERS

Although many people think that careers involving e-business require advanced technological knowledge of hardware and software, in fact these requirements are limited to specific areas of the organization, such as the installation of software systems and the writing of customized software applications. Interestingly, much e-business activity demands the same skill set needed in any business setting—such as the ability to understand customer needs, communicate with customers and fellow staff, and report on changes and trends in the external and internal environments. For example, a firm like IBM needs to understand the forces of globalization that are at work in different parts of the world in order to build a better e-business plan. Individuals with this expertise are as important a part of the team that is designing IBM's e-business strategic plan as the software engineers.

ASSIGNMENT

1. Write a brief job description for a nontechnology position whose mission is to help the organization build a better e-business plan by gaining an understanding of the external and internal environmental forces it faces.
2. Explain what skills this individual should have and why.

IMPROVING COMMUNICATION SKILLS

The website set up by your academic institution is primarily designed to serve the current student body, potential students, and the community at large. The images and information it displays reflect the understanding of the designers of the school's e-business plan regarding the groups the school is trying to communicate with online as well as their informational needs. In many ways, the presentation is very similar to messages and designs used at other institutions because students are similar, regardless of where they attend school. And most academic institutions try to communicate similar messages concerning their scholarly staff, hard-working students, and pleasant surroundings conducive to higher learning.

ASSIGNMENT

1. Describe the sociocultural environmental forces at work at the institution you attend. In other words, describe the student body in sociocultural terms.
2. Explore your institution's website and summarize the key messages it communicates.
3. Explain why, in your opinion, the messages are either successful or not in light of the sociocultural forces at play at your institution.
4. What message would you add to the website? Explain your reasoning.

Exploring Useful Websites

These websites provide information related to the topics discussed in the chapter. You can learn more by visiting them online and examining their current data.

1. IBM's e-business website, **www.ibm.com/ebusiness/**, contains strategic e-business information, case studies, white papers on emerging issues, and information on software and hardware.
2. The World Trade Organization's website, **www.wto.org**, is a primary source of information favoring the globalization movement.
3. The online community iVillage.com (**www.iVillage.com**) provides information on a variety of topics designed to appeal mostly to women.
4. Forrester Research, Inc. (**www.forrester.com**), Nielsen/NetRatings (**www.nielsen-netratings.com**), and Jupiter Media Metrix (**www.mediametrix.com**), now part of ComScore Networks Inc. (**www.comscore.com**) are good sources of online statistics and usage behavior.
5. Siebel Systems Inc. provides informational technology courses through its website at Siebel University, **www.siebel.com**, as well as through instructor-led classroom sessions.

6. Recording Industry Association of America (**www.riaa.com**) reports on industry activity and is especially concerned with the increasing popularity of file-sharing (P2P) software like KaZaA (**www.kazaa.com**), Grokster (**www.grokster.com**), and Morpheus (**www.morpheus.com**). New legal sites have emerged, including Apple Computer Inc.'s i-Tunes Music Store (**www.apple.com/itunes**), Roxio's Napster (**www.napster.com**), RealNetworks Inc.'s Rhapsody (**www.real.com**), and MusicNet (**www.musicnet.com**), which is supported by AOL Time Warner, Bertelsmann AG, and EMI Group.

7. In response to falling European sales attributed to file-sharing websites like Limewire (**www.limewire.com**) and iMesh (**www.imesh.com**), British-based retailer Virgin Megastore (**www.virgin.com**) launched an online pay-per-play plan. In the U.S., Wal-Mart (**www.walmart.com**) accounts for approximately 14 percent of CD sales and has also launched a downloading service on its site. Virgin is among several other retailers and technology firms including Microsoft and Tiscali (**www.tiscali.com**) that are licensed to resell more than 200,000 songs from British technology firm OnDemandDistribution OD2 (**www.od2.com**).

8. Eastman Kodak Company (**www.kodak.com**) is losing traditional old-technology revenues to stiff competition in the emerging digital photography market. The Photo Marketing Association International **http://www.pmai.org/** researches the digital photography industry.

chapter 3

Ethical, Legal, and Social Concerns

LEARNING OBJECTIVES

1. Explore a framework for understanding the ethical, legal, and social concerns related to e-business and the online environment.

2. Discuss the concerns over privacy and confidentiality.

3. Examine security issues and cybercrime.

4. Understand the special problems related to digital property, copyright, and distribution.

5. Explore the regulatory role played by government and related issues such as cybercrime and taxation.

INSIDE e-business

Zero-Knowledge Systems Inc.—Providing Privacy and Security Online

If there is one clear area of common concern among both consumer and business Internet users, it is privacy and security. Internet users face major problems such as viruses, computer system invasions, and the theft of confidential and important identity-related data as well as somewhat less important but annoying and time-wasting disruptions by unsolicited pop-up advertisements and e-mail. To deal with these and other issues, a growing industry of players has emerged, offering both markets a range of hardware and software solutions.

Zero-Knowledge Systems Inc. (**www.zeroknow ledge.com**), of Montreal, Quebec, and San Francisco, California, is a leading provider of Internet security and privacy solutions for consumers and businesses. Its bundles of Freedom software services (**www.freedom.net**) can provide users with antivirus protection, a firewall to protect their computer from unwelcome intrusion when connected to the Internet; a form filler that saves them the trouble of entering common information like passwords and identification each time they register at a new site or buy something; a cookie manager that controls unauthorized surveillance of their Internet activities, such as sites visited and information entered; a pop-up ad blocker that filters out unwanted advertisements as they browse, thereby speeding up generation of webpage screens; parental control of websites and content their children can view; and a keyword alert feature that prevents any data, such as names, passwords, credit card numbers, or any other item that the user records, from being sent out unintentionally.

To build market share, Zero-Knowledge distributes its basic bundle of services without charge over the Internet so users can sample its product. Then, much like a magazine publisher, the firm hopes that satisfied users will be converted into paying subscribers after the trial period and will also trade up to the more sophisticated web services it offers. In addition, Zero-Knowledge works with distribution channel partners who are able to offer their clients a value-added service and generate additional revenue streams. For example, RBC Royal Bank (**www.rbc royalbank.com/freedom/**), Canada's largest bank, offers its security-conscious online clients one year's free use of the software as a promotional tool. And Canada's largest telecommunications firm, Bell Canada Inc., partners with Zero-Knowledge through its Internet service provider (ISP) division, Sympatico.ca (**www.sympatico.com**). Small monthly charges allow customers to tailor their online security needs and provides Sympatico.ca with additional sources of revenues.

A somewhat controversial web service available to subscribers is Freedom's WebSecure, which acts as a shield to prevent anyone from tracking a user's surfing habits and personal information. The software encrypts and reroutes a user's connection requests through Zero-Knowledge's proxy servers with 128-bit encryption so the user's personal information cannot be found. When surfing without WebSecure, users may unknowingly provide information about themselves to the sites they visit. Using WebSecure, surfers can also establish *nyms*, or substitute anonymous identities that are known only to them. In effect, an online user can visit any website, shop online, or exchange e-mail under several different names. Advocates argue that this feature enhances free speech and the exchange of ideas, particularly in chat rooms, because the identity of the speaker is shielded. As a result, the speaker need not be concerned with retribution or the consequences of expressing ideas and opinions in a public forum.

What makes this service controversial, however, is the protection this same software affords to unethical and even illegal actions by motivated individuals who take advantage of the identity protection. The irony is that a product that was created to protect Internet users from unscrupulous individuals online or to allow users to avoid unwanted participation in online data collection and corporate consumer profiling strategies can also assist criminals, terrorists, hate mongers, and other undesirables in functioning anonymously online. Furthermore, this sort of software can help them evade the efforts of law enforcement agencies and ISPs to control their use of the Internet and thus can abet their undesirable behaviors. The efforts of law enforcement agencies to prevent crime will clearly be handicapped if they are unable to trace online exchanges. However, this ability to shield one's identity is a vital communications tool for political dissidents in undemocratic countries, informants who wish to remain anonymous in order to protect themselves from retaliation, and possibly even victims of abuse. Privacy and encryption software like that developed by Zero-Knowledge is likely to continue to be the object of more government study and popular debate as we attempt to balance the needs of societies with the legitimate rights of individuals to protect their freedom and privacy.[1]

In addition to the complex mix of environmental forces (presented in Chapter 2) that can influence e-business planning and practice, managers must also deal with the special circumstances of operating in a new frontier—a world without geographic borders or much in the way of governmental or other organizational control or regulation. For better or worse, the cyberworld of e-business is an emerging industry. It presents great beneficial opportunities for businesses and customers but equally great concerns about social behaviors. These behaviors are for the most part **self-regulated behaviors**, meaning that individuals and firms generally police themselves by choosing to do things that, in their view, are ethically correct and to avoid doing things that are not.

Gradually, global standards are emerging. For instance, the U.S.-based Better Business Bureau (BBB) website, located at **www.bbbonline.org/Reliability/code/**, provides an international code of ethical behaviors that the BBB developed jointly with the Federation of European Direct Marketing (FEDMA) and the Association of European Chambers of Commerce. The site promotes a trademark that identifies member businesses that adhere to the organization's rules of conduct. By organizing and creating an international symbol, the group hopes to establish an instantly recognizable sign that can reassure buyers who are dealing with firms online. The BBBonLine website provides a variety of information related to ethical online behavior and ways users can file complaints if they believe they have been mistreated.

This chapter will explore the ethical, legal, and social concerns related to e-business as well as the unique and artificial social environment created by the Internet. In addition, we will examine the role of governments and the ideas of control and regulation of Internet activity, as well as privacy, security, copyright, trademark, crime, and taxation issues.

A Framework for Understanding Ethical, Legal, and Social Behavior

self-regulated behaviors
The idea that individuals and firms generally police themselves by choosing to do things that, in their view, are ethically correct and to avoid doing things that are not.

The ethical, legal, and social environmental forces that are at work in e-business can be explored using the same basic models that apply to all businesses, regardless of whether they have any connection to the Internet. The general framework for approaching these subjects and making judgments about individual and organizational behaviors begins with an examination of ethics. **Ethics** is the study and evaluation of what constitutes proper or correct behavior as defined by a community of people. In other words, if the answer to the question "Is this behavior acceptable to the people here?" is "Yes," then, ethically speaking, the behavior meets the moral standards established by the community.

FIGURE 3.1   The Scale of Ethical Behavior and Community Evaluation
            of a Specific Behavior

Higher-Level Behaviors   Lower-Level Behaviors

Socially   Ethical   Not Ethical but   Not Legal
Responsible   Still Legal

Communities judge whether a particular behavior is more or less ethical than other behaviors. Highly ethical
behaviors are considered socially responsible and positive, whereas lower-level behaviors may even be illegal as
defined by the community.

ethics
The study and evaluation
of what constitutes proper
or correct behavior as
defined by a community of
people.

    Communities develop a sort of continuum, or scale, of ethical behaviors. Behaviors are viewed as tending toward higher or lower levels on that continuum. In other words, people make judgments as to whether a specific behavior is more or less ethical than other behaviors and position that behavior in their minds relative to those other behaviors. Specific behaviors that are deemed to be at the higher end of the scale—and the individuals and firms that engage in them—may be regarded as being more *socially responsible* and beneficial for the community as a whole, whereas those behaviors that cross the line set by government legislation may even be *illegal*. In between these limits are behaviors that are judged by the community to be *ethical* but of no special benefit to the community and those that are seen as *unethical*, but are still legal. Figure 3.1 illustrates the scale of ethical behavior with the community evaluation label attached to specific behaviors.

Understanding the Ethical Decision-Making Process

Whether we are examining the behavior of an individual or an organization, we must always remember that only people can actually make a decision and behave in some way. Behind the anonymity of organizational identities are the people who run those organizations. The question we will attempt to answer next is how people make ethical decisions, whether on behalf of an organization they represent or simply for themselves as users of services available on the Internet.

    Figure 3.2 illustrates the three primary factors that influence an individual's ethical decision-making process. The first of these factors, and perhaps the most influential, is the *individual* him- or herself. Who and what an individual is, ethically speaking, will determine how that individual processes information and ultimately decides how to behave. An individual who has strong ethical values and moral judgment enters the decision-making process equipped differently from someone at the opposite end of the moral character scale. However, we also must recognize that individuals make decisions within the context of a

FIGURE 3.2   Primary Factors Influencing the Ethical Decision-Making

Individual Factors   Social-Environmental Factors   Opportunity

Ethical Decision Making

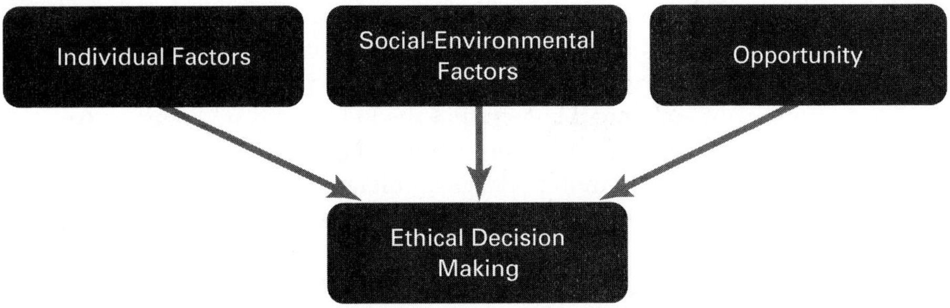

social situation in which they are also subject to the influences of *social environmental factors*, such as their peers, coworkers, family, and the general community. Finally, we recognize that an individual's decision to behave in some manner is subject to the *opportunity* available to that individual. Someone who is alone on a desert island will have little opportunity to embark on many behaviors that might be ethically questionable. As religious leaders are apt to tell their congregants, no one worries what you will do while inside the house of God—the problems begin once you leave and face the temptations offered by the greater society outside.

Let's look at an example of how decision-making might be influenced by each of these three factors and how these influences might be changed. Suppose we consider someone who would be considered a typical representative of North American culture and social values—someone who knows the basic rules of right and wrong as defined by the North American community and routinely tries to live by them. While at his place of work, he notices that most employees use their computers to reply to personal e-mail, shop for products, and surf the Internet for questionable entertainment during the workday. No one in the firm has ever been reprimanded for these behaviors, even though the firm has a policy against employee use of its high-speed Internet connection for anything but business purposes. The culture of the firm supports a relaxed social environment, and employees often send instant pop-up messages to one another during the day. Some of these might disturb the receiver's concentration and undermine his or her productivity. The individual we introduced at the beginning of this scenario gradually finds himself falling into the same pattern of behavior as his coworkers. He recognizes that his behavior is somewhat unethical and not particularly responsible socially, but apparently it is not illegal. His decision to follow the crowd and do what everyone seems to do is a result of his own individual character, the social environmental influences at the workplace, and the opportunity made available by his employer.

To change the level of ethical behavior of this or other employees, one or more of the three factors in the current equilibrium would have to change. First, it might be possible to strengthen the moral character of the individual and other employees so they would resist the temptation to violate the company policy concerning Internet usage. The firm might seek out and screen for employees who it believes will be of the highest moral character to start with. Training programs covering what the firm considers to be right and wrong decisions can be launched. Second, making it known that the behavior is no longer acceptable can change the social environment and culture. Managers might issue reprimands to employees, stating that although the firm tolerated this behavior in the past, it will not do so in the future. To be credible and to have any validity with employees, this change must be adopted companywide and be applied without exception. Finally, the firm might choose to reduce the opportunities available to employees to engage in undesirable behaviors. For instance, a software program can be installed on the firm's LAN that demands that an entry be made in a log before an employee is granted access to the Internet. Knowing that the websites employees visited and the activity keystrokes they enter there are being recorded and possibly analyzed for violation of the firm's policy is likely to reduce employees' abusive behaviors.

Needless to say, each of these approaches to changing the ethical decision-making of employees is itself ethically questionable. Many critics are alarmed by the possibility that people will begin to develop psychological disorders because of the fear engendered by continuous supervision and monitoring of their behaviors. Ultimately, a balance has to emerge that reflects both the needs of the firm to regulate the activities occurring under its auspices and the needs of individuals to feel free in an open society.

Behavior in Online Social Environments

We have established that the individual factors that define a person, the opportunity to take some action, and social environmental factors are the primary influences on that person's decision-making and behavior. The many artificially created social environments that exist in cyberspace present special circumstances for social interactions between people and may contribute to behaviors online that would not occur if it were not for the artificial reality defined by the site. For example, some people will reveal personal information about themselves and others in an online chat room that they would never tell other people in a face-to-face setting. The online social environment of a chat room tends to precipitate this sort of behavior by encouraging a false sense of privacy and security through the use of temporary online user identification names. When someone joins a website exchange identified only as "Bob from New Jersey," he may feel at liberty to say and do things that he might not say and do if his true identity were not shielded.

The website chat room gives people an opportunity to behave in any way they choose. Simply put, people have an invitation to change their traditional *persona* (the face that they normally show the world) when they are online. And even if they do not do so, the effect of being online automatically changes them to some degree. Thus, they may buy things, say things, and do things that they otherwise would not buy, say, or do because of the effect on them of being in the virtual environment created by the Internet. None of this should be surprising. People behave differently when they are on vacation, at a party, or watching a baseball game in a stadium with thousands of other fans. The social environment that people are in—whether it is a real environment or one created in cyberspace—affects who they are at that particular moment and creates opportunities for behaviors that might not exist in other situations.

e-BUSINESS insight

Can Socially Undesirable Online Behaviors Be Stopped?

Many people have concerns about how easily the Internet can be used to enable what they consider to be socially undesirable behaviors, such as online gambling and the distribution of adult entertainment. Together, these areas represent by far the greatest proportion of Internet commercial activity. The convenience and anonymity provided by the Internet are clearly the primary factors that facilitate and encourage individual decisions to become involved.

According to a Media Metrix study, 30 percent of Internet users, almost 85 percent of them men, visit adult entertainment sites each month (however, Nielsen/NetRatings reports that the figure is only 16 percent). Control and regulation are complicated by the fact that websites may be located anywhere in the world, beyond the reach of law enforcement officials in North America. For example, the World Sports Exchange (**www.wsex.com**), the largest sports gambling website, is located in Grand Cayman Island. Although many of its gaming activities are illegal in the United States, players can access the site with a credit card or establish an account, making control by American authorities difficult. In the end, without a technology to control access to foreign websites, no government agency can hope to control what individuals choose to do on the Internet.

According to the U.S. General Accounting Office, Internet gambling operators have established nearly 1,800 online wagering sites operated from outside the United States. Although fifty-four countries compete in the online gambling marketplace, within the United States, five states have outlawed certain aspects of Internet gambling, and most state laws that prohibit some types of online wagering generally apply to Internet gambling as well. As a result, global revenues from Internet gambling were projected to exceed $5 billion in 2003, with 50 to 70 percent coming from Americans. To combat this effect from the offshore industry, the House of Representatives passed the Unlawful Internet Gambling Funding Prohibition Act, which prohibits financial institutions from making credit card payments to online casinos. Furthermore, according to the U.S. Justice Department, the long established Wire Act prohibits the transfer of funds to overseas gambling operations. The U.S. action triggered Antigua and Barbuda, a Caribbean island nation that is a major nexus for the Internet gambling industry, to complain to the World Trade Organization. Claiming that U.S. laws restrict cross-border access to services, Antigua and Barbuda have seen their online gambling industry fall to 40 firms from more than 100 in the 1990s.

Question for discussion: Do you agree or disagree with the idea that government officials should attempt to curb offshore gambling and other online behaviors?[2]

As might be expected, issues such as privacy, distributing ethically questionable content, and engaging in ethically questionable online behaviors are likely to remain concerns for the foreseeable future. Most ISPs and browsers allow users to block out URLs that have been identified as adult in nature, and many chat rooms are supervised so that unacceptable language or behavior can be stopped. Nonetheless, given the Internet's openness and its relative absence of regulation, aside from that exercised by individuals, firms, and ISPs, each participant online will have to develop her or his own strategies for handling the difficult ethical challenges presented by the Internet.

Privacy and Confidentiality Issues

One questionable ethical practice in cyberspace is the unauthorized access to and use of information discovered through computerized tracking of users once they are connected to the Internet. There are several ways to collect data with and without the knowledge of the user, including placing "cookies" on user's computers, analyzing log-file records, and mining the data in customer transactions and registration records.

Cookies Track Online Behavior

cookie
A small piece of software code that may allow the sender to track which pages the user visits on the site and how long the user stays at any particular page.

A user who visits a website may unknowingly receive or willingly accept as a condition for entry what is euphemistically referred to as a cookie. A **cookie** is a small piece of software code that may allow the sender to track which pages the user visits on the site and how long the user stays at any particular page. However, a cookie that is left on the user's computer may also continue to track the sites on the Internet that the user subsequently visits and report that information back to the site that placed the cookie. Although this ability can provide the site with valuable information about the customer as she or he browses through an online mall, it can also be viewed as an invasion of privacy, especially since the customer may not even be aware that these movements are being monitored and analyzed.

Generally speaking, ethical website managers will inform users as soon as they access a website that a cookie is going to be installed on their computer and give them the choice of opting out. Cookies are often presented as shopping agents that will help users as they explore the site, and, as such, they may appear innocent enough. Because the cookie is software and must be recorded on the user's computer, however, the browser will display a message alerting the user that the site is attempting to write something and ask the user's permission before it allows the transfer to proceed. When there is any doubt as to the security risk posed, it is best to err on the side of conservatism and refuse the download of any questionable content. As a last resort, users can employ their browser to search the designated cookie storage area on their hard drive to locate cookies that may reside on their computer. The cookies can then be deactivated or removed.

Surveillance and Analysis of Log-File Records

According to research by the University of Denver's Privacy Foundation Workplace Surveillance Project, more than one-third of the 40 million U.S. employees who work online—about 14 million—are under continuous surveillance by their employers, using commercially available software. Given that the average annual cost of this software is only $5.25 per employee, the number of surveilled employees is likely to increase. As a result, the debate over how much employers are ethically and legally entitled to monitor employee behavior online versus an employee's right to privacy is likely to intensify. The Privacy Foundation study suggests that at the very least, employers need to disclose and publicize the level of their surveillance of employees and consider their motivations for monitoring employees' behavior. The reason that surveillance is likely to grow is the increasing availability of low–cost software that allows employers to monitor their employees' online actions easily. Because the opportunity to monitor behaviors is there, it is done—regardless of whether it is really productive in any way.[3]

log-file records

Files that store a record of the websites users have visited.

Monitoring an employee's **log-file records**, which record the websites visited, may help employers police unauthorized Internet use on company time. However, the same records can also give the firm the opportunity to observe what otherwise might be considered private and confidential information. This is especially true when a firm does not have a policy restricting personal use of the firm's computer resources on company time. Many firms might consider occasional personal use of the firm's local area network (LAN) facilities to be an employee benefit that costs the firm little and can in fact produce greater employee satisfaction and motivation at work.

Data Mining Customer Transactions and Records

data mining

The practice of searching through data records for meaningful and strategically useful information.

Data mining refers to the practice of searching through data records for meaningful and strategically useful information. Customer registration forms typically require that a variety of information be provided before a user is given access to a site. When this is combined with customer transaction records, data mining analysis can provide what might be considered private and confidential information about individuals or groups. For example, suppose a website offering free access to health information requires users to fill out a detailed registration form before they are granted a user identification and password. As a result of this voluntary disclosure, website operators can easily uncover correlations between users' demographic factors, such as age and gender, and the specific health topics and issues that interest them. The website operators could then conceivably sell this marketing intelligence to pharmaceutical firms. The information sold might suggest that there is a high level of interest in a particular type of medication that the firm manufactures among, say, a particular group of people living in Michigan. Subsequently, advertising campaigns and other marketing decisions might be changed because the firm is aware of this information.

Advocates for better control of the way user information is collected and distributed to interested third parties such as businesses point to the potential misuse of information—intentionally or otherwise. For example, if an individual frequents a website that provides information about a life-threatening disease, an insurance company might refuse to insure this individual, on the belief that some-one who wants more information about this disease poses a higher risk of having it. Perhaps the individual does have the disease, or thinks she might, but perhaps she is only writing a research paper for a school project or has been asked to look into this topic by an acquaintance who does not know how to search the Internet. Sometimes, a little bit of information about an individual can be dangerous and can be used to harm him or her. This risk is compounded if the information is in-correct or misinterpreted.

Industry Self-Regulation

To help deal with this issue and to support industry self-regulation, the U.S. Federal Trade Commission (FTC) approved the formation of the Network Advertising Initia-tive (NAI) in 1999. The NAI, 90 percent of whose membership is Internet advertisers, including the industry leaders DoubleClick (**www.doubleclick.com**) and 24/7 Media (**www.247media.com**), was established to set rules and guidelines for collecting and using personal data. The NAI prohibits the collection of personal data from health and financial services websites that individuals visit. However, the NAI permits the cross-referencing of personal and Web-collected data, provided the user is in-formed that this is taking place and is allowed access to his or her records. In line with the NAI guidelines, browser software such as Microsoft's Internet Explorer is programmed to routinely prevent cookies from collecting user information without first receiving the user's permission through a pop-up window. By requiring users' consent and by opening the process somewhat to scrutiny, the NAI has helped make online data collection more ethical than it used to be. It lends support to the argu-ment that the Internet can regulate itself without undue government interference.

The ability to collect and analyze personal data is critical for the industry if it is going to compete for advertisers' spending, and so it must learn to do this ethically. The great advantage of the Internet is its interactive communication features, which allow third-party vendors of products to target advertisements and other promotional messaging to small niche markets. Just as television is a mass com-munication medium for delivering messages that appeal to relatively large audi-ences, so the Internet is attempting to carve a position in the communications industry by identifying smaller niche markets that television or other mass media could not economically reach and delivering highly specific and timely informa-tion to them. To achieve this advantage, Internet-based firms will need to analyze personal data in order to cross-reference products and services with perceived needs and wants. We will explore this topic and other marketing-related issues in Chapter 8, Creating the Marketing Mix.

Security Concerns and Cybercrime

According to research conducted by Computer Security Services Inc., 85 percent of the firms it surveyed in 2001 had detected online security breaches. However, by 2004, this figure had fallen to 53 percent—the fourth year in a row of decline—

suggesting that although the security threat remains commonplace for any computer connected to the Internet, the effort to fight back is succeeding. Denial of service was the number one violation followed by unauthorized theft of software. For businesses as well as individuals, this reality compels an understanding of how best to engage the Internet.[4]

For all intents and purposes, the Internet remains an unregulated frontier. Therefore, both individuals and business users must be cognizant of the security risks and dangers they may encounter online.

Internet-Facilitated Fraud

Aside from the risks posed by the unauthorized use of data collected through the Internet, individual users and businesses must watch for criminal activities, including fraud and larceny. According to research by Gartner Inc. (**www.gartner.com**) 3.4 percent of the American population have been victims of identity theft, and the rate is growing. The ease with which the Internet can be used to masquerade as a retriever of critical information such as dates of birth and social security and credit card numbers has contributed to the problem. For instance, fake e-mails have been sent en masse to customers of EarthLink and eBay, asking users to provide personal information on a look-alike website that appears to be legitimate. Unwary customers may be convinced to enter data, which is then used to steal their identities. Because the Internet allows easy creation of websites, access from anywhere in the world, and anonymity for participants, it is almost impossible to know with certainty that the website, organization, or individuals you are interacting with are what they seem.[5]

Consider the following simple examples of fraud, which will help to illuminate the risks posed to unsuspecting users and illustrate how easy it is to orchestrate misrepresentations online.

First, an individual who is intent on perpetrating fraud can build a website that falsely presents him- or herself as, say, a legitimate charitable organization dedicated to raising funds for some worthy cause. Through various online promotional efforts, such as e-mail campaigns and banner advertising, unsuspecting individuals may be enticed to make a quick donation by entering their credit card information in an online form conveniently displayed on the website or by putting a check in the mail (typically addressed to a post office box). In the former case, the website operators are now in a position to make further illegal use of the credit card information, which they now possess, before their fraud is uncovered and authorities shut down their credit card processing capability. In any case, they may well be able to keep the donations.

A second type of fraud that is facilitated by the Internet occurs when a website offers to sell products at an unbelievably low price, but never delivers the products after collecting the funds. By the time authorities are made aware of the fraud, the website operators have usually abandoned the site and set up another that promises to deliver some other low-risk common product, such as a compact disc or a magazine subscription. These scenarios are similar to old-style mail fraud. However, they are more complex and difficult to control because fraudulent websites can be set up anywhere in the world, and operators will often locate them in areas where the authorities are reluctant to interfere with them.

Although online auction fraud at sites like eBay and Yahoo! occurs only rarely (less than one one-hundredth of 1 percent of all eBay auctions result in any confirmed case of fraud), both the Internet Fraud Commission Center (**www1.ifccfbi.gov/index.asp**) and the nonprofit National Consumers League (**www.natlconsumersleague.org/**) reported to a congressional committee investigating Internet fraud that auction websites were by far the most common targets of the complaints they receive. The most popular form of fraud, and one that is difficult for auction website operators to control, is called *shilling*. This is the process of bidding up the price of an auction item by people who have no intention of buying it. These fraudulent bidders may be either the vendor or people in cahoots with the vendor. All of the website auction operators attempt to protect the integrity of their auctions by insuring transactions and monitoring activity closely. As always, *caveat emptor* (let the buyer beware) is good advice to follow, whether on the Internet or off.[6]

Network Security and Encryption

In addition to the fraudulent website schemes that are clearly visible to users and can be avoided through investigation, businesses and individual users must also guard against nonvisible intrusion into their computer systems and the theft by electronic means of data, passwords, credit card numbers, and so forth.

In the past, businesses created **private networks**, which were secure LAN systems that were closed to outside access. Only computers that were actually connected to the private network by wires could access the information there. The only real concern was that someone with access to the system, such as an employee, might violate the system's security, copy information, and remove it from the business's premises without authorization. Today, the need to connect outside users such as customers, sales representatives, and suppliers to the firm's system has led to the rise of **virtual private networks (VPNs)**, which extend the firm's private network using secure third-party vendors' services and **encryption systems**, which scramble the data sent over the Internet.

The technological basis for a growing number of popular encryption systems today is referred to as **public-key cryptography**. The system relies on two *keys* or *codes* for **encrypting** (locking) and **decrypting** (unlocking) data transmitted by a sender to a receiver. Each party has a pair of keys, one of which is publicly available and the other of which is private. Both keys are needed to encode and decode data. The sender uses the receiver's public key to encrypt a message, and the receiver uses its private key to decrypt the message. Should an intruder capture data while it is in transit, that intruder would be unable to unlock the data without both keys. Public keys are also the basis for **digital signatures**, which are used to authenticate the sender of data.

To alleviate consumers' concerns about online purchasing, the major credit card organizations like MasterCard and Visa have instituted various programs to protect cardholders against fraudulent use of their cards on the Internet. In addition, the effort to develop stronger encryption systems that can help prevent

private networks
Secure LAN systems that are closed to outside access.

virtual private networks (VPNs)
Software-generated extensions of a firm's real private network made possible by secure third-party vendors' services and encryption systems.

encryption systems
Systems that scramble data that are sent over the Internet.

public-key cryptography
A form of encryption that relies on two keys or codes for encrypting (locking) and decrypting (unlocking) data transmitted by a sender to a receiver.

encrypting
Locking data sent between a sender and receiver.

decrypting
Unlocking data sent between a sender and receiver.

digital signatures
Devices used to authenticate the sender of data.

secure electronic transaction (SET)
An encryption process developed by MasterCard, Visa, IBM, Microsoft, and Netscape that prevents merchants from ever actually seeing any transaction data, including the customer's credit card number.

digital wallets
Devices that store consumer information, such as a consumer's name, address, credit card numbers, and so forth, and enter this information automatically when the consumer shops online.

agent
Software code that will automatically seek out information on the Internet.

viruses
Computer instructions that are designed to disrupt normal computer and software functions.

worm
Computer instructions that penetrate and attach to a computer's operating system and then release viruses that cause damage to files on a network.

spamming
The sending of massive amounts of unsolicited e-mail.

the theft and fraudulent use of credit card and other information continues to receive a great deal of attention. For example, the **secure electronic transaction (SET)** encryption process (**www.setco.org**), which was developed by MasterCard, Visa, IBM, Microsoft, and Netscape, prevents merchants from ever actually seeing any transaction data, including the customer's credit card number. This is accomplished by creating a system that requires the merchant, the customer, and a trusted third-party holder of shared information to exchange partial data. The system also makes use of **digital wallets**, which, as the term suggests, store consumer information, such as a consumer's name, address, credit card numbers, and so forth, and then enter this information automatically when the consumer shops online. This not only saves time by freeing the consumer from inputting the same data for each transaction at a different website, but also authenticates the buyer.

Agents, Viruses, and Spamming

One of the reasons many businesses are reluctant to make their computerized records accessible through the Internet is the risk that some programmer might be able to breach the security firewalls that protect the firm from intrusion. A programming expert who is capable of writing code that will automatically seek out information on the Internet—code that is known as an **agent**—is likely to also be capable of writing code that can venture into a firm's computer system and retrieve records, without leaving any trace that it was there. It is therefore understandable that a niche in the software industry dedicated to security and access control features has emerged. Some firms deal with the risk of intrusion by establishing separate Internet-accessible computers that are not connected to the rest of the firm's LAN. Others make use of hosting firms that provide advanced security features or choose to distribute only what would be considered noncritical data to users over the Internet.

Computer **viruses** are computer instructions designed to disrupt normal computer and software functions. Viruses or other forms of unwanted interference with computer operations can originate from anywhere in the world. Indeed, a software security industry has emerged to protect businesses and individuals from these risks in cyberspace. Norton's AntiVirus program, distributed by Symantec (**www.symantec.com**), and McAfee's VirusScan (**www.mcafee.com**) are two well-known commercial products that help to screen out incoming files containing viruses.

The Sircam series, which first appeared in 2001, is an example of a **worm**, a program that penetrates and attaches itself to a computer's operating system before releasing viruses that cause damage to files on a network. Worms do not need to be attached to any program, such as e-mail, in order to spread, which makes them even more difficult to avoid. As long as undesirable data can be easily sent out, viruses and other forms of online harassment will remain a security issue and a business opportunity for firms like Symantec and McAfee, which must continuously revise their software to deal with newly created viruses.

Although not a security violation in the same sense as releasing a computer virus, **spamming**—the sending of massive amounts of unsolicited e-mail—may also be considered, if not a security issue, then certainly an ethical issue. Sorting through what many recipients view as *junk e-mail* is, if nothing else, a waste of resources that can cost individuals time and their employers money. Most e-mail software programs and most firms' mail servers have many control features that allow an individual or firm to block mail from senders that are not recorded on a list or from senders that have been identified as undesirable. Furthermore, most ISPs provide their customers with screening capability, so they may choose to block any mail or connections to websites that the ISP considers to be adult or hateful in nature. We will revisit this issue as it relates to marketing campaigns in Chapter 8. There we will discuss how firms that want to use the communication power of the Internet in an appropriate and socially responsible manner can do so while respecting the rights of individuals to control the volume of information that bombards them.

e-BUSINESS insight

Spam Is More Than a Nuisance

According to a study by the Radicati Group (**www.radicati.com**), if nothing is done to curb the growth of spam, by 2007 more than 33 billion corporate spam e-mails will inundate businesspeople each and every day. The study estimated that the cost of filtering out these unsolicited and for the most part unwelcome intrusions will be nearly $200 billion annually. Furthermore, the group projects that spam could account for 49 percent of all corporate e-mail traffic by 2007, compared to 24 percent in 2003, causing increasing problems for businesses and people as they attempt to cope. Interestingly, however, a survey conducted by Insight Express and Symantec Inc. found that more than half of all workers did not agree with the commonly perceived view of their IT managers that spam was a significant problem in their workplace.[7]

A Canadian COMPAS Inc. (**www.compassmc.com/North_America/home_nam.htm**) survey conducted in 2003 found that employees waste an average of 12 minutes each workday purging business in-boxes of unsolicited mail. This suggests that the average businessperson is wasting an hour each week, or more than a week each year, cleaning unwanted e-mail from her in-boxes. According to the researchers, this lost productivity will likely continue to grow as spam grows, leading to a paradoxical call for government regulation to help fix the problem.[8]

But spam is not just a business problem or an annoyance for the general Internet user. According to a survey by Symantec Inc., unsupervised children are regularly exposed to spam of an adult nature. Specifically, the survey found that more than 80 percent of children using e-mail receive inappropriate mail; 47 percent of children between 7 and 18 years old have received pornographic spam; 21 percent have read spam; nearly a third said they do not know if spam is good or bad; and 22 percent said their parents have not talked to them about spam.[9]

Question for discussion: How would you suggest we deal with the problems associated with spam?

Digital Property and Distribution Rights

A major concern for businesses that use the Internet to distribute content is controlling digital property that can easily be replicated and distributed over the Internet. According to research by the Business Software Alliance (BSA, **www.bsa.org**), an organization whose mandate includes educating software users, piracy declined in 2002 after two consecutive years of increases. BSA estimated that the piracy rate for business software—the only software considered by the study—dropped to 39 percent from 40 percent in 2001. The most common form of piracy happens when a company illegally installs copies of an application on several of its own computers after purchasing rights to just one installation. Although the BSA attributed the decline in piracy rates in part to its educational efforts, Rob Enderle of Forrester Research Inc. has suggested that the decline may simply be due to the increasing importance of the software support that is packaged with technical support and upgrades, making the software alone difficult to work with.[10]

copyright
The inherent right of owners to be the only ones permitted to replicate and distribute material they have created or paid someone for the rights to distribute.

The legal issue of **copyright**, or the inherent right of owners to be the only ones permitted to replicate and distribute material they have created or paid someone for the right to distribute, is somewhat controllable today. This is because firms are moving to regular updating and licensing arrangements rather than selling individual complete copies of their software. Furthermore, complexity—that is to say, software that requires the user to seek support from its producers in order to use it has also helped limit unauthorized replication and distribution. And producers of entertaining games now design software to function in conjunction with specially designed hardware play devices such as PlayStation and Xbox. However, the copyright problem is clearly exacerbated by the lack of controls available to the music and publishing industries.

Music and Publishing

The music and publishing industries have for a long time had to deal with new technologies that allowed individuals to make and distribute copies of a firm's property. In the recent past, the music industry had to contend with unauthorized replication and distribution of its content through audiotape and CD technologies. Now, with Internet technologies such as MP3 (**www.mp3.com**), anyone can digitize a song into a file and then send it to someone else, without ever paying the copyright holders.

As far as the industry is concerned, every copy of a song that is passed along for free on the Internet represents a loss of sales revenue from a customer who might otherwise have made a purchase. To deal with this intrusion, some music companies have begun to sign distribution contracts with online selling firms, enabling them to gain greater control over the distribution of their content. Another solution has been for firms to establish a software mechanism of their own making that allows music to be distributed online but prevents its free distribution by those who are unauthorized. For example, MusicNet (**www.musicnet.com**), a service set up jointly by RealNetworks, AOL Time Warner, EMI Group, and Bertelsmann AG's BMG, was established to control legal distribution of the music industry's content. According to research conducted by Jupiter Media Metrix, the online music industry will be worth over $6 billion by 2006, suggesting how financially significant the stakes are for the industry.[11]

Use of Names and Trademarks

cybersquatting
Establishing a web URL name that clearly should rightfully belong to someone else.

Consider the case of Kevin Spacey, the Academy Award–winning actor, who sued a firm that used his name and identity without his permission. Spacey accused the firm of **cybersquatting**—that is, establishing a web URL name that clearly should rightfully belong to someone else—when it created a website called **www.kevinspacey.com**. Spacey claimed that the firm uses the names of famous people to link web surfers to the firm's commercial site, located at **www.celebrity1000.com**, and thereby drive up traffic at that site for its own benefit without the permission of the people who make this possible. Furthermore, he argued, association of his name with this firm's website undermines his ability to market himself.[12]

Currently available technology makes it quite easy to copy and use a company name or recognized trademark, like McDonald's golden arches, without permission. Most firms post information about how their highly visible and recognizable names and trademarks may legally be used and under what circumstances links to their sites can be made. However, it should be stated that many people see the Internet as an open and unregulated environment, and believe that no government or company should be able to control the distribution of information once it reaches the Internet. Given these sorts of security and legal issues, it is no wonder that some firms have been reluctant to open their doors too wide to the Internet public.

Government Regulation and Taxation

For the most part, government regulators view the Internet as simply an extension of the regular business activity of firms operating in these governments' jurisdictions. They see rules and regulations as applying to all businesses, even if they exist entirely or partially online. For that reason, you would think that governments would make firms responsible for collecting the appropriate sales taxes on products sold online and then remitting them to governments on the basis of where the firms' customers are located. This is not the case, however. Although state and local governments are working toward a uniform sales tax policy for online sales, online vendors are legally treated like mail-order companies, which collect sales taxes only if they have a physical presence or nexus in the customer's state. American buyers are expected to pay local use taxes on products bought in other states, but the responsibility for doing this is the customer's, not the selling firm's. Canadian online vendors, however, are required to collect sales taxes and remit them to both federal and provincial governments. American firms selling to Canadian buyers can either collect sales taxes for their customers and remit them to the appropriate governments or leave them uncollected until delivery, when they are paid directly to the delivery agent by the buyer.

The absence of tax collection obviously provides an unfair benefit to those firms that can take advantage of the current law. To prevent the loss of potentially huge amounts of sales tax revenue, a consortium of American states is presently working to develop a uniform sales tax system so online firms will not be able to avoid collecting taxes or gain a competitive advantage over traditional bricks-and-mortar firms that are located in jurisdictions that levy sales taxes. Today, the existence of software services that can identify the appropriate tax authorities and their respective tax rates based on the address products are shipped to has given firms little excuse for not collecting sales taxes and remitting them to the proper jurisdictions. The online tax-free holiday will be ending shortly.[13]

Government Regulation of Restricted Products

One interesting aspect of online business is the sale and distribution of restricted products such as pharmaceuticals. In most jurisdictions, a doctor's prescription for medication must be presented to a pharmacist, who then fills the order. The Internet allows anyone to buy medications online; in some cases, they only need a credit card and the ability to claim they have a prescription. As a result, pharmaceuticals can be bought illegally with relatively little difficulty and subsequently sold into the illicit drug market. Just as it is in the bricks-and-mortar pharmacy on Main Street, it is legally the responsibility of the online pharmacist to verify the validity of the order and to look for abusive patterns, such as doctors prescribing unusually large quantities of certain drugs for one patient. Although it should be emphasized that most firms attempt to conduct their online activity fairly and legally, the Internet presents a great opportunity for illegal activity, for which profits can be a major motivator. In the absence of stricter government enforcement, this is both a legal and an ethical issue that will become even more pronounced as more firms migrate their traditional businesses to the Internet.

The U.S. Government Electronic Commerce Policy site, located at **www.commerce.gov**, is the definitive portal for finding current information and regulations related to online business, both within the United States and internationally. Since U.S. commercial interests drive the vast majority of Internet business, the focus of legal attention on the United States is understandable. The U.S. Department of Justice site, located at **www.usdoj.gov/criminal/cybercrime/compcrime.html**, provides more information about efforts to police cybercriminal activities.

Public Attitudes

As for the public's view, the Markle Foundation, a nonprofit group that focuses on public policy and technology, conducted a major yearlong study of the American public's attitudes about accountability on the Internet. Its findings suggest that Americans want a national governing commission to be created to ensure that Internet technologies reflect democratic decision-making values in the ways they deal with privacy, quality of information, and consumer protection issues. Although these surveys, which used telephone and online polling and focus group discussions indicated widespread enthusiastic support for the Internet, more than

**Go to the Web:
e-Business Online**
For tutorials and more on the topics in this chapter, visit the student website at **http://business.college.hmco.com/students** and select "Canzer e-Business."

half of respondents expressed concerns about pornography and privacy issues on the Internet and wished there was a central authority they could contact if they felt victimized by online fraud or scams or had other Internet-related problems. Interestingly, however, although more than two-thirds said they wanted government regulations to protect people, about 60 percent believed that Internet rules should be developed and enforced primarily by online businesses themselves.[14]

Conclusions

Socially responsible and ethical behavior on the Internet by both individuals and businesses is a major societal concern that has simply extended its reach from the general social environment to the special virtual environment of cyberspace. The individual, the social environment, and the opportunity to engage in unethical or even illegal behavior are the primary factors determining whether unethical behavior will take place. Unfortunately, the Internet provides a cover of anonymity and detachment for both individuals and firms, which might suggest why certain behaviors have surfaced on it.

This chapter provided an overview of the **Ethical, Legal, and Social Concerns** component of the **e-business plan** and concludes our introduction to the major themes in the study of e-business. A more detailed tutorial on the preparation of the e-business plan is available on the textbook's website.

In the next chapter, we will examine e-business models in greater detail in order to better understand and emulate the strategic approaches that are available to e-business planners.

 RETURN TO
inside e-business

CASE STUDY

The website for Zero-Knowledge Inc., **www.zerokn owledge.com**, provides a variety of information about encryption processes, new products coming onto the market that use new encryption processes to assure protection of information, articles emphasizing the need for Internet users to educate themselves about privacy issues, and links to relevant websites related to online security. No matter how convincing any promotional material might be, however, the fact remains that eventually all coding systems are vulnerable to someone or some organization that is willing and able to break the code. To further convince users of the need to use Freedom services, Zero-Knowledge has demonstrated this fact itself by exposing weaknesses in computer components and popular software like

Microsoft Office. Like vendors of security devices of many sorts, such as car alarms and dead-bolt locks, Zero-Knowledge is selling potential customers on the idea that security can be purchased. But just as in the real world, there are reasonable limits to security that individuals must recognize and learn to live with in order to function.

ASSIGNMENT

1. What are your views on the importance of using online security software?
2. Should the government be able to prevent a firm from selling this sort of shielding software in order to prevent criminals from benefiting from it?

Chapter Review

SUMMARY

ACE Self-Test
For a quick self-test of the content in this chapter, visit the student website at **http://business.college. hmco.com/students.** Select "Canzer e-Business."

1. **Explore a framework for understanding the ethical, legal, and social concerns related to e-business and the online environment.**

   The ethical, legal, and social environmental forces that are at work in e-business can be explored using the same basic models that apply to all businesses, regardless of whether they have any connection to the Internet. The general framework for approaching these subjects and making judgments about individual and organizational behaviors begins with an examination of ethics. Communities develop a sort of continuum, or scale, of ethical behaviors, in which behaviors are viewed as tending toward higher or lower levels on that continuum. Three primary factors determine ethical decision-making: the individual, the social environment the individual is presently in, and the opportunity the individual has to behave in some manner. To change the level of ethical behavior, one or more of these three factors in the current equilibrium would have to change.

2. **Discuss the concerns over privacy and confidentiality.**

   A questionable ethical practice in cyberspace is the unauthorized access to and use of information acquired through computerized tracking of users once they are connected to the Internet. There are several ways to collect data both with and without the user's knowledge, including placing cookies on the user's computer, analyzing log-file records, and mining data on customer transactions and their registration records. Advocates for improved control of the ways in which user information is collected and distributed to interested third parties such as businesses point to the potential for the misuse of information— intentionally or otherwise. However, the ability to collect and analyze personal data is critical if the industry is going to compete for advertisers' spending, and so it must learn to do this ethically.

3. **Examine security issues and cybercrime.**

   For all intents and purposes, the Internet remains an unregulated frontier in business. Therefore, both individuals and business users must be cognizant of the security risks and dangers they may encounter online. In addition to the risks associated with the unauthorized use of data collected through the Internet, individual users and businesses must watch for criminal activities, including fraud and larceny. Because the Internet allows the easy creation of websites, access from anywhere in the world, and anonymity for users, it is almost impossible to know with certainty that the website, organization, or individuals you are interacting with are what they seem. To alleviate consumer concerns about online purchasing, the major credit card organizations like MasterCard and Visa have instituted various programs to protect cardholders against fraudulent use of their cards on the Internet.

4. **Understand the special problems related to digital property, copyright, and distribution.**

   A major concern for businesses that use the Internet to distribute content is the control of digital property that can easily be replicated and distributed over the Internet. The legal issue of copyright, or the inherent right of owners to be the only ones permitted to replicate and distribute material they have created or paid someone for the rights to distribute, is best illustrated by the problems facing the music and publishing industries. With today's Internet technology, such as MP3, anyone can digitize a song into a file and then send it to someone else, without ever paying the copyright holders. As far as the industry is concerned, every copy of a song that is passed along for free on the Internet represents a loss of sales revenue from a customer who might otherwise have made a purchase.

5. **Explore the regulatory role played by government and related issues such as cybercrime and taxation.**
   For the most part, government regulators view the Internet as simply an extension of the regular business activity of firms operating in these governments' jurisdiction. They see rules and regulations as applying to all businesses, even if the businesses exist entirely or partially online. For that reason, you would think that governments would make firms responsible for collecting the appropriate sales taxes for products sold online and then remitting them to governments on the basis of where the firms' customers are located. This is not the case, however. Although state and local governments are working toward a uniform sales tax policy for online sales, online vendors are legally treated like mail-order companies, which collect taxes only if they have a physical presence or nexus in the customer's state.

REVIEW QUESTIONS

1. Describe the scale of ethical behavior.
2. What is the connection between the scale of ethical behavior and community judgment about specific behaviors?
3. Describe the ethical decision-making process.
4. What is a cookie?
5. How is the use of a cookie a security and privacy issue?
6. What is data mining?
7. How is data mining a security and privacy issue?
8. What is spamming?
9. Explain what the term *digital property rights* means.
10. Explain the issue of taxation as it relates to the sale of products over the Internet.

DISCUSSION QUESTIONS

1. Discuss the difficulties that face employers that are trying to set and administer policies concerning ethical employee behaviors.
2. Using the ethical decision-making process model, describe how you might try to change unethical behavior in an office environment. Explain your reasoning.
3. Discuss security issues and how they can be addressed.
4. How can digital property rights be protected?
5. What are the threats to digital property rights?
6. Discuss the role of government as it relates to the regulation and taxation of e-business.

Building Skills for Career Success

EXPLORING THE INTERNET

One of the security problems related to exchanges of documentation is confirming the identities of senders and receivers. To help solve this problem and expedite the development of e-business, the U.S. government has passed legislation for a digital authentication standard called *Digital Signature Standard* (DSA). You can learn more about this important development and other topics related to security and government involvement in it at **www.itaa.org/infosec.**

ASSIGNMENT

1. What is a current hot topic discussed at this website?
2. How would you describe government concerns about Internet security issues?

DEVELOPING CRITICAL THINKING SKILLS

According to Internet law expert Lawrence Lessig, a professor at Stanford University in California and author of the bestseller *Code and Other Laws of Cyberspace*, innovation and creativity are threatened by attempts to regulate intellectual property. Lessig states that before the digital age, copyrights were limited rights that expired in time and allowed a certain degree of fair use by others. However, technology, which is now capable of allowing individuals and organizations to freely create and distribute content as never before, can also be designed to block and control content forever through the use of encoding software. As a result, the necessary creative good that comes from having content in the public domain is gradually becoming more and more restricted by legislation and the technology of firms that wish to protect what they perceive as their rights. The problem that will eventually arise, says Lessig, is a decline in overall creativity as a result of the absence of freely available—public domain—content. Lessig argues that society needs to question the very notion of copyright in our digital age and points to Disney's use of classic writer Victor Hugo's *The Hunchback of Notre Dame*. Had copyright law prevented Disney's use of Hugo's work and other such works, the world would be without the animated creations that exist today.[15]

ASSIGNMENT

1. Do you agree or disagree with Lessig's arguments on copyright protection and its effect on creativity? Explain your thinking.
2. What would you consider a fair copyright arrangement for original works?

BUILDING TEAM SKILLS

In general, government-owned or government-controlled corporations have always been considered unfair competitors to regular businesses and an impediment to industry investment. After all, the argument goes, if a government agency is going to build a business and offer products or services free of charge or at subsidized rates, how can a for-profit business expect to compete? However, the Canadian government and the Internet industry may have found a model for a compromise solution through their creation of Ebiz.enable (**http: //strategis.ic.gc.ca/epic/internet/inee-ef.nsf/vwGeneratedInterE/Home**) and SourceCAN (**www.sourcecan.ca**). Ebiz.enable is an information website clearinghouse where small and medium-sized businesses can find information about moving operational processes such as supply-chain management onto the Internet. SourceCAN is an umbrella public- and private-sector e-marketplace where Canadian firms can find domestic and international buyers and sellers of services and products, participate in virtual trade shows, post and view electronic catalogs, and use applications that support online procurement, supply-chain management, and logistics services—free of charge. The site encourages the participation of Canada's large private-sector business-to-business (B2B) sites, such as Bell Canada's BellZinc.com (**www.bellzinc.com**). Should buyers or sellers conclude a deal with a participant that does charge a fee, the fee is paid only to that participant—not to the operators of the SourceCAN site. The result, developed after consultations with business leaders in the field, is a one-stop site for those who wish to consult a large number of competitors all at once. Considering that the development costs were only C$450,000 for Ebiz.enable and C$1.4 million for SourceCAN, the strategy might be a model for governments in countries where a lack of business investment to provide online information and services is impeding e-commerce development.[16]

ASSIGNMENT

1. Describe your group's perception of the Ebiz.enable (**http://strategis.ic.gc.ca/ epic/internet/inee-ef.nsf/vwGeneratedInterE/Home**) and SourceCAN(**www.source can.ca**) websites.
2. Discuss the idea of government's helping to expedite the development of the Internet, and report your group's position.

RESEARCHING DIFFERENT CAREERS

The mission of the nonprofit organization DigitalEve (**www.digitaleve.org**) is to level the playing field and encourage women to enter traditionally male career fields in technology through local seminars and mentoring programs. According to its study in collaboration with Jupiter Communications Inc., women look at the Internet differently from the way men do. Whereas women relate to the communications aspect of technology, men focus on the hardware technology. Over 10,000 organization members belong to the twenty chapters of DigitalEve in North America, Europe, and Asia.[17]

ASSIGNMENT

1. Describe how the DigitalEve website, (**www.digitaleve.org**), appeals to women.
2. Are any of the strategies used on the website just as applicable to men?

IMPROVING COMMUNICATION SKILLS

Although out-of-court third-party arbitration is a well-established method for solving business disputes quickly, a Toronto, Ontario, law firm believes that its Internet-based software, NovaForum (**www.theelectroniccourthouse.com/main/index.html**), can provide an even faster alternative solution. Opposing parties to a dispute anywhere in the world follow an eight-step online process that leads them to a legally binding solution that is rendered by the law firm within seventy–two hours. The $2,500 cost is a far cry from the $50,000 that the typical law firm client needs to pay for an average of 600 hours of legal services. The firm's website provides a free-access walk through a sample case study to illustrate the process for clients.[18]

ASSIGNMENT
1. Describe the steps involved in the sample case study presented on the website.
2. Do you think the process is as fair as a face-to-face situation? Explain your thinking.

Exploring Useful Websites

These websites provide information related to the topics discussed in the chapter. You can learn more by visiting them online and examining their current data.

1. Zero-Knowledge Systems Inc. (**www.zeroknowledge.com**) is the leading provider of Internet privacy technologies and services for consumers and businesses. Its current version of its Freedom software, available as a free download over the Internet (**www.freedom.net**), provides users with the ability to create their own personal firewalls and other features.

2. The Better Business Bureau website, located at **www.bbbonline.org/Reliability/code/**, details an international code of ethical behaviors that it developed jointly with the Federation of European Direct Marketing (FEDMA) and the Association of European Chambers of Commerce.

3. DoubleClick (**www.doubleclick.com**) and 24/7 Media (**www.247media.com**) are the industry's leading online advertisers.

4. The secure electronic transaction, or SET, encryption process (**www.setco.org**) was developed by MasterCard, Visa, IBM, Microsoft, and Netscape; it prevents merchants from ever actually seeing any transaction data, including the customer's credit card number. Both the Internet Fraud Commission Center (**www1.ifccfbi.gov/index.asp**) and the nonprofit National Consumers League (**www.natlconsumersleague.org/**) reported to a congressional committee investigating Internet fraud that auction websites were by far the most common targets of the complaints they receive.

5. Norton's AntiVirus program, distributed by Symantec (**www.symantec.com**), and McAfee's VirusScan (**www.mcafee.com**) are two well-known commercial products that help screen out incoming files that contain viruses.

6. With Internet technology such as MP3 (**www.mp3.com**) anyone can digitize a song into a file and then send it to someone else, without ever paying the copyright holders. MusicNet (**www.musicnet.com**) was established to control the legal distribution of copyright content.

7. Kevin Spacey sued the firm behind **www.celebrity1000.com** for using his name in the URL **www.kevinspacey.com** without his permission.

8. The U.S. Government Electronic Commerce Policy site, located at **www.commerce.gov**, is the definitive portal for current information and regulations related to online business, both within the United States and internationally. The U.S. Department of Justice site, located at **www.usdoj.gov/criminal/cybercrime/compcrime.html**, provides more information about the effort to police cybercriminal activities. To help expedite the development of e-business, the U.S. government has passed legislation for a digital authentication standard called *Digital Signature Standard* (DSA). You can learn more about this important development and other topics of concern related to security and government involvement at **www.itaa.org/infosec**. The Business Software Alliance (**www.bsa.org**) is an organization whose mandate includes educating software users in order to reduce the theft of copyright material.

9. The Canadian government and the Internet industry may have found a strategy for helping to boost Internet commerce by creating Ebiz.enable (**http://strategis.ic.gc.ca/epic/internet/inee-ef.nsf/vwGeneratedInterE/Home**) and SourceCAN (**www.sourcecan.ca**). Ebiz.enable is an information website clearinghouse where small and medium-sized businesses can find information about moving operational processes such as supply-chain management onto the Internet. SourceCAN is an umbrella public- and private-sector e-marketplace where Canadian firms can find domestic and international buyers and sellers of services and products, participate in virtual trade shows, post and view electronic catalogs, and use applications that support online procurement, supply-chain management, and logistics services—free of charge. The site encourages Canada's large private-sector B2B sites, such as Bell Canada's BellZinc.com (**www.bellzinc.com**) to participate.

10. The World Sports Exchange (**www.wsex.com**), the largest sports gambling website, is located in Grand Cayman Island, and although many of its gaming activities are illegal in the United States, players can access the site with a credit card or establish an account, making control by American authorities next to impossible.

11. The mission of the nonprofit organization DigitalEve (**www.digitaleve.org**) is to encourage women to enter traditionally male career fields in technology through local seminars and mentoring programs.

12. The Internet-based software NovaForum (**www.theelectroniccourthouse.com/main/index.html**) can provide opposing parties to a dispute with an alternative method for obtaining a legally binding solution rendered by a law firm.

Strategic Business Planning for the Internet

Module II examines the strategic business planning process in greater detail. We focus our attention on the three key components of strategic planning: research, analysis, and the formulation of an e-business plan. First, in Chapter 4 we present a structure for organizing and understanding the variety of e-business models, and we discuss how each model serves to direct the entire organization in its search to generate revenues and create a competitive advantage online. In Chapter 5 we examine these activities from the point of view of strategists working at each of the three primary organizational levels of the firm: the corporate, division/strategic business unit, and operating/functional levels. In Chapter 6 we detail the research and information-gathering process, and then in Chapter 7 we explore online communication and user behaviors. The module provides a broad base of information about what e-business models and their strategies can help the firm to achieve and how they can be incorporated into the existing organization and business plan. Managerial details and operational implications of any e-business plan will be addressed in the third module.

chapter 4

Developing
e-Business Models

INSIDE
e-business

Amazon.com—Selling Online Services to Other Retailers

Like his fellow entrepreneurs who started eBay and Yahoo!, Jeff Bezos, founder and CEO of online retailing giant Amazon.com, is among those few brazen mid-1990s e-business visionaries who managed to create a globally recognized online brand name where none existed before. Amazon.com, which for many early Web shoppers was the only known name for online retailing, managed to survive the growing pains of establishing the firm. But it also finally emerged from steady losses (more than $1.4 billion in 2000) into the glow of respectability and profit in 2003, something many once doubted was possible.

Amazon.com began by offering customers easy-to-handle merchandise such as books, videotapes, and music. Gradually, more categories were added, and today a wide array of products, from electronics and cameras to games and clothing, are available to the more than 33 million Amazon.com shoppers around the world. Many online retailing ideas were developed at Amazon.com and have become de facto standard features of the better online retailers. These include keeping track of the customer's previous buying behavior and preferences, displaying product-specific opinions posted by other shoppers, and providing sample excerpts from books. Amazon.com is expected to generate $4.8 billion in sales revenues in 2003 and more than $6 billion in 2004.

Being a first mover can mean enjoying benefits that competitors may never match and an advantage they may never overcome. However, along with the advantages of being the first to the market with a new idea or product also comes the risks associated with doing things for the first time. In the field of retailing, Amazon.com provided others with a view of the emerging online world by taking the lead. The successes and failures at Amazon.com provided needed guidance to other online retailers as the nascent industry learned how to build brand recognition and website traffic and function profitably. Amazon.com demonstrated the importance of warehousing and other fulfillment requirements as it developed ways to assure quick delivery of orders at costs that would provide profit. Today, Amazon.com remains the most visible example to retail developers watching for strategies to emulate or surpass.

Currently, Amazon.com's management is building revenues by capitalizing on the firm's expertise in software design and running online retail operations. Retailers like Target, Toys 'R' Us, Marshal Field's, and Office Depot have partnered with Amazon.com to set up their online operations. Amazon.com's software developers and Web operators provide their expertise in online retailing to these and any other retailer that wants to partner with Amazon.com in exchange for shared commissions. In this way, Amazon.com can symbiotically offer its customers a greater selection of merchandise than other retailers. In 2003, 22 percent of items sold on Amazon.com, in fact, were from other sellers.[1]

Amazon.com is considered by many to be the first online retailer to seriously challenge the conventional "bricks-and-mortar" method of selling products to consumers. Although catalog, mail-order, and direct-to-customer marketing were well-established strategies, no one had yet tried to take on a globally distributed marketplace using the Internet as a communications vehicle and simultaneously build a brand name from scratch. As the Amazon.com method of conducting business evolved, others—both new creations and existing old-economy retailers like Barnes & Noble (**www.barnesandnoble.com**)—studied the successes and failures that tested and proved models of success.

Changes, opportunities, and challenges to existing strategies, as well as discussions about how management should respond, are best understood when they are presented within an organizing structure. For instance, what researchers and business practitioners want to learn when they look at successes like Amazon.com and Yahoo! as well as celebrated failures such as Boo.com and Pet.com is a simplified description of how each business was intended to work. To answer this fundamental question, they need information about how the firm planned to earn revenues, the sources of those revenues, the identity of target customers, pricing, promotion, and other strategies that were part of the overall plan. In this chapter, we will examine a structure and related terminology that will allow us to organize and analyze information and approach e-business decision-making in a methodical manner.

Exploring e-Business Models

model
A representation of an actual device.

To understand how anything works, especially complex, large-scale devices like a manufacturing assembly line or warehouse distribution system, it is common to construct a **model** or a representation of an actual device. Engineers build small-scale models of buildings and bridges and test them for design integrity, appearance, and other factors before they commit themselves and investors to the costs of building the real thing. Much can be learned from a model. The fundamental characteristics are usually the focus of the model's design, and less-important details may be omitted so attention is directed to the important areas alone, without complicating distractions.

business model
A group of shared or common characteristics, behaviors, and methods of doing business that enables a firm to generate profits by increasing revenues and reducing costs.

Models of a particular type tend to share certain characteristics. For instance, most models of cars have four wheels and a steering wheel. By examining models, engineers can gain insight into the basic components that are likely to be present in their own specific designs. Precisely the same concept prevails within the confines of a business model. A **business model** is a descriptive representation of the fundamental components of a business, which we described in Chapter 1 as a group of shared or common characteristics, behaviors, and methods of doing business that enables a firm to generate profits by increasing revenues and reducing costs. For example, the business model for the book retailer Barnes & Noble is similar to that of most other retail establishments: targeted customers' reading needs are satisfied through the business activities of stocking the store shelves with desirable products at acceptable prices, and so forth. How Barnes & Noble specifically carries on its business is detailed in its business plan. But the basic model of who and what Barnes & Noble is as a business is much simpler to describe: *Barnes & Noble makes money by selling books and other products in a physical retail environment to clearly identified target customers.* Anyone else who wants to emulate this successful retail business model can study the model and replicate it with whatever additions or deletions are seen as necessary. Perhaps instead of books, another retailer might sell clothing or sports equipment. With few exceptions, the retail business model is common to a variety of individual businesses whose efforts to further customize the model are detailed in their respective business plans.

e-business model

A descriptive representation of the fundamental components of a business that operates partially or completely on the Internet.

An **e-business model** is a descriptive representation of the fundamental components of a business that operates partially or completely on the Internet. Barnes & Noble's e-business model for its online operations overlaps somewhat with its traditional bricks-and-mortar business model. Although there are similarities between the two, business operations in each model are significantly different in many ways. For example, the retail business model is based on selling and distributing a product to customers who walk into the retailer's stores. But the e-retailer can accommodate online customers who are dispersed throughout the world by using courier services for delivery and does not operate any actual, physical stores. All customers may enter the same "virtual door" if that is the way the online operations are designed. Alternatively, a different virtual entrance to shopping can be created for, say, young customers under the age of eleven, or there can be one virtual entrance for boys and another for girls. The choice of entrances and the method of offering an online shopping experience to each target market is entirely the choice of the firm. The costs of designing multiple gateways to the Barnes & Noble online store are relatively low in comparison to the costs of building a real store and staffing it with personnel who are trained to cater to a specific target group. On the other hand, both the online and the bricks-and-mortar business operation models include equivalent warehousing and distribution logistics and costs. Regardless of whether the merchandise is sold online or at a physical retail outlet in a mall, the warehousing operation for maintaining proper inventories is going to be similar.

Although a firm's business model comprises several key features that describe how the business functions in the world, to many people the term really means only one important thing: "How does the firm earn revenues?" Although this view might be considered somewhat myopic, it focuses attention on the single most critical point—revenue sources. It also sheds light on the feasibility of what the firm is trying to do and whether the analyst examining the business model thinks there is much point to continuing to investigate the rest of the firm's business model or business plan. For example, suppose that the basic premise of a business model is to make money by selling, on the Internet, used sports equipment like football and hockey pads to individuals, schools, sports teams, and organizations. Suppose also that an analyst believes that this is just not a very good idea, both because people need to try out sports equipment before they purchase it and because the costs of shipping are too high given the profit margins typically available for used sports equipment. The analyst in other words can save a great deal of time and effort by focusing immediately on the basic foundation upon which the rest of the business model and business plan rests.

Finally, it is important to recognize that, in most cases, any particular e-business operation is likely to be a blend of more than one e-business model. For example, Yahoo! and MSN are examples both of advertising and portal e-business models. It is useful to look at the component e-business models that constitute a complex Web-based operation in order to simplify and better understand the strategic actions taking place. In this chapter, we will next explore each e-business model in greater detail by looking more closely at the core operations and strategic actions of several firms. To focus further on business objectives and the strategic actions firms employed to achieve them, this segment of the chapter also contains in-depth strategic profiles of E*TRADE and Yahoo! in the e-Business Insight features.

Brokerage e-Business Model

brokerage e-business model

An e-business model that encompasses online marketplaces in which buyers and sellers are brought together in an organized environment to facilitate the exchange of goods.

The **brokerage e-business model** encompasses online marketplaces where buyers and sellers are brought together in an organized environment to facilitate the exchange of goods and services. Brokerage firms often specialize in a particular product classification and may even be organized by a major supplier or vendor of these products. This is the case with the auto-parts exchange organized by General Motors and the airline industry supply exchange set up by Air Canada. Though the vast majority of brokerage activity is conducted among businesses, the popular and profitable eBay (**www.ebay.com**) provides both businesses and consumers with access to a communications structure for buying or selling virtually anything.

Brokerage sites may also specialize by providing a particular type of product or service. They thereby attempt to satisfy needs within a niche market that might be better served online than through conventional means. For example, research suggests that less than 1 percent of an estimated $57 billion of excess merchandise is currently sold through online brokers. But that is likely to change dramatically as e-commerce sites specializing in redistributing unwanted inventories spring up to handle the task of finding buyers for these goods. AMR Research Inc. estimates that about 14 percent of unwanted goods are sold online through sites like RetailExchange.com (**www.retailexchange.com**), and Overstock.com (**www.overstock.com**), which answer the inefficiencies inherent in the non-Internet-based system, in which buyers are found through phone calls and faxes. Often the merchandise may be slightly damaged or simply a poor-selling style or color that was overproduced by enthusiastic manufacturers. Wholesalers who overestimated demand and got stuck with too much merchandise as well as vendors who have declared bankruptcy make up the bulk of the oversupply industry. Huge discounts, which might reduce prices to 10 percent of regular wholesale prices, help to motivate buyers who believe they have customers who would willingly buy—at the right price.[2]

Adbargains Inc. (**www.adbargains.com**) is a good example of an even more specialized excess inventory brokerage e-business model that uses the communication power of the Internet to solve logistical problems and make money where none could have been made before. A Toronto, Ontario–based start-up serving North American media buyers and sellers, Adbargains presents an easy-to-use website where sellers of excess advertising space in any medium can connect with buyers seeking last-minute bargains or supplementary supply to increase their current advertising commitments. Like other brokerage models such as eBay, the site is automated and generates revenue equal to 25 percent of the value of any advertising space sold. Without Adbargains, media sellers would have to forgo potential sales of unsold available space and buyers would be unable to boost their current advertising campaigns.

Brokerages employ a variety of structural designs to facilitate the exchange process, typically using those that reflect the real-world environment users are already familiar with. Therefore, virtual shopping malls often have a look and feel that is not different from the physical environment they already know, right down to the shopping cart icon indicating the merchandise they have selected for purchase. On the business-to-business (B2B) side of the brokerage model, designs include regular auctions, reverse auctions, classified listings, and so forth, all of which also tend to reflect buying and selling environments that users are likely to easily understand and feel comfortable with. Firms like Charles Schwab (**www.schwab.com**) and E*TRADE (**www.etrade.com**) focus on facilitating the exchange of financial securities between buyers and sellers. As in all brokerage businesses, revenues are earned mostly through commission charges that are based on the value of the securities bought and sold. In addition, the brokerage firm may charge a membership fee and collect advertising revenues by selling display space on its screens. In the case of a securities brokerage firm like Charles Schwab or E*TRADE, the firm earns money in traditional ways too, such as on the spread between the interest rates it charges for the money it lends to clients and what it has to pay to borrow those funds.

e - B U S I N E S S
insight

Profile of a Brokerage e-Business Model—E*TRADE (www.etrade.com)

- **Target Audience for the Business**

Retail, institutional, and corporate financial services customers.

- **Primary Purpose for the Website**

E*TRADE provides personalized and fully integrated brokerage, banking, and lending financial services. The site serves as a gateway to customers who may buy and sell securities, conduct common banking transactions, and borrow money. The primary purpose of the site is to facilitate and promote the sales of these products and services, which are available exclusively online, or through call centers and automatic teller machines (ATMs) worldwide.

- **Actions Taken on the Site**

The home page (**www.etrade.com**) contains a high-level organizational menu bar, which is placed across the top. It clearly directs current customers and potential new ones to the various product and service areas. For example, the Accounts, Investing, Banking, Lending, and Plan and Advice items in the menu bar reduce complexity and send the message that the business is mainly concerned with these

services. Current customers can quickly access their accounts. Current and potential customers can seek further information and services from one of the other high-level menu choices. In addition, the home page contains a variety of complementary financial information such as current stock and bond market summaries, a stock quote look-up service, and interest rates on saving and borrowing. Presumably, E*TRADE's analysis has suggested that the high-level menu offerings of its home page structure can best serve current and potential customers. By examining E*TRADE competitor Charles Schwab (**www.schwab.com**) we can see that the industry leaders have arrived at a common design and structure, with minor differences.

The focus of E*TRADE's well-designed gateway is providing quick access to the many products and services it offers to current and potential customers. These are organized under pulldown menus that are promotional in their design as well. For example, consumer loans are listed under Auto, Motorcycle, and RV & Boat Loans. The pulldown menu allows users to access specific information and application forms. In addition, the home page displays banner advertisements that highlight and direct customers to current promotions such as a limited-time-offer special fee rebate plan on mutual funds.

• **Actions Taken to Achieve Business Success**

To continue growing, the E*TRADE brokerage model needs to focus on building brand recognition and website traffic in a crowded and competitive marketplace. The next logical task would be to convert as many as possible of those who visit into customers. The third task would then be to increase the number and volume of services all current customers buy.

Building brand awareness and driving traffic can be accomplished through conventional media advertising as well as through online campaigns. In addition, firms can list their sites with search engine databases and directories such as Google.com. Furthermore, paid advertising placements that appear on screen alongside unpaid regular search engine results can be especially useful for building awareness and traffic because people searching for specific sites are more likely to see and act on the sites that are displayed on the first page of search engine results.

Using direct mail and e-mail advertising to selected databases of interested potential customers can be a successful strategy for building awareness and drawing potential customers. These lists can be purchased from third-party sources or compiled from potential customers who may enter their e-mail addresses in order to receive investment information such as stock market projections by the firm's "experts."

Finally, all businesses should take full advantage of any opportunity to promote their website by placing their URL on all business cards, letterhead paper, invoices, packaging, and so forth.

Question for discussion: What changes would you make to the website?[3]

etrade.com

(*Source:* © 2004 E*TRADE Financial Corp. Reprinted with permission.)

Advertising e-Business Model

An **advertising e-business model** is based on earning revenues in exchange for the display of advertisements on a firm's website, in much the same way as other media such as television, radio, newspapers, and magazines earn revenues. Advertisers' sponsorship of distributed online entertainment or information is likely to continue to be readily accepted by audiences, who see advertising as the price they have to pay for receiving free content online. But in contrast to conventional media, where engaging the consumer is often problematic, the Internet provides both the advertiser and the website content provider with the opportunity to create unique design and interaction with the targeted audience.

In the near future, the biggest online content provider is likely to be AOL, since its merger with Time Warner has combined the massive audience base of AOL subscribers with the huge vault of multimedia content from the Time Warner group. However, the advertising model for the Internet has also stimulated the entry of small production studios and entertainment artists, who are seeking to earn advertising revenues as well as to sell their products online. In contrast to the situation in television and radio, Internet barriers to entry are low, and virtually anyone with something that will attract an audience can get started quite easily. The advertising model has also been used by consultants such as financial advisers and lawyers, who might provide free articles about topics specific to their expertise and practice. For example, a lawyer who specializes in real estate business might set up a website that contains articles related to the legal issues arising from the buying and selling of real property. Besides serving to advertise the lawyer's own services, the website would also interest banks that seek to make mortgage loans, moving and storage firms, and of course real estate agents. Although the lawyer in this case may view a professional website as a promotional tool rather than a revenue source, many small start-ups hope to find a huge global audience and the advertising revenues that go along with it. Others hope to be discovered by a larger firm that wishes to add their website content to their own. From the very large to the smaller-scale firms, the e-business advertising model can provide a financial and promotional contribution to the overall business plan.

The critical factor that determines the success of the advertising and for that matter most e-business models is the level of traffic generated by the website offering—whatever content it happens to be. The level of traffic is, in turn, a function of how appealing the site is to those who know of it and how effective the company has been in building brand awareness among those who don't. To accomplish both objectives, management might advertise, list on search engines, and encourage visitors to refer friends and others who they believe would be interested to visit their site. This can be done by encouraging visitors to send an article from a subscription e-business site or other content item to others. For example, the distribution channel member e-business model used by the Hallmark (**www.hallmark.com**) website encourages visitors to e-mail greetings cards free of charge. These bring recipients to Hallmark's website to view their cards, giving them knowledge of the site and its other products and services.

Subscription, Pay-per-View, and Membership e-Business Models

subscription
An e-business model in which access to a site is controlled by a subscription fee.

pay-per-view
An e-business model in which access to a site is controlled by a charge for viewing single items.

membership e-business model
An e-business model in which access to a site is controlled by membership fees.

Website content providers may elect to earn revenues by using a **subscription**, **pay-per-view**, or **membership e-business model**, in which access to the site is controlled by a subscription fee, a charge for viewing single items such as a report, or a membership fee, respectively. Often these sources of revenue are combined with advertising revenue. The subscription model, which is popular with publications and research organizations, often provides samples of the site's content free of charge and then seeks to induce interested clients to subscribe to the full range of products and services available. A common strategy is to offer a trial subscription for a limited time period and at a substantial price reduction to entice new subscribers.

Both Forrester Research Inc. (**www.forrester.com**) and *Business Week* (**www.businessweek.com**) magazine provide free content and then attempt to sell further services through subscription. Like other magazines that display online content, the venerable *Reader's Digest* (**www.rd.com**) surrounds its free-access magazine articles with advertising. The hope is that the free sample will ultimately lead people to subscribe to the print version of the magazine. This approach is also common for online learning and educational institutions that sell courses and programs through the Internet.

In some cases, content providers request only that users register to gain wider access to the providers' products and special services. IBM's small business and e-business website, for example, will send registrants daily bulletins containing links to its database of articles. The purpose of registration is to get information about the person and possibly use that information to control the number of visitors to the website. Furthermore, this information can be used to offer sales on products from the firm or from others, if the member has agreed to this as a condition of membership.

Distribution Channel Member e-Business Model

distribution channel member e-business model
An e-business model that encompasses the activities of retailers, wholesalers, and manufacturers conducting business through the Internet.

The **distribution channel member e-business model** encompasses the activities of retailers, wholesalers, and manufacturers conducting business through the Internet. It is a natural choice for businesses that are currently active at any of these levels in the distribution system of products to end users. Taking product offerings into a global and virtual environment is easier than ever, because e-commerce software that facilitates this is available for relatively small fees from hosting firms, which also provide everything required to get started. Furthermore, firms can easily scale up if their initial activities produce positive results. Newcomers to the Internet might wish to place only their top-selling products in an online facility, gradually building up an entire online catalog in tandem with their bricks-and-mortar retail or wholesale operations.

Retailers such as Wal-Mart (**www.walmart.com**), Staples (**www.staples.com**), Sears, Roebuck (**www.sears.com**), and of course, Amazon.com (**www.amazon.com**) provide easy and convenient online shopping experiences for virtual shoppers. In addition, shoppers may simply be using the retail website to gather the information they need to make an informed decision before finalizing their purchase within the walls of one of the company's stores. Regardless of whether the website promotes sales within the company's stores or is the primary avenue for more frequent shopping by busy or geographically dispersed customers, companies regard providing some level of online shopping assistance to be a prudent and effective means of serving customers today.

Wholesalers and manufacturers have found that the Internet can be a productive new tool for reducing costs and finding new sales. In addition to putting their product catalogs online, wholesalers and manufacturers are increasingly making use of brokerage websites as well as managing their own site activities. Perhaps the most celebrated Internet-related manufacturing success story is that of Dell Computer, which is credited with helping to establish a new model for tying manufacturing to orders entered online and for building relationships with component manufacturers and customers.

Affiliation e-Business Model

**affiliation
e-business model**

An e-business model that involves payments to website operators for customers who find their way to a company's site and either buy merchandise or services or perform some other action, such as registering and providing certain information.

The **affiliation e-business model** involves payments to website operators for customers who find their way to a company's site and either buy merchandise or services or perform some other action, such as registering and providing certain information. This model was popularized by Amazon.com (**www.amazon.com**), which, like other operators of affiliate programs, has automated the process of registering and creating an online link to the destination site. Any website operator that wants to earn a share of the revenues from books and other products sold through the Amazon.com website to customers that the website operator has sent there simply has to make a few clicks at the Amazon.com registration site. An Amazon.com link will then appear on the affiliate's website. Amazon.com currently pays a 15 percent finder's commission for customers sent its way, which helps to explain why the program is such a success with website operators.

This affiliation model is now commonplace for firms that are seeking to build sales through partnerships with website operators who believe that their audience will find a reason to click on the affiliation link. Regardless of the affiliate website operator's actual level of success, such an affiliation link costs little to try out and maintain and tends to increase the value image of the host site. The only true cost is the space on the screen that is taken up by the affiliation site icon, and this is why the programs are so attractive to both parties. Affiliation programs are really a form of advertising that is paid for only when sales are made. Thus, Amazon.com receives huge amounts of exposure from anyone who is willing to become an affiliate. The real costs to Amazon.com are practically nothing, since this is a software application that is entirely automated. For better-known brands, using affiliate programs rather than spending on massive advertising campaigns can do the job more effectively and save funds for other activities. However, an affiliation program is not likely to work well for an unknown brand unless there is no need for branding. For example, a site that specializes in the sale of science fiction titles may not be widely known. However, someone who is reading an online article and sample chapter about a new science fiction book would be likely to click on the affiliation icon to order the book without caring too much about what the book distributor's name was.

Community e-Business Model

The **community e-business model** is built around the idea that a group of online users can be regularly brought together at a commonly used website for commercial purposes. The sorts of communities that are brought together can vary widely and can include people who share an interest such as playing bridge or poker, wish to exchange their opinions about politics and public affairs, or wish to find old high school classmates with whom they would like to reestablish contact.

Communities are the great growth opportunity for any individual or organization that can think of a reason why someone would be interested enough in its site to make the effort to visit it. Online communities such as those set up by educational institutions and religious organizations can be self-supporting by associating themselves with their respective larger organizations and implementing fee structures for members or donors. These online communities are generally regarded as simply another method by which members can communicate with one another and are usually free of any revenue-generating aspect. However, online communities, along with the advertising and shopping services that are unique to their focus, continue to flourish as a niche for small and special-interest groups. For example, Oxygen (**www.oxygen.com**), Oprah Winfrey (**www.oprah.com**), and iVillage (**www.ivillage.com**) have all developed large numbers of regular users by focusing mainly on topics that are of interest to women. GeoCities (**www.geocities.com**), Yahoo!'s build-your-own-web-site-for-free service, provides an environment for individuals who wish to explore their creative skills by constructing a website. In all of these communities, advertising, affiliate programs, and online shopping provide the revenues needed to make the communities viable. The success of this model is obviously based on building awareness among interested users and spreading the word. Therefore, most site operators offer incentives such as rewards and prizes to current members who enlist new users.

Infomediary e-Business Model

The **infomediary e-business model** is based on the collection and sale of online information. For example, Bizrate.com (**www.bizrate.com**) provides a comparative shopping guide to vendors' products, which consumers find through the firm's search engine. Like other search processes, the results are rated, and users can locate the vendor of choice based on price or other criteria. Another infomediary e-business model is ClickZ.com (**www.clickz.com**), formerly known as CyberAtlas.com, the popular research website that presents published statistics and articles on a wide range of Internet-related topics from a variety of sources.

Many sites, especially communities, are in a position to analyze their users' online interests and behaviors and sell the results of this research to other interested parties, such as advertisers. In addition, communities can earn revenues by providing informational services from advertisers to users who accept the offer, usually in the form of e-mail advertisements or other types of announcements. Without a community site that has a large numbers of users, no data collection activity is really possible unless the infomediary firm uses other methods to attract online users and motivate them to volunteer information. In some cases, this is done by providing free Internet access or free access to a website and its content in exchange for registration and permission to collect online behavior data, send out e-mail advertisements, and conduct other such activities.

Gomez.com (**www.gomez.com**) is an infomediary that pays users for permission to track their movements on the Internet and sell the information to advertisers and other interested parties such as website managers that want to know more about the online behaviors of visitors to their sites. The research approach is similar in design to the television research techniques used to monitor the viewing habits of paid participants who allow a recording device to be hooked up to their television sets. After registering, users load a software program that tracks their online behavior. Not all applicants are accepted, however. After a trial period, Gomez.com decides whether the applicant matches the research needs of their clientele and pays them amounts that reflect the value of time they spend online.

portal e-business model
A type of infomediary that earns revenues by drawing users to its site and serving as a gateway or portal to information located elsewhere on the Internet.

horizontal portals
Portals that have a wide general reach into different informational topics.

vertical portals
Portals that have a narrow focus into a particular informational topic.

Portal e-Business Model

The **portal e-business model** is a type of infomediary that earns revenues by drawing users to its site and serving as a gateway or portal to information located elsewhere on the Internet. Some portals, such as search engines, have a wide general reach into different informational topics and are referred to as **horizontal portals**, whereas others have a narrow focus on a particular topic and are called **vertical portals**. Both types of portals can earn revenues by selling advertising, providing search services to users who are seeking merchants and products, and charging finder's fees for customers sent to a particular merchant.

e-BUSINESS insight

Profile of a Portal e-Business Model—Yahoo! (www.yahoo.com)

- **Target Audience for the Business**

Yahoo! was among the first portals established for general entry to the Web and remains a globally popular launch site.

- **Primary Purpose for the Website**

Yahoo! was among the first search engine and directory sites to establish its brand on the Internet, earning its revenues primarily from banner and other style advertisements on its various webpages. As the frequency and duration of users' visits to Yahoo! pages increased, the firm increased the advertising revenue it could generate.

- **Actions Taken on the Site**

Yahoo! offers a variety of mostly free services to attract and keep visitors on its webpages as long as possible. Search engine and directory listings for employment, real estate, travel, e-mail and personal webpage space, news, stock market information, classified advertisements, auctions, communities, chat rooms, entertainment and games, web hosting, and so on give customers more reason to return to Yahoo! and stay longer on one of its display pages.

• **Actions Taken to Achieve Business Success**

To continue growing, Yahoo! needs to focus on maintaining its high brand recognition and website traffic in an increasingly crowded and competitive marketplace. This horizontal portal that appeals to a wide audience will continue to face stiff competition from vertical portals that may appeal to more narrowly defined markets that wish to launch their computers on the Internet at a news site, like CNN.com (**www.cnn.com**) or *USAToday* (**www.usatoday.com**), that also provides search engine services, stock market reports, weather reports, and other common services.

Yahoo! websites are customized to better cater to geographic and linguistic markets than less developed portals. For example, Yahoo! sites are presented in Spanish, French, Chinese, and other languages in appropriate countries. Interestingly, Yahoo!'s American site is also available in Spanish and Chinese so as to better serve customers inside and outside of the country who wish to interact in these languages instead of English.

Question for discussion: What other services would you suggest Yahoo! add to improve growth?[4]

Yahoo.com

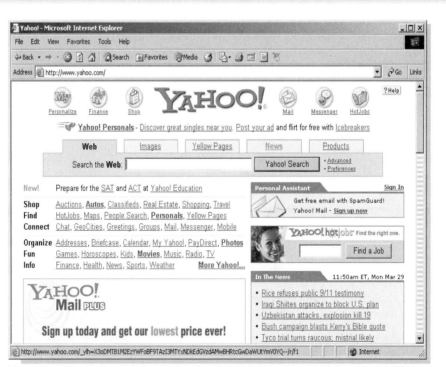

(*Source:* Reproduced with permission of Yahoo! Inc. © 2004 by Yahoo! Inc. YAHOO! and the YAHOO! logo are trademarks of Yahoo! Inc.)

Internet-Based Software and e-Business Solutions

One of the e-business models we have just examined, or some variation on them, will generally form the core of an organization's e-business plan. In other words, a firm's selection of one or more of these models determines the basic framework for its e-business plan. In addition to these basic e-business models, the primary Internet-based software tools that vendors sell as e-business solutions for communications and other applications, are worth a closer look.

In this section we will examine these primary Internet-based software solutions in order of their complexity and difficulty of implementation within the firm's operations. We will also examine the strategic use of these solutions within the context of the topics to be presented in the remaining chapters of this textbook. The purpose of introducing these topics here is to point out their relationship to e-business models and to resolve the confusion created by firms that market these software products. Vendors of these products typically promote them as the only part of an e-business plan that the buyer needs to be concerned about—as though e-business begins and ends with selecting a software solution and modifying the firm's behavior and processes to match the solution created by the software. The important thing for students to recognize is that planning begins at a much more fundamental level—the e-business model level. Once the firm decides what it wants to do to earn revenues and serve customers, it can study software solutions and select the one(s) that will allow it to achieve its planned objectives. All too often, decision-makers look for a software solution without considering the overall effect the adoption of this software solution must necessarily have on the firm's business practice. Although any software solution can be "patched in" to the current business plan successfully, firms need to stand back and consider the bigger questions through a complete e-business plan that requires answers before they commit to one software solution.

E-mail

Today, e-mail is considered a standard communication tool for all business-people. Whether it is used for internal or external communication, the benefits derived from implementing e-mail are well established. Because it was the first Internet-based software application, e-mail has had the longest amount of time to develop and evolve variations. Instant messaging and live online meetings are two examples of e-mail-related software that contributes to individual and group productivity. The benefits and low cost of e-mail make it the easiest Internet-based software solution to rationalize. Every individual should have her or his own e-mail accounts, and any communication that contains a name, address, and phone number should also provide an e-mail address. E-mail allows individuals to request information and receive quick responses without necessitating other time-consuming interaction. When questions are not specific to any one person, they can be answered routinely by a rotating group of employees. For example, customer service questions could be addressed 24 hours a day, 7 days a week to "customerservice@anyfirm.com." Experts can be hired to deal with the questions customers send by e-mail, thus relieving other employees who might have been contacted in the past for other tasks, such as the sales representatives or the company's telephone receptionists, of the need to answer routine or difficult product-related questions.

Regardless of a firm's e-business approach, e-mail and its many more advanced software variations—which may include calendar functions and sales-force automated data sharing and messaging—are primary solutions for improving productivity and efficiency. Every firm should be employing e-mail solutions and transforming its processes so as to take advantage of the improvements inherent in the adoption of e-mail communications strategies both inside and outside of the firm.

Website

Every organization can benefit from adding a website. Consider the benefits that accrue to the people at Comedy Central (**www.comedycentral.com**) because all the firm's television programming and entertainment are promoted to a community of viewers who can check schedules, view sample vignettes, and buy DVDs.

As with e-mail, the low costs and high associated benefits of websites make the decision to establish a website an easy one to rationalize. Also, as with e-mail, the organization's Web address should be included on its stationery, business cards, press releases, advertisements, and any other form of communication. The website serves as the organization's primary visible presence on the Internet as well as a communication hub for customers, suppliers, investors, and the general public. How well or poorly the website presents the organization to the world will have a significant impact on whether users decide to continue their contact. Therefore, the design, structure, and management of the site are critical to its strategic success. We will look at these strategies in the third module of this text. However, suffice it to say that even a simple and inexpensively designed website can provide basic information about the firm, its products and services, its prices, which people to contact, press releases and other public announcements, along with an e-mail address users can write to get more information.

Although a small business may view a simple website as little more than a low-cost and effective addition to its promotional effort, organizations that depend on large volumes of user traffic to generate either advertising revenues or user behavior information for analysis must be particularly concerned with their websites' long-term attractiveness and appeal. The maintenance costs for continuously updating and servicing a website are high. However, if a website is what the e-business model requires, then an appropriate budget for a website operation of the proper scale needs to be included in the plan.

e-Commerce

A logical next step for sellers of products that can be readily sold over the Internet, such as books, music, DVDs, compact discs, and other similar items, is an

LLBean.com

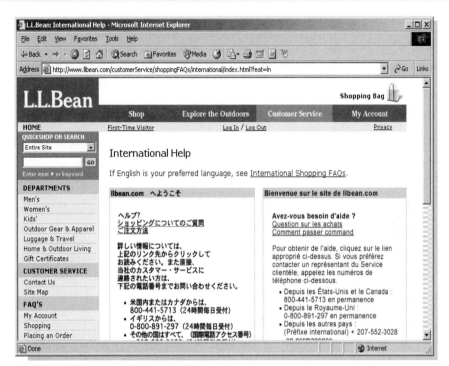

(*Source:* © L.L. Bean, Inc. 2004. L.L. Bean® is a registered trademark of L.L. Bean, Inc. Reprinted with permission.)

e-commerce capability. This can be part of the firm's website and accessible through icons on the site, or it can be independent. Catalog sellers can obviously benefit by selling their products to a global marketplace over the Internet. For example, consider the operations at L.L.Bean's (**www.llbean.com**) and the international screens it provides to assist global shoppers.

In the most rudimentary e-commerce system, a firm can simply use its website to receive orders by e-mail and then invoice its customers using its current regular procedure. However, the use of the Internet to buy and sell products is constantly evolving. Today, firms need not concern themselves with all of the complexities of designing and maintaining an e-commerce site. Instead, hosting firms can provide merchants with complete software services on a fee basis. Even a small business that wishes to explore global sales opportunities or better serve local and regional markets can now subscribe to a variety of simple plans. For example, a small monthly fee would typically allow the firm to post a catalog of its products, often with space for photographs and short product descriptions. e-Commerce service providers like eBay (**www.ebay.com**) generally fit the small firm into one or more of the business categories that eBay has devised to help buyers find the vendors and products they are looking for. The plan package would also provide credit card processing for the vendor, making it relatively painless for firms to establish e-commerce. As sales volumes increase, the vendor may choose to work more independently of the service provider, thus creating the image that it has its own virtual buying environment rather than a shared one. The real task facing sellers, regardless of their size or how they first entered the e-commerce environment, is building their traffic and sales through the e-commerce site so as to make the whole effort worthwhile.

Customer Relationship Management

customer relationship management (CRM)
Software solutions that incorporate a variety of means for managing the tasks of communicating with customers and sharing this information with employees so as to create more efficient relationships.

Several large firms now sell complete **customer relationship management (CRM)** software solutions that incorporate a variety of means to manage the tasks of communicating with customers and sharing this information with employees in order to create more efficient relationships. The concept behind CRM is to establish a seamless system for handling any and all information that involves customers' interactions with the firm's employees. For example, a customer in St. Louis that sees a television advertisement for a car rental deal calls the 800 number to find out more. The question is not only whether the call-center customer service representative who takes the call will have all the information needed to deal with this particular promotion, but also additional information that might help him or her do the job better. If the customer's records can be easily retrieved from the firm's database by entering a telephone number, any customer service representative in the network will have immediately available a complete history of that customer's buying history. Ideally, the service representative would have a record of important information about this customer, including, for example, the customer's request never to be put in a subcompact car, regardless of the cost. The conversation could then be more personalized as well as informed and lead to more efficient service and better customer relations.

CRM software is often discussed in terms of *front-end* or *back-office* applications, with firms marketing one or both. Front-end applications involve direct dealings with customers, such as the car rental call center in the example just provided or the e-commerce website Flowers.com (**www.flowers.com**) which takes orders online. Back-office applications involve activities that are not visible or obvious to customers, such as accounting, warehousing, inventory and ordering management, sales force automation software, and so forth. Some smaller firms may need only part of a full CRM software package. One marketing strategy employed by vendors of CRM software is to sell users additional modules of different CRM solutions as they need them. Users understand each additional module quickly because menus and other design elements are similar across the integrated system and the users are already familiar with them. Siebel Systems Inc. (**www.siebel.com**) is the largest software solution vendor and provides an abundance of literature about CRM modules at its site, as well as the opportunity to try demonstration versions.

IBM is a firm that both sells CRM solutions and practices good CRM management as an example to its clients. According to IBM's (**www.ibm.com/ebusiness/**) own published reports, the more than 41 million annual technical self-service inquiries handled over its website result in more than $750 million in cost avoidance and productivity gains for the global computer hardware and consulting services giant. By showing how it uses the Internet to improve its own customer services and save money, IBM is illustrating practical applications of the Internet to clients and others who are seeking case studies in e-business solutions. But this is only one illustration of the three primary CRM strategies that IBM promotes by its example to potential clients seeking advice and consulting services.

To begin with, IBM has established an *online community* for users of IBM products. One example is a dedicated chat room that allows users of IBM's Think-Pad portable computer to discuss technical and operational issues related to the product. Besides facilitating the exchange of opinions, ideas, and other useful information among users, IBM technicians are able to survey the comments users enter and use this customer feedback to develop future ThinkPad enhancements and new product designs.

Second, IBM's strategy is to maintain an *ongoing dialogue* with its customers and to continuously analyze its communications with them. This may mean monitoring what customers view while they are on the IBM website or what they say in chat rooms, responding to e-mail requests for information, or using registration forms that offer customers a long list of topics, ask them to select those that interest them, and then send them free informative messaging via e-mail. The objective is to better understand customer needs and to project when customers will most likely be open to buying a product or service that the firm can sell.

A third customer relationship management strategy demonstrated by IBM is improving *personalized value* by gathering and packaging resources to meet the needs of each individual customer. For instance, the firm tries to use information about a customer that it has gathered and analyzed to help it guide that customer toward a satisfactory purchase. Consider the following example. A customer dialogue may have been initiated by a television or newspaper advertisement that promotes the sale of several models of the ThinkPad computer line. The potential customer may then be motivated to continue the dialogue by connecting to IBM's website, where more information is provided and the customer's purchase order can be entered on an online form. At various moments, pop-up windows might offer intelligent suggestions for the customer to consider. For example, if the customer is unable to decide how much memory to order, a short quiz that calculates input data might appear, allowing IBM to better understand the customer's needs.

Should this computer-generated information be insufficient to close the sale, the customer can reach a customer service representative at the telephone number provided on the screen. The customer service representative is able to join the buying process and facilitate the customer's decision-making by offering recommendations based on the information the customer has entered online, along with any data about this customer that IBM may have previously recorded. In this way, IBM spends time and financial resources only with customers that want assistance and call for it, thereby improving the efficiency and productivity of its operations even further.[5]

Supply-Chain Management

supply-chain management (SCM)
Software solutions that focus on ways to improve communication between the suppliers and users of materials and components, enabling manufacturers to reduce inventories, improve delivery schedules, reduce costs, and so forth.

Just as CRM software solutions help firms create more efficient relationships with their customers, **supply-chain management (SCM)** software solutions focus on ways to improve communication between the suppliers and users of materials and components. By providing their production requirements and planning information directly to their suppliers, manufacturers can reduce inventories, improve delivery schedules, and reduce costs, which can quickly show up as improved profitability. For example, AeroXchange (**www.aeroxchange.com**) is a thirteen-member B2B global airline procurement system that was set up using Oracle Exchange Marketplace software. Designed to improve members' supply chains and streamline procurement of airplane parts and other supplies, the Dallas, Texas–based organization is being spearheaded by Air Canada. AeroXchange is a communication hub that coordinates the purchasing of the parts and supplies required by all its members and secures better pricing and services from vendors. Member airlines that require parts on short notice are able to secure these from fellow members rather than placing rush orders with suppliers. Air Canada alone expects to save $25 million a year by using the system.[6]

Fundamental Characteristics of Internet-Based Software and e-Business Solutions

In the previous section, we examined a range of Internet-based software and associated e-business solutions, from simple e-mail to full-scale CRM and SCM systems. In this section, we will examine the fundamental shared characteristics that explain why these e-business solutions are growing in popularity as firms increasingly move to solve their problems and improve their operations through the Internet. We will also examine how businesses can systematically make informed decisions about whether to adopt or reject an e-business solution option.

Efficiency and Productivity

At the core of a business's decision to adopt any e-business solution is the belief that it will result in more productive and efficient use of resources. Recall that e-business resources include human, material, informational, and financial resources. Therefore, in considering an e-business solution, the improvement in the effective use of resources should be weighed against the costs of implementing such a solution. The strategy, then, is to look at the costs and benefits of the current procedure in comparison with those of a procedure that is based on e-business and then make an intelligent decision as to whether the change is best for the firm.

Let's use an example to illustrate the evaluation process. Efficiency typically means doing things at a lower cost, whether that means reducing direct costs or time spent performing a current work activity. Suppose a firm is considering establishing a customer service bureau that will allow customers to communicate by e-mail in addition to using the firm's 800 telephone number. Its analysis of current operations shows that each of the firm's twenty call-center operators receives an average of about six telephone calls per hour. If the operator is unable to satisfy the caller's requirement, the call is routed to a technical or knowledge expert within the firm. Research suggests that an experienced operator can answer almost all of the calls within about 10 minutes, since the dialogue with the customer almost always yields one of fifty common requests or inquiries, which are easily retrieved on the operator's computer screen. The call center, which is located outside Chicago, operates 12 hours each business day so as to accommodate customers located in all time zones in North America. More operators are available during the peak period of the day and fewer at the start or end, when customers in different time zones may not be at work. Since the total cost of running the call center, including salaries, training for new employees, overhead, and telephone charges, is calculated to be $1.25 million per year and the firm handles approximately 3.6 million calls per year, the average cost per call works out to about $0.35.

As the firm expects to double in size within five years, it can use these figures to project the costs of serving customers. Although the firm does not intend to reduce its current call-center operation, it is anxious to know what savings it can generate by transferring the expected increase in customer service requests to a less expensive but equally effective system. The firm conducted research and analyzed tests to learn about the feasibility of directing customers to an e-mail-based customer service bureau. The findings suggest that customer e-mail requests would be readily understood by experienced customer service representatives and that the responses they sent back would satisfy the customer's needs almost all of the time. Furthermore, the research suggests that e-mail-based customer service representatives could comfortably handle twelve e-mail messages per hour, twice the number handled by telephone. In addition, the research experiment, which was conducted with the help of experienced telephone customer service operators, revealed that many of the operators would prefer a break from telephone work during the day and would welcome the opportunity to switch to an e-mail-based system for part of the time. In addition, some operators said that they would be willing to service e-mail-based inquiries from home rather than at the call center because it would eliminate the time required to travel to work and give them the option of working hours more suitable to their family lifestyle. It was found that the cost of installing Internet software that would allow employee-only access from home or from the firm's premises was not significant and that the software could be programmed to record and report employees' activities whether the employees were at home or on the firm's premises. This would allow the firm to pay employees who were working from home on a per-service-call-reply basis.

Based on an analysis of the savings in new overhead for an expanded call center and the estimated number of e-mail replies that employees could handle who were working from home, the firm arrived at the following conclusion. A new telephone-based call center would cost another $1.25 million; an e-mail-based center on the firm's premises would cost about half that, since operators would be twice as efficient. The third possibility, employees working from home on a pay-per-call e-mail basis, would further reduce the costs associated with the overhead for a new call center, to approximately $500,000. Based on these factors alone, the informed decision-makers in the firm decided to establish a group of reliable at-home employees. To assure success, employees would have to prove their online ability by working on the company premises for a trial period before working from home. Another benefit of this strategy was that it enabled the firm to process requests from customers around the world who might not be able to telephone or converse in technical English, but would manage fine online.

Quality, Standardization, and Customization of Products and Services

A second common fundamental characteristic of Internet-based software and e-business solutions is the drive toward quality, standardization, and customization of the delivery of products and services. Software solutions usually demand a particular way of performing functions such as processing a customer's order. They therefore lend themselves well to the establishment of performance standards for quality, time, costs, and so forth, as illustrated in the e-mail-based versus call-center customer service bureau. Both present clear standardized processes and procedures for employees to follow. Like operations in a manufacturing environment, such work is measurable, and benchmarks based on industry standards, corporate historical records, and management goals can be employed to measure the efficiency of individual employees' performance as well as the performance of the entire organization. At the same time, because input and output screens can readily be designed to best suit individual users, software allows for a great deal of customization and adaptation to the user.

Adding Value and Creating Competitive Advantage Online

Finally, a third commonality among Internet-based software and e-business solutions is the concept of creating additional customer value. In our case example, customer value could include more convenience and less time spent communicating with the customer service center. Creating customer value is at the core of establishing and sustaining a competitive advantage over other firms in the industry. In the case of e-businesses that are attempting to outdo competitors in the eyes of current and potential customers, a competitive advantage may be created online by providing better-quality products or wider selection of products, better order-taking and delivery choices, lower selling prices, more attractive and

Go to the Web: e-Business Online
For tutorials and more on the topics in this chapter, visit the student website at **http:// business.college .hmco.com/students** and select "Canzer e-Business."

better online shopping environments, and so forth. Creating an online competitive advantage works in tandem with the firm's overall business strategy to create added customer value.

Conclusions

This chapter introduced the value-adding approach to creating competitive advantage, along with a variety of solutions for creating a competitive advantage through the Internet. These solutions ranged from the introduction of simple e-mail and group communication software to full CRM and SCM software. The chapter emphasized the creative thinking needed to understand processes as they exist now and how by changing these to better online processes, an organization can transform itself into an improved needs-satisfying and value-adding company for both customers and employees. The challenge for strategists is to creatively use the e-business models and e-business tools we have just examined to build a sustainable competitive advantage in the marketplace.

This discussion provided a closer look at the various models available for building an **e-business plan.** A more detailed tutorial on the preparation of the e-business plan is available on the textbook's website.

In the next chapter, we will explore how these concepts come together in the context of strategic planning within the firm.

RETURN TO
inside e-business

CASE STUDY

Recognizing the opportunities available in the e-commerce search technologies market, Amazon.com established its A9.com division to compete with search engine developers at Google and Yahoo!. According to Alison Diboll, an A9 spokeswoman, "A9.com is a new, separately branded and operated company to create the best e-commerce search technology available to Amazon and third-party websites." Search sites that direct customers to shopping sites receive commissions from retailers for delivering customers. The market for this software and the programs customers use to find products within the retail databases is estimated to be worth $2 billion annually and provides another revenue stream to Amazon.com.

But the challenges will be great. Some analysts see A9.com as a prelude to a battle between Google, Yahoo!, and eBay to become the leading search and shopping site on the Web. As Rob Leathern, director and senior analyst at Nielsen/NetRatings put it, "They'll be fighting it out to be one of the prime places for people to start out online to look for products and services."

ASSIGNMENT

1. Who do you think will win this battle for shopping referrals?
2. How else can Amazon.com capitalize on its brand recognition to build other sources of revenue either independently or in partnerships with other firms?

Chapter Review

1. **Explore the various e-business models.**

   An online broker brings buyers and sellers together, often specializes in a particular product classification, and may even be organized by a major supplier or vendor of the products. An advertising e-business model is based on earning revenues in exchange for the display of advertisements on the firm's website. Website content providers may elect to earn revenues through subscription fees, charges to view single items such as a report (pay-per-view), or membership fees for gaining access to the site. The distribution channel member model includes the activities of retailers, wholesalers, and manufacturers conducting business through the Internet. Affiliation programs pay website operators for customers who find their way to a company's site and either buy merchandise or services or perform some other action, such as registering and providing certain information. The community model is built around the idea that a group of online users can be regularly brought together at a commonly used website. Infomediaries sell information such as online customer behavior to advertisers and other interested parties. The portal e-business model is a type of infomediary that earns revenues by drawing users to its site and serving as a gateway or portal to information located elsewhere on the Internet.

2. **Understand the range of Internet-based software and e-business solutions.**

   Today, e-mail is considered a standard communication tool for all business-people. Whether e-mail is used for internal or external communication, the benefits derived from the implementation of e-mail are well established. As with e-mail, the low costs and high associated benefits make the decision to establish a website an easy one to rationalize. The website serves as the organization's primary visible presence on the Internet as well as being a communication hub for customers, suppliers, investors, and the general public. A logical next step for sellers of products that can be readily sold over the Internet, such as books, DVDs, CDs, and other similar items, is an e-commerce capability. The concept behind CRM is to establish a seamless system for handling any and all information that involves customers' interaction with the firm's employees. Just as CRM software solutions help firms create more efficient relationships with their customers, so supply-chain management (SCM) software solutions focus on ways to improve communication between the suppliers and users of materials and components. By providing their production requirements and planning information directly to their suppliers, manufacturers can reduce inventories, improve delivery schedules, and reduce costs, which can quickly show up as improved profitability.

3. **Describe the fundamental characteristics of Internet-based software and e-business solutions.**

   At the core of a business decision to adopt any e-business solution is the belief that more productive and efficient use of resources will result. A second common fundamental characteristic is the drive toward quality, standardization, and customization of the delivery of products and services, and a third is the concept of creating additional customer value.

1. What is the difference between a business plan and a business model?
2. What is the primary point of interest in a firm's business model?
3. Why is the brokerage e-business model so popular?
4. In which sort of website is the advertising e-business model more likely to be used successfully?
5. Explain the differences between the subscription, pay-per-view, and membership e-business models.
6. How does the affiliation e-business model work to the advantage of both sides?
7. How does a community e-business model generate revenues?
8. What do infomediaries do to earn revenues?
9. Describe each of the primary Internet-based software and e-business solutions.

1. Discuss the relative advantages and disadvantages of employing a payment-based e-business model versus one that is free of charge to users.
2. Do you agree that websites that are free of charge to users are the best choice for both users and website managers?
3. Discuss the relative importance of each characteristic that is common to Internet-based software and e-business solutions.

Building Skills for Career Success

EXPLORING THE INTERNET
Check the list of websites you have visited recently by opening the "History" record on your web browser. Select one site whose e-business model is clear and that you feel can be profiled using the same categorical descriptions we used in the example provided in the chapter.

ASSIGNMENT
1. Identify the website you have selected, and explain why you believe it is an example of one or more of the e-business models we examined in the chapter.
2. Following the same structure used for the e-business model examples presented in the chapter, prepare your own profile of the website.

DEVELOPING CRITICAL THINKING SKILLS
One of the reasons why community e-business models like Oxygen (**www.oxygen.com**), Oprah Winfrey (**www.oprah.com**), and iVillage (**www.ivillage.com**) are popular is that they provide an environment in which members share a

clearly defined interest of some kind. Therefore, like special-interest magazines, they deliver an audience to advertisers and vendors of products that are targeted to this group of potential buyers. Examine one of these online community sites or some other site that you are more interested in.

ASSIGNMENT
1. Identify the community and then describe it in terms of how the site attracts the target audience.
2. List the community's revenue streams and your estimate of how significantly each of them contributes to total earnings. Explain your thinking.

BUILDING TEAM SKILLS
Working in a team, develop a website concept that would serve the unique needs of people living in your neighborhood. Rather than trying to create a site that would attract users who are dispersed around the world, try to think of the sorts of things that would interest only a small group of users who lived, say, on your college campus, or off-campus in their own apartments.

ASSIGNMENT
1. Describe the concept for your website.
2. Explain which e-business models you would employ.

RESEARCHING DIFFERENT CAREERS
Each of the e-business models discussed in the chapter would require employees with specialized content knowledge. For example, operating a brokerage site for computer components requires people who have both product knowledge and knowledge of the way traditional brokerage businesses operate. Brokerage sites require people who understand the way traditional brokerage business practices can be transferred to a website. Examine a website representative of one of the e-business models and check for any job opportunities it has posted.

ASSIGNMENT
1. Identify the site and describe the e-business model the firm is following.
2. Describe one specialized job that is specific to that e-business model.

IMPROVING COMMUNICATION SKILLS
Some e-business models seem to complement each other and fit together well, as in the case of a combination of the advertising and community e-business models. For example, since a community of alpine skiers would generally be interested in advertisements from product vendors, tour operators, and sellers of other related services, advertising would be welcomed and easily blended into a website, just as it is in magazines. To help get a better understanding of the relationships between these e-business models, create

a two-dimensional grid that shows the models listed horizontally in columns and vertically down the left-side margin as illustrated here.

	Brokerage	Advertising	Subscription	Distribution	Affiliation	Community	Infomediary	Portal
Brokerage								
Advertising								
Subscription								
Distribution								
Affiliation								
Community								
Infomediary								
Portal								

ASSIGNMENT

1. Mark on the grid those combinations of models that would work well together.
2. Explain how the models in the combinations you have marked would complement each other.
3. Identify a website that illustrates one of the combinations you have marked.

Exploring Useful Websites

These websites provide information related to the topics discussed in the chapter. You can learn more by visiting them online and examining their current data.

1. Amazon.com (**www.amazon.com**) is the largest and best-known online retailer. Barnes & Noble (**www.barnesandnoble.com**) is an example of a firm that has added an online presence to its established bricks-and-mortar operations.

2. Brokerage site eBay (**www.ebay.com**) provides both businesses and consumers with access to a communications structure for buying or selling virtually anything. Firms like Charles Schwab (**www.schwab.com**) and E*TRADE (**www.etrade.com**) focus on facilitating the exchange of financial securities between buyers and sellers. Adbargains (**www.adbargains.com**) presents an easy-to-use website where sellers of excess advertising space in any medium can connect with buyers seeking last-minute bargains or supplementary supply to increase their current advertising commitments.

3. Community sites like Oxygen (**www.oxygen.com**), Oprah Winfrey (**www.oprah.com**), and iVillage (**www.ivillage.com**) have developed large numbers of regular users by focusing mainly on topics that are of interest

to women. GeoCities (**www.geocities.com**), the build-your-own-web-site-for-free service provided by Yahoo!, provides an environment for individuals who wish to explore their creative skills by constructing a website. Gomez.com (**www.gomez.com**) is an infomediary that pays users for permission to track their movements on the Internet and sell that information to advertisers and other interested parties. ClickZ.com (**www.clickz.com**) is an infomediary that makes statistics and articles from a variety of sources available to readers.

4. Siebel Systems (**www.siebel.com**) is the largest software solution vendor and provides an abundance of literature about CRM modules at its site as well as the opportunity to try demonstration versions. AeroXchange (**www.aeroxchange.com**) is a thirteen-member B2B global airline procurement system set up using Oracle Exchange Marketplace software and is designed to improve members' supply chains and their procurement of airplane parts and other supplies. RetailExchange.com (**www.retailexchange.com**) and Overstock.com (**www.overstock.com**) find buyers online for excess inventory and unwanted goods.

chapter 5

Strategic Planning: A Multi-level Organizational Approach

CHAPTER OUTLINE

Inside e-Business: Home Depot.com—Serving Customers Through Online Strategies

An Overview of the Strategic Planning Process

Mission Statement of the Organization
Analysis of External and Internal Information
Planning Strategies and Objectives Throughout the
  Organization
Implementation and Control of Plans

Strategic Planning at the Three Primary Organizational Levels of the Firm

Corporate-Level Planning
Division/Strategic Business Unit-Level Planning
Operating/Functional-Level Planning

Strategic Planning and the Value Chain

Primary Activities in the Value Chain
Support Activities in the Value Chain
Creating and Sustaining Competitive Advantage

Building an Online Presence for an Existing Business

Complementing Existing Non-Internet-Based Plans
Complexity and Time Concerns
Motivating Acceptance of e-Business Plans

Industry- and Global-Level Issues Related to e-Business Planning

The Industry Supply Chain
A Fragmented Industry Environment
Industry Life Cycle Issues
Global-Level Strategic Planning Issue

LEARNING OBJECTIVES

1. Describe the fundamental characteristics of the strategic planning process.

2. Examine the strategic planning process at each of the three primary organizational levels of the firm.

3. Define the value chain and ways to create competitive advantage.

4. Explore issues related to building an online presence for an existing business.

5. Explore the industry- and global-level strategic planning issues facing the firm.

INSIDE
e-business

Home Depot.com—Serving Customers Through Online Strategies

A do-it-yourselfer who visits the Home Depot website (**www.homedepot.com**) for the first time might be forgiven for thinking that she has stumbled upon one of those PBS television shows' companion websites, like Home Time (**www.hometime.com**) or This Old House (**www.pbs.org/wgbh/thisoldhouse/**). What the visitor to the Home Depot website is likely to find is an array of handy tips and step-by-step informative instructions on anything from installing ceramic tile to remodeling an outdated kitchen. And if that isn't helpful enough, home decoration and planning ideas, such as how to make better use of a small closet space and which paint colors make a room look and feel more spacious, which would make Martha Stewart proud (**www.marthastewart.com**), are also available free of charge.

Of course, all of these informational services are also provided inside the more than 1,500 bricks-and-mortar Home Depot stores in the United States, Canada, Mexico, Puerto Rico, Chile, and Argentina during regular in-store demonstrations by employees. Furthermore, informed Home Depot personnel assist shoppers by providing answers to technical questions and suggestions to help them solve their home decoration, renovation, and repair problems. The Home Depot website complements this strong customer service orientation by providing free 24/7 access to the answers to service questions commonly asked by potential buyers about the firm's enormous selection of products. Customers will, of course, eventually need these products to carry out a specific project. By developing a reputation as a website where repair and renovation projects can be researched and planned at the customer's convenience, Home Depot's web presence becomes an extension of the time-consuming preliminary services that companies must provide to potential customers before they are ready to decide on their purchase requirements. Some customers may need weeks or months

of information gathering before they are ready to place their actual order, decide to hire a contractor, or elect instead to undertake the project themselves. The website, then, helps customers and develops goodwill so the customer is more likely to think of Home Depot when purchasing materials.

The Web's efficiency in delivering standardized, easy-to-understand step-by-step procedures that answer a customer's informational needs helps Home Depot continue to build on its well-deserved reputation for providing excellent customer service at competitive prices. In fact, the website provides these services in a form that some customers may prefer. For example, some may be unable to attend in-store presentations, and others may be considering a project but have not researched important points such as cost estimates and materials and labor requirements sufficiently to crystallize what they want their project to actually be. This is especially true for larger-scale undertakings, which might include the need for financing. Conveniently, Home Depot's website provides a loan application service, which saves the firm the cost of processing a loan in the store and provides the customer with an understanding of the budgetary limits on their home renovation project as well.

Although the Internet has opened the way for e-commerce opportunities, Atlanta–based Home Depot remains firmly a bricks-and-mortar retailer—opening a new store every 43 hours to better serve the more than 23 million customers who walk in each week. Online retailing will allow customers to place orders and either pick up materials and tool rentals at local store locations or have them delivered. This time- and money-saving service is of particular value to tradespeople like carpenters, electricians, and plumbers, who must take time away from their work to select and pick up the building materials they need. Generally speaking, they will send a lower-paid assistant to the building supply center to get the required materials, but when it is critical that the right material be selected, many tradespeople prefer to pick up materials themselves rather than risk an incorrect selection and a delayed project. Given that the average Home Depot bricks-and-mortar store stocks more than 40,000 different kinds of building, home improvement, and garden products, its e-commerce facility not only becomes a way to reach more customers more conveniently but also complements the search and selection process that customers must inevitably go through either in the store or online before they find what they need for their home project.[1]

In comparison to many other home renovation centers' websites, Home Depot's offers the advantages of lower prices, wider product selection, more knowledgeable support staff, an easier shopping environment for customers to navigate, and close ties with the company's bricks-and-mortar retail operations across North America. Together, these competitive advantages allow Home Depot to perform better than its competitors, providing superior value to

customers and ultimately returning more profit to stockholders. Creating a competitive advantage over other industry competitors is the primary goal that guides the strategic planning process for any firm.

In this chapter we will see how the e-business models and tools that we introduced in the previous chapter can be used to help create a competitive advantage by finding new ways to create more customer value. We will examine how the strategic planning process is an integrated effort at all three primary organizational levels of the firm: corporate, division/strategic business unit, and operating/functional. In addition, we will explore the strategic issues that face a firm as it builds an online presence, transforms itself from an old-economy business into a new one, and considers industry-level and global positioning concerns. First, let's take a closer look at the strategic planning process, the key relationships between its components, and how creating a competitive advantage and delivering additional value to customers are incorporated throughout the enterprise.

Reprinted by permission. The Home Depot is a registered trademark of Homer TLC, Inc.
(*Source:* **www.homedepot.com**.)

An Overview of the Strategic Planning Process

The **strategic planning process** involves a sequence of steps taken by management to develop new plans, modify existing plans that may require revision, and discontinue plans that are no longer justified. The strategic planning process requires first establishing and then maintaining a plan of action that everyone in

strategic planning process

A sequence of steps taken by management to develop new plans, modify existing plans that may require revision, and discontinue plans that are no longer justified.

the organization is expected to follow. A well-managed strategic business plan is one in which each individual employee's work contribution is consistent with the goals set for the organization as a whole. The strategic planning process is about designing, monitoring, and revising a plan of action for everyone working for the organization. The expressed understanding is that deviations from planned results and any changes in the business environment are to be researched and the resulting feedback used to revise the current plan.

The strategic planning process has four key components: the mission statement, analysis, planning, and implementation. Figure 5.1 summarizes the continuous flow of activity as new strategic plans are developed and existing plans are monitored, modified, and possibly replaced if they are no longer considered a good fit with current conditions or management objectives.

FIGURE 5.1   The Strategic Planning Process

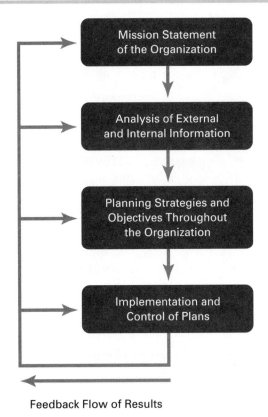

Feedback Flow of Results

After the organization's mission statement has been established, analysis of relevant information leads the firm to develop strategic plans and subsequently implement them. Feedback links assure that new information is continuously incorporated at all steps of the process.

Mission Statement of the Organization

mission statement
A basic description of the fundamental purpose for the organization's existence.

Strategic planning begins with the establishment of the firm's **mission statement**, a basic description of the fundamental purpose for the organization's existence. The mission statement is developed at the highest level of the firm's management and ownership structure, including its board of directors. Mission statements should be relatively stable over long periods of time and should provide a general sense of direction for all other decision-making throughout the firm. The mission statement tells managers at lower levels of the firm in what directions their strategic thinking may possibly go as well as the directions it should avoid. The firm and its management will encourage opportunities for business growth and the development of competitive advantages that fit within the structure established by the mission statement. Those that are beyond the boundaries set by the framers of the mission statement will be rejected.

Mission statements should not change unless fundamental changes have occurred that are forcing a major rethinking of the firm's business practices. These may be the result of radical changes in competition or in any other area of the business environment. For example, AOL's first mission statement was probably limited to setting a corporate goal of building a base of subscribers to its Internet connection services. In those early days of the Internet, only a handful of competitors vied for subscribers who would pay fees for connecting to the Internet. More recently, however, especially after the somewhat troubled merger with Time Warner and subsequent reorganization, it is likely that AOL's very essence and its long-term goals have changed more than once to reflect its changing role as a division of Time Warner. For example, soon after the merger, AOL's website stated that the firm's mission was "to become the world's most respected and valued company by connecting, informing, and entertaining people, everywhere in innovative ways that will enrich their lives." But by 2004, the mission statement was revised "to build a global medium as central to people's lives as the telephone or television . . . and even more valuable." This reflected AOL's divisional responsibility as both a communications company and as a firm that is playing an important role in building the base of connected customers for the Time Warner group of product-specific divisions.[2]

analysis
The study and evaluation of both external and internal factors to the firm that are considered important environmental forces acting upon customers, current strategies, and new plans still under development.

external factors
Sociocultural, technological, legal and regulatory, political, economic, and competitive forces.

internal factors
The organization's human, material, informational, and financial resources; structure; operational style; culture; and other characteristics that are at work within it.

Analysis of External and Internal Information

Information is derived from the **analysis** of factors, both external and internal to the firm, that are considered important environmental forces acting upon customers, current strategies, and new plans still under development. **External factors** include sociocultural, technological, legal and regulatory, political, economic, and competitive forces. **Internal factors** include the organization's human, material, informational, and financial resources; structure; operational style; culture; and other characteristics at work within it. Any new plan will have to reflect the reality of both the external world and the internal dynamics of the organization. We examined these environmental forces that affect planning and business practice in Module I of this text. Chapter 6, Researching and Analyzing Opportunities for Growth, presents methodologies for researching these areas and for staying in front of continuously and rapidly changing events that can affect current and future planning activities.

Planning Strategies and Objectives Throughout the Organization

planning
Organizing and detailing all of the strategies that will be undertaken throughout the firm and their expected or targeted objectives and results.

corporate-level planning
Planning that determines the overall direction for the firm.

division- (strategic business unit [SBU]-) level planning
Planning that focuses on a major area or group of related products offered by the firm.

operating- (functional-) level planning
Planning that occurs within specific departments of the organization.

implementation
The actual tasks that must be carried out in order to realize a strategic plan.

control
How well an intended objective is likely to be realized.

feedback
The evaluation of activities that are reported back to management decision-makers.

Planning is concerned with organizing and detailing all of the strategies that will be undertaken throughout the firm and their expected or targeted objectives and results. Planning is organized hierarchically from the top down. Therefore **corporate-level planning** and objectives, which determine the firm's overall direction, become the starting point for **division- (strategic business unit [SBU]-) level planning**. This lower level of planning focuses on a major area or group of related products offered by the firm. These plans, in turn, become the starting point for the third level of planning: **operating- (functional-) level planning**, which involves more local plans within specific departments of the organization. For example, when Home Depot's corporate-level planners decided that the firm would have an Internet presence, the decision precipitated planning activities within a team at the divisional/SBU level of the firm that would be charged with fulfilling the task. Within this divisional/SBU-level team, many operating or functional groups, such as Web designers, e-commerce customer service representatives, software administrators, and others, would then be expected to develop specific plans for their areas that were consistent with the planning laid out at the divisional/SBU level.

Implementation and Control of Plans

Implementation refers to the actual tasks that must be carried out in order to realize the plan. This includes a control and feedback system that can direct useful information to the various levels of the firm that are involved in the ongoing planning process. **Control** refers to how well an intended objective is likely to be realized, given current conditions. Control strategies may simply involve evaluating daily reports of website activity in order to assess the success or failure of the current strategy. If the expected volume of Web users and the number of transactions are in line with expectations, then the plan is judged to be under control. **Feedback** refers to the evaluation of activities that are reported back to management decision-makers. Reports to management may trigger decisions to stay the course or to make changes. In this way, progress toward the successful achievement of the plan can be measured, and information that may be useful to the development of emerging plans can be directed to those who can incorporate these findings. We will explore these topics in greater detail in Chapter 11, Implementation and Control of the e-Business Plan.

Strategic Planning at the Three Primary Organizational Levels of the Firm

Perhaps the best way to develop an understanding of the complexities of strategic planning is by examining the activities that are undertaken at each of the three primary organizational levels of the firm. Although management might focus on the planning at one particular level, it is critically important to recognize that it must make an effort to integrate strategies consistently across all levels of the organization in order to assure success.

Corporate-Level Planning

Planning at the corporate level answers fundamental questions about the nature of the business. What business are we in? What is our business model? What is our mission statement? How will our corporate plans be understood and carried out by the division/SBU teams in our firm? Who are our customers? What sorts of products are we selling? Will we operate globally? Will we have strategic alliances and, if so, with whom? These questions and their answers can be summarized at the corporate level into a few generic competitive strategies that the firm may choose to employ in pursuit of growth and profitability.

Let's first examine the use of strategic alliances and partnerships with other firms. A **strategic alliance** exists when the strategic planning of one firm is dependent on the cooperative strategic planning of another. For example, IBM (**www.ibm.com**) maintains a strategic alliance with Siebel Systems Inc. (**www.siebel.com**), the largest developer of customer relationship management (CRM) software. In essence, IBM chose to enter into a strategic alliance with Siebel Systems and to sell Siebel Systems' products rather than developing its own. Why would the venerable IBM choose such a course of action, and what's in it for Siebel Systems? The answers are quite simple. Advantages accrue to both firms. In the case of IBM, the firm does not have to develop, continuously update, and maintain a software solution that would be only one of many. Instead of directing resources to create a costly SBU that is focused on competing with Siebel Systems and other firms that produce CRM software solutions, IBM can instead sell CRM solutions from several vendors. Should Siebel Systems' products lose their appeal in the marketplace, IBM can switch to other vendors' products. Siebel Systems wins because a strategic alliance with IBM gives it access to IBM's client base. IBM's endorsement of Siebel Systems' products adds value to these products in the customer's eyes, and Siebel reaches a larger potential client base through IBM's network of sales teams than it would ever be able to reach independently.

An important point should be made here. Although software sales are a significant part of revenue for both IBM and Siebel Systems, most revenues are earned from installation and software customization programming. For IBM, the game is won by getting a contract to install a solution—regardless of which software is used to create that solution.

The difference between a strategic alliance and a partnership is one of degree. A **partnership** represents a more permanent and longer-term commitment between firms, whereas strategic alliances are generally considered weaker arrangements that may not receive the same level of involvement by the firms. For example, Lotus Development Corporation offers a partnership program to firms that wish to act as local representatives of the firm and its products. In essence, when a prospective customer contacts Lotus and asks for information or a sales presentation about Lotus software solutions, the firm notifies a local partner and that partner takes over the responsibility on Lotus's behalf. Local Lotus partners may undertake the sale of any product, installation, or training. Thus, Lotus does not need to maintain sales representation offices everywhere and can make use

strategic alliance
An arrangement in which one firm's strategic planning is dependent on the cooperative strategic planning of another firm.

partnership
An arrangement that represents a more permanent and longer-term commitment between firms than a strategic alliance.

of the goodwill, reputation, and knowledge of its local partners. This is particularly important in international markets, where the vendor needs information on a variety of local issues and details in order to conduct business properly. Should the local partner be unable to handle the entire project, other partners that may be more skilled in a particular part of the job can join the "Lotus team" in order to complete the task. In this way, local firms gain the competitive advantage of having access to a variety of skills and knowledge that they might need to secure certain contract work for their clients.

AOL Time Warner, the world's biggest media company, invested $200 million into a strategic partnership with Legend Holdings Ltd., China's biggest personal computer manufacturer, to co-develop Internet services. An estimated 30 million people regularly log on to the Internet in China, and analysts estimate that this number will grow to 100 million users within the next few years. Although China is the world's most populous country, with more than a billion people, some are concerned that many Chinese will not be able to afford AOL's Internet services and content. By partnering with Legend Holdings, AOL shares the risk and opportunity with a knowledgeable firm that is able to help guide its strategy.[3]

Another generic competitive strategy at the corporate level is the decision to merge with or acquire another firm. A **merger** is the combining of two more or less equal firms into a new firm, whereas an **acquisition** usually implies that a larger firm has bought a smaller operation and subsumed it into its organizational structure. Sometimes a merger or acquisition is not apparent to clients and employees because the two firms continue to operate independently, much as they did before. The motivation for acquisitions varies, but it is generally related to the perception that the competencies of the acquired firm will contribute to the acquiring firm's value in some way. Rather than trying to generate these competencies on its own, the acquiring firm may consider it more economical, efficient, and practical to simply buy another firm that has these competencies and resources. For example, IBM merged with or acquired, depending on how one views the relationship, Lotus Development Corporation. IBM, which was not known for its smaller computer software solutions, saw an opportunity to gain that expertise by joining with the leader in the field. On the other side of the deal, Lotus could capitalize on IBM's large global computer client base and reputation. Perhaps more fundamentally, Lotus's principal owners and managers realized an opportunity to convert the years of work they had put in developing the firm into personal riches and then move on.

Mergers and acquisitions are a common route followed by smaller firms that have grown sufficiently large to be attractive to larger organizations. Often start-up firms have a product with potentially great sales or have a customer base, skills, or expertise that another firm may desire or need. Sometimes, in order for a firm to grow, a variety of elements are needed, such as capital and global geographic sales representation. Instead of moving to the next level by conventional means such as internally generated growth, strategic alliances, and partnerships, management may choose to be bought outright by a larger firm that can supply these needs, thereby expediting growth to the next level. In these situations, the management of the acquired firm may join the larger firm, and the acquired firm may continue to operate

merger

The combining of two more or less equal firms into a new firm.

acquisition

A larger firm buying a smaller operation and taking it into its organizational structure.

as a divisional SBU. Senior executives from each division would probably become part of corporate-level planning committees, where synergies between divisional operations of the firm can be examined for mutual benefit. This approach can be seen in AOL's mergers with Netscape, ICQ, and more recently Time Warner. Each of these combinations has rewarded both firms by providing AOL with new competencies and by providing greater growth opportunities to the firms that chose to merge rather than continue growing independently. Hindsight shows that not all mergers bring guaranteed success, as illustrated by the AOL Time Warner experience.

vertical integration
A strategy of growth based on moving into more activities, either further up or further back in the production process.

Vertical integration refers to a strategy of growth in which a firm takes on more activities either further up or further back in the production process. For example, many Internet retail vendors focus their effort on selling products to customers and contract with another firm for warehousing and shipping services. If they established their own distribution services, these firms would be able to earn the revenues associated with providing these services as well. Why would a firm not wish to seek growth through vertical integration? The answer may be as simple as its decision that the added value or contribution to profitability gained by the additional activity does not justify the use of the firm's resources in this way. In order to be successful in some of these areas, a large-scale operation may be required. If the firm's scale of operation is too small, it would be counterproductive for the firm to attempt to include that operation in the channel. Consider that for many firms it is generally more advantageous to use computer hosts for e-commerce than to maintain their own software and maintenance operations. Instead, the firm's resources are directed to those areas where the firms can best exploit them for optimal value creation and profitability. Similarly, it should not be surprising to learn that Atlanta, Georgia–based United Parcel Service (UPS) (**www.ups.com**) generates over $30 billion of its revenues and continues to grow by using Internet technologies to handle logistical solutions for its customers. UPS delivers more than half of all goods ordered over the Internet, a major portion of the 13 million packages it delivers each day, and also maintains warehousing logistics for many of its customers.[4]

As these broad-based questions suggest, corporate-level strategic planning takes a wide and long-term view of business operations. The fundamental identity of the firm is decided at this level, and the decisions taken here determine which divisions or strategic business units the firm will establish and what their individual mandates will be. For instance, a decision to create a website with e-commerce services for customers will generally result in the establishment of a division or SBU that is responsible for achieving the objectives set by corporate-level planners. Exactly how those objectives are to be achieved are set by planners at the SBU level.

Division/Strategic Business Unit-Level Planning

The division or strategic business unit level of the firm concerns itself with those items that we generally consider when we think about the "nuts and bolts" meaning of planning. What products will we sell, and to whom? What price will we charge, and how will the product be delivered? These are fundamental marketing issues, and we will explore them in greater detail in Chapter 8. Here, however, the focus is on fundamental strategic questions concerning the competitive advantages enjoyed by the firm. Generic strategies available to the firm for creating competitive advantages include cost leadership, focus on a particular target market, and differentiation of its products.

A **cost leadership** strategy implies that the firm is able to channel its distinctive competencies into lowering its costs of operation. It thereby gains competitive advantage by being able to sell its products or services to customers at lower prices or by selling at the market price and benefiting from the extra profit. For example, Dell Computer's success is mainly attributed to its ability to reduce costs in several areas, including order taking, inventory, and selling. By producing excellent-quality products at competitive, but not the cheapest, prices Dell has established itself as the premier online computer vendor for both industry and consumer markets. Dell's just-in-time delivery scheduling with suppliers and its strategy of producing products as customers enter orders on Dell's e-commerce website have produced a model of manufacturing excellence that is used as a benchmark both inside and outside the computer and technology industries.

Market segmentation analysis might suggest that certain target groups are more profitable and better matches for the distinctive competencies of the firm than others. A **focus** strategy is based on creating value by satisfying the wants and needs of specific targeted groups of customers. For example, Web-based magazines such as Businessweek.com and retailers such as Gap.com focus on a particular target customer. In most situations, the firm's Internet-based strategy is an obvious extension of its primary strategy. This niche approach to marketing can permit higher selling prices when customers are seeking specialized products and can't easily find alternative sources of supply.

In the third generic strategy, **differentiation**, the firm directs its distinctive competencies into differentiating its products from those of its competitors. By creating a unique product, the firm is able to more readily distinguish itself in the marketplace and either charge higher prices for its products or simply draw a customer base that is attracted to its unique offerings. For example, online providers of content such as information, articles, animation, and music enjoy a competitive advantage if the content they produce is perceived by customers as being of value. The more distinctive the content the website provides, the more likely it is that the content-providing firm will be able to carve out a niche market that is willing to pay premium dollars to view the content. This can be offered on a subscription or pay-per-view basis, or, if the website is sponsored, the firm can profit from higher advertising revenues. Forrester Research Inc., for example, sells reports costing as much as several thousand dollars each that can be downloaded from its website as needed. Businessweek.com online subscribers have access to a variety of content that is not available in the free viewing public areas, which are advertising-sponsored, and that supplements the print version of the magazine.

Combinations of differentiation, focus, and cost leadership strategies are common and should be employed whenever possible, as they allow the firm to transform more competencies into specific competitive advantages. For example, iVillage.com, like many content providers on the Internet, differentiates itself and its products by focusing on a niche market of women and by providing a wide range of information and services that either generate revenues directly or provide the opportunity to charge higher advertising rates. CDNow (**www.cdnow.com**) and Egghead (**www.egghead.com**), which are now in alliances with Amazon.com,

cost leadership
A strategy that implies that the firm is able to channel its distinctive competencies into lowering its costs of operations.

focus
A strategy that is based on creating value by satisfying the wants and needs of specific targeted groups of customers.

differentiation
A strategy in which the firm directs its distinctive competencies into differentiating its products from those of its competitors.

compete both by using a cost leadership strategy and by offering differentiated products at low prices. Although one of these three generic strategies may be emphasized at the SBU level, it is common to find that a combination is employed to carve out a position in the marketplace.

Operating/Functional-Level Planning

efficiency
Doing things at a lower cost.

At the operating or functional level of the firm, the work of building distinctive competencies is channeled through the effort to provide superior efficiency, quality, innovation, and customer responsiveness. **Efficiency** means doing things at a lower cost. For example, processing orders through e-commerce can reduce costs by reducing or even eliminating the time that employees spend entering and processing orders. Superior efficiency can be generated by improving employee training and by providing employees with software solution tools such as CRM. This, in turn, can help to reduce the rate of customer attrition (loss). Keeping existing customers longer, increasing the number of customers, and increasing the effective service provided to those customers reduces the average fixed costs of any business operation, such as the installation of an e-commerce system or CRM software. The opportunities to improve efficiency through management and leadership techniques, performance bonuses for employees, and interdepartmental cooperation are just a few areas for management to explore.

quality improvement
Making a better product and, in so doing, increasing customers' perceived value.

Quality improvement means making a better product and, in so doing, increasing customers' perceived value. This can be achieved in a variety of ways, including better manufacturing and automation and by using superior components, which are affordable despite their higher prices because of efficiencies derived from economies of scale. Dell Computer is recognized for its excellent quality and reliability, which in turn generates more sales and customer loyalty.

innovation
Creating new products, designs, styles, and other features that are attractive to customers.

Related to issues of quality is **innovation**, which refers to the idea of creating new products, designs, styles, and other features that are attractive to customers. Innovation is critical for a firm's survival in many businesses, especially for a computer manufacturer like Dell or a content website such as Businessweek.com, where customers will become bored and move on if magazine content is not continuously refreshed.

customer responsiveness
How well the firm is serving and responding to the needs of its customers.

Customer loyalty is a major concern and a reason why firms focus on customer responsiveness as a means to create competency. **Customer responsiveness** refers to how well the firm is serving and responding to the needs of its customers. Once again, a CRM software solution may be considered part of an overall effort to improve customer responsiveness and efficiency. For example, providing excellent online customer support can be a critical part of selling CDs on CDNow.com. Unless the customer service representatives who are tied in to the Web-based selling effort provide efficient and high-quality customer attention, the overall strategy would be unlikely to succeed.

To briefly summarize this section, then, the effort to develop new distinctive competencies is generally a mix of many different functional-level activities, not all of which are necessarily Internet-based activities and concerns. Most strategic planning involves an overlap between functional areas and departments. Senior management must make a concerted effort to tie together all the participants in the overall plan and to ensure that a consistent objective is shared and integrated throughout the three primary levels of the firm.

Strategic Planning and the Value Chain

Harvard Business School professor Michael Porter has contributed seminal ideas about the firm's value chain and management's need to be vigilant in monitoring the "five forces" in the business environment that create both opportunities and threats to the firm's competitive advantage. Porter's thinking provides a guiding framework for managers to employ in the strategic planning process. In a recent look at e-business, Porter uses the same five-forces model—namely (1) the risk of entry by new competitors, (2) the level of rivalry among established competitors, (3) the bargaining power of buyers, (4) the bargaining power of suppliers, and (5) the threat of substitute products or services—to examine how the Internet is affecting existing competitive arrangements (see Figure 5.2).

Porter points to the obvious empowerment of buyers, who can use the Internet to find better sources of supply at lower prices, and of suppliers, who can also readily seek buyers around the world and use the Internet to reduce their operating costs.

FIGURE 5.2   **The Five-Forces Model**

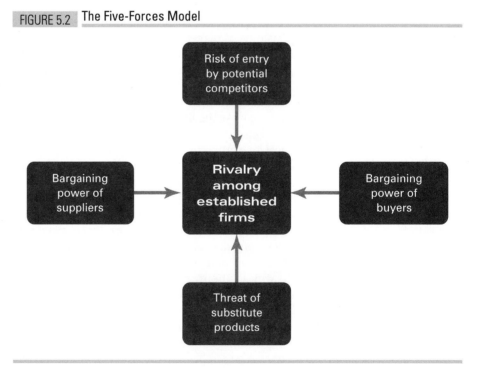

(*Source:* Adapted and reprinted by permission of *Harvard Business Review.* From "How Competence Forces Shape Strategy" by Michael E. Porter, March/April 1979. Copyright © 1979 by the Harvard Business School Publishing Corporation; all rights reserved.)

In addition, the Internet has low barriers to entry, which allows virtual firms to enter the market and meet any fulfillment gaps through strategic alliances with other firms. One example is the arrangement between AOL and AutoNation (**www.autonation.com**), in which AutoNation allows AOL to share in the huge and growing online market for the sale of new and used autos, and AOL gives AutoNation access to AOL's database of customers. Not surprisingly, Porter envisions increasing competitive rivalry among players and increasing numbers of substitute products and services becoming available online.

According to Porter, understanding and properly deploying Internet strategies are critical if firms are to remain competitive. Porter suggests that every activity in the firm essentially involves the movement of information, and that since the Internet has the special ability to link previously separate activities in real time, it plays a vital role in the entire value chain. The successful deployment of Internet-based solutions, from supply-chain management activities on one end to customer relationship management on the other, will strengthen the company and its brand. The challenge for managers will be to break the traditional structural barriers within the organization so cross-functional solutions involving people in all company departments can be developed.[5]

Much strategic planning effort focuses on finding ways to add customer-perceived value to the value chain. The **value chain** refers to a view of the firm as an organization of activities concerned with transforming inputs into customer-valued outputs (see Figure 5.3). The underlying thinking that guides strategic

value chain

A view of the firm as an organization of activities concerned with transforming inputs into customer-valued outputs.

FIGURE 5.3   The Value Chain

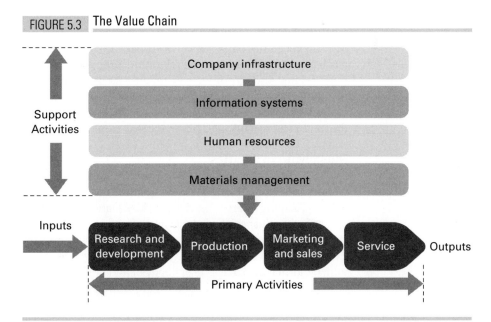

(*Source:* Adapted from Charles Hill and Gareth Jones, *Strategic Management,* Sixth Edition. Copyright © 2004 by Houghton Mifflin Company. Reprinted with permission.)

planning is to select activities that are superior to other choices and, in so doing, deliver superior customer value. Superior value will, in turn, provide the firm with a competitive advantage and thereby lead to greater profitability.

Primary Activities in the Value Chain

The primary activities in the value chain are research and development, production, marketing and sales, and service. Next, let's examine these value-creating opportunities in greater detail and look at the opportunities for creating competitive advantage in the marketplace that they give the firm.

Research and Development

Research and development focuses on generating innovative products and services that are recognized as offering superior value to customers. For example, online securities trading services offered by innovative firms like Charles Schwab provide investors with an alternative method for trading and monitoring their investment portfolios. Furthermore, online brokerage firms differentiate themselves through various unique online services, such as providing information and advice about current economic and investment conditions.

Production

Production is concerned with the creation of a product or service. A bank website can provide quick processing and approval of a loan application based on information entered by customers online. In a sense, the production of the loan is accomplished on the website. The website provides a more efficient means of production, creating value by reducing costs and saving time for both parties. Rather than a loan officer of the bank sitting in front of the same data input screen and asking a customer questions over the telephone or in the bank's offices, the entire activity is automated and customer-controlled. The bank saves on the costs of the loan officer and on overhead and processing costs. The customer saves time, can access his or her bank accounts at any time it is convenient, and probably will benefit from the bank's savings through lower, more competitive interest charges as well.

Marketing and Sales

Marketing and sales activities allow firms to distinguish themselves from their competitors and create unique customer-perceived value in a variety of ways. For example, AOL, the leading Internet service provider, stands out in the industry by providing its subscribers with special products and services that are not available to others on the Web. *Business Week* magazine gives subscribers to its print edition access to an extended online version. Marketing and sales activities can also provide useful customer information, such as user behavior and preferences, that the firm's research and development staff can use in developing future products and activities.

Service

Providing superior customer service is a popular focus for firms adding value and attempting to distinguish themselves from competitors. For example, online retail customers may abandon the purchasing process if information and assistance are not readily available when they need it. If the buying process is stalled at some point, a quick exchange over the telephone with a customer service representative who can see the current screen being used by the customer may be needed to solve the problem. In that case, a firm like Dell Computer (**www.dell.com**), which provides this service, will be perceived as superior and as having a competitive advantage. Given the importance of providing high-quality service, CRM software solutions are commonly deployed by firms that can afford the relatively high cost of operating them. Customer expectations are an important part of the decision whether or not to deploy a full CRM solution as part of a Web strategy. Large firms that provide superior customer quality in their bricks-and-mortar operations will be expected to at least match that quality level in their website activities. Smaller firms or those that are unknown to customers may be given a grace period as the Web effort is unfolded. However, if these firms face competitors that are already established and are providing high-quality service, management should be concerned about erosion of customer loyalty and the reputation of the corporate brand. It might be advisable to delay a public Web effort until management has confidence in the quality of the service rather than risk the damage that might be done by a poor solution.

Support Activities in the Value Chain

In addition to the primary activities in the value chain that we have just examined, there are also support activities, which include the company infrastructure, information systems, human resources, and materials management. Support activities facilitate the primary activities in the value chain.

Company Infrastructure

company infrastructure
Those things that define the structure within which the value-chain activities take place, such as the firm's culture, leadership, organizational structure, control systems, and other such activities.

The **company infrastructure** refers to those things that define the structure within which the value-chain activities take place, such as the firm's culture, leadership, organizational structure, control systems, and other such activities. A firm that encourages innovation and rewards initiative can develop superior competency in a variety of activities, such as research and development and marketing and sales. Firms that fail to innovate and develop a competitive advantage may find that their problem lies here and that they need to shake up their long-established managerial methods of thinking and practice. Creative thinking can be learned, but doing so is affected by the environment in which any such effort takes place. Establishing a good supporting environment that encourages risk taking and thinking out loud in meetings (where rejection can easily be personalized) is a major challenge for all organizations that are hoping to create new value.

Information Systems

The firm's various information systems engage in a broad range of activities involving intelligent decision making that can lead to competitive advantage. Information that produces better understanding of warehousing and distribution strategies and customer-related information about products and prices are only a few of the information support activities that tie in with the primary value-chain activities. Sales force automation software is one solution that provides a network of databases and cross-referenced information about customers, products, and sales activities that can help the sales and marketing management team by providing them with superior communication and knowledge.

Human Resources

The human resources activities that are needed to contribute to the firm's value chain center on maintaining an appropriate number of trained, skilled, motivated, and properly rewarded employees to carry out the primary activities in the value chain. The sales force needed to help customers complete online orders at the firm's website must have a great deal of information about the firm and its products and services, as well as knowledge of online customer selling strategies. Training, CRM, and other Web-based software solutions can help distinguish the firm from its competitors by enhancing the abilities of its human resources.

Materials Management

materials management (logistics)
A support activity that involves the procurement, production, and distribution of physical product throughout the value chain.

Materials management (logistics) is a support activity that involves the procurement, production, and distribution of physical product throughout the value chain. For example, Amazon.com must order and warehouse inventories of books, CDs, and other products in order to be able to distribute them quickly to customers. One way to differentiate one online retailer from another is by the quality and efficiency of this activity. Poor materials management may mean lost customers, who will not purchase again if the delivery of their orders is delayed. On the other hand, good materials management can translate into better customer service, lower costs, and other savings as a result of more efficient logistic operations. As demonstrated by both Dell and Amazon.com, real-time transaction of orders, automated customer-specific agreements and contract terms, and customer access to delivery status are Web-based strategies for creating a competitive advantage.

Creating and Sustaining Competitive Advantage

distinctive competencies
The ability of the firm to provide superior efficiency, quality, innovation, or customer responsiveness.

The value chain provides strategic planners with a map of the primary and supporting activities that the firm carries out as inputs are transformed into customer-valued outputs (products and services). Next, we will look at how the value-chain concept provides a structure for identifying opportunities for creating a competitive advantage over competitors and more profits for the firm. As illustrated in Figure 5.4, the model suggests that the firm's resources (human, material, informational, and financial) and capabilities (skills and abilities to make productive use of available resources) lead to the development of **distinctive competencies,** or the ability to provide superior efficiency, quality, innovation, or customer responsiveness. Superiority in these areas can permit the firm to differentiate its products, lower its costs, or both and thereby create a valued competitive advantage over competitors in the marketplace that generates higher profits.

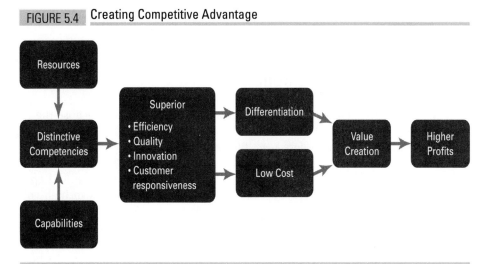

FIGURE 5.4   Creating Competitive Advantage

(*Source:* Adapted from Charles Hill and Gareth Jones, *Strategic Management,* Sixth Edition. Copyright © 2004 by Houghton Mifflin Company. Reprinted with permission.)

Let's look at an example to illustrate the process. Radio Shack's ubiquitous chain of retail stores and its e-commerce website operations were recognized as significant resources that could allow the consumer electronics distributor to create a distinctive competency. One of the advantages that Radio Shack (**www.radioshack.com**) enjoyed over most of its web-based competitors was the ability to make use of any local Radio Shack retail location to better serve customers who might want to pick up the merchandise that they had ordered online instead of using a delivery service. Besides saving on the delivery charges, customers who wanted to see the merchandise before they finalized their purchase could simplify the order-processing procedure by using the e-commerce website to place their orders. Furthermore, many shoppers are reluctant to buy online because of concerns over the return of unwanted or unsatisfactory merchandise. Once again, the local Radio Shack retail stores provide the human contact, which offers a value-added service to those customers who perceive the abundance of local retail stores as a critical part of their buying decision.

The superior services that Radio Shack can provide its online customers allow the firm to differentiate itself from its competitors. They perhaps also enable Radio Shack to offer products at lower selling prices because of savings on the handling of returned merchandise and reduced inventories facilitated by the presence of retail community stores. All of these value-added services ultimately result in a competitive advantage for the firm and higher profitability.

Competitive advantage originates with the firm's distinctive competencies, which allow it to provide superior efficiency, quality, innovation, and customer responsiveness in the value chain. In order to sustain a competitive advantage for

competitive advantage
A benefit that originates with the firm's distinctive competencies, which allow it to provide superior efficiency, quality, innovation, and customer responsiveness in the value chain.

e-BUSINESS insight

Just Send Flowers.com

When Flowers.com added Internet-based ordering, consumers had the new value-added option of placing their orders over the Internet rather than through a retail store or through an 800 telephone number, two value-added services it supplied to customers. By using the firm's website and e-commerce facility to place their orders, customers can view available floral arrangements and then select one that suits their taste, eliminating the time and inconvenience of finding and going to a retail store. Furthermore, the e-commerce order-taking process costs considerably less than order taking by either a telephone operator or a retail store clerk. Because the customer is the only participant in the order-placing procedure online, the only cost is that of the software and website maintenance. That cost becomes lower and lower with each transaction and approaches relatively insignificant levels in high-volume operations. Selling flowers over the Internet works especially well because the product is well known to buyers and because online advertising and visual displays can readily trigger impulse buying.

Question for discussion: What other products do you think have similar characteristics to flowers and would sell well online?

---

benchmarking
The use by a firm of comparisons between its performance and the performance standards established by other firms inside or outside of its industry.

the long term, however, the firm must continuously work at cultivating new resources and capabilities that feed the development of new, distinctive competencies—something easily said, but challenging for any firm to carry out. In addition, the firm needs to maintain a high level of focus on finding ways to continuously improve its efficiency, quality, innovation, and customer responsiveness and to seek excellent practices. By **benchmarking** or comparing itself to performance standards established by other firms inside or outside of its industry, the organization can measure its progress toward the goal of sustaining its competitive advantage.

Building an Online Presence for an Existing Business

In this chapter, we have expanded on the understanding of the e-business models and Internet-based software tools and solutions that were introduced in Chapter 4 by adding the concept of creating value and developing a competitive advantage in the marketplace through superior competencies. In addition, we have looked at the planning process that takes place at the three primary levels of the organization, emphasizing the relationships between the three levels. Although these concepts apply to any business, whether it is a new venture that intends to operate exclusively online or an existing operation with bricks-and-mortar investments, it is particularly important to recognize the unique planning concerns entailed in introducing web-based solutions into a functioning operation. In this section of the chapter, we will examine how an existing business firm should frame the development of its online presence, which critical factors it needs to weigh, and which guidelines planners should use as the planning process is carried out at each level of the firm.

Complementing Existing Non-Internet-Based Plans

The development of the firm's online presence should be guided by one key objective: to complement the existing non-Internet-based business plan. Whatever the firm's objectives, the e-business plan must be in line with them, supporting and, it is hoped, enhancing the current plan. If customer responsiveness is considered a weakness that can be solved by bringing a companywide CRM solution into play, then planning will be required at each of the three levels of the firm in order to properly integrate this strategic option. Clearly, the worst situation for a firm is one in which it is making a local- or department-level effort to use the Internet, but people in other areas of the firm who need to be part of the total effort are left out of the planning process. For example, if one SBU is using a CRM solution to increase customer responsiveness and other SBUs are not, customers may be confused by the lack of consistency across the operations of the business. The same would follow with the introduction of a webpage that promotes one SBU but not others in the firm.

Complexity and Time Concerns

In addition to having a consistent overall companywide policy toward building the e-business plan, the firm must also be concerned about complexity and time. Solutions such as introducing e-mail or a simple company website to help the staff of all SBUs communicate better with suppliers, customers, and one another can be developed and installed without undue delay, cost, or disruption of current work responsibilities. However, as the complexity of the plan increases, so too does the amount of time required to design, install, and test the new solution and then train the staff to use it. All of this is further complicated by the need to educate customers and suppliers, who will be expected to change their current behavior and shift to a new, perhaps unfamiliar method of placing orders, making requests for information, and so forth. For example, although Internet banking is growing in popularity with each passing day, customers moving to this method of recording transactions for the first time must pass along a learning curve. A strong customer support system is critical to help those customers who may be confused about the online screen menus, computer and connection problems, and anything else they may need assistance with. The telephone contact channel of a complete CRM solution should allow the service representative to view the same screen the customer sees. Furthermore, the customer service representative needs to be knowledgeable and skilled not only with the bank's online software, but with computer systems and their common problems as well.

A good overall e-business plan requires firms to research and gain an understanding of the behaviors demonstrated by users of websites as well as Internet-based solutions. For example, how long will it take the typical bank customer to adapt to the online banking system? What behavioral problems can planners anticipate and prepare for in order to assure potential users' acceptance of the system? These behavioral issues and other important topics related to online communication will be examined in greater detail in Chapter 7.

Motivating Acceptance of e-Business Plans

A business that already has a physical location (bricks and mortar) and a customer base generally looks at e-business as a way to expand sales to current customers and to add new customers who are beyond the reach of the firm's geographic location. Firms also look to improve their operations by developing superior competencies that are available as part of an Internet-based software solution. For example, retail firms like Radio Shack, Sears, the Gap, Barnes & Noble, and many others have turned to the Internet to sell more products through e-commerce or to lead customers to a local bricks-and-mortar store to finalize a purchase. Customers who are seeking the convenience of shopping online and receiving delivery as well as those who are simply using the website to view a retailer's catalog of merchandise and promotions before buying in their local store outlet can use the firm's website to satisfy their personal shopping needs. These retailers can improve efficiencies and customer responsiveness by combining website content with CRM solutions.

Every business must be prepared to give customers, suppliers, and staff sufficient time to adapt to the new methods of operation necessitated by the installation of e-business solutions. If the newly introduced solution is seen as an improvement—for example, if it reduces employees' workload by increasing their efficiency and making their tasks easier and more enjoyable—then planners might expect motivated users who are eager for the transition to the new system. The message here is simply that planners must recognize the motivation level of those involved. The more that an e-business plan complements existing operations and improves life for individual users, the more likely it is that it will be well received, learned quickly, and adopted. Even though the firm sees the installation of a new system as a positive course of action, if the users' perception of the planned changes is negative, the firm can expect resistance and a desire to maintain familiar behaviors. This was the case when banks first introduced automatic teller machines (ATMs) in the 1980s. Many customers were hesitant to exchange the tradition of lining up to transact business with a live teller for the time-saving efficiency of the ATM. Although ATMs were first offered as a way to extend bricks-and-mortar banks' operating hours, the general population switched over to ATMs in large numbers only when the ATMs were networked, making far more locations available, and in some cases when banks began levying charges for transactions conducted at a teller. The lessons learned with ATMs seem to have been applied when online banking was introduced, as banks generally provide online banking services as an additional service, in addition to telephone and ATM banking, for clients who really do not need the services of a teller and can manage autonomously.

e-BUSINESS insight

Hosted CRM Solutions

According to research by Boston-based Aberdeen Group (**www.aberdeen.com**), CRM spending will continue to increase steadily from $13.7 billion in 2002 to $17.7 billion in 2006. This represents a 6.7 percent compound rate of growth. Because the high initial cost of software was a barrier for many firms that wanted to adopt CRM solutions to build competitive advantage, hosted, subscription-based software offerings from independent software vendors and systems integrators are now expected to drive growth. Revenues for subscriptions are expected to soar from $246 million to $2.8 billion in 2006 whereas total worldwide application license sales (using the perpetual license model) are expected to decline 17.8 percent from $3.01 billion to $2.48 billion. By subscribing to CRM software instead of purchasing complete systems, firms gain access to CRM solutions at lower entry costs and are assured of continuously updated versions. Reflecting American businesses awareness that CRM can enable them to better serve customers and reduce their operating costs, the U.S. is expected to remain the dominant CRM market, representing 52 percent of global sales.

Question for discussion: What other online products do you think could be sold by subscription?[6]

Industry- and Global-Level Issues Related to e-Business Planning

The strategic planning process model we have presented focuses on the strategic choices that are available to management at each of the three corporate levels of the organization and on the interconnectedness of decisions. But just as the decisions taken at the corporate level set the stage for the selection process at the divisional level and on to the operational level, the firm must view itself as a member of an industry that is part of a global network of organizations competing within and across national borders. In this closing section of the chapter, we will examine the nature of both environments and the corporate-level strategic choices that must reflect the influences of these environments on the firm's e-business plan.

supply chain
The firms along the distribution channel that deliver valued services as the product is processed and moved along a path to the final buyer.

The Industry Supply Chain

Just as the firm can be viewed as a value chain of activities that transform inputs into customer-valued outputs, so it can also be viewed as a contributing member of the industry supply chain. The **supply chain** refers to the firms along the distribution channel that deliver valued services as the product is processed and moved along a path to the final buyer. So just as there is a value chain within a single firm, we can also recognize an industry-level chain that involves suppliers, producers, service providers, and so forth, who in combination deliver value to the final customer.

The logistical concerns of warehousing, sorting, packaging, and transportation are only a few examples of the many activities in the chain that add value. The focus for businesses here is always, "What new and better customer-perceived value can be added to the current arrangement?" Current and potential participants in the supply chain compete to uncover a new value-added service or a better way to manage the current supply-chain activities. Obviously, any activity that reduces costs along the channel will be of benefit to final customers. For example, a brokerage firm that facilitates the exchange process among all industry suppliers by providing an easy-to-use website is contributing a value-added service to the supply chain that delivers products to business customers. This service might result in lower prices or a wider selection of products for others further down the supply chain. Regardless of the value added to the supply chain, the service is judged to be an improvement to the way the supply chain was operating previously. By looking at itself as a component of a larger infrastructure (the supply chain), the firm can expand on its internal view of its own value chain.

A Fragmented Industry Environment

fragmented industry
An industry in which there are a large number of small and medium-scale firms that typically employ a focus strategy at the SBU level of their organizations.

Corporate strategic planning should also reflect the competitive conditions present in the industry. Industries can be classified as fragmented, growth-oriented, mature, or declining. A **fragmented industry** is one in which there are a large number of small and medium-scale firms that typically employ a focus strategy at the SBU level of their organizations. The strategic focus may be based on specialized products or services, a particular target audience, or a particular geographic area. On the Internet, many industry environments can be considered fragmented, meaning the customer often has difficulty differentiating one firm from another and therefore selecting one firm over another. For example, consider online retailing of CDs, books, clothing, and other consumer products. Just as consumers may have dozens of bricks-and-mortar retail locations to choose from in their geographic area, the Internet also creates even greater fragmentation problems for vendors of these easily compared products. To take advantage of the organizational strategies inherent in Internet solutions, firms will tend to graduate toward some sort of online organizational structure, such as an online mall, that can consolidate this fragmented situation and thereby take advantage of economies of scale and cost savings. This is precisely the same reason why local firms will join in strategic alliances and partnerships with larger-scale firms, as was described earlier in the IBM-Lotus partnership program. In short, the solution for managers in a fragmented industry is to seek a unifying organization on the Internet that can bring shared economies and other benefits to smaller firms that are trying to expand their operations online.

Industry Life Cycle Issues

The **industry life cycle** refers to the stages that an industry and its firms pass through over time as their product sales soar in *growth,* level off in *maturity,* and finally *decline.* Characteristics of a *growth industry* environment usually include the introduction of innovative products and services by firms that hope to capture higher prices for their inventions and solutions. The strategic choices for an innovative firm in a growth industry are to either go it alone, if the firm possesses the competencies needed to properly exploit the available opportunities; to seek a strategic alliance or partnership; or to license the right to distribute or produce its product. For example, the online entertainment industry is certainly a growth environment, with innovative products and services emerging every day. In the area of peer-to-peer file-sharing software, which allows superior distribution of music on the Internet, more partnerships are likely to develop between software firms and industry giants in order to quickly exploit the technology before another takes its place.

A few dominant large-scale firms with established, long-selling, familiar products and brands typically characterize *mature industries.* On the Internet, these firms might be retailers like Amazon.com and Barnes & Noble. Whether the Internet presence of these firms is mature or not is beside the point. What is important is the customers' perception of the products and services being sold to them. The primary strategy for vendors of mature commodity products like books and CDs is to focus on cost-reducing efficiencies and superior customer responsiveness. Price reductions and other promotional efforts can also help to better position the firm and its brand association.

In a *declining industry,* where sales are falling and some competitors are leaving the market, the surviving firms can develop strategies for picking up abandoned customers and focusing on niches in the marketplace that they still consider viable. Although we have already witnessed a major shakeout of so-called dot.coms or Internet-only firms, it would be inappropriate to identify any industry as an example of a declining online industry. However, as is the case with mature industries and their products, any declining industry with products to sell may find that the expanded opportunities and efficiencies the Internet provides will create a new venue for finding and serving customers.

Global-Level Strategic Planning Issues

The Internet opens the door to global strategic planning opportunities for even the smallest of organizations. An **international strategy** is a firm's attempt to benefit by transferring its competencies to markets that lack them while providing a minimal amount of customization to suit local conditions. Developers of online game sites may customize their entry screens with instructions and advertising in the local user's spoken language, but the rest of the game display is likely to be unchanged, especially since the game display is visual and the added sound effects are readily understood across cultures and language barriers. A **multidomestic strategy** recognizes the need to customize the firm's operations to reflect selected local conditions. For example, Microsoft's network, msn.com, has more than a dozen versions that use different languages and are customized for different regions in the world. A firm with a more involved **global strategy** would set up

transnational strategy
A strategy in which a firm combines a variety of operations in different countries to create the firm's overall operations.

some operations in foreign countries to take advantage of local economies. A firm with a **transnational strategy** combines a variety of operations in different countries to create the firm's overall operations. For example, many high-tech American-based firms have established their programming operations in India, where expertise is available at lower costs.

To conclude, global-level Internet-based strategies should reflect the corporation's degree of commitment to the globalization of its other operations. The Internet can provide a cost-effective means for drawing together strategic alliances, partners, and divisions that are scattered across geographic distances.

Conclusions

In this chapter, we described the strategic planning process as a methodical approach toward understanding and building an e-business plan of action for any organization. We emphasized that the planning process takes place within the firm at the three primary levels of the organization. Understanding the relationships between the three levels is critical to overall successful planning. Planning objectives set at the corporate level set the conditions for planning at the divisional level, and this in turn sets the conditions at the operational level. We explored the basic thinking behind the strategic planning model, which sees as its primary objective delivering value to customers and developing competitive advantage through superior competencies. Furthermore, we recognized the position of the firm within its industry and global planning as sources of influence on the planning process.

This discussion provided a structural understanding for developing and structuring a firm's Internet-related plans as part of an **e-business plan.** A more detailed tutorial on the preparation of the e-business plan is available on the textbook's website.

In the next chapter, we will examine the research process that planning should follow as information is collected, analyzed, and used to create and maintain the strategic planning process.

 RETURN TO
inside e-business

CASE STUDY

Home Depot's Internet presence is clearly designed to assist customers with their home improvement planning before they enter the stores. Besides providing important information about interior design and product selection, the site acts to develop and nurture long-term relationships with customers. In many ways, the website's design and style are not unlike those of the sites associated with not-for-profit PBS shows like Home Time and This Old House. All sites clearly must have a commercial aspect that will generate revenues, or they must be sponsored. Otherwise, their business model cannot work.

ASSIGNMENT

1. What design additions would you make to the Home Depot site to increase customers' perception of its value? Explain your suggestions.

2. Does the Home Depot enjoy any online competitive advantage that it is not presently exploiting through its website? If so, what would you suggest it do?

Chapter Review

SUMMARY

ACE Self-Test
For a quick self-test of the content in this chapter, visit the student website at **http://business.college. hmco.com/students.** Select "Canzer e-Business."

1. Describe the fundamental characteristics of the strategic planning process.

The strategic planning process involves a sequence of steps taken by management to develop new plans, modify existing plans that may require revision, and discontinue plans that are no longer justified. After establishing the organization's mission statement, the firm analyzes relevant information, which leads to the development of strategic plans and their subsequent implementation. Feedback links assure the continuous incorporation of new information at all steps of the process. The strategic planning process requires first the establishment and then the maintenance of a plan of action that everyone in the organization is expected to follow. A well-managed strategic business plan is one in which each individual employee's work contribution is consistent with the goals set for the organization as a whole. The strategic planning process is about designing, monitoring, and revising a plan of action for everyone working for the organization, with the expressed understanding that deviations from planned results and any changes in the business environments are to be researched and the resulting feedback used to revise the current plan.

2. Examine the strategic planning process at each of the three primary organizational levels of the firm.

Planning is organized hierarchically from the top down, and therefore plans and their objectives at the corporate level become the starting point for planning at the next lower level, which is the division or strategic business unit level. The plans approved at this level become the starting point for creating plans at the local operating or functional level of the organization. Most strategic planning involves an overlap between functional areas and departments. Senior management must make a concerted effort to tie together all the participants in the overall plan and to ensure that a consistent objective is shared and integrated throughout the three primary levels of the firm.

3. Define the value chain and ways to create competitive advantage.

The value chain refers to a view of the firm as an organization of activities that are concerned with transforming inputs into customer-valued outputs. The primary activities in the value chain are research and development, production, marketing and sales, and service. In addition to these primary activities, there are also support activities, which include the company infrastructure, information systems, human resources, and materials management. Support activities facilitate the primary activities in the value chain. The underlying thinking that guides strategic planning is to select activities that are superior to other choices and, in so doing, deliver superior customer value. Superior value will, in turn, provide the firm with a competitive advantage and thereby lead to greater profitability. Opportunities identified within the value chain can be turned into a competitive advantage and hence more profits for the firm. The firm's resources (human, material, informational, and financial) and capabilities (skills and abilities to make productive use of available resources) lead to the development of distinctive competencies, or the ability to provide superior efficiency, quality, innovation, or customer responsiveness. Superiority in these areas can permit the firm to differentiate its products, lower its costs, or both. This thereby creates a valued competitive advantage over competitors in the marketplace, which generates higher profits.

4. **Explore issues related to building an online presence for an existing business.**
   The development of the firm's online presence should be guided by one key objective: to complement the existing non-Internet-based business plan. Whatever the firm's objectives, the e-business plan must be in line with them, supporting and, it is hoped, enhancing the current plan. As the complexity of the plan increases, so too does the amount of time required to design, install, and test the new solution and then train the staff to use it. A business that already has a physical location (bricks and mortar) and a customer base generally looks at e-business as a way to expand sales to current customers and to add new customers who are beyond the reach of the firm's geographic location. Firms also look to improve their operations by developing superior competencies that an Internet-based software solution makes available. Businesses must be prepared to allow sufficient time for customers, suppliers, and staff to adapt to the new methods of operation necessitated by the installation of e-business solutions. If the newly introduced solution is seen as an improvement, then planners might expect to have motivated users who are eager for the transition to the new system.

5. **Explore the industry- and global-level strategic planning issues facing the firm.**
   Just as the decisions taken at the corporate level set the stage for the selection process at the divisional level and on to the operational level, the firm must also view itself as a member of an industry that is part of a global network of organizations competing within and across national borders. Corporate strategic planning should reflect the competitive conditions present in the industry. Industries can be classified as fragmented, growth-oriented, mature, or declining. Global-level Internet-based strategies should reflect the corporation's degree of commitment to the globalization of the firm's other operations. The Internet can provide cost-effective means for drawing together strategic alliances, partners, and divisions of the firm that are scattered across geographic distances.

REVIEW QUESTIONS

1. Explain each of the key steps in the strategic planning process.
2. How is planning different at each of the three primary organizational levels of the firm?
3. Explain the meaning of the value chain.
4. What are the five forces that influence a firm's competitive thinking?
5. What is meant by competitive advantage? Describe some examples.

6. What advantages does a bricks-and-mortar business have as it develops its e-business plan?
7. What industry-level issues should e-business planning consider?
8. What global-level issues should e-business planning consider?

<table>
<tr><td>DISCUSSION
QUESTIONS</td><td>1. The strategic planning process is an integrated business effort across the firm. Discuss.
2. Discuss how the value chain relates to the strategic planning process.
3. How are e-business models and Internet-based software solutions related to the strategic planning process?
4. Is it easier or more difficult for an existing firm to create an e-business strategic plan in comparison to a business that is just starting up?</td></tr>
</table>

Building Skills for Career Success

EXPLORING THE INTERNET

Microsoft's central website operation at **www.msn.com** is the firm's gateway for contact with global users seeking sources of news, chat rooms, communities, links to other Internet websites, and a variety of other valued content and services. Content distributors like Microsoft and the British Broadcasting Corporation (**http://www.bbc.co.uk/**), the most popular site in the United Kingdom, can easily modify and customize their display screens to better serve the global marketplace, which wants content that is culturally and linguistically suited to its needs. Taking the theme of customization one step further, both sites provide users with a variety of personalization choices, including the ability to select local news and weather services by entering a postal code. The Microsoft site allows users to select the magazine article title links that they prefer to see each time they load their personalized webpage. The ability to interact with individuals and offer them independent control of what they see on their screen is a prime attraction of the globalization effort.

ASSIGNMENT
1. Select a website that allows the user to customize it. What sorts of options are provided to users?
2. How beneficial do you believe this strategy is for the website you have selected, in terms of attracting and keeping loyal users?

DEVELOPING CRITICAL THINKING SKILLS

Michael Porter's value chain and five-forces model play an important role in the strategic planning process. By examining the current situation facing a firm and the industry it competes in, planners can develop an inventory of opportunities for growth that the firm can consider and can better understand the threats to any competitive advantage the firm may enjoy. Use the Internet to learn more about a firm that currently enjoys a competitive advantage in its industry.

ASSIGNMENT
1. Describe the reasons for the competitive advantage that the firm currently enjoys.
2. How much risk is there to this advantage from the entry of new competitors? From substitute products?
3. Describe the level of rivalry among established competitors.
4. Describe the bargaining power of buyers and suppliers.

BUILDING TEAM SKILLS

The SBU level of the firm concerns itself with those items that we generally consider when we think about the "nuts and bolts" meaning of planning. What products will we sell, and to whom? What price will we charge, and how will the product be delivered? Generic strategies that are available to the firm include *cost leadership, differentiation,* and *focus on a particular target market.* Search the Internet together and select three websites, each representing one of these generic strategies.

ASSIGNMENT
1. Describe each of your selections and how it conforms to the definition of the generic strategy.
2. Which was the easiest site to select? Which was the most difficult? Explain why you think this is so.

RESEARCHING DIFFERENT CAREERS

Learning Tree International (**www.learningtree.com**) is a leading private information technology (IT) training organization that provides courses on software, systems design, and so on in both teacher-led and multimedia student-controlled learning environments. The typical two- or three-day seminars it holds in hotels around North America are usually bundled with CD-ROM packages and online learning that continues after the learner has completed the seminar. You can learn about IT careers and the knowledge requirements demanded of IT personnel by examining the course descriptions and promotional material provided for Learning Tree's targeted learners. You can also learn about some of the current software used by IT professionals by exploring Learning Tree's promotional site at **www.GetTechTips.com**.

ASSIGNMENT
1. Describe the categories of courses offered by Learning Tree.
2. What software training programs seem to be popular, and who are the target learners?

IMPROVING COMMUNICATION SKILLS

Benchmarking involves comparing an organization's performance to standards established by other firms inside or outside of the industry. Performance standards can cover a wide range of activities, from how well customer services are provided to the visual quality of the firm's website. Understanding the criteria that are useful and informative for benchmarking can be as important as the actual data for the compared firm. Select a firm that you are familiar with, such as a search engine or a news site.

ASSIGNMENT

1. Identify the selected site and list its competitors in its industry.
2. List the criteria that you believe would allow a comparison between the chosen website and its competitors.
3. Create a scale or some other measurement that allows you to score the firms on each criterion you have selected. For instance, you might use a scale of 1 through 5, where 1 represents a low and 5 a high degree of performance.
4. Present the criteria and your scores for the site and the industry in the form of a grid. Indicate whether the firm was above or below the industry standard scores and to what degree by placing an asterisk on the grid line.

Exploring Useful Websites

These websites provide information related to the topics discussed in the chapter. You can learn more by visiting them online and examining their current data.

1. The Home Depot (**www.homedepot.com**), Home Time (**www.hometime.com**), This Old House (**www.pbs.org/wgbh/thisoldhouse/**), and Martha Stewart (**www.marthastewart.com**) websites provide handy tips and step-by-step informative instructions on everything from installing ceramic tile to remodeling an outdated kitchen.
2. The Internet has low barriers to entry, which allows virtual firms to enter the market and meet any fulfillment gaps by forming strategic alliances with other firms, such as the arrangement between AOL and AutoNation (**www.autonation.com**).
3. One of the advantages that Radio Shack (**www.radioshack.com**) enjoyed over most of its web-based competitors was the ability to make use of any local Radio Shack retail location to better serve customers who might want to pick up merchandise they ordered online instead of using delivery service.
4. IBM (**www.ibm.com**) maintains a strategic alliance with Siebel Systems Inc. (**www.siebel.com**), the largest CRM software developer.

5. United Parcel Service (UPS) (**www.ups.com**) generates over \$30 billion of revenues and continues to grow by using Internet technologies to handle logistical solutions for its customers.

6. CDNow (**www.cdnow.com**) and Egghead (**www.egghead.com**) compete by using a cost leadership strategy and by offering differentiated products at low prices.

7. Microsoft's central website operation at **www.msn.com** and the British Broadcasting Corporation (**http://www.bbc.co.uk**), the most popular site in the United Kingdom, can easily modify and customize their display screens to better serve the global marketplace, which wants content that is culturally and linguistically suited to its needs.

8. Learning Tree International (**www.learningtree.com**) is a leading private IT training organization. Learning Tree's promotional site at **www.GetTechTips.com** provides informational tips on popular software.

chapter 6

Researching and Analyzing Opportunities for Growth

LEARNING OBJECTIVES

1. Examine the primary reasons for conducting e-business research.

2. Identify the steps in the e-business research process.

3. Describe the types of research data available.

4. Examine the methods used for successful e-business research.

INSIDE
e-business

Forrester Research Inc.—Providing Information and Guidance for e-Business Growth

According to a 2003 study by Forrester Research Inc. (**www.forrester.com**) of Cambridge, Massachusetts, portals will be the primary means by which most online consumers will be introduced to comparison shopping online. The strategic implications of this research for planning at portal websites is obvious: prepare for this behavioral trend on the part of online shoppers and reap the benefits. Fail to offer this service, or fail to offer it in a way that users will consider satisfactory, and your portal will likely lose traffic and revenues to competitors that do. This study is only one among the hundreds of reports Forrester Research prepares each year. Forrester is recognized as one of the leading Internet-industry research firms that analyze the future of technology change and its impact on businesses, consumers, and society. The firm's success in this highly competitive field is reflected in the respect and status it has earned as a primary resource center for e-business clients wishing to make informed decisions and develop better strategies. Forrester accomplishes this, in part, by combining the consulting services it offers through its Giga Information Group (**www.gigaweb.com**) with its reports, which are distributed online through the infomediary e-business model.

Forrester organizes its cross-referenced research reports into three primary categories so its clients gain a unique combination of data, analysis, and unified guidance on customers, business strategies, and technology investments.

Forrester's TechStrategy® category provides qualitative industry and technology research that analyzes the impact of technology change and supplies clients with information for strategic decision-making. For each report, TechStrategy analysts interview thirty to fifty business strategists, IT professionals, and marketing executives; twelve to twenty relevant technology vendors; and other key influencers, such as scientists, regulators, or academics. Reports are categorized for a wide variety of industries such as automotive, telecommunications, retailing and health care, which simplifies the search for information. A part of TechStrategy, called the Forrester Wave®, is a visual-mapping tool that helps companies select vendors and products by evaluating the strength of their current offering, strategy, and market presence.

The Technographics® category provides users with comprehensive quantitative research for determining how technology is considered, bought, and used by consumers and businesses. The research is divided into two main categories. Consumer Technographics data are based on surveys of more than 260,000 households in North America and Europe, and Business Technographics data are gathered from more than 3,000 large North American companies. Descriptive categories of buyers, which include "Fast Followers" and "Cautious Onlookers," help marketers understand the types of market segments they face.

TechRankings™ research uses lab-tested evaluations to deliver analysis and online customization tools so users can select and implement software infrastructure and application products. TechRankings provides advice on enterprise software selection and implementation, offering more than seventy product evaluations based on more than 300 attributes. It combines data from hands-on lab testing and vendor research with strategic market analysis and insight about technology users' needs.

Finding high-quality information that can be trusted as the basis for planning e-business strategies is a daunting challenge. Executive decision-makers are continuously bombarded by advertising hype and anecdotal references suggesting that organizations that do not get on board the Internet revolution today will be left behind forever. Knowing how far ahead or behind your business practices are in relation to those of competitors and other industry players is critically important and helps explain the role played by research and consulting firms like Forrester.[1]

Information is a primary business resource essential for individual and collective decision-making throughout any organization. Information, like other assets, has value, and like any other tangible asset of the firm, it must be created. Somehow, somewhere, somebody has to invest time and effort to learn about something, organize the relative importance of the facts and their interpretation, and then prepare a summary of that information for others in the firm to use. Many of the clients that firms like Forrester Research serve are planners and decision-makers who need to know a range of often fast-changing and complex information, especially so in the e-business area.

In this chapter, we will examine the complex challenge of researching e-business and explain how managers might begin the process that leads to discovering, evaluating, and finally adopting specific e-business solutions. We will structure our approach by first examining the fundamental reasons for conducting e-business research and then look at a common model of the research process as it applies to e-business concerns and activities.

Primary Reasons for Conducting e-Business Research

management information system (MIS)
A system for researching and maintaining a continuous flow of useful information to those in the organization who need to know it.

In the absence of complete and perfect information, all decision-making involves a certain degree of risk. However, greater information can lower the risk that a specific plan or decision being taken will be wrong or a poor choice. Researching and maintaining a continuous flow of useful information to those who need to know it is a vital part of any good organizationwide **management information system (MIS)**. Research can be thought of as the principal activity that provides information for this system and helps management make better-informed decisions. This is particularly important given the growing effort to find e-business solutions and incorporate them into overall strategic plans.

e-business information system
A more narrowly defined system than MIS that serves the needs of the organization as part of a larger management information system.

There are a variety of often overlapping reasons for conducting e-business research and maintaining, as part of a larger management information system, a more narrowly defined **e-business information system**. We will structure our discussion by focusing on three primary purposes: gathering business intelligence, managing problem solving and decision-making, and discovering new opportunities for growth.

Gathering Business Intelligence

A good e-business information system will provide managers at each level of the organization with timely and pertinent data through reports that are written in a style and format that is appropriate for the intended user. Business intelligence requires the continuous gathering and reporting of information about a firm's industry, suppliers, competitors, or customers, or even background data on a single potential client. A good system will not overload the user by providing more information than the user can digest or information that is superfluous to the user's current research needs. In addition, to be an effective and productive tool, the system must anticipate the likely search behavior of users. For example, to help them focus their search of the many available reports and databases, Forrester Research first has its clients fill out a descriptive profile of the sorts of research they are most likely to find useful. In addition, this support system recalls which reports a user selected in the past and can make intelligent decisions that identify other related reports that may also be of interest to the user. Furthermore, Forrester provides a search engine that can employ key words and phrases to intelligently help to guide clients to the information they seek.

Most e-business information systems that are designed to help users quickly find information online provide a search engine, especially those systems that hold a large and complex volume of stored data. The firm using such systems can choose from among many of the search engines used on popular websites, then add key words, names, and phrases tailored to the contents of its data-collection needs.

Search Results of "Business" from college.hmco.com

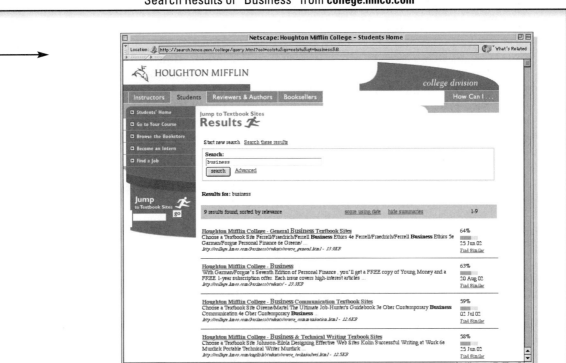

Reprinted by permission of Houghton Mifflin Company. (*Source:* **http://search.hmco.com/college/ query.html?col=colstu&qc=colstu&qt=business&B**.)

Search engines typically provide a ranking of each item or "hit" they return to the user's screen. This ranking is based on an intelligent evaluation by the engine's software of how closely the search criterion the user entered matches the listed item. This is often displayed as a percentage figure such as "95%," which would suggest that the software believes the item is highly associated with the search criterion and is "95% certain" the user will find it useful. The screen shot shown here displays a screen of data received from the Houghton Mifflin search engine after the firm's database catalog was searched for "business" books.

competitive intelligence (CI)
A type of business intelligence that focuses on continuously gathering information on clients and competitors and then incorporating this information into the firm's strategic decision-making process and business plan.

A special type of business intelligence called **competitive intelligence (CI)** focuses on continuously gathering information on clients and competitors and then incorporating this information into the firm's strategic decision-making process and business plan. Gathering CI involves searching publicly available databases and journals; interviewing suppliers and employees; and using other intelligence-gathering strategies to develop and maintain an awareness of what one's industry competitors are up to. California-based Palo Alto Management Group Inc. estimates that the global market for CI currently exceeds $100 billion and will continue to grow. You can learn more about CI from the Society of Competitive Intelligence Professionals (**www.scip.org**), a nonprofit organization that offers training seminars and acts as a network for its 6,750 worldwide members. Hundreds of private-sector firms specialize in CI services, such as Fuld & Company of Cambridge, Massachusetts.[2]

Entering the term *competitive intelligence* as the search criterion in the Forrester Research website's search engine will yield a list of reports tagged with that term, allowing clients to find and purchase needed reports quickly and easily. This primary strategy for gathering business intelligence online is a basic starting point for researchers who need to learn techniques for successfully searching both their firm's information system and externally available sources.

Managing Decision-Making and Problem Solving

management decision-making process
A continuous activity that requires management to take a creative approach to understanding the problems or opportunities its organization faces and then generating solutions or means to take advantage of opportunities that might not last for long.

A second primary reason for carrying out e-business research and maintaining an e-business information system is to help management make intelligent decisions and solve problems. To do this, management must be committed to the **management decision-making process**, a continuous activity that requires management to take a creative approach to understanding the problems or opportunities its organization faces and then generating solutions or means to take advantage of opportunities that might not last for long. The logical connection between the firm's business information system and its construction of an organizational culture that nurtures individual contributions to a creative problem-solving and decision-making process should be readily seen: Without a good system in place, the organization's ability to carry out any problem-solving and decision-making effort will be weakened. For example, the open-style culture nurtured by Forrester Research founder George Colony is regarded as a fundamental reason for the firm's rapid growth as it seeks ways to serve clients' research and information needs. Rather than simply presenting reports and databases on its website for clients to access, Forrester's staff works with clients as part of their total research team. If a

Forrester service representative is unable to find existing documents that would serve a client's needs, then he or she might suggest that Forrester begin a new research report, providing new growth for Forrester. As another example of problem solving, Eastman Kodak Company's recent entry into digital films—projection, editing, and distribution to theaters and movie studios—when announced, helped boost the firm's sagging share value 5 percent in one day. This new area of product development illustrates how looking at e-business solutions can revitalize at least in the short term a firm that many believed was unable to break from its original but aging technology.[3]

It remains to be seen whether Kodak manages the shift to digital technologies in film and photography that will facilitate distribution of entertainment content over the Internet or ultimately fails in this endeavor. However, investors perceived the decision to be a positive move by management to change strategies to reflect customers' needs. Clearly, other firms have failed to respond properly to technological changes, littering the business landscape with disappointments. For example, Polaroid failed to deal with its aging instant photography technology because management was unable to make proper decisions to revitalize the firm. Surely, the Polaroid brand could have found a place in digital photography had better decisions been taken in time. To help managers think creatively and differently when solving problems and to recognize opportunities to improve current business operations, we will examine the decision-making steps that are typically recommended, as presented in Figure 6.1.

Step 1: Analysis of the Business Environments

The first step in the decision-making process is the ongoing analysis of business environments both internal and external to the firm. Managers involved in decision-making need to be well informed about trends in their industry, recent strategic moves by competitors, technological developments, and so forth. Contributing to the firm's e-business information system and using it on a regular basis automatically stimulate management participation in the first step of the decision-making process. Individuals and groups that are responsible for specific products or perhaps operating divisions within the firm will often maintain their own online discussion forum that focuses on developing a greater shared understanding of the changes occurring within the firm or in the industry. For example, how will the trend toward greater use of wireless communication technologies like phone sets and other palm-held devices affect access to our website and our e-commerce business? And now that digital photography has shifted activity away from centralized photo-processing labs to desktop computers and printers, how should traditional photo supply firms like Kodak and printer manufacturers like Hewlett-Packard respond? This forum can be a place for comparing ideas and floating thoughts or suggestions in an environment that should encourage creative thinking. A forum monitor should regularly prepare short summary reports on the dialogue and add these to the firm's database, or perhaps send a monthly e-mail providing highlights of the forum's discussion to an "interested-parties" list. Anyone examining the archived summaries in the firm's database would gain a quick history of the sequence of discussions on the topic.

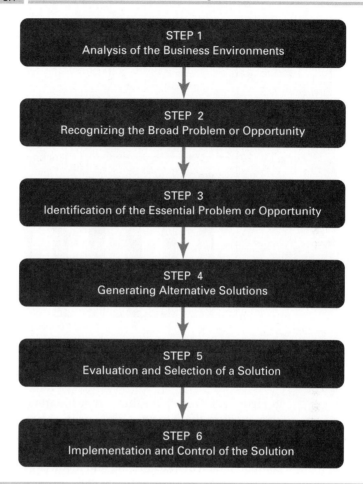

FIGURE 6.1   The Management Decision-Making Process

STEP 1
Analysis of the Business Environments

STEP 2
Recognizing the Broad Problem or Opportunity

STEP 3
Identification of the Essential Problem or Opportunity

STEP 4
Generating Alternative Solutions

STEP 5
Evaluation and Selection of a Solution

STEP 6
Implementation and Control of the Solution

Step 2: Recognition of the Broad Problem or Opportunity

Eventually, analysis of the process will allow an individual, a group, or the firm as a whole to recognize a problem that demands a solution or an opportunity that awaits exploitation. At this point, management will recognize only the general nature of the problem and perhaps express it in descriptive terms such as "our customer satisfaction ratings are falling," "customers do not consider our prices as competitive as they used to," or "we don't have a competitive online presence in a growing new market."

As an example, the customer satisfaction problem could have been recognized by analyzing customers' e-mail to the firm, as illustrated by the graphical presentation

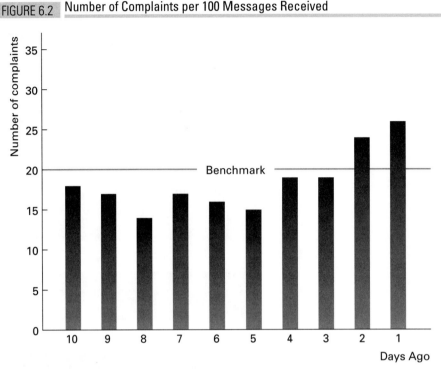

FIGURE 6.2   Number of Complaints per 100 Messages Received

in Figure 6.2. This figure shows that the trend in the number of complaints has been upward; the rate has clearly risen above the acceptable benchmark performance level set by the firm. After reading one of these e-mails and dealing with the customer's concerns, the customer service representative could generate complaint data by categorizing and recording the nature of the e-mail complaint. An alert report might be automatically triggered if the acceptable benchmark level is exceeded for more than two consecutive days. To better understand the reasons behind the complaints, management would probably want to read recent messages and try to identify any common characteristics.

Step 3: Identification of the Essential Problem or Opportunity

In this step of the decision-making process, the specific nature of the problem or opportunity is established. For instance, research into a fall in customer satisfaction ratings may discover that it is directly attributable to the excessive time required for customers to receive responses to their questions about use of the firm's products and that no one has complained about the products themselves. Before any serious amount of time and effort is devoted to generating solutions, decision-makers must be confident that they have clearly identified the true problem. Otherwise, any solution taken may be misdirected at the very least and completely off target in an extreme situation. For example, if this customer satisfaction problem can be solved through new and improved methods of train-ing employees, then the process will have succeeded. However, if the source of customer dissatisfaction is in no way related to employee behavior, then any effort spent on training will be wasted. The execution of a solution is usually the more expensive portion of the decision-making process. Management therefore needs to be satisfied that the problem has been clearly defined and pinpointed before proceeding with a solution. However, as with all decision-making, even after a substantial research effort and much expert opinion, the risk remains that the understanding of the problem may be incomplete or wrong.

Step 4: Generation of Alternative Solutions

Management's belief it knows the true problem leads next to the creative work of generating alternative solutions that can solve it. Here managers will assemble as-sumptions about current and future conditions and the likely costs and benefits associated with each potential solution. In the customer satisfaction example, perhaps more customer service staff should be hired to deal with the workload, or perhaps the firm needs to develop better computer-assisted problem-solving software to improve employee productivity and thereby reduce response time to customers. Of course, the alternatives available to management will be con-strained by the need to make a decision within a reasonable amount of time, es-pecially given the relative importance of the problem and the limitations on such resources as staff abilities and money. Undoubtedly, Kodak's move was a result of management's recognition of the severity of the problem facing the firm as in-creasing numbers of customers shifted to digital photography.

Step 5: Evaluation of Alternatives and Selection of a Solution

The next decision-making step is where management proves its worth to the firm, for the right decisions are often not obvious or clear-cut. Management must evalu-ate the alternative solutions available, weigh the consequences of selecting each one, and then decide which choice is best. Perhaps improved staff training really is the solution in the customer satisfaction case. Perhaps, because of this firm's high staff turnover, the benefits of allocating extra funds for better training will have a short life, and therefore perhaps computer-assisted problem-solving software might better serve the firm. For example, in addition to assisting full-time staff, the investment in software might make the use of part-time employees more at-tractive, since the average cost and time for training can be substantially reduced if the software is used by many employees instead of just a few.

Step 6: Implementation and Control of the Solution

Once a solution is selected, a plan of action needs to be laid out, complete with a timetable and an identification of who will be responsible for carrying out specific actions in the plan. Milestones set on a calendar can allow management to track whether planned actions are unfolding as scheduled and can help guide the suc-cessful rollout of the solution. Information the firm learns during the plan's imple-mentation can provide new data for the firm's e-business information system and thus contribute to future decision-making.

Discovering New Opportunities for Growth

The third primary purpose for carrying out e-business research and maintaining an e-business information system is to help management identify and assess new opportunities for growth through e-business solutions. This means employing and extending the management decision-making process into an aggressively creative research force that is on the prowl for good ideas that will increase revenues and reduce expenses. Often research into current market activities, and especially competitors' clear successes, will uncover ideas that management will wish to follow. For example, although IBM is well known today for selling a variety of services to small businesses, historically the firm was associated more with providing large-scale computer hardware and software solutions to large-scale organizations. IBM recognized that it did not have to abandon its traditional markets in order to reach out to new ones. It saw that it would have to change its business thinking and its strategies if it wished to serve small-scale business operations, such as a sole proprietor who may be operating a business alone from an office set up in his or her own home. To reach this market, IBM and other firms interested in the same market make greater use of mass media (television, magazines, and newspapers) than they ever did in the past. Online e-business strategies such as e-commerce and website service centers that focus on small business needs are designed to help serve niche markets in conjunction with mass media advertising campaigns. IBM was not the first to follow this route and probably borrowed strategies from successful competitors like Dell Computer. Dell paved the way by selling directly to businesses and proved these techniques would work.

The e-Business Research Process

Now that we have established why e-business research is so important to the effective management of an organization, we will focus on a model of the research process that explains how this process should be conducted. To understand the tasks involved, which staff should be assigned to these tasks, and the status of work in each area, it is useful to view the research process as a sequence of steps, as illustrated in Figure 6.3. The labels for each step are fundamentally the same as in the marketing or general business research process. What is distinctive in our discussion here are the details related to e-business that apply within each step.

Step 1: Define What Information Is Needed

The research process is goal-directed. This means that every research project should have a stated purpose, even if that purpose is expressed simply as continuing to gather useful intelligence about the current state of the industry and the market, competitors' and customers' behavioral trends, or changes in market prices for products. For example, e-retailers like the Gap and Sears, Roebuck need to conduct ongoing research so they can modify their selling strategies as circumstances warrant. However, research projects may also be of short duration, rather than continuous, if the information is needed for a one-time decision. For

FIGURE 6.3   The e-Business Research Process

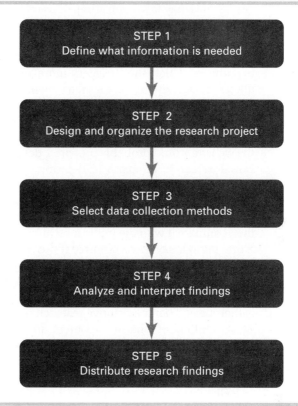

example, Sears may need to know whether a line of power tools would sell well to online gift-buying shoppers. If the study returns a positive result, suggesting that the firm should go ahead and introduce the product line to its web-based shopping catalog, then the need for this particular project will have been satisfied and the project completed. The results of a research project will often precipitate new needs assessments and trigger new research projects to supply more information. For Sears, this might focus on the best way to market the line of tools, pricing and promotional strategies, and so forth.

Step 2: Design and Organize the Research Project

The best way to design and organize any research project will depend on a variety of factors, such as the nature of the information, its importance to the firm, what the costs and benefits of the research effort are to decision-makers, and the relative need for reliability and validity in the data collection process. The basic research design may focus on the testing of a **hypothesis**, which is simply a statement that we want to prove true or false, based on the data collected. For example, the statement "men and women are equally comfortable navigating our website" is a hypothesis that we can show to be true or false, and the *null hypothesis*, "men

hypothesis
A statement that we want to prove true or false, based on the data collected.

and women are not equally comfortable navigating our website," suggests that a gender bias may favor one group of users.

To gather data, researchers may elect to conduct **exploratory research** to seek out appropriate information related to a research question or hypothesis, if one has been formulated. Exploratory research often leads to the clarification of a hypothesis, which then triggers more research targeted more precisely at the question. **Descriptive research**, as the term suggests, focuses on helping to shed light on some area of interest. For instance, the research question "how do men navigate our website?" might be answered through descriptive research. A skilled researcher who is capable of explaining the observed behavior of men while using the website would probably prepare a descriptive report. A third type of research, **causal research**, attempts to determine whether there is a causal relationship between two variable items—for example, "Would the display of a photograph of a star athlete change the daily volume of traffic on our website?" To test the hypothesis, we would first establish a benchmark or current traffic volume level and then compare it with the traffic level after placing a photograph on the website for a trial period, say three months. If the results showed no statistically significant difference in traffic after the placing of the photograph, we would conclude that it had no effect on traffic. Of course, researchers are generally interested in finding out what does attract more traffic and might conduct exploratory research to first gather ideas. Then descriptive research might be employed to help formulate an understanding of what web content and techniques are popular on websites in general and on websites of firms like their own in particular. Lastly, causal research might be used to test for the mix of specific content that best suits the target audience for the firm's site and generates the greatest traffic.

Reliability is a measurement of the ability of the research method to report what it is intended to report each time it is used. Reliability is generally regarded as a critical element of design quality. A wooden ruler is usually a very reliable instrument for measuring length, since it returns the same length for a given item each time it is used. In e-business research, we are interested in discovering and using methods of data collection and measurement instruments that will return more or less the same results in successive trials. For example, an online survey that attempts to measure customers' satisfaction with their online purchase experience would be considered very reliable if the results are shown to be about the same each time another sample of customers is surveyed, within the time frame established for data collection (which should be a time frame within which the results would not be expected to change). If, say, between 68 and 70 percent of all randomly selected samples of 1,000 customers returned a positive customer response, the research team would likely be satisfied that the method (survey) and the instrument (questionnaire) being used to measure customer satisfaction levels are reliable.

Validity is a measurement of how accurately the research method and instrument measure what they are intended to measure. Validity is also regarded as a critical design quality factor. For example, if a question on the survey is misunderstood by a large number of the customers, then even though the results may be reliable (the same results occur with each sample), they do not necessarily measure what the researchers wanted to know. Selecting good methods and designing reliable and

exploratory research
Research that seeks out basic information related to a research question or hypothesis.

descriptive research
Research that focuses on helping to shed descriptive light on some area of interest.

causal research
Research that attempts to determine whether there is a causal relationship between two variable items.

reliability
A measurement of the ability of the research method to report what it is intended to report each time it is used.

validity
A measurement of how accurately the research method and instrument measure what they are intended to measure.

valid measuring instruments such as survey questions is a complex field of study beyond the scope of this textbook. Reliability and validity are mentioned here simply to draw students' attention to the importance of questioning the results of any research project they may be presented with and asked to pass judgment on. If the design and organization of the information-gathering process is suspect, then it follows that the value of the rest of the research process will be questionable too.

Step 3: Select Data-Collection Methods

A variety of research methods and techniques can be used to gather data about e-business. However, surveys, experiments, observation, website content analysis, focus groups, and individual interviews with customers and suppliers are the most common methods because they deliver good-quality results within a relatively short time and on a limited budget. In addition, these conventional methods can be adapted to online data collection, so the firm can take advantage of the automated data-collection tools established at various customer "touch points," or moments when customers are in direct contact with the firm. These tools would include data entry by customer service personnel who take orders, provide product information, or receive complaints from customers by e-mail, telephone, or regular mail. Furthermore, retail bar code scanners at the check-out counter and credit card purchase data provide information on the quantities and types of products purchased as well as data that are useful for creating customer purchasing profiles and patterns. Interviews can often take the form of unstructured conversations with randomly selected sample groups of customers about their experiences using a firm's website. The dialogues provoked within focus groups of six to eight people can often reveal information that would not be uncovered through one-on-one interviews. Surveys can be done online, by telephone, or by e-mail, and these methods are familiar to the subjects providing the data as well as to the researchers. Surveys can direct subjects' responses through multiple-choice, true/false, or fill-in-the-blank selections; use open-ended complete-the-sentence statements; and so on. We will examine each method in greater detail later in this chapter.

Step 4: Analyze and Interpret Findings

Once the raw data are collected, the tasks of organizing, analyzing, and interpreting what they mean to the firm and to decision-makers in particular begins. **Information** can be defined as data that have been transformed into a form that is meaningful to users. A long list of data, such as thousands of readers' ages entered on a questionnaire at a magazine's online site, can be summarized using statistics. A **statistic** is a calculated measurement that summarizes a characteristic of a large group of numbers. Suppose that the following statistics resulted from the survey data that users entered when they sought a password for access to the online magazine. The **mean** (arithmetical average) age of the respondent was 19.5 years old, the **mode** (the age with the most entries) was 19 years, the **median** (the age at which half of the total number of entries, arranged in order, are higher and half are lower) was 19 years, and the **standard deviation** (a measure of the relative difference

information
Data that have been transformed into a form that is meaningful to users.

statistic
A calculated measurement that summarizes a characteristic of a large group of numbers.

mean
The calculated arithmetical average of a group of numbers.

mode
The group or class of data with the most entries.

median
The data item at which half of the total number of entries in an ordered list are higher and half are lower.

standard deviation
A measure of the relative difference between each data entry and the mean for the entire group.

between each entry and the mean for the entire group) was only 0.23. These statistics indicate that the age distribution of users is quite narrowly clustered around 19 years and that there are very few entries by users whose age deviates substantially from the group mean.

What this information might mean for the website content developer and the marketing manager can be quite different. To the website content developer, the information helps create a better profile of the users' characteristics. By extrapolating what is known in general about 19-year-olds and their lifestyles, interests, and motivations, the website developer can possibly create a more attractive site that will generate greater satisfaction and loyalty. The marketing manager might consider this information to be a sort of alarm bell if the intended target audience of the magazine is 18- to 24-year-olds. These statistics would indicate that only a narrow part of the entire target audience is exploring the site. Further research might then be called for to determine why this is the case. Perhaps potential readers above and below the age of 19 don't like the look of the site or don't know about it. Whatever the reason, the information can now stimulate an appropriate planned response by management.

Step 5: Distribute Research Findings

The distribution of research findings can follow one or more of the many methods that firms employ to build a solid knowledge-based organization. Generally speaking, the research findings, the methods used to collect and analyze data, the assumptions made, the recommendations for actions to be taken, and so forth will be documented in a full written report. Typically, full reports can run from a few pages long to more than a hundred pages.

executive summary
A shorter version of a longer report that highlights only the key points.

An **executive summary** is a shorter version of a longer report that highlights only the key points of concern. Executive summary reports will normally be no more than two or three pages long. High-level managers are busy people and prefer a well-written short version. Should they desire or need to read the details, the full version should be readily available to them through a link to the firm's computer-based **documentation warehouse**, which stores and catalogs cross-referenced reports for easy retrieval. For instance, after reading the full report, an executive might wish to call up a list of other reports that contain the client's name. Lotus Development Corporation's popular trademark software, Lotus Notes, when used in combination with its Document.com software, facilitates the storage, retrieval, and management of documentation and attached multimedia files.

documentation warehouse
A facility that stores and catalogs cross-referenced reports for easy computerized retrieval.

In a simplified distribution system, reports and their executive summaries may simply be circulated through e-mail lists and specialized e-mail group discussion software such as Microsoft Corporation's Outlook Express. Corporate websites and electronic newsletters are also popular methods for distributing documents. To help direct the circulation of new information to individuals who need to know it as soon as possible, software systems typically use a categorical coding approach when storing the documents, so that anyone who has registered to receive documents in a particular category is assured of immediate e-mail notification.

Researchers generally expect to present their findings in person to their superiors or to peers at meetings that have been arranged specifically to share information and stimulate discussion about strategic reactions to the findings. These meetings may be regularly scheduled on a weekly, monthly, quarterly, semiannual, or annual basis or they may be called on demand when the findings are deemed urgent enough to justify convening such a meeting. Strategic planning committee meetings are often the setting for PowerPoint multimedia presentations about research findings that relate to a targeted brand, to customer perceptions, to industry developments, and so forth. The PowerPoint slides prepared for such committee meetings are often posted on the firm's internal information website along with the research report documents. If they are designed well, the PowerPoint slides should convey the essential characteristics of the actual presentation and often may contain audiovisual recordings of the exchanges between participants and recorded notes. Microsoft Corporation's NetMeeting is one of many popular tools that firms use to facilitate the exchange of information by participants in different locations.

Understanding the Types of Research Data Available

Data that are collected during the e-business research process are classified, first, according to whether they originate externally to the firm or internally and, second, whether they are primary or secondary in character. The significance of each classification is examined next.

External and Internal Sources of Data

External sources of data include a variety of Internet-based and traditional publishing sources, such as research firms and government agencies that provide databases and published reports on e-business industry facts, conditions, and trends. Often some of the research data are published and made available for no fee as a marketing strategy to publicize the research firm and attract clients interested in the collection, analysis, or reporting of more specific data. For example, Forrester Research (**www.forrester.com**), Nielsen//NetRatings (**www.nielsen-netratings.com**) and ComScore Networks (**www.comscore.com**) are well-known sources of free Internet-based information. Like most research firms, they provide a regular newsletter that highlights recent findings that those who have signed up at the firms' respective websites can receive. The research firms are motivated to do this because they believe that brand awareness can be built up over time and that when a firm that has been receiving the newsletter wants to hire a research organization, Forrester, Nielsen//NetRatings, or ComScore will be at the front of the client's mind. This strategy is also followed by a variety of firms selling all sorts of products and services, including industry giants such as IBM and Oracle as well as smaller-scale management consultants. Every firm that can publicly publish data and reports, and so can create a portrait of expertise in the potential client's mind, should do so to take advantage of an inexpensive method for promoting its business activity and building its brand identity.

In order to take advantage of this wealth of externally and usually freely available data and reports, researchers should assemble their own personal list of the websites they find worthwhile. Thus, the next step should be the creation, with other researchers, of a common website that pools the researchers' lists. In this way, duplications can be eliminated from a master list, and an annotated description of the sort of information that can be found and why it is considered useful can be part of the firm's e-business information system and website. This gives the firm the opportunity to share a categorical listing of useful external sources with whomever else may be interested, both within the organization and outside of it. To publicize its own business through the Internet, the firm may choose to make its research site accessible to its clients, suppliers, and other parties who might also be interested in this valuable service. The website for this textbook contains our list of good sources of research data and is designed to serve a broad audience interested in learning about e-business.

Internally generated data and reports can originate from the firm's own research and data-collection activities. The firm's computerized accounting system can provide a range of facts, lists, charts, and profiles about customers, products, and sales staff performance. External sources tend to be broader in scope and to be applicable and useful to both the firm and its competitors, whereas internal sources tend to be specific to the firm and not generally in public distribution, unless the firm wishes to make them so. The firm is likely to have greater confidence in the quality and interpretation of its own data and reports than in those produced by external sources for a wider public, which are also intended to promote the image of the research firm.

Sales representatives are valuable sources of information about the firm's clients, trends in the sales of specific products and categories of products, and so forth. A good research site will collect this information and have divisional team members prepare summary reports so everyone in the firm can share in developing the company's view of customers and markets.

e-BUSINESS insight

Research into B2B e-Commerce

The quarterly survey and report of manufacturing and nonmanufacturing members of the Institute for Supply Management (**www.ism.ws**), which is prepared in collaboration with Forrester Research Inc., sheds a high-quality light on the behavior patterns that are emerging in the B2B e-commerce field. The first issue of this report, presented in 2001, showed that only about half of the firms surveyed were at a very early stage in adapting both to new Internet technologies and to the buying processes available through the Internet, such as e-commerce and other procurement activities. However, these firms viewed the Internet as an important part of their future procurement planning, which suggested that B2B adoption was still at a very primitive stage of development, with much growth still to come. For example, only about 40 percent of organizations bought their direct manufacturing materials online, and only 15 percent used online auctions during the three-month period studied. The survey also found that organizations were using the Internet to identify potential new suppliers and to collaborate with current suppliers. Meanwhile, only 20 percent of organizations reported being satisfied with their suppliers' online capabilities, which suggested that these suppliers needed to improve or face losing customers to other suppliers who could provide better online services.

However, by 2003 a steady rise in business adoption of online purchasing was clearly evident from data provided by 294 supply management executives surveyed. Of the companies surveyed, 85 percent had made at least some progress toward adopting the Internet for purchasing—and only 4 percent did not plan to use it at all. Still, the majority were less than halfway along toward their objectives, with only 14 percent claiming to be mostly or fully adopted. As expected, large companies outpaced lower-volume purchasers, with 20 percent mostly or fully adopted. More companies reported savings from online purchasing—35 percent, up from 30 percent in the previous quarter—and a steady 40 percent of firms indicated that the Internet would remain important or critical to their purchasing decision-making in the following year.

Question for discussion: Why do you suppose bigger firms are more likely to adopt online solutions?[4]

Primary and Secondary Sources of Data

primary data
Data that have been collected through the original efforts of a firm and presented in reports.

primary research
Research effort that produces primary data and original information.

secondary data
Someone else's primary research and data.

secondary research
The use of someone else's primary research and data.

Data that have been collected through the original efforts of a firm and presented in reports are called **primary data**, and the work involved is called **primary research**. This original research data and research effort are referred to as **secondary data** and **secondary research**, respectively, when they are used by a second party, such as a researcher from another firm who reads the report and makes use of the original data, analysis, and so forth. It is generally preferable to make use of secondary data and reports whenever possible because these are generally a less expensive (sometimes even free) means of deriving information than through company-led primary research. Large-scale research studies that look at common industry trends and characteristics, such as consumer behavior issues, are generally expensive and time-consuming to produce. Purchasing a copy of a report written by a research firm that has conducted broad-based research in the field is therefore almost always a preferable strategy. For example, the ISM/Forrester report on e-business, which tracks organizations' adoption of Internet-based purchasing, can provide a wealth of information at relatively little cost. This is because its contents are of interest to many subscribers, who therefore effectively share the cost of developing it. Furthermore, firms may be able to purchase only those portions of certain reports that are most important to them. On the other hand, reports on broadly focused topics, whether offered for free or sold for fees, are not likely to contain the detailed information that is important to firms. In these situations, firms will probably weigh the costs and benefits of conducting their own primary research to satisfy their information needs. Often, large research organizations can be hired to do research on behalf of a client for that client's confidential or exclusive use, thus preventing competitors from knowing the client's business intelligence.

Firms' need for research on broad-based e-business topics that are common to the industry as a whole is most likely to be satisfied by using secondary research. In practical terms, these topics are the dynamic environmental forces that, as discussed in Module 1 of this textbook, will strongly influence the strategic planning process. As such, firms should monitor and use them continually.

Methods for Successful e-Business Research

The decision to select any particular research method over the alternatives is generally a reflection of the perceived advantages and disadvantages inherent in the selected method. Among the research methods available for understanding e-business, the use of surveys, particularly online surveys, stands out from the rest in benefits offered. In this segment of the chapter, we will examine the online survey method, introduce the online research survey that is located on the website for this textbook, and discuss how you can contribute to and supplement your use of these survey results for your own research projects. First, we will briefly examine several other research methods and their application to e-business research.

Observation

Watching what the subjects in a research study are doing can provide information that those subjects might not consciously understand. For example, how long would you wait for a webpage to download over the Internet and appear on your computer screen before canceling your effort and moving on to another site? This is an important question for website managers, who must weigh the value of including entertaining or revenue-generating content such as advertisements on their webpage against the quick reflex action of the user's finger on a mouse button. Although high-speed Internet access is growing in popularity, most users are still using slower modem connections, and so website managers must consider the slowest common denominator in their design or risk losing a large portion of the global Internet audience.

A popular belief holds that webpages must be able to load on a user's computer screen within 8 seconds to minimize the risk that the user will become frustrated with waiting and simply move on to another site. Research has uncovered something that website designers and site managers have long known intuitively: superfluous downloads that slow the process are often unwelcome and can be the cause of lost viewers not only for the offending page but, by association, for the entire site as well. As a result, producing designs that are simple, quick to download, and created with the intended user in mind is the best strategy to follow. Although snappy animations may be possible and might look better, they are useless if the viewer has already left the page.

One way to gain this and other information on user behavior is by observing targeted users. A computer lab at a school or library and volunteer subjects who don't object to the researcher's monitoring their behavior will provide acceptable data on a variety of behavior patterns. Although only a stopwatch is needed to measure the time spent waiting for a page to load, the research technician's time may be a significant cost for this type of research, especially if several technicians are needed to observe many subjects.

Observation-based research also has more serious drawbacks, however. There is the error risk associated with technicians not accurately recording the start and stop moments. Measuring short time frames is particularly problematic when the range is measured in seconds. A better solution would be to have a computer-assisted measuring instrument built into the computers, that would accurately record the time required for a page download and how long the user waited for an incomplete download before moving on. Another major concern inherent in this method is the behavior that subjects demonstrate while they work under conditions that have been set up to efficiently observe them and collect primary data. Is the observed individual behaving normally? That is to say, is any subject under observation behaving as he or she would when in front of the computer screen at home or in the office? A host of issues can distort the value of the data collected using this design. However, as with any research effort, the researchers must weigh these risks against the real value derived. If the results of this method seem to be consistent with those derived through other methods, then those results can be used with a higher degree of confidence.

Observation research is highly dependent on the skill of the observer. Aside from the technical skill needed to identify the start and stop moments, what skill would the research technician need if a firm wanted a descriptive report on users' emotional responses to webpages? Were the subjects having fun? Did they seem to be enjoying themselves? Were the pages entertaining enough to create long-term goodwill for a particular site? The more complex the research questions are, the more skills the research technician will need to recognize the behaviors and then interpret their meaning. And at what point do we trust the individual researcher's interpretation of the observed situation? Did the 6-year-old subject rush away from the computer screen out of frustration at navigating the page, or did he have to get to the washroom quickly? The more we rely on research on observed behavior, the more we need to know about the people who prepared the data and reports. In a sense, this triggers the need for an underlying faith in the validity of the researcher, or at the very least a cursory review of the researcher's credentials, before value can be attributed to his or her report.

Interview

The interview process is also a relatively inexpensive method that is highly dependent on the technical skills of the researcher. To follow the same example we introduced in the discussion of the observation method, the interviewer could simply talk to subjects before, during, and after they used webpages to uncover their attitude toward waiting. Using this method, the researchers might not hear a simple answer. For example, when asked, "How long would you wait for a page to download before moving on to another?" subjects might say, "It depends on the site, how busy I am, how tired I am, my mood, what's on television," and so forth. Interviews allow the researcher to explore a theme with the subject and to pursue information that might be difficult or impossible for the subject to formulate independently. A good interviewer can uncover a wide range of information by skillfully navigating through a list of directional conversational questions.

Long-term studies of behavior changes and learning are particularly well suited to this method. This is because the individual subjects are generally known to the researcher and can be remunerated for their time and effort. For a small cost, usually under $100 for a one-hour session, a research firm can track changes in the online behavior of regular research subjects over time. Furthermore, paid subjects will generally feel an obligation to be truthful and "earn" their payment by helping the researchers find what they are looking for.

Focus Group

In much the same way that interviews can uncover online attitudes toward waiting, focus groups can stimulate the flow of information by interacting with the members of the focus group. Because the opportunity exists for interaction among the members of the group, individuals' responses may differ from what they would be in a one-on-one interview. For example, suppose a subject in the focus group started the discussion by saying, "Anyone who waits more than 5 seconds for a webpage to appear is a fool. I never wait, and ever since I got hooked up at home to my high-speed Internet service I won't use anything else that is slower." How might others in the focus group react to these statements? Would a user of older technology hide the fact out of embarrassment or concoct totally false information about his or her behavior to conform to the group attitude that emerges when they interact? On the other hand, focus groups can provide great opportunities for generating ideas for improving a webpage and site. Simple leading questions about what the subjects like best and dislike the most can open up a cornucopia of creative ideas for improving the design and content of a site.

Experiment

Experimental methods can also be used to answer the research question of how long subjects will wait for a webpage to download before abandoning the page and moving on to another. One way to ascertain this information would be to conduct experiments in which the length of time subjects spent waiting is measured under controlled conditions. Suppose the researchers set up a site that they believed would be interesting to targeted research subjects. For instance, if it was a site designed to focus on a variety of topics related to Alpine skiing, the research subjects chosen would qualify only if they were ski enthusiasts. As the subjects progress through the simulated and controlled website, the researcher reduces the download speed of each of the pages as the subject requests them, in 1-second intervals.

FIGURE 6.4   Frequency Distribution of Waiting Times Before Abandoning a
Webpage Download

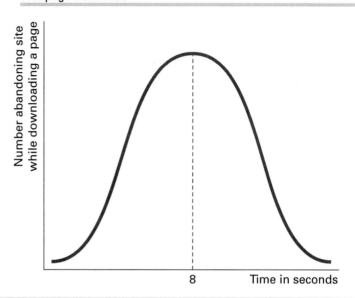

Therefore, the first page would appear in 1 second, the second in 2 seconds, and so forth. The software is designed to record the moment at which a subject first interrupts a page download and moves on to another page instead.

A variety of analytical techniques can be applied both to the list of subjects and to the number of seconds each of them waited before abandoning the page download. Suppose the research results showed that subjects waited an average of 8 seconds, suggesting that the results have a strong measure of consistency with what was assumed before the experiment. Additional information could be derived by analyzing a frequency distribution that showed how many subjects abandoned downloads at any given second. The distribution illustrated in Figure 6.4 appears to be normal: few subjects have very low or high waiting times, and the mass of subjects are bunched together at about the average wait time of 8 seconds.

Content Analysis

Content analysis is concerned with understanding the nature of the content in some medium, including a website. For example, researchers for a small corporation who are considering the design of a website for the corporation might want to know what content is typically presented by other firms of similar size in the same industry. They would use a fair and systematic method for selecting websites, and would gather data on the content found. Suppose that over 90 percent of the websites they surveyed provided an e-mail link to facilitate contact with the firm and help users gain information about the company and its products. However, only 30 percent of the websites provided e-commerce services to help users purchase the firm's products and services online. It is important for researchers to know information on how much content is static, or basically not changed very often, and how much is replaced or updated daily, weekly, monthly, or on some other schedule. These facts, along with descriptive reports on the website designs that users found to be easy to navigate and artistically pleasing, would be useful in guiding the firm in its design approach. As with other methods that depend on researchers' ability to accurately report what is often a personal value judgment, they should consider error risks before accepting any reports prepared using this research method.

Survey

Researchers using the survey method may collect data over the telephone, through face-to-face contact with the subject, on paper forms sent through the mail, or

e-BUSINESS insight

Research Shows Growth Opportunities Exist for Older Media

According to research conducted by Houston, Texas-based The Media Audit (**www.themedia audit.com**), newspaper websites, rather than cannibalizing sales of their print editions, are actually complementary additions. Robert Jordan, co-chairman and co-founder of International Demographics, Inc., parent company of The Media Audit, suggests that research shows that newspapers and their websites are really one media as opposed to two. "Newspaper websites are an extension of the newspaper and add audience to the reach of the printed edition. Also, newspaper websites are updated throughout the day, which improves a newspaper's ability to compete with television news programs with up-to-the minute breaking news information."

This research helped shed light on how customers are reacting to the proliferation of online media. It suggests that newspapers enjoy great advantage by serving the "heavy-user segment" of the market, who are defined as those who spend more than 60 minutes a day reading the newspaper. Since more than 60 percent of Internet heavy users have household incomes of $50,000 or more and more than half have one or more college degrees, they represent a desirable target audience for advertisers and an attractive source of advertising revenues for the newspapers that can deliver them.

Furthermore, newspapers are using their websites to extend their reach to difficult-to-reach market segments who traditionally do not read newspapers. For example, *The Houston Chronicle* reaches 34.5 percent of young upscale adults, who are defined as college-educated 21- to 34-year-olds, in technical, professional, proprietor, or managerial jobs through its print edition, plus an additional 10.3 percent of nonprint readers through its web edition, for a total market reach of 44.3 percent. The Internet technology, which was once feared as a threat to the older medium, is in fact turning out to be an opportunity for growth.

Question for discussion: How would you strategically approach the threats and opportunities facing a radio station based in a city like Houston, Texas?[5]

online through electronic forms. The questionnaire may limit respondents' choices by asking true/false or multiple-choice selections, or it may be open-ended and allow written answers to incomplete sentences. These and other style and format techniques for using this well-established research tool are available to e-business researchers. However, the most interesting are online research designs that take advantage of the fact that subjects are momentarily connected to a site or are subscribers, clients, or suppliers of the firm.

Just as mailing lists facilitate the distribution of paper survey forms, so e-mail lists can be compiled from the firm's internal sources of data or purchased from external sources. There are businesses that prepare and maintain updated categorical lists of e-mail addresses of people who have indicated a willingness to receive solicitations online. The lists are often created through online advertising and promotions at popular websites. They usually reward participants by entering them in a contest in exchange for filling in a profile data sheet and agreeing to receive other solicitations through e-mail. A popular form of data collection and means of building an e-mailing list is the online survey questionnaire that customers must fill out before they can gain access to the firm's website, documents, and services. By providing information such as gender, family income level, educational level, achievement, and so forth, website users trade valuable information about themselves and their online behavior each time they navigate the site. When done in an unobtrusive manner, short surveys that demand little of a user's valuable time and attention can become great sources of current information that is useful for firms improving their marketing to targeted customers.

Although online surveys are inexpensive to launch and easy to distribute, they are often suspect for many reasons. These reasons include the quality of the questions that are asked; how the respondents were selected or came to be presented with the survey form; the large number of potential respondents who ignore e-mailed requests or pop-up surveys, which interrupt another activity online and so they refuse to participate; the danger of bias when a benefit is offered to respondents to entice their participation; and the risk of a motivated individual submitting multiple entries.

**Go to the Web:
e-Business Online**
For tutorials and more on the topics in this chapter, visit the student website at **http://business
.college.hmco.com/
students** and select "Canzer e-Business."

Conclusions

This chapter has presented a broad overview of the research process and the reasons for maintaining an active and up-to-date e-business information system. We discussed the tasks involved in research, the sources of information available, and the methods used to find, analyze, and distribute reports, along with the importance that must be placed on the quality of the information produced.

This discussion also provided a methodical understanding for researching and analyzing information that is vital for the development of an **e-business plan**. A more detailed tutorial on the preparation of the e-business plan is available on the textbook's website.

In the next chapter, we will examine the communication process that takes place online as individuals interact with website content and other people.

RETURN TO
inside e-business

Forrester Research Inc. was established in 1983 and taken public in 1996 by its founder and driving force, chairman and CEO George F. Colony. Since then, the fast-growing Nasdaq-traded (FORR) star of the Internet-research industry has more than doubled the number of clients it serves, from 885 to 1,763. Today's 549 employees, more than four times the 134 it employed in 1996, provide clients with research and guidance as they transform their operations and adapt to the new Internet-based economy. Revenues, which have grown at a compounded rate of 52 percent since the company went public, continue their stellar performance. Unlike many other new firms in the industry, Forrester has consistently earned a profit, which reached $20 million on $159 million of revenues in 2001. Like most technology firms, Forrester experienced serious revenue decline during the post–2000 technology crash as many client firms cut back on research spending. Its profit fell to $11 million on revenues of $96 million in 2002. However, 2003 results showed improvements over 2002.

Like the clients it serves, Forrester is not immune to the rapidly changing forces in the e-business environment and has recently transformed its entire business model. The new model places a greater emphasis on electronic formats and distribution methods to clients that take advantage of the Internet, new products, and the development of strategic partnerships for collecting and reporting research. For example, to build on its reputation and continue its successful growth, Forrester entered into a strategic alliance with the Institute for Supply Management (**www.ism.ws**) to produce a new product called the ISM/Forrester Report on Technology in Supply Management. The quarterly report tracks the adoption of Internet-based purchasing by both manufacturing and nonmanufacturing organizations through a jointly developed survey of business-to-business (B2B) e-commerce activity. This valuable resource helps more than 47,000 supply management ISM members as well as the business community gain a general understanding of the impact of e-commerce on their operations and so plan accordingly.

Strategic alliances such as the one between Forrester Research and the Institute for Supply Management are popular tools for growth among e-businesses. The synergistic goals of both organizations support this strategic alliance. The task of collecting good-quality research data is often the single most difficult issue facing research firms. The response rates of randomly solicited participants are often quite low, which may compromise the usefulness of the data and reported findings. By partnering with ISM, Forrester gains access to a large membership that is more likely to participate voluntarily in research efforts. On the other side of the alliance, ISM benefits from the expertise Forrester brings to its research program and taps into the historical knowledge base that Forrester has already established. By co-operating with Forrester, ISM fulfills its mandate to provide members with the education and research resources to help expand their professional knowledge and improve their business practices.

ASSIGNMENT

1. What other benefits for these two firms do you see emerging from this strategic alliance?
2. What other strategies can you think of that could help Forrester Research continue its successful growth?

Chapter Review

ACE Self-Test

For a quick self-test of the content in this chapter, visit the student website at **http://business .college.hmco.com/ students**. Select "Canzer e-Business."

1. Examine the primary reasons for conducting e-business research.

Research is conducted in order to gather business intelligence, manage problem solving and decision-making, and discover new opportunities for growth. Since information can lower the risk that a specific plan or decision being taken will be wrong or a poor choice, e-business research can help improve a firm's activities in all three of these areas. In the absence of good information, managers lack an understanding about what their competitors are doing in the marketplace, how best to select one solution to a problem out of many possible solutions, and how to maintain the firm's competitive position by discovering new business opportunities for growth. Researching and maintaining a continuous flow of useful information to those who need to know it is a vital part of any good organizationwide management information system. A good e-business information system will provide managers at each level of the organization with timely and pertinent data through reports on the firm's industry, suppliers, or competitors, or background data about a particular client.

2. Identify the steps in the e-business research process.

The e-business research process follows these consecutive steps. First, the researcher defines what information is needed. Next, the research project is designed and organized; data collection methods are selected; and data are gathered, analyzed, and interpreted. Finally, the research findings are distributed to those who need to know them.

3. Describe the types of research data available.

Data that are collected during the e-business research process are classified on the basis of, first, whether they originate externally or internally to the firm and, second, whether they are primary or secondary in character. External sources of data include a variety of Internet-based and traditional publishing sources, such as research firms and government agencies that provide databases and published reports of e-business industry facts, conditions, and trends. Internally generated data and reports can originate from the firm's own research and data collection activities. The firm's computerized accounting system can provide a variety of facts, lists, charts, and profiles about customers, products, and sales staff performance. Data that have been collected through the firm's original efforts and presented in reports are called primary data, and the work involved is called primary research. These original research data and effort are referred to as secondary data and secondary research, respectively, when they are used by a second party, such as a researcher from another firm who reads the report and makes use of the original data, analysis, and so forth.

4. Examine the methods used for successful e-business research.

The decision to select any particular research method over the alternatives is generally a reflection of the perceived advantages and disadvantages inherent in the selected method. Among the research methods available for understanding e-business that experts consider most likely to produce successful results are observation, interviews, focus group interviews, experiments, content analysis, and surveys.

1. What is an e-business information system?
2. What role should an e-business information system play in management?
3. Explain the meaning of business intelligence gathering.
4. List the steps in the management decision-making and problem-solving process.
5. List the steps in the e-business research process.
6. Explain the differences between external and internal data.
7. Explain the differences between primary and secondary data.
8. List the primary methods used for successful e-business research.

1. Describe the primary reasons for conducting e-business research. Discuss the relative importance of each reason.
2. Discuss the reasons for conducting primary and secondary research. Provide situations in which one would be preferable over the other.
3. Discuss the problems facing researchers when they analyze and interpret secondary reports.

Building Skills for Career Success

EXPLORING THE INTERNET

In addition to the home pages of industry research firms like Forrester Research, ComScore, and Nielsen//NetRatings, students can find a great deal of information about the recent activities of these firms from their press releases and briefs. These items, which generally contain key bits of useful information such as statistics or critical findings about changes or new breakthroughs, are usually accessible from the sidebar menu. The information that such websites freely display helps to promote the firm's products, services, and expertise to potential clients. By examining this material, potential clients can better assess whether the research firm will be able to help them with their research needs. Often enough, the purchase of full reports or paid subscription to periodic summary reports can serve the information needs and fit within the budget constraints of smaller firms. You can find links to the websites of several research firms that are good sources of e-business information by going to the information gateway for this text, located on the *e-Business* website at **http://business.college.hmco.com/students**.

ASSIGNMENT

1. Examine the home webpage for one of the research firms and describe some of the areas currently being studied.
2. Select a research firm that presents its press releases and briefs in chronological order. What can you learn about e-business from these items? About the firm?

DEVELOPING CRITICAL THINKING SKILLS

The e-business research process described in this chapter sets out the steps that are required to conduct research systematically. Select a problem or question that you consider worth exploring. For instance, is there a difference between the way men and women shop online? You may choose to test a hypothesis or write an exploratory report. The choice is yours as you follow the research process and prepare your report.

ASSIGNMENT

1. Briefly describe your research problem or question.
2. Following the recommended structure for the research process, write a short report that describes what you would do at each step.

BUILDING TEAM SKILLS

Select a question to research that is of interest to all members of your group. For instance, how do students in your class divide the time they spend online? How much of their time is spent checking e-mail, in chat rooms, doing research for class assignments, and so forth? Discuss the methods of research that are available and select two methods that you consider to be better than the rest. Divide your group equally and assign one method to the first team and the second method to the other. Working independently, conduct the required research and then compare the results from each group.

ASSIGNMENT

1. Present the two reports to your class and compare the results.
2. Explain why you believe the results turned out to be the same or different.

RESEARCHING DIFFERENT CAREERS

A career in research requires good conceptual, analytical, and communication skills. Researchers need to be able to recognize business problems, select effective methods of information gathering, and report their findings effectively. These skills develop and improve with experience. Competitive intelligence focuses on gathering information about competitors and buyers in an industry. The answers to questions like "Which new products or services would customers want to buy?" and "What new products are competitors planning?" are important pieces of information to firms that wish to stay up to date. The Society of Competitive Intelligence Professionals is a nonprofit organization that offers training seminars and acts as a network for its 6,750 worldwide members.

ASSIGNMENT

1. Explore the Society of Competitive Intelligence Professionals website, **www.scip.org.**
2. Describe the information you find there that you consider useful to someone interested in a career in research.

IMPROVING COMMUNICATION SKILLS

Conducting interviews and focus groups can uncover a great deal of information. Often these research methods can be excellent exploratory tools for understanding complex behaviors and decision-making processes. Organize a focus group to discuss some complex issue, such as how people use the Internet for shopping or for researching information before they shop in a bricks-and-mortar store. Then interview one member of the focus group alone to review the results of the focus group discussion.

ASSIGNMENT

1. Briefly describe the research question that you want to explore.
2. Describe the characteristics of the focus group you have selected.
3. Prepare a report that summarizes what was communicated during the focus group.
4. What, if any, new information was uncovered by conducting an interview with only one member of the group?

Exploring Useful Websites

These websites provide information related to the topics discussed in the chapter. You can learn more by visiting them online and examining their current data.

1. Forrester Research (**www.forrester.com**) entered into a strategic alliance with the Institute for Supply Management (**www.ism.ws**) to produce a new product called the ISM/Forrester Report on eBusiness. The quarterly report will track the adoption of Internet-based purchasing by both manufacturing and nonmanufacturing organizations through a jointly developed survey of B2B e-commerce activity.

2. ComScore (**www.comscore.com**) and Nielsen//NetRatings (**www.nielsen-netratings.com**) are well-known sources of free Internet-based information.

3. The website for this textbook contains our list of good sources of research data and is designed to serve an audience that is interested in learning about e-business. You may reach our *e-Business* website at **http://business.college.hmco.com/students**.

4. The Society of Competitive Intelligence Professionals (**www.scip.org**) is a nonprofit organization that offers training seminars and acts as a network for its 6,750 worldwide members.

chapter 7

Understanding Online Communication and Behavior

INSIDE
e-business

Measuring Internet Behavior One Click at a Time

Several firms approach the task of researching individual online behavior by enlisting subjects who agree to have their computer entries monitored and search results passed along for analysis. Firms like the Media Metrix division of ComScore Networks (**www.comscore.com**), Nielsen//NetRatings (**www.nielsen-netratings.com**), and Gomez (**www.gomez.com**) are among this group. They collect data from Internet users who are compensated in some manner for allowing them to examine their behavior one keystroke at a time. The objective is to learn about audience traffic and usage, website ratings, advertising impact, and e-commerce activity. Without the critical information that these firms independently gather, analyze, and report, little would be known about the success or failure of any given website's strategic plans, what advertisers should be willing to pay for display space, and which sites are more likely to produce the desired results.

ComScore Media Metrix (**www.comscore.com/metrix/default.asp**) collects data from a sample of more than 100,000 globally representative Internet users. The firm's database is constantly fed by tracking the click-by-click behavior of users who have been categorized by demographic, geographic, and other criteria. The sample is composed of randomly recruited individual and business users who have agreed to allow a software program to track their online behavior and report the data back to ComScore Media Metrix. A variety of data are recorded, such as the identity of the user, which is determined through a log-on procedure; which sites the user's browser visits; how long the user stays; the number of pages viewed; and even whether the user switches to other digital activities such as a spreadsheet or word processor. By analyzing these data, website developers can test the appeal of various types of online content, how much time and information customers require to make their buying decisions,

and whether customers leave the site and are lost after a particular screen is displayed, which perhaps suggests a flaw in the design or presentation of that screen.

Using information gathered through its research system, ComScore Media Metrix reported that the estimated 152 million American Internet users spent a record average 27.6 hours online during the month of December 2003, and much of it related to holiday shopping. "Our year-end sales data have confirmed that 2003 online holiday retail spending grew by 30 percent, to a record $12.5 billion," said Peter Daboll, president of ComScore Media Metrix. "Consumers actively used the Web to buy online and guide their shopping offline, leaving their mark in traffic patterns across a range of retail categories from Flowers, Gifts & Greetings to Department Stores to Toys." Consistent with expectations for this time of year, the AmericanGreetings website had the largest jump in website ranking, moving up 22 spots to number 13. Other properties that posted a double-digit increase in rank included Best Buy, moving up 17 spots to number 30; Target Corporation, up 15 spots to number 27; Sears, up 11 spots to number 38; and Dell, up to the number 50 position. More than 22 million visitors logged on to delivery firms' sites, such as UPS.com, USPS.com, FedEx.com, much of the time to check up on the status of gifts bought online. As a result, the shipping retail category recorded the second-largest gain, with every site in the category seeing an increase in visitation of more than 30 percent from November to December. The jewelry, luxury goods & accessories category was the third-largest gainer in December 2003. A 500 percent increase in visitors to OmahaSteaks.com helped propel the retail-food category up 27 percent from November to December, making it the fifth-largest gaining category. Interestingly, Nielsen/NetRatings reported a 35 percent increase in seasonal online buying to an even greater record $18.5 billion. Apparel, toys/video games (hardware and software), consumer electronics, computer hardware and peripherals, and video/DVD generated the most revenue. Online shoppers spent $3.8 billion on apparel, a 40 percent increase from 2002; toys and video games (hardware and software) drew $2.2 billion, jumping 33 percent from the previous year; and consumer electronics spending totaled $2 billion, a rise of 2 percent year over year. The computer hardware/peripherals category also attracted significant attention from online shoppers with total revenue of $1.7 billion in 2003. Video/DVD had a strong season; shoppers spent $1.6 billion, up 46 percent.[1]

The Internet is a relatively new interactive medium for users and content providers, as well as for researchers who are interested in understanding both individual and group online behaviors. Although the Internet is similar in many ways to older and more established media such as television, radio, and print journals, it provides the unique capability of allowing user interactivity and two-way communication. This critical difference changes the design considerations completely from the passive approach employed by noninteractive media such as television, which simply "talks" to an audience. Advertisements on television, for instance, generally hope to attract the audience's attention for a few moments and then, ideally, generate a positive response to the advertisement at a later time when the viewer makes a purchase at a retail store. On a website, the design objective is more likely to be to provoke an immediate user response, which occurs when the viewer clicks through to the next screen or on a link taking her or him to another site. Ultimately, the design of an e-commerce website is intended to lead the user to make a purchase online. However, all commercial websites try to keep viewers for as long as possible and to make them as loyal as possible.

The online behavior of customers, staff, and suppliers must be better understood if strategic plans are to have any chance of succeeding. In order to accomplish this task, we will build on a commonly used model of communication and explore the primary factors that can influence the online behaviors of suppliers, employees, and others who use the Internet to communicate with one another. Finally, we will examine a series of related psychological theory-based models that provide a framework for understanding moment-to-moment online behavior and can help firms develop new strategic plans to direct their future online behaviors.

Understanding the Online Communication Process

online communication process
A sequence of steps that successfully transfers multimedia content and information from one person to another through the Internet.

The **online communication process** model involves a sequence of steps that successfully transfers multimedia content and information from one person to another through the Internet. The model is built around several component points of reference: the *sender of a message*, the *encoded message* that the sender intends to send to the targeted receiver or audience, the medium used to distribute the message, the *decoded message* that is actually received and interpreted by the targeted *receiver of a message*, and finally the *feedback* response by the receiver to the sender reflecting his or her reaction to the message received. Figure 7.1 presents a graphic illustration of the structure of the model and the flow of communication

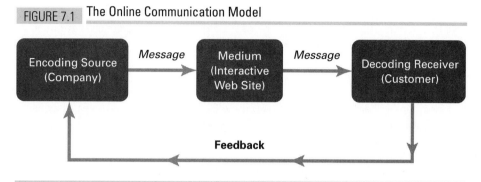

FIGURE 7.1   The Online Communication Model

(*Source:* From Carol H. Anderson and Julian Vincze, *Strategic Marketing Management Theory*, Second Edition. Copyright © 2004 by Houghton Mifflin Company. Reprinted with permission.)

that can help us focus on the reasons for both successful and unsuccessful communication. In this chapter, we will examine the model's architecture further and at the same time bring into our discussion strategic details related to online communication.

Sender or Source of a Message

sender of a message
The initiator or source of a message; in most online communications this is the individual or group that is responsible for preparing the organization's online content and Internet presence.

The **sender of a message** is the initiator or source of the entire communication process. In most online communications this is the individual or group that is responsible for preparing the organization's online content and Internet presence. In a simple situation, the sender could be someone who composes an e-mail message or posts a webpage of information that describes the attributes of a product or service the firm is selling. In more complex situations, there are usually designated individuals who are responsible for designing and developing content for distribution over the Internet.

A managerial structure is in place to control the production of content. The designers and developers of content will often work in tandem with someone else. This may be a content expert or a division in the organization that wishes to create communication for a specific strategic purpose, such as to provide marketing support to sales representatives in the field or to post press announcements to generate public awareness of the organization and present its official response to information others are circulating about it. In situations like these, it is critical to successful communication that the design team and those who wish to send out the message work well together. This is especially critical when designing the firm's webpages and posting content. Once active, the communication between the firm's webpages and Internet users is generally automated, and any content errors can be costly because they may send confusing or incorrect information to the public. The possible damage such errors could cause to the firm's brand equity and goodwill makes the careful design of the website a critically important first step in the online communication process.

Encoded Message

encoded message

The many different ways in which the sender may prepare a message for the targeted receiver, using appropriate and meaningful images, symbols, and jargon.

The **encoded message** component of the model refers to the many different ways in which the sender may prepare a message for the targeted receiver. Just as advertising messages for children's television are different from those for adults, so too should Internet-delivered messages reflect the sociocultural specifics of the targeted receivers. Obviously, this means encoding messages in the language the receiver understands and using appropriate images, symbols, and jargon. In this respect, designing and encoding Internet-based messages is not all that different from designing and encoding messages for other media. Consider how different the encoded messages are for the broad-based target audience of MSN (**www.msn.com**) versus the much narrower target audience of Warner Bros. entertainment (**http://www2.warnerbros.com/web/music/jukebox.jsp**). Whereas MSN presents news and information more conservatively in a magazine-style format, Warner Bros. uses bold visual images of highly recognizable actors from its recent film and television productions to attract users and generate an exciting online environment.

The specific purpose and function of the message the sender intends to send to the targeted receiver should be identifiable. Is the message supposed to inform, persuade, or elicit a specific reaction or response from the targeted receiver? If these basic questions are unclear, then the design of the message is likely to be unclear as well. Whether it is a basic text message or sophisticated audiovisual content in an interactive webpage, each message can be viewed as an effort by designers to transfer specific information to the intended receiver. Consider the home page for Yahoo! (**www.yahoo.com**), which presents a broad range of multimedia content, including links to online shopping sites as well as an interactive screen of information categories and a search engine to assist researchers. The page design and the words chosen to describe the categories of databases that Yahoo! has organized for searching are simple and relatively stable, so users can gradually learn how to use the Yahoo! site to find the information they seek. The hierarchical structure within the categories is consistent with the way people organize and remember information, further facilitating the search procedure and making use of the website a comfortable and non-frustrating experience. The relatively large amount of print information as opposed to graphics allows the site to jam a great deal of information into the start screen. This contrasts with MSN (**www.msn.com**), which makes greater use of graphics to attract users to articles on a wide range of topics, often related to general interests such as home decoration and health care. Visitors to Yahoo! are motivated by the desire to use the site to search the Web for information. Visitors to MSN, on the other hand, are perhaps more likely to see the site as an online magazine and will come back often if the site provides a satisfactory balance of real news and what can be called *entertaining news.* The motivation of each design team is fundamentally the same—to draw and retain users. The demographics of the users of Yahoo! and MSN might also be quite similar. However, they expect fundamentally different interaction from each of these sites. The lesson to be learned is not to try to be *all things to all people,* but instead to create and support your brand presence and clear identity. It would be an error for Yahoo! to try to be a magazine as well as a primary search engine. The brand identity that Yahoo! wishes to reinforce with each subsequent visit is that it is the user's search engine of choice.

Medium

medium
The vehicle that delivers the message to the receiver; online, this includes the Internet and the network of communication devices such as desktop and laptop computers, interactive television, and wireless telephones that use the Internet.

The **medium** is the vehicle that delivers the message to the receiver. The online communication medium includes the Internet and the network of communication devices such as desktop and laptop computers, interactive television, and wireless telephones that use the Internet. Because of the convergence of technologies, content that is traditionally associated with one device can now be accessed by other devices. For example, users can check their e-mail messages on any of these devices that is the most convenient at a particular moment. As a result, the e-mail alerts that Internet-based securities trading firms like E*TRADE and Charles Schwab send out on stocks held by their investors may be viewed on any of these devices.

Designers need to consider which device receivers will use to access Internet-based information. A large-screen display on a computer monitor or television works well for reading text and scanning colorful images. However, only short messages or menus may be practical for the small display area on a wireless telephone. The 1970s media guru Marshall McLuhan's famous observation that "the medium is the message" takes on new meaning in the age of the Internet. How users see the Internet and the information transmitted through devices tied to the Web influences their understanding of the messages they receive. Some users may view the Internet as simply a source of entertainment and therefore not use it for any business transactions such as banking or online shopping. For others, the Internet is a practical business tool that saves time and money. Knowing the means through which any targeted audience views the medium is critically important before firms begin encoding the message and designing the webpage.

Decoded Message

decoded message
The message that is understood by the targeted receiver.

The **decoded message** is the message that is understood by the targeted receiver. Using whatever perceptual, conceptual, and intellectual skills and knowledge they possess, receivers will create in their minds a model of what they believe was the intended message. Whether their perceived model of the message and the message the sender intended to send are in fact the same generally will require verification. Suppose MSN (**www.msn.com**) uses a photograph that shows a child playing with a puppy. The image can communicate a wide range of information and emotion for many viewers, perhaps for some even standing out from much of the rest of the content on the screen. However, though this image might be attractive and appealing to, say, a mother with young children who are about the same age as the child depicted in the photograph, it might be quite uninteresting to an unmarried older male business executive. In fact, he might not even notice the graphic display.

Consider also how a pop-up advertisement that unexpectedly appears and overlays a large portion of the user's screen might be decoded. Suppose the advertisement offers the user a free trial subscription to a parenting magazine. The young mother we just mentioned is a potential new subscriber and may welcome the ad, leading to the desired outcome—a new subscriber. On the other hand, the older businessman may perceive the ad as an annoyance or even as an obstruction or intrusion into his personal space. Knowing how the communication effort will be decoded or understood by the receiver is critical to its successful utilization and placement.

Receiver of a Message

receiver of a message
The targeted audience of a message; in most online communications, this is the individual receiver of e-mail or the group that views the organization's web content, such as customers, suppliers, and employees.

Much of the success or failure of any communication effort will be determined by the comfort and degree of familiarity that message designers have with their targeted audience—the individual **receiver of a message.** The research methods presented in Chapter 6, such as focus groups and surveys, can help designers gain this familiarity. The mother and the older business executive mentioned in the last section might both use the same MSN website, but they are very different people who are likely to use quite different sociocultural references when interpreting the images displayed. Therefore, each is likely to derive different meaning from them, which will consequently trigger different responses. It is incumbent upon designers to know the targeted receivers of their messages well so they can better direct successful images and create successful messages. However, it is also important that they be aware of the fact that many diverse users in addition to the intended target audience may be exposed to the message. Designers must be careful not to create messages that might be well received by the target audience but others visiting the same website might consider offensive. The results might prove to be counterproductive to the overall communication effort.

Feedback

feedback
Responses from the message receiver that are communicated back to the original sender.

noise
Any disturbance in the environment that prevents the receiver from fully receiving the intended message.

The online communications model suggests that communication is an ongoing process, in which **feedback** responses from the receiver are communicated back to the sender. Feedback tends to drive the next round of communication, as the feedback demands a response from the original sender. A lack of response from the receiver can also be interpreted as feedback. If viewers are expected to click on the graphic image of the child playing with the puppy and few of them do so, then this feedback, in the form of a low click rate, is a clear indication of that the message for the intended audience was designed poorly or of some other flaw. Often the message must be repeated because of "noise."

Noise is any disturbance in the environment that prevents the receiver from fully receiving the intended message. The phone ringing and distracting the user's attention from the computer screen is a form of noise, as is a pop-up advertisement window overlaying the screen being viewed. More likely, the feedback will indicate successful communication of the message and a shared understanding with the target audience. However, when feedback indicates that communication has been unsuccessful, the next round of communication should be designed in such a way as to incorporate this vital piece of feedback into the process.

Content analysis of customer feedback, such as e-mail and other customer relationship management (CRM) inputs gained through customer contact opportunities, can provide the firm with insight into the success of its design effort. Often the comments customers made or the way the user expected to navigate the website can indicate where the design failures or successes lay. According to researchers at Greenfield Online Inc. (**www.greenfieldonline.com**), online polls are an inexpensive and popular strategy for creating feedback and interactivity with viewers. People like expressing their opinions and comparing themselves to others. Furthermore, online polls are good for generating content and entertainment for virtual communities. According to an online poll (about online polls), about half of the respondents said that they were an amusing diversion. Although highly unscientific, such polls can also be successfully used to generate traffic at website communities and to direct users to chat rooms to discuss the results.[2]

Clearly, the best chance for successful communication starts with the designer having an understanding of the characteristic makeup of the targeted receivers of the message. Designing websites that communicate successfully with potential customers requires an understanding of those customers' buying processes, which is our next topic.

Consumer and Organizational Buying Processes

Both the buying processes of consumers and organizations follow similar steps, or stages, which logically resemble the management decision-making process we discussed in Chapter 6. After all, the whole point of the process is to make a good buying decision for oneself or one's organization. In either situation, the decision is driven by the desire to optimally satisfy needs or wants through the particular buying decision being taken. For example, online buyers might be motivated to save time or money when shopping for products or services. Other common reasons for buying online include convenience, delivery services, and selection. A starting point for any understanding of why customers are or are not shopping at a firm's website is the fundamental question of why they have chosen to be there instead of at any of the other e-commerce sites or bricks-and-mortar options that are available. Failure to satisfy that basic need will logically undermine any other positive effort to attract customers and keep them coming back.

FIGURE 7.2   The Consumer and Organizational Buying Process

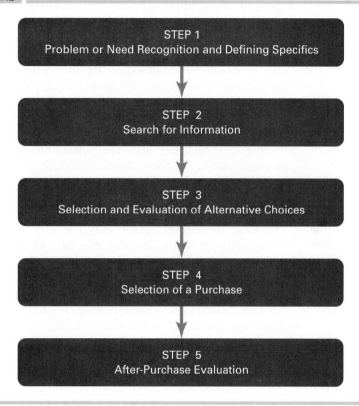

STEP 1
Problem or Need Recognition and Defining Specifics

STEP 2
Search for Information

STEP 3
Selection and Evaluation of Alternative Choices

STEP 4
Selection of a Purchase

STEP 5
After-Purchase Evaluation

Step 1: Problem or Need Recognition and Defining Specifics

As illustrated in Figure 7.2, the buying decision process begins with the *problem or need recognition and defining specifics* stage. In this stage, potential customers must first become aware of a need or want and then define the specifics of that need as much as possible to help narrow the scope of the task they face. This stage can be stimulated automatically, as when an organization's inventory-reporting system indicates low levels of supplies, or stimulated spontaneously, as when a consumer decides it's time to plan a summer vacation. The problem-recognition stage includes defining as specifically as possible just what the problem or need is and what purchase will be required to satisfy the need. Generally speaking, the more clearly defined the need is in the buyer's mind, the easier it will be to find a purchase solution. However, consumers are often not clear about what they want—and may not know what they wanted until after they have found it. Websites that encourage browsing or that offer suitable gift suggestions can generate customer loyalty if the shopping experience is satisfactory, whereas frustrated browsers are unlikely to return. Sites like Amazon.com (**www.amazon.com**) keep track of what customers have bought in the past and direct them to possible new purchases that are intelligently related to their past buying preferences.

It is useful to categorize the buyer's perception of the purchase in terms of its complexity and the level of the buyer's involvement in the purchase decision. *Routine* or *simple purchases* require minimal search and analysis effort. For example, reordering paper and ink cartridges for office printers and photocopy machines is generally automatic. Typically, the specifications of the needed items are known, and suppliers are routinely contacted when an order is required. Often buyers establish long-term relationships with certain suppliers so as to take advantage of discounts and minimize transportation charges, and prices are generally not a major part of the decision process. According to office supplies retailer Staples (**www.staples.com**), the average spending by small-business customers of Staples' bricks-and-mortar stores increased from $600 to $2,800 when they shifted to the firm's website. As a result, online sales have risen to more than 5 percent of the overall $10 billion Staples earns each year.[3]

An example of a *moderately complex purchase* involving moderate buyer involvement would be a product, such as a computer, that is acquired less frequently. The buyer probably has a great deal of information from previous purchases and experiences with vendors and brands, but the existence of many new technological features may still make the decision a bit complex. Finally, on the extreme of the continuum are *complex purchases* and buying situations that demand a high level of buyer involvement. For example, buying a Caribbean cruise package or selecting an e-commerce host for a firm for the first time is no small undertaking for most people. There are many issues and concerns to weigh, and the time required to finalize a purchase decision will reflect the degree of complexity. Finally, it should be mentioned that what may be a simple, routine buying decision for one person or organization may be quite the opposite for another. Someone who routinely takes cruise ship vacations in the Caribbean and a first-time buyer may both end up on the same ship but have made their decisions in fundamentally different ways. Website designers and operators must cater to both types of buyers if they are to succeed at satisfying the needs of each type of customer.

Step 2: Search for Information

The *search for information* stage will reflect the buyer's prior knowledge and experience. If a buyer's prior experiences at certain sites were positive, it is likely that the he or she will at least begin by revisiting those sites. For instance, a buyer might choose to visit the site where she booked her last Caribbean cruise (a site that specializes in cruise vacations) or to begin at Microsoft's travel central, Expedia.com (**www.expedia.com**). From there, if her search proves unsatisfactory, the buyer may back up to a more general search environment by entering a few descriptive keywords into a search engine. The organizational buyer who is reordering paper and office supplies might simply search the e-commerce site of the firm's supplier to determine whether new products or price changes might influence his purchase decision before he enters the order online. There are also a wide range of influences and sources of information in addition to what a potential buyer might find online. We will explore these factors later in this chapter.

Step 3: Selection and Evaluation of Alternative Choices

After the buyer is satisfied with the available information and understands the decision he or she needs to make, the *selection and evaluation of alternative* choices stage begins. In this stage, the potential buyer must first select the alternative choices he or she considers worthy of evaluation and then evaluate the advantages and disadvantages of each. It is at this stage that the important motivational factors directing the purchase decision will emerge, and the vendors will have the opportunity to differentiate their products. Perhaps price is truly the key issue determining which purchase the buyer will make in the end, or maybe the delivery dates available from various suppliers will be more important. Ultimately, to be successful, an online strategy must reflect whichever factor or factors the buyer considers pivotal at this point in the process. Online agents can search the sites selected by potential buyers or search the Internet seeking close matches with a set of specified criteria. The results of this search can help sort out the large number of potential alternative choices. Commercial websites such as those at IBM and Dell Computer allow visitors to enter the criteria for the sort of computer system they need and also provide online direction and answers to commonly asked questions. Together, all of these online strategies help potential customers make an informed and satisfactory needs-driven decision.

Step 4: Selection of a Purchase

When the buyer is satisfied with the decision or the time he or she has available to continue the search and evaluation of alternatives runs out, the *selection of a purchase* takes place. How the firm handles the recording and completion of the sale is critical to determining whether the sale will in fact be finalized. If the website confuses the buyer or if the buyer requires online support to complete the required forms, then the firm must be sure to provide effective customer service and support or it risks losing the sale. It is here that a good CRM solution helps tie together the total selling strategy, since telephone-based customer support staff can not only talk to the buyer while she or he is entering information on the firm's screen but can also see exactly what the buyer sees at the same time.

A variety of statistics have been published suggesting that large numbers of online sales have been lost because customers become frustrated and drop out of the online purchasing process. No doubt few of those who abandon a purchase effort at this stage of the process are likely to return to the site again. The permanent damage caused by the loss of potential customers cannot be overstated. Designers and e-commerce managers must provide the support required not only by new customers having first-time navigation problems but also by regular customers who need assistance. Finding customers and bringing them to the website for the first time is a difficult and costly task. It is tragic if customers are lost because the support needed to keep them is absent.

Step 5: After-Purchase Evaluation

The *after-purchase evaluation* stage reflects the buyer's experience not only with the product or service but with the entire buying experience as well. If the cruise was a vacation dream come true and the online booking process was simple to understand and navigate, then the buyer can be expected to repeat what was essentially a totally positive experience. If there were problems with the online booking process, then the buyer might choose to take her business to another online site or perhaps to a bricks-and-mortar travel agency the next time she is considering a Caribbean cruise vacation. That purchase experience will be feedback into the reservoir of knowledge with which the buyer will begin the process the next time around. Therefore, it is critical that online vendors monitor just what buyers are learning about their products and their online support, as well as any other vital information that can lead to strategic improvement. This is especially important for organizational vendors for whom routine and highly automated B2B buying is the basis of their business. For them, losing one customer to a competitor can translate into large revenue losses.

Sources of Influence on Buyer Behavior and Decision-Making

Now that we have established the sequence of steps that buyers take as they make their way to a purchase decision, we will turn our attention to some of the major influences or factors that can affect buyers' decision-making and how businesses can use this knowledge to better develop their online strategic presence. Influences on buyer behavior fall into three primary categories: social, personal, and psychological factors.

Social Factors

social factors
Cultural and social influences on individual buyers' behavior; these can include an individual's social roles and the influence of family, peers, opinion leaders, and reference groups.

Social factors are cultural and social influences on individual behavior. These can include an individual's social roles and the influence of family, peers, opinion leaders, and reference groups. Social roles are associated behaviors that an individual person engages in within the context of some social situation or environment. A manager, whoever else he or she might be outside of the workplace, is expected by his or her superiors, subordinates, and customers to behave in a way consistent with his or her role or position within the firm. This may mean, for instance, that the manager is expected to solicit advice about which CRM system the firm should acquire before he or she makes a final decision. Similarly, the manager might be influenced by family members, peers, industry opinion leaders, and managers in other departments in the firm who constitute a reference group from which the manager seeks advice and guidance.

e-BUSINESS insight

College Students and Teens Demonstrate Different Online Shopping Behavior

A recent study sponsored by the College Stores Research and Educational Foundation, the research arm of the National Association of College Stores, uncovered a variety of interesting facts about college students' online buying behavior. First, college students are highly influenced by the college environment itself and quickly become comfortable with online shopping once they have left home. More than half shop online, spending only about $330 a year on music (38 percent), books (34 percent), travel (33 percent), concert tickets (22 percent), and computer software (18 percent). Also, the survey reveals that low prices, selection, and personal knowledge of the brand sold are the top three reasons that students select one online retailer over another. About 60 percent of students find out about a website through an online search engine, of which the leaders are Yahoo!, AltaVista, and Excite. Interestingly, recommendations from socially relevant others such as friends and family were a distant second source of information about where to shop. Although students were generally satisfied by the service provided, the survey reported that they cited difficulties in locating online stores and navigating their websites.

However, teens demonstrate far different online shopping behavior. Research by Jupiter Communications, part of the ComScore Media Metrix group (**www.comscore.com**), suggests that the Internet serves primarily as a source of information for preteens and teenagers, and they make their purchases later at a bricks-and-mortar store. The survey of 12- to 17-year-olds suggests that this group is likely to spend $4.9 billion annually online by the year 2005, but will spend $21.4 billion at regular retail outlets after first researching the purchase decision on the Internet. According to the survey, girls are more likely than boys to be influenced by online marketing efforts directed toward brands and so should be the preferred target of online advertising effort. Boys seem less interested in following brand names online. Since teens' main online activities are instant messaging, chatting, and searching, marketers are advised to incorporate "viral" or word-of-mouth communication strategies, which let teens share their opinions about brands and products with other teens by sending messages to their friends that include links to brand websites.

Question for discussion: How would you design websites that cater to college students and websites that cater to teens?[4]

Personal Factors

personal factors
Those general characteristics that are closely associated with the individual buyer; they can be categorized as demographic, lifestyle, and situational.

Personal factors are those general characteristics that are closely associated with the individual buyer. They can be categorized as *demographic, lifestyle,* and *situational.* Demographic factors, which include individual descriptive characteristics such as age, gender, occupation, income, and so forth, are traditional tools that strategists use to help them understand customers and their behavior. For instance, knowing that married couples between 25 and 55 years old make up a large part of the cruise ship travel market suggests how the designers of the Celebrity Cruises Inc. (**www.celebritycruises.com**) website might consider communicating with the likely visitors to its site. The images that appeal to this target group and the comfort its members feel navigating the Web can easily be researched through focus group studies. Similarly, lifestyles or psychographic factors that describe people in terms of their categorical activities, opinions, and interests can help strategists identify special niche markets among visitors to their sites. For example, Celebrity Cruises might design webpages that are of particular interest to frequent cruise vacationers, scuba divers, adventurers, and other lifestyle-defined groups. Researchers must also recognize the importance of situational factors that can influence individual buyers' behavior. For instance, while an individual is examining free access to *Business Week* magazine online, a pop-up promotional advertisement for a highly discounted cruise of the Caribbean may influence that person to take some positive buying action at that particular moment. Although the individual had not been intending to consider a cruise ship vacation, the situation presented conditions that could precipitate a sale.

Psychological Factors

psychological factors
General types of behavioral influences that can influence individual buyers' behavior and that are widely shared by individuals, including motivation, perception, learning, attitude, personality, and self-concept.

Psychological factors include general types of behavioral influences that are widely shared by individuals regardless of any individual characteristics they may have, such as their demographic or lifestyle circumstances. Psychological factors that influence human behavior include motivation, perception, learning, attitude, personality, and self-concept.

Motivation is what we call the force that drives an individual to achieve goals associated with the fulfillment of his or her needs, wants, and desires. In social situations, individuals generally seek to satisfy their needs for *power, achievement, affiliation, and control.* For example, researchers who are seeking to understand the motivation of visitors to the online lifestyle community iVillage.com might discover that all of these needs are being satisfied in one way or another through visitors' activities and interaction with others on the website. The job for web designers is to maintain a steady supply of online content that can regularly meet the need requirements of visitors and thereby keep them coming back.

Motivated behavior is often explained as a person's attempt to satisfy a combination of these needs simultaneously. For example, shopping online at a website for the first time might be explained by the shopper's need to express power by proving that she can locate merchandise, click where she must, and conclude a purchase—something that not everyone can do with confidence. The ability to then tell all her friends about this shopping experience allows her to share her personal sense of achievement and to feel that she belongs to a relatively small community of special people who know about Internet shopping firsthand. Finally, the shopper might also feel that she has learned to control her life just a bit more by demonstrating to herself that she has the ability to control technology rather than having technology control her. Managers need to be tuned into the needs that are important motivators for individuals' online behavior and develop websites accordingly.

Perception refers to the ways in which an individual selects, organizes, and understands information and thereby creates personal meaning about the world. It is important for successful web communication. For example, web designers need to understand just how viewers of a particular site will perceive those ubiquitous interrupting pop-up advertising boxes. Perhaps there are moments when the advertised offers are more likely to be well received than others. It is commonly accepted that much banner advertising is not even noticed by viewers, let alone read or acted upon. Research has been relatively weak into how to break the protective barriers that individuals naturally erect to prevent themselves from being overwhelmed by information overload. Our understanding of online perception is fairly limited and provides a wide-open opportunity for research.

Learning is considered to have occurred when a change in individual behavior can be attributed to acquired experience or knowledge. Web designers should consider what they are teaching users through the online learning experiences at their websites. Are customers gaining valuable insight into an important purchase decision, or are they learning that the website operators know little about their product? Often the impression that the customer comes away with will be a lasting one. A poorly designed opening screen that looks unprofessional may be all that a new visitor to the firm will ever see. First impressions are important, and webpage designs need to be given the attention and budget they rightly deserve if the firm is to create good first-time learning experiences for web visitors.

Attitude can be thought of as a combination of factors, including an individual's knowledge, understanding, or beliefs (the cognitive factor); feelings (the affective factor); and likely behavior or tendency to act (the behavioral factor). For instance, someone who believes (cognition) that he would not enjoy a cruise ship vacation in the Caribbean and feels uncomfortable (affective) about the idea of being on a ship far away from the sight of land is unlikely to even search out a website containing information on cruises (behavior), let alone book a vacation online. In short, this person's attitude toward cruise ship vacations is not a positive one. There is a consistency or equilibrium between the three component factors that make up his attitude toward cruise ship vacations. How attitude is formed and can be changed is beyond the scope of this textbook. However, it should be apparent that changing one of the component factors that make up a current attitude structure would provoke a change in the others. For example, providing information about a website (cognition) can provoke a change in the motivation to examine a website and thus in behavior. We will revisit this important part of understanding individual behavior later in this chapter.

Personality refers to an individual's characteristics and consistent behavioral tendencies in a particular situation. For example, employees working online at a call center may demonstrate aggressive behaviors and other personality quirks that they do not normally demonstrate when they are communicating face to face with customers. Trainers need to recognize that an individual's personality can vary widely as the social situation changes, possibly resulting in undesirable behaviors. Furthermore, the notion of *self-concept* is closely related to personality. It refers to how the individual views or perceives him- or herself and how the individual thinks others see him or her, especially in particular social situations. Thus, an online call center customer service representative can be trained to adopt a particular personality and to see herself, at least while answering the phone, in a way that is highly effective for the organization's purposes.

e-BUSINESS insight

The European Experience After Ten Years of the Internet

According to Nielsen/NetRatings' European analysts, the Internet has had tremendous influence on the behavior of Europeans during the decade in which it has developed into a mass medium. To summarize those developments, the analysts prepared a list of what they considered to be the top ten websites and the Internet applications that they feel have had the greatest impact on the development of the Internet and on European social behavior.

(1) Google.com. Searching for websites is now a flexible mixture of online explorative activity; (2) eBay.com. Buying and selling anything is possible; (3) Microsoft Outlook. Ubiquitous e-mail; (4) AOL Instant Messenger. A new way to communicate using text messaging; (5) Napster. Paving the way for P2P file sharing; (6) Amazon.com. Pioneering personal selling and e-commerce; (7) Friends Reunited (**www.friendsreunited.co.uk**). A social community that helped paved the way for the wider acceptance of online dating and matchmaking services; (8) Easyjet (**www.easyjet.co.uk**). Still the number one web-only budget airline; (9) Kelkoo (**www.kelkoo.co.uk**). Comparison shopping made easy; (10) Blogger. A tool that lets you publish your own web diary.

Question for discussion: Do you agree with the analysts' top ten list?[5]

A Framework for Understanding Moment-to-Moment Online Behavior

Explaining and understanding users' online behavior is certainly facilitated by studying the social, personal, and psychological influences that affect those individual. What is still required, however, is a model that can help guide research into online user behavior and develop an understanding of that behavior, especially while it is occurring from one moment to the next. For example, one might rightly feel confident in suggesting that women choose to visit iVillage.com because it reflects a lifestyle community that appeals to a class of women in the general population and satisfies a variety of their needs. However, what is perhaps more difficult to measure and explain is why an individual woman chooses to behave the way she does from moment to moment while she is navigating the iVillage website. Rather than simply seeking to explain how and why a website can attract its targeted user audience, we will conclude this chapter by presenting a series of related psychological theory-based models that attempt to provide a framework for understanding why an online visitor to a website chooses to make the next selection that he or she makes, whether that is to click on a pop-up advertisement, read content, or perhaps leave the current site completely.

Value-Expectancy Theory

value-expectancy theories
Theories based on the belief that the individual rationally weighs the advantageous and disadvantageous outcomes associated with a specific behavior and their expectations that each outcome will occur as a result of their behavior.

All of the models we will examine are derived from value-expectancy theories of human behavior. **Value-expectancy theories** are based on the belief that the individual rationally weighs the advantageous and disadvantageous outcomes associated with a specific behavior and their expectations that each outcome will occur as a result of her or his behavior. In other words, the individual asks him- or herself, "What is the likely outcome of this behavior, and how valuable is it to me?" The individual is expected to maximize the value of that decision by choosing the behavior that represents the greatest measure of outcome benefit or the least amount of loss.[6]

Table 7.1 illustrates a user's value-expectancy-based decision to remain at a current website or switch to the next one. She is researching information for a class term paper and is progressing down a list of potential sites that a search engine has produced. In this highly simplified situation, her behavior is restricted to only two possible choices: remain or switch to the next site on her list.

First, she creates a list of outcomes for each behavior. Here, researchers find that the same two outcomes apply to both behaviors: a belief that the site will provide useful information and that it will be easy to find that information. A seven-point bipolar scale is used to allow the individual to weigh the value or importance of each outcome associated with remaining at the current website and switching to the next. For instance, assigning a "3" value for "Will provide useful information" indicates a high value level for this particular outcome. This means that the individual places a great deal of value and importance on this particular outcome, and therefore it is an important motivating factor for that user.

Similarly, the individual uses the same bipolar scale to indicate his or her expectancy that the behavior will actually deliver the outcome. The 3 indicates that the individual user has a high expectation that remaining at the current website will in fact provide useful information. The combined score of 9 for the value expectancy of

TABLE 7.1	Value $\times$ Expectancy Decision Structure for Deciding to Remain at the Current Website or Switch to the Next Website on a List

Outcomes	Value $\times$ Expectancy $=$ Score				
Remain at Current Site					
- Will provide useful information	3	$\times$	3	$=$	9
- Will be easy to find information	-2	$\times$	3	$=$	-6
Total value of choosing this behavior					3
Switch to Next Site					
- Will provide useful information	3	$\times$	1	$=$	3
- Will be easy to find information	-1	$\times$	3	$=$	-3
Total value of choosing this behavior					0

Strongly Negative		Neutral		Strongly Positive		
-3	-2	-1	0	1	2	3

the first outcome indicates that the user has a high level of confidence that remaining at the current site will deliver the information she is seeking. Why she believes this to be true to the degree indicated is another matter. Perhaps she has been to this site previously and has been successful in finding information, or perhaps her professor has suggested that it is a good source of information for the topic she is writing about. Regardless of the reasons, the model helps researchers focus on the user's motivation at a particular moment. Will the score remain the same if the user has not found any useful information after an hour of searching the site? One would expect not.

Let's examine the other scores that help predict what the decision-making behavior will be. The second outcome score (−6) is derived from a strong expectation (3) that finding information at this site is not going to be easy (−2). The combination of the two scores (3) suggests that there is a relatively strong positive chance that this behavior will be selected. But we cannot predict which of the two behaviors will be chosen until we consider the scores for the only other choice. The second behavior has a lower positive score, reflecting the user's belief that the website will provide the information she is seeking (3). Although the value of the outcome (3) is the same for both behaviors, and logically it should be the same for any site the user selects, the user's expectancy score (1) changes. Perhaps the user has never been to the next website on the list and has no real way of knowing what the likelihood is that she will find the information she seeks. Whatever the reason, on this factor the first behavior wins by a difference in score of 6 points. However, with respect to the belief about how easy it will be to find information on the website, the score is less negative (−3) for the next website on the list than for the current site (−6). On this factor, the scores suggest a movement toward switching to the next website.

To predict which choice will be made, we need to compare the total scores for the different behaviors. According to the total value-expectancy scores for this individual, remaining at the current website would deliver a higher result (+3) than switching to the next site (0) on her list. Hence, the model would predict that this rational decision-maker would opt for remaining at the current website on the basis of her self-reported measure of the value to be gained. The message for website designers is to research the important outcomes and their respective expectancies for a user group and develop strategies that improve the scores for those factors that will contribute to positive online behaviors, such as remaining at the site longer, and reduce the scores for alternative behaviors, such as switching to another site. We will examine these strategies in more detail in chapter 8.

The principles of value-expectancy theory form the basis for more elaborate models useful for predicting rational decision-making and behavior. In a sense, other value-expectancy models have evolved out of the generic form just described. We will examine several other theories to further develop our understanding of this area and its utility in online behavior research.

Theory of Reasoned Action

The theory of reasoned action is a widely used technique for predicting and explaining behavior in a variety of social situations, including those involving consumer behavior.[7]

The simplicity of the model and its ease of use suit it well for many research situations in which prediction of behavior is desired. The theory of reasoned action is a value-expectancy model in which outcomes, beliefs, expectancies, the strength of the beliefs, and the opinions of socially influential others are organized into two groups, or factors. The first group measures attitudes toward the behavior and is composed of measures related to outcomes attributed to the individual performing the behavior. This part of the model is similar to but not exactly the same as the original value-expectancy model we have just examined. The second part of the model measures the opinions of important sources of social influence, which represents socially normal behavior for the individual. These opinions are referred to as the subjective norms.

Mathematically, behavior (B) is expressed by the equation

$$B = BI = w_1(A) + w_2(SN)$$

The theory behind this model suggests that the closest antecedent, or prior state, to actual behavior (B) is behavior intention (BI), meaning the intended behavior of the individual at some moment. Behavior intention in turn is dependent on two weighted factors (weights w_1 and w_2), attitude toward the behavior (A) and subjective norms (SN) about the behavior. The calculation of the weights for these two factors can be derived through research or established more simply by making an educated guess as to how much decision-making in the particular social situation under study is influenced by the individual and how much by his or her social environment. For instance, assigning a weight of 70 percent to w_1 and 30 percent to w_2 suggests that social sources of influence have a smaller effect on decision-making in this particular situation, regardless of the individual scores for each factor.

Attitude Toward the Behavior

Mathematically, attitude toward the behavior measures both the strength of the person's belief that performing the behavior will result in a specific outcome and the individual's evaluation of the outcome, as expressed by the following equation:

$$A = \sum_{i=1}^{n} b \times e$$

where A = the attitude toward performing the behavior
b = the strength of the person's belief that performing the behavior will result in outcome i
e = the person's evaluation of outcome i
n = the number of relevant outcomes

The individual's attitude toward the behavior (A) is explained by the strength of his or her beliefs about the action and the result of taking the action as well as by his or her evaluation of the outcome. For example, an individual who strongly believes that her action of searching a website (b) will lead to finding useful information (i) and who evaluates the outcome of finding useful information (e) as a very positive outcome will have a strong positive attitude toward the action of searching the website.

TABLE 7.2   Measurement of Attitude

Outcomes of Shopping at Amazon.com	b	e	score
1. Will provide products I want to buy	3	2	6
2. Will be easy to find products	−1	3	−3
3. Will save me time	2	1	2
4. Will save me money	−3	2	−6
Total attitude score			−1

Consider the hypothetical data for an individual given in Table 7.2, which illustrate the relationship between the individual's beliefs (b), evaluations (e), and attitude.

The first attitude component, or outcome, which is based on the belief that the website will provide products that the user wants to buy, contributes a relatively high positive score (6), since the belief is strong (3) and the user's evaluation of the importance of finding products also has a relatively high positive score (2). However, the fourth attitude component counters the first because the user does not believe shopping at Amazon.com will save him money (−3) and this factor is given the same importance (2) as the first factor. Therefore these two forces contributing to the total measurement of the user's attitude toward shopping at Amazon.com effectively neutralize each other.

The second attitude factor, based on the belief that products will be easy to find, contributes a negative value (−3), while the third attitude factor, based on the belief that shopping at Amazon.com will save time, contributes a positive value (2). On the whole, we would evaluate this individual's attitude score (−1) as relatively neutral. The positive attitude would be weaker if the individual did not hold strong beliefs about the likelihood of the website's being able to provide the products he wanted to buy or if this were not evaluated as an important outcome. To produce a more positive attitude score and thereby increase the probability of keeping this customer, website designers should focus on increasing the scores on those beliefs that are important to the user. Positive experience using a website will strengthen the user's scores, whereas frustration or poor shopping results are likely to result in scores so low that the customer might not return.

Subjective Norms

Mathematically, the individual's subjective norm score is measured by summing the products of beliefs about whether a significant source of social influence approves or disapproves of the individual's performing the behavior and the strength of the individual's willingness to comply with the norms set by these sources, as expressed by the following equation:

$$SN = \sum_{i=1}^{k} b \times m$$

TABLE 7.3	Illustration of Measurement of Subjective Norms		
Social Influence	b	m	bm
1. Parents	-2	-2	$+4$
2. Peers	$+1$	$+2$	$+2$
3. College professor	$+2$	$+2$	$+4$
4. Best friend	-2	$+2$	-4
Subjective norm score			$+6$

where SN = the individual's subjective norm regarding the behavior
   b = the belief that social influence group or person i thinks the individual should or should not perform the behavior
   m = the person's motivation to comply with the norms set by social influence i
   k = the number of relevant sources of influence for this behavior

Consider the hypothetical data for an individual given in Table 7.3, which illustrate the relationship between beliefs about what socially important others think about the behavior (b), the strength of the individual's motivation to comply with their view (m), and the resulting measurement of subjective norms.

Although both parents and the person's best friend (sources 1 and 4) think shopping at Amazon.com is a bad behavior choice (–2), the negative motivation to comply with parents (–2) results in a +4 score, in comparison to a –4 for the best friend. Given that these two sources mathematically cancel out each other's influence, the remaining positive scores from peers and college professor combine to create a strong positive +6 subjective norm score.

Interpretation of Scores

The attitude toward the behavior score (-1) is not as strong a force in determining behavior intention as the subjective norm that favors the behavior (+6). The final predictive value of the model requires the weights for each factor, which would probably have been derived from preliminary studies using linear regression and are beyond the scope of this text. If they were 0.7 (70 percent) for w_1 and 0.3 (30 percent) for w_2, then

$$B = BI = w_1(A) + w_2(SN)$$
$$= 0.7(-1) + 0.3(+6)$$
$$= -0.7 + 1.8$$
$$= 1.1$$

This final score indicates a low probability of shopping at Amazon.com. The relative strength of the BI for one person or one group can easily be compared with that for another by examining this score. For example, a score of 2.5 would indicate a higher probability of shopping at Amazon.com than one of 0.4.

Self-Regulatory Theories of Behavior

Self-regulatory models regard behavior as being goal directed. That is, an individual's behavior is activated in order to achieve a perceived desirable goal. Action is taken to close the perceived gap between what is and what is desired. A feedback mechanism actively compares the individual's present circumstances with the desired future state and activates behaviors that work toward eliminating the perceived discrepancy in reality. Understanding is therefore achieved by identifying the goals and the processes that are connected with the behaviors the individual undertakes to reach those goals.

The social settings in which behaviors take place are fluid, presenting a continuously changing environment for individuals to navigate. Although previously learned behaviors may be routinely activated, the opportunity to select alternative, nonroutine behaviors is always present.[8]

It is at this level that the theories attempt to understand individual social behaviors by trying to explain why some choices are made and not others.

Research into cognitive psychology and information-processing theories suggests that long-term memory has a hierarchical structure that is made up of clusters or nodes of related items.[9]

In addition to the factual component of a node, it is useful to acknowledge an affective or emotional dimension as well. For example, the emotional affect of frustration that is experienced by an individual who cannot find the product he or she wishes to buy online is likely to contribute to a long-term negative association in their mind with the website and to other related nodes in the situation.

Similarly, associated with factual and affective knowledge are stored "scripts" or behavior sequences, which are part of an individual's complete cognitive network.[10]

Hence, the procedure for logging on to the Amazon.com website and reviewing the current list of suggested products that interest the buyer can be treated as a memory unit of related nodes.

Festinger suggested back in the 1950s that people generally undertake behaviors that are consistent with their attitudes. When there is a discrepancy between the two, the individual suffers dissonance until the attitude-behavior consistency is reestablished. This is usually accomplished by changes in attitude to fit the expressed behavior.[11]

Bem's self-perception theories, which date from the 1960s, argue that cognitive dissonance works only when the individual has strong attitude-behavior definitions. When they are weaker or undefined, he argues, attitude may be rationally defined after the behavior has been performed.[12]

Regardless of which philosophical approach is taken by researchers, the common theme of consistency or congruence between behavior and attitude is remarkable in its simplicity and utility. The task becomes one of choosing which of the two is easier to change or whether an attack on both would expedite the transition process. Festinger suggests that when an individual changes his or her attitude, his or her behavior will fall into line in order to eliminate the stress of dissonance. Likewise, should an intervention strategy force or persuade individuals to adopt a different behavior first, Bem suggests that attitudes will fall into line later.

This research suggests that managers need to know whether the current attitude-behavior relationship among their online customers is firmly rooted or relatively weak. Consumer marketing strategies have successfully applied these theories by advertising the consumers' need to try the product so they know what to think about it. To get consumers to try products when their attitudes toward those products are weak or relatively undefined, firms can provide a free trial membership or access to a website. Managers recognize that generating the motivation to pay for something requires providing the first step toward the formation of a positive attitude. This approach is certainly a well-used strategy for firms like AOL, which attracts new clients with free trial membership offers.

Self-regulatory theories of behavior suggest that the difficulty will be greatest with people who are strongly entrenched in an alternative attitude-behavior relationship. Weakening these bonds will require offering a variety of alternative behaviors that can disrupt their existing strong support for the present behavior. In general, a person's behavior, such as shopping, can be explained in terms of a goal, in this case finding and buying desired products. The cognitive network of factual information, behavior pattern, and goal achievement is common to cognitive information-processing models of behavior.[13] The question of why some behaviors are attempted and others not, and why some are completed while others are not, is the subject of much debate and theorizing. Ajzen has transformed the theory of reasoned action into what he calls the theory of planned action to underline the gap between the individual's present behavior intention and the point in time when the individual can carry out or actualize the behavior. As the gap in time closes, Ajzen points out, the strength of the behavior intention increases. Ajzen explains the problem in terms of intervening or interrupting factors that interfere with the original behavior intention. Ajzen argues that the individual experiences a continuously active cognitive processing of information up until the very moment when the behavior is actualized. He leaves the discussion on this point: the closer one is to the moment of actualizing the behavior, the greater the probability of its execution, since there is less time, and hence opportunity, for influences to change the intended behavior.[14]

Action Control Theory

Although Ajzen helps to narrow the focus of the issue by suggesting the importance of the time dimension, he does not attempt to explain the cognitive competition that is occurring within the mind of the decision-maker except to say that some "thing" may act to strengthen or weaken the intended behavior. Julius Kuhl and Jurgen Beckmann developed a cybernetic (feedback) explanation for why people often fail to complete their intended actions, such as shopping at a website. This body of cognitive psychology, called action control, focuses on self-regulatory mechanisms, which mediate the formation and enactment of behavioral intentions. A distinguishing feature of the theory is the attention it pays to the formation and change of action intention.[15]

According to action control theory, whether an individual will carry out a current behavior intention depends on how difficult it is to carry out the behavior relative to the efficiency of the self-regulatory processes involved. The difficulty of carrying out the behavior is determined by the strength of the external forces working against the behavior, such as social norms; the strength of the internal forces working against the behavior, such as competing action tendencies; and the individual's predisposition toward change-prevention (state-oriented) or change-inducing (action-oriented) behavior.[16]

According to Kuhl, an individual's predisposition to behave in a particular way in some situation lies somewhere between two extreme reference points, which are referred to as action and state orientation. A person is action-oriented with respect to carrying out some behavior when all four of the following conditions are met: The person is focused on (1) his or her present state or condition, (2) a future state or condition, (3) a discrepancy between the two states, and, finally, (4) an action that can eliminate the perceived discrepancy. If any of these four conditions is lacking, the individual is classified as being state-oriented—that is, incapable of action.

This simple structure provides management with an understanding of how to discourage undesirable actions and encourage alternative choices. For example, suppose research confirms that a subject fails to perceive a gap between a present state and a more desirable future state (conditions 1, 2, and 3). If the subject responds with, "I see no advantage to shopping online at Amazon.com and have no desire to change my current practice of shopping at the local mall," then Amazon.com's management may be able to initiate change by creating awareness in the subject of the advantages of shopping at Amazon.com. Or suppose research confirms that the issue is not the subject's lack of awareness, but instead the absence of buyer strategies (condition 4). By providing the subject with needed advice through CRM solutions that meets the individual's needs and respond to his or her concerns or doubts about self-efficacy, management can intervene to promote change.

The action environment is a defined subset of the larger environment with which the individual interacts. For example, an individual who is visiting iVillage.com is in a clearly definable social environment that involves many previously learned, hierarchically arranged nodes of useful information and behavior patterns (scripts), such as talking to people in chat rooms, reading articles, and examining merchandise for sale. Every action environment has its own goals, which are subjectively and normatively defined. That is, each person at the site has her or his own definition of the goals or purposes for being at the site and shared understandings with people who are sources of social influence. For example, most people would agree that the site is a place to find useful information about products and events of interest. In addition, each person holds a personal definition of the goal or purpose of the action environment. It is likely that the subjective and normative definitions will be closely related, but some situations may produce great differences between the two.

According to Kuhl, the action environment or situation is composed of competing action tendencies. An action tendency is a behavioral predisposition to carry out an action that is goal directed in a specific action environment. For example, an individual who feels confused might adopt an action tendency that involves first the intention and then the action of using the help menu on the site. The goal is to eliminate the current state of confusion, and the individual has probably learned the action sequence necessary to succeed at this through experience at other sites or by observing others.

While the individual is engaged in this particular action tendency, any one of several other action tendencies may interfere with his or her successful completion of the intended action. For example, while exploring the help menu for information, the individual might notice the 1-800 CRM number and choose instead to telephone a site representative who is available to assist visitors. At this point, the strength of the competing action tendency (talking to the CRM representative) may win out and therefore replace the initial action tendency (searching the help menu).

The strength of an action tendency relative to competing action tendencies determines whether the action tendency will be interrupted or will reach its goal. Goals can be completed by protecting action tendencies from interference by alternative action tendencies. However, expectancy theory suggests that the individual is continuously weighing the value of goal completion against the appeal of alternative goals in the network.[17]

Another way to think of an action tendency is as the strongest behavior intention associated with some social environment, or the one with the highest probability of being invoked. An action tendency does not occur in a vacuum; it emerges as a possible course of behavior in the context of an action environment. Asking for help while shopping may occur as an action tendency at a retail location or online at Amazon.com. This action tendency is one of several possible action tendencies that might occur at any moment in the particular action environment. Whether it will emerge is primarily a function of its strength relative to that of other familiar and unexpected action tendencies that are present at the time.

One action tendency may be programmed to trigger the activation of another so that the second action tendency emerges as dominant when the first is completed. For example, the familiar and strong action tendency of checking e-mail or updating virus screening software is likely to be cued by sitting down at one's computer for the first time that day. The more linked the action tendencies are, the more familiar and stronger they are.

The task for managers, then, is to understand the complex structure of customers' action environments of competing behavior patterns and networks of cognitive decision rules. In essence, the question becomes, "How does one support customers' positive action tendencies and disrupt negative ones through interventions?"

The simple, heuristic answer is based on research findings that indicate that an action tendency will remain in effect until it is completed or replaced. Therefore, the strategy for managers should be to build informative and persuasive campaigns that support potential customers' positive action tendencies and to attempt to disrupt negative action tendencies by offering alternative/competing action tendencies or by weakening the cognitive/affective network that supports the action tendency.[18]

If, as Kuhl argues, it is necessary to disrupt only one of the four components that identify an individual in an action environment, then a strategist might seek ways of disturbing the existing formation if it is associated with an undesirable action tendency and then maneuvering an alternative action tendency to replace it.

Researchers should be looking for "new" substitutes and components that will alter the strength of customers' present action tendencies. Success is likely to be quicker with action tendencies that are familiar and that are strong in other action environments. The idea of crossover is a popular one in commercial advertising and can be readily explained in the context of this approach. Also, people are more easily moved to take small steps away from a familiar behavior. Therefore, moving a bank customer to full Internet banking is likely to be easier if the customer has already made the move away from the bricks-and-mortar branch and is using the automatic teller machines. The next step to online banking is not that great for those who have already taken the first step. Similarly, Home Depot's online information services prepare customers for the next step, which is actually shopping online.

An individual's selection of an action tendency may be based on his or her belief that that behavior will best satisfy a multitude of goals in the action environment. For example, in making the decision to shop at Amazon.com, the shopper's goal may encompass an improved self-image, saving time, feeling empowered, and so forth. In a sense, the individual's selection of an action tendency may go beyond the achievement of the immediately perceived goal and the present action environment. In terms of reasoned action theory, the online shopper may be making his or her choice of behavior based on a desire to optimize time or mental energy. Online shopping may emerge as the "best" activity to engage in at the moment, in order to satisfy a variety of needs.

**Go to the Web:
e-Business Online**
For tutorials and more on the topics in this chapter, visit the student website at **http://business.college. hmco.com/students** and select "Canzer e-Business."

Conclusions

This chapter has attempted to construct a comprehensive model of online user behavior to help guide management's strategic decision-making. We started with the communication process and the primary sources of influence on individual behavior, and were then able to consider a variety of psychological theories of individual behavior. Given how important it is to know how and why online users choose to make their next decision in the ways they do, the series of value-expectancy models discussed here provided a framework for understanding the moment-to-moment choices that individuals make while online. Though ideally we would like to be able to reduce individual decision-making to a few simple factors, such as economic gain or self-image enhancement, we recognize the complexity of human behavior. Individuals may often be motivated to achieve goals they, let alone the researcher, are not even aware of.

This discussion also provided an understanding into researching and analyzing the individual online behaviors that must be done to develop an **e-business plan.** A more detailed tutorial on preparing the e-business plan is available on the textbook's web site. The next module of the text (Chapters 8 through 11) will explore the micro-level of strategic planning, where detailed marketing, management, and financial strategies are planned out and mechanisms for implementing and controlling the overall e-business plan are set.

RETURN TO
inside e-business

Fortunately for student researchers, ComScore Media Metrix makes many of its key research findings available on its website as a promotional tool to attract potential clients. For example, one of its reports suggested that online retail sales were being driven by a growing and more diverse base of customers, greater access to broadband services (38 percent of American connections are now broadband), and an increasing variety of product choices available online.

ASSIGNMENT

1. Report some of the recent research content that is available at the ComScore Media Metrix websites.
2. What changes would you make to improve the site and increase the chances of attracting new customers? Explain your suggestions.

Chapter Review

SUMMARY

ACE Self-Test
For a quick self-test of the content in this chapter, visit the student website at **http://business. college.hmco.com/ students.** Select "Canzer e-Business."

1. **Examine how the communication model can be used to understand online communications.**
   The online communication process involves a sequence of steps in which information is successfully transferred from one person to another through the Internet. With respect to online communications, we generally think in terms of people and machines communicating text, images, and sounds with each other. The model is built around several component points of reference: the sender or source of a message, the encoded message that the sender intends to send to the targeted receiver, the medium used to distribute the message, the decoded message that is received and interpreted by the targeted receiver, and finally the feedback response the receiver transmits to the sender, reflecting his or her reaction to the message received. The model suggests that communication is an ongoing process, with feedback to the sender acting to drive the next round of strategic effort so as to either repeat or modify what was communicated previously. Often repetition of the message is needed because of noise, that is, any disturbance in the environment that prevents the receiver from fully receiving the intended message.

2. **Explore the similarities and differences between consumer and organizational buying processes.**
   Both the consumer and organizational buying processes follow similar steps, which logically resemble the management decision-making process. After all, the whole point of the process is to make a good personal buying decision or one for the organization. In either situation, the decision is driven by the desire to optimally satisfy needs or wants through the particular buying decision

that is being taken. The sequence of steps is (1) problem or need recognition and defining specifics, (2) search for information, (3) selection and evaluation of alternative choices, (4) selection of a purchase, and (5) after-purchase evaluation.

3. **Examine the sources of influence on buyer behavior and decision-making.**
Influences on buyer behavior fall into three primary categories: social, personal, and psychological factors. Social factors are cultural and social influences on individual behavior; these can include an individual's social roles and the influence of family, peers, opinion leaders, and reference groups. Personal factors are those general characteristics that are closely associated with the individual buyer; they can be categorized as demographic, lifestyle, and situational. Psychological factors include general types of behavioral influences that are widely shared by individuals regardless of any individual characteristics they may have, such as their demographic or lifestyle circumstances. Psychological factors that influence human behavior include motivation, perception, learning, attitude, personality, and self-concept.

4. **Explore a framework for understanding moment-to-moment online behavior.**
This chapter presented a series of models based on value-expectancy theories in an attempt to provide a framework for understanding why an online visitor to a website chooses to make the next selection that he or she makes. Value-expectancy theories are based on the belief that the individual rationally weighs the advantageous and disadvantageous outcomes associated with a specific behavior and the expectancy that each outcome will occur as a result of her or his behavior. In other words, the individual asks him- or herself, "What is the likely outcome of this behavior, and how valuable is it to me?" The individual is expected to maximize the value of that decision by choosing the behavior that represents the greatest measure of outcome benefit or the least amount of loss. The theory of reasoned action is a value-expectancy model in which outcomes, beliefs, expectancies, the strength of the beliefs, and the opinions of socially influential others are organized into two groups, or factors, that predict the behavior. Self-regulatory models regard behavior as being goal directed; that is, an individual's behavior is activated in order to achieve a perceived desirable goal. Action is taken to close the perceived gap between what is and what is desired. A feedback mechanism actively compares the individual's present circumstances with the desired future state and activates behaviors that work toward eliminating the perceived discrepancy in reality. Understanding is therefore achieved by identifying the goals and the processes connected with the behaviors undertaken by individuals to reach these goals. According to action control theory, whether a current behavior intention will be carried out depends on how difficult it is to carry out the behavior relative to the efficiency of the self-regulatory processes involved. The difficulty of carrying out the behavior is determined by the strength of the external forces working against the behavior, such as social norms; the strength of the internal forces working against the behavior, such as competing action tendencies; and the individual's predisposition toward

change-prevention (state-oriented) or change-inducing (action-oriented) behavior.

1. Explain the communication process in terms of the flow of information from a sender to a receiver.
2. How is the Internet like other media? How is it different?
3. What is feedback?
4. Describe the steps involved in the consumer and organizational buying processes.
5. Referring to the categories described in the text, which sources would be likely to influence a manager's decision whether to advertise a firm on the Internet?

1. Why is it so important to know how the receiver is likely to decode a message?
2. How are the consumer and organizational buying processes similar? How are they different?
3. Discuss the main sources of influence on buyer behavior and decision-making.
4. Discuss the basic concepts involved in the value-expectancy model and their ability to explain individual online behavior.
5. What are some competing behavior intentions that might be at work while an individual is searching a website?

**Building
Skills
for Career
Success**

EXPLORING THE INTERNET

The Stanford Research Institute Consulting–Business Intelligence (SRIC–BI) (**www.sric-bi.com**) group manages the now famous VALS (Values and Lifestyles) survey, which was first developed in the 1970s by Arnold Mitchell. Mitchell created VALS to explain changing American values and lifestyles. In 1989, VALS was redesigned so consumers would be segmented on the basis of enduring personality traits rather than social values that change over time. The VALS (Values and Lifestyles) survey, which categorizes U.S. adult consumers into mutually exclusive groups based on their psychology and several key demographics, is probably one of the best-known surveys of its type. It can provide students with a great deal of understanding of how large-scale surveys are designed and their results interpreted. The survey organizes respondents into psychographic types and identifies specific attitude statements that have a strong correlation with a variety of consumer preferences in products and media. Recent research by SRIC–BI (based in Menlo Park, California) has helped to explain attitudes toward technologies and the Internet. You can contribute to their database of responses and learn about the VALS survey at (**www.sric-bi.com**).

ASSIGNMENT

1. Describe your impressions when taking the VALS survey questionnaire.
2. What are the segment types or categories that VALS has identified?
3. Which segment type are you?
4. How would you describe your online behavior?
5. Are other students in your class who have the same segment type as you similar to you online?

DEVELOPING CRITICAL THINKING SKILLS

The online communication process model presented in this chapter provides a guided structure for explaining the flow of information between a website and the target audience. Select a website you are familiar with and consider the communication effort it directs at viewers.

ASSIGNMENT

1. Identify the website you have chosen and describe its likely target viewer.
2. Prepare a report that describes the communication process, using the steps in the model.

BUILDING TEAM SKILLS

The model of the consumer and organizational buying process that is presented in this chapter provides a structure for explaining how individuals and organizational decision-makers make their purchases. Select a product that all of the members of your team would normally be motivated to purchase, such as a laptop computer or cellular telephone. Make a group decision to purchase the product that satisfies the most number of people.

ASSIGNMENT

1. Using the model as a guide, prepare a report that describes how your group arrived at the purchase decision.
2. What were some of the most influential factors that determined the choice?

RESEARCHING DIFFERENT CAREERS

Online behavioral research is an emerging field of specialized study. Social scientists such as psychologists and sociologists are likely to lead the research effort to understand and predict online behaviors. Management research will also have to expand its traditional limits of study to look at how employees communicate using rapidly emerging technologies.

ASSIGNMENT

1. Describe the sort of work social scientists do that is related to online behaviors.
2. Describe one emerging work-environment problem that might require the professional services that social scientists provide.

IMPROVING COMMUNICATION SKILLS

Using one of the value-expectancy models presented in the chapter, conduct a survey to measure and predict the likely behavior of your entire class. To do this, just calculate average scores with the model you use for analysis. For instance, you might try to predict whether or not the class would book travel reservations online using Expedia.com.

ASSIGNMENT

1. Which model did you choose to use? Why?
2. Prepare a report that explains the results you derived from the survey, using the model structure to help communicate your thinking.

Exploring Useful Websites

These websites provide information related to the topics discussed in the chapter. You can learn more by visiting them online and examining their current data.

1. The Media Metrix division of ComScore Networks (**www.comscore.com**), Nielsen/NetRatings (**www.nielsen-netratings.com**), and Gomez (**www.gomez.com**) are among a growing group of research organizations that collect data from Internet users.

2. Expedia.com (**www.expedia.com**) is Microsoft's online travel center.

3. The Stanford Research Institute Consulting–Business Intelligence (SRIC-BI) (**www.sric-bi.com**) group manages the now famous VALS (Values and Lifestyles) survey.

4. Greenfield Online Inc. (**www.greenfieldonline.com**) is a research firm.

Implementing the e-Business Plan

In **Module III,** we join the strategic thinking concepts examined thus far to the specific *marketing, management,* and *financial* plans of action. These three functional components are universally recognized as the core foundations for any strategic business plan. Therefore, we incorporate each of these subject matter areas into our study of the design and creation of the complete e-business plan while examining related issues that affect e-business strategy. Additionally, each chapter can help to guide e-business planners toward the development of detailed answers to questions in each of these core subject areas. The final chapter in this unit concludes our discussion of the entire planning process by looking at how the e-business plan can be integrated into an organization's current structure, and then controlled, measured, and evaluated for future decision-making.

chapter 8

Creating the Marketing Mix

INSIDE
e-business

Office Depot—Creating Online Business Communities

When Office Depot Inc. of Delray Beach, Florida, was founded in 1986 it had only a single retail outlet to serve the office supply needs in the Fort Lauderdale vicinity. Today, it is the world's largest seller of office products and an industry leader in every distribution channel, including stores, direct mail, contract delivery, the Internet, and business-to-business electronic commerce. Office Depot can serve its customers 24 hours a day, 7 days a week, anywhere in the world. Customers can shop for more than 14,000 products—anything from furniture to paper supplies—by phone, fax, or the Internet and at 1,020 retail stores in nine countries. Most people know that Amazon.com (**www.amazon.com**) is the biggest online retailer, but some might be surprised to learn that Office Depot is the second biggest. Its online retail operations, located at **www.officedepot.com**, were established in 1998 to complement its existing direct mail catalog, telephone call centers, and retail outlets, and today generate about $1 billion of sales—at a profit.

Office Depot already had good relationships with customers and suppliers and had in existence proven logistical distribution (fulfillment) systems made up of its own vehicle delivery and warehousing network. As a result, the addition of Internet retailing was not as difficult as it would probably have been for an entirely new firm, which would have faced the multiple tasks required to create an infrastructure from scratch. For Office Depot, the Internet was an additional tool to serve its existing and growing customer base and was readily integrated into the existing business plan, which had already been tested by years of experience.

The website not only provides convenient online shopping for busy customers but is also an online community where customers are encouraged to create their own websites, promote their businesses, and network with potential customers. Managed in collaboration with Microsoft's bCentral (**www.bcentral.com**), the site provides businesses with a rich selection of information through posted articles and links to other useful sites that provide such things as guides for writing business plans, research, and so forth.

Rather than just providing another convenient method for placing orders, **www.officedepot.com** gives customers additional reasons to return to the website. As a result, the brand recognition, which was strong from the start because of Office Depot's long-established retail and catalog distribution system, has been successfully transferred to the Internet, offering an important lesson for other firms seeking to develop successful Internet strategies. Furthermore, the website provides the firm with additional opportunities for nurturing customer goodwill through value-adding informational services that might be tied to partnerships with vendors of office products and services. An endorsement by Office Depot can assure customers that products with lesser-known brand names are to be trusted and represent good value for the money—otherwise Office Depot would not be offering them to its valued customers.

This transparent cooperative marketing strategy between an established and trusted Internet brand that can deliver many potential customers and firms with lesser-known brand names that are seeking customers is likely to produce better results than could be generated by Internet advertisements alone. We are likely to see the continued use of this strategy, in which an established and well-recognized brand like Office Depot manages its website so as to develop an online community of attractive shoppers for vendors of the products it markets. Instead of buyers just searching the Web for products and services from any site, we will probably see trusted brands like Office Depot serving as the endorsing gateway for buyers who want assurances about what they are actually buying and from whom.[1]

So far in this text, we have explored what might be called the *macro level* of topics related to e-business strategic thinking and planning. Beginning with this chapter, we will turn our attention to the *micro level,* where planning decisions are made within an individual firm. We will start by exploring the "nuts-and-bolts" decision-making process that takes place in strategic marketing and ways in which e-business considerations can be accommodated as part of overall planning. As we do this, the guiding structure that firms should follow to develop effective marketing strategies within the e-business plan will become evident.

The **marketing management process** is the comprehensive term used to refer to the ongoing planning, organizing, and controlling of marketing activities that the personnel at all levels of a firm are engaged in. This includes **e-marketing**, or those activities that are mainly associated with the use of the Internet. Although the marketing management process is by definition a continuous series of activities, new projects, such as Office Depot's web initiative, must begin somewhere. Logically, a firm needs to first identify potential markets and then select those customers that will be targeted by its marketing effort. Then a marketing mix of strategies related to product, price, place, and promotion is developed in order to successfully reach each targeted group. This chapter will examine the steps in the marketing management process that are central to the preparation of an e-business plan.

Identifying and Describing Potential Markets

marketing management process

The comprehensive term for the ongoing planning, organizing, and controlling of marketing activities that the personnel at all levels of a firm are engaged in.

e-marketing

Those marketing management activities that are mainly associated with the use of the Internet.

market

A group of customers with a common need or desire to acquire some product and that represents an estimated amount of dollar or unit sales over some period of time.

At the heart of any good business plan are well-thought-out, detailed answers to basic marketing questions. e-Business planners need to first identify and then select markets of potential buyers that will be the targets of their strategic effort. An important consideration for planners who are considering an online strategy to complement their existing business is whether the market they can reach online is fundamentally made up the same people the firm is presently reaching through its bricks-and-mortar operation. In some cases, a firm may be reaching out to new markets that are geographically dispersed and quite different in a variety of ways from the customers it serves locally or in its physical stores. The more complex the differences between these two markets, the more challenging it will be to develop strategies that will appeal to each targeted group. For instance, besides the obvious differences in language usage, a website selling a product like clothing or footwear must be sure to give sizes in the forms that are used in the different markets around the world. But designing a website that can successfully communicate to each market and cater to individual online behavior raises additional challenges for online vendors far greater than simply assuring culturally appropriate size references.

Defining Broad Markets

A **market** is characteristically defined by customers who have a common need or desire to acquire some product and who represent an estimated amount of dollar or unit sales over some period of time. For example, we might describe the market for high-speed Internet service access in terms of all the individuals and organizations, including businesses and governments, that desire fast Internet connection services. According to a report by Jupiter Research, increased competition between cable and DSL providers will cause the broadband market to explode, with access expected to more than double to more than 46 million households in the United States by 2008, up from 21.5 million at the end of 2003.[2]

Firms like Cisco Systems, Nortel Networks, and others whose sales of products and services are directly linked to the growth of this market adjust their strategic plans based on an estimate of the current number of broadband subscribers and the expected market growth over the next few years. For firms like Cisco, the market is primarily made up of telecommunications firms that use Cisco's computer products to deliver high-speed service to individual customers, as well as larger organizations that need Cisco's products to handle these connections and deliver data to the individual users connected to the organization's local area network (LAN). Cisco Systems' sales are considered bellwethers by other firms in the industry, and announcements that Cisco intends to either expand or reduce the production or inventories of its products can trigger an industrywide response by competitors and other firms selling related products.

consumer markets
Markets composed of individuals making purchases for their own use.

In broad terms, markets are classified by the type of buyer making the purchase decision. **Consumer markets** are composed of individuals making purchases for their own use, whereas **organizational markets** are those composed of businesses, governments, the military, nonprofit groups, and any other group in which purchasing is done by an individual or a committee on behalf of the entire organization. British children's author J. K. Rowling made good use of the Internet to launch her international marketing effort for *Harry Potter and the Goblet of Fire*. The book launch became an event, enjoying unheard-of advance sales of 5.3 million copies in its first international print run. Many of these sales took place through Amazon.com and Barnesandnoble.com by customers who ordered online and had the books shipped as gifts to children for their summertime reading.[3]

organizational markets
Markets composed of businesses, governments, the military, nonprofit groups, and any other group in which purchasing is done by an individual or a committee on behalf of the entire organization.

On the other hand, Dell Computer built its online B2B business by first serving the growing number of technically knowledgeable organizational buyers and only then, more recently, making an effort to appeal to the individual consumer. The decision to increase its penetration of the consumer market likely follows from Dell's expanded product selection, which by 2004 included MP3 players, flat-panel TV screens, and other consumer electronic products.[4]

market segments
Identifiable groups of customers within larger consumer or organizational markets that share characteristics such as a common lifestyle or demographic.

Market segments are identifiable groups of customers within the larger consumer or organizational markets that share characteristics such as a common lifestyle or demographic. For example, we have identified the market for iVillage.com as being a community of women who are brought together online by shared interests in health education, financial issues, lifestyles, and so forth. A careful examination of the attractiveness of the market segments that make up a larger market helps firms select and develop the mix of marketing strategies that it will use to cater to specific customers' interests and needs. Marketers use segmentation criteria to help define these segments.

Using Market Segmentation Criteria

The principal consumer segmentation criteria (also referred to as *variables* or *factors*) that firms use to define market segments are demographic, geographic, psychographic, and behavioristic criteria. Regardless of the primary market the firm intends to focus on, segmenting the broad market using these basic descriptive criteria will help it create a clearer understanding of the identity of each group of potential customers within that market.

Demographic criteria reflect the descriptive characteristics of consumers, such as their age, gender, family status and size, social class, religion, occupation, educational level, and so forth. For example, families that can afford a home computer and high-speed Internet access are likely to have a higher-than-average income. The parents are likely to have higher levels of education and to place a higher value on the need to use computers and the Internet to improve their children's academic performance. *Geographic* criteria describe where individuals are physically located, the density of the local population, climatic conditions, and so forth. Cost-effectiveness considerations suggest that densely populated urban areas are likely to receive fiber-optic cables and other high-speed infrastructure installations from telecommunication firms like WorldCom and AT&T before less densely populated suburban and rural areas do. *Psychographic* criteria include lifestyle, personality traits, and psychological factors such as motivation. For example, part of the personal lifestyle statement for many Internet users is to have the latest computer gadgets and technology. This psychological characteristic generally leads these people to want the fastest Internet connection service available. This segment can be trusted to be the first to graduate to the latest high-speed service as new technology is introduced into their geographic market. Finally, *behavioristic* criteria can be thought of in terms of how individuals use a product or service, such as heavy versus light usage; their intended purpose for using the product; and the benefits they seek. One might assume that heavy users of the Internet, as defined by the amount of time spent uploading and downloading data like music files, are more likely to be customers for high-speed access because of its benefits: faster data transfer rates, greater work productivity, and less frustration caused by waiting for screen displays.

The principal criteria used to define large organizational market segments are similar to those used to segment consumer markets. They may include geographic, type, size, and product usage variables. For example, Dell Computer manufactures Internet computer servers for large, high-usage firms as well as lower-capacity units. Each machine is designed to match the different needs of a particular market segment, such as directing e-mail within an organization or serving up content files to web browsers who have come to a site in search of information.

However, the conventional categorical variables such as industry type, size, and location generally do little to explain or predict how businesses make their decisions. Instead, it might be more useful to segment organizational markets into groups by using clearly identifiable characteristics related to each group's willingness to spend funds on new technologies, attitude and progress toward using new technologies, and buying style. Forrester Research Inc. of Cambridge, Massachusetts, has developed a new system for segmenting the market, for predicting how and why businesses make their technology buying decisions, and for determining what decisions they will make. Based on a survey of more than 1,000 senior business and information technology executives of firms with revenues greater than $1 billion, the firm's *Business Technographics's* segmentation focuses on three key dimensions of e-business culture: risk tolerance, executive commitment, and buying style. A combination of these dimensions can identify a segment that might, for example, comprise more risk-tolerant buyers of newer technology, who have strong backing from executives and are supported by a coordinated buying process for products like supply-chain and wireless applications. Other segments might be slow to adopt new technologies but maintain a coordinated buying process for new products. To market successfully, vendors need to know which segments they are dealing with and then use appropriate strategies for each one—regardless of whether the market segments are consumer or organizational.[5]

Defining Markets According to Size

After segmenting the broad market into identifiable segments, planners will then be able to organize and rank them in order of size and potential sales value. A **mass market** is characteristically large, with little, if any, important differentiation among its segments and offers great potential for revenue generation. A **niche market**, on the other hand, is smaller in size and more specialized in character. A niche market tends to encompass consumers who share a single lifestyle characteristic or issue, such as teenagers interested in science and technology or weekend campers in Wisconsin. We can distinguish, then, between e-business strategies that employ websites that appeal to a mass market of teenagers and those that appeal to the more narrowly defined niche market of teenagers who are motivated to learn more about science and technology, career choices, and so forth.

The potential for revenue enhancement gained from serving a mass market tends to attract many competitors who have different market share strategies for drawing customers. For example, Time Warner's AOL division is the largest Internet service provider in a mass market of customers who seek basic connection and services. To compete with AOL , competitors will have to offer something outstanding to draw away satisfied customers. Time Warner has differentiated itself from its competitors by offering access to online content that other providers do not have. Meanwhile, some competitors have responded by offering lower-priced services to draw customers who are more attracted by cost savings than by exclusive online content.

On the other end of the size continuum, the Internet has lowered the barriers to identifying globally dispersed niche markets of customers, who now have a powerful medium for communicating and distributing a wide array of products and services. As we have emphasized throughout this text, the Internet has become the "great equalizer." It allows smaller businesses to compete on a global scale and niche markets of customers to receive better service from firms by using web tools such as websites, e-commerce sales presentations, and so forth. For example, BackcountryStore.com (**www.backcountrystore.com**), which was set up with only

mass market
A market that is large, has little, if any, important differentiation among its segments, and offers great potential for revenue generation.

niche market
A market that is smaller in size and more specialized in character than a mass market.

$2,000 by two self-described ski bums—six-time U.S. Nordic ski-jumping champion, Jim Holland, and former editor of *Powder* magazine, John Bresee— has been profitable for five straight years and generated an estimated $15 million of sales in 2003. The number-two site for online outdoor gear, after REI.com (**www.rei.com**), BackcountryStore.com credits its success to the fact that it serves the niche market of trail enthusiasts as well as other more conventional lovers of outdoor adventuring but also to the fact that it makes newly arrived merchandise available on the firm's website within the hour, relies on data-mining search requests and web traffic logs instead of conducting more costly surveys, and uses analytical services from Atomz (**www.atomz.com**) and WebSideStory (**www.WebSideStory.com**) to determine how customers navigate through the site toward their purchase decision. Furthermore, instead of competing on price, the firm distinguishes itself by paying fellow ski bums with free merchandise that they have personally tested. They can then serve as phone representatives, answering questions from customers who are looking for personal endorsements from the experts.[6]

Although North America is still the dominant commercial market in the world, its market share continues to shrink as Internet usage in other areas grows. According to the study "A Nation Online: How Americans Are Expanding Their Use of the Internet," published by the *National Telecommunications and Information Administration* and the *Economics and Statistics Administration,* more than half of the American population, approximately 140 million people, now uses the Internet regularly, and usage is growing at the rate of 2 million people every month. Furthermore, although the most popular use for the Internet is still e-mail, which is used by 45 percent of the overall population, approximately one-third of Americans use the Internet to search for product and service information (36 percent, up from 26 percent in 2000). Among Internet users, 39 percent are making online purchases, and 35 percent are searching for health information. According to a report by Jupiter Research (**www.jupiterresearch.com**) U.S. online retail sales were expected to reach $65 billion in 2004, and grow by a compound annual rate of 17 percent through 2008 to more than $117 billion—rising from $540 to $780 per buyer. The report also suggests that the online buying population will grow by 14 percent in 2004, representing 30 percent of the U.S. population. By 2008, one-half of the population is expected to be making purchases online. Although consumers look for items not readily available in their local market, they also want to trust the retailer from whom they purchase. So, according to the study, small businesses are advised to be sure that they have legitimate and very strong vendor ratings wherever consumers may find their products, such as on comparison-shopping sites. Furthermore, small businesses are advised to add consumer feedback sections to their sites to help build their credibility with shoppers.[7]

But the trend is also clearly toward more international business growth as well as the expansion of the commercial use of the Internet. More than half of all the half-billion Internet users worldwide logged on from outside the United States in 2003. Furthermore, China, with 79.5 million Web surfers is now the second-largest country of users after the U.S., having grown 34 percent in 2003, according to a report by the China Internet Network Information Center (CNNIC) of Beijing. China has only three Internet service providers—ChinaLink Networks, Netaway, and

VPM Internet Services, Inc.—and the majority of Internet use comes from dial-up connections to the home and about 45 percent from Internet cafes scattered throughout the country. Also, nearly 25 percent of the country's Internet access comes from leased lines, while about 10 percent of users have a broadband connection. Meanwhile, European consumer e-commerce is expected to grow from about €5 billion in 1998 to over €400 billion in 2003 and an estimated €100 billion by 2008. Germany is expected to account for the largest portion of e-commerce revenues in 2008 at €25.8 billion, closely followed by the UK (€24.3 billion), then France with €16.6 billion, Italy (€6.5 billion), Spain (€4.6 billion), the Netherlands (€4.5 billion), Sweden (€2.9 billion), Belgium (€2.1 billion), Switzerland (€2.0 billion), and Denmark (€1.7 billion). Japanese online buying is expected to expand twentyfold over five years, from $3.2 billion in 1999 to $63.4 billion in 2004. Whether these predictions turn out to be overly optimistic or not, the numbers clearly suggest a belief in increased opportunities for firms that have an online global capability.[8]

Analyzing Markets and Targeting Strategies

The process that leads firms to decide which market segments to target and which to ignore requires that management be able to weigh risks and rewards and assess the firm's likelihood of succeeding at each available choice. After a satisfactory amount of analysis, an overall targeting strategy will emerge that reflects the number of markets the firm will target and the level of sales expected for each. We will begin this section of the chapter by examining a popular analytical framework for developing strategies that lead to selecting and targeting markets.

Using SWOT Analysis

SWOT analysis

An acronym for a process of organizational self-study and evaluation in which a firm focuses on its overall *strengths* and *weaknesses,* along with the *opportunities* and *threats* it faces in the marketplace.

SWOT analysis is an acronym for a process of organizational self-study and evaluation in which a firm focuses on its overall *strengths* and *weaknesses,* along with the *opportunities* and *threats* it faces in the marketplace. A SWOT analysis should be undertaken before market selection decisions are made so the firm is better able to choose those opportunities that offer it the greatest reward relative to the accompanying risks. In essence, marketers should select opportunities that fit well with the firm's strengths and increase the chances that the firm will be successful. At the same time, marketers need to be vigilant and guard against threats from competitors that might take advantage of the firm's weaknesses in the marketplace. Eastman Kodak, Canon, Hewlett-Packard, and many other digital technology firms have recognized the opportunities presented to them by the growth of digital photography. According to Info Trends Research Group of Boston, in 2000 consumers spent about $1.2 billion on digital cameras, which allow them to edit their photographs, create online albums, print pictures on their own printers, and e-mail images over the Internet. However, a Gartner Group Dataquest study predicted that digital camera penetration would reach about 17 percent of U.S. households by the end of 2002 and exceed 50 percent by 2006. In fact, cameras and camera-cellphones sales have soared, creating opportunities for firms like Sunnydale, California-based SanDisk Corporation (**www.sandisk.com**), which makes the ubiquitous flash memory cards used in digital cameras. According to Photo Marketing Association International of Jackson, Michigan, digital camera sales were expected to surpass regular camera sales for the first time in 2003. Although rapid growth in digital cameras sales only began in 1998, they were expected to exceed 12 million units in 2003, about half of all cameras sold, and grow to more than 17 million units in 2004. Meanwhile, camera-cellphones' global sales in 2004 were expected to reach 93 million units, a 63 percent jump over 2003 sales. This suggested that consumers were also more than just accepting of the greater visual communications capacity provided by the devices and that there were opportunities for the telecommunications industry and others who could capitalize on the trend.[9]

Smart business strategists can use SWOT analysis to help them identify who their target market should be as well as the viability of catering to any particular segment in the larger market. For example, suppose a well-known print-based publisher like the National Geographic Society was considering the introduction of an online publication focusing on science and technology. The firm enjoys a strong reputation for its educational publications across a broad range of readership. Suppose preliminary research suggested that there are many market segments that currently are not being well served in this area and might be receptive to the effort. For example, a publication dedicated to the needs of secondary school children and one aimed at community college students might be only two of many specific market segment possibilities. The task for marketers is to select the best one.

Before committing major resources to any online effort, however, the organization needs to determine whether there are a sufficient number of potential viewers in the target market to make the project viable. Furthermore, given that there are many potential niche markets, it is important for the organization to conduct research studies to establish the range of possible market segments and the potential benefits that can accrue by serving each one before it commits to any individual market segment. Using a SWOT analysis framework, the organization might conclude that it has many *strengths*, such as strong brand recognition among both students and educators, a knowledgeable staff that is capable of handling this new project, and a large inventory of multimedia content that it can use for the intended online publication. However, *weaknesses* also exist, such as limited experience working in an online environment, challenges related to the product's design, and the difficulty of setting prices given that online users are not used to paying for information. Finally, there are the *threats* from other publications that might replicate the design of this publication and fragment the market further. Since barriers to entry are weaker in the online marketplace than in the print world, National Geographic can expect many more competitors to consider entering the market. All of these factors must be properly weighed so management can move forward with a fuller awareness of the risks and benefits associated with the *opportunities* it may select.

Targeting Strategies

concentrated targeting strategy
A marketing strategy that focuses on only one market from among many.

After identifying each of the available market segments and conducting a SWOT analysis, a firm may opt for a **concentrated targeting strategy** and choose to focus only on one market. The selected single target market might be a niche market that has little appeal for larger competitors, thus providing a good opportunity for a firm that wishes to be left alone. Selling prices in such a market might be higher than they would be in larger markets where competitors vie to attract customers. Concentrating on a neglected niche market is often considered a good way to get started in business and is sometimes the choice of entrepreneurs. Most online communities like iVillage.com are examples of e-business start-ups that were looking for a way to cater to the growing number of niche markets that wanted information, products, and services that are tailored to their needs and delivered to them through the Internet. Interestingly, many of these firms gradually came to offer traditional printed versions of their products to customers who wanted to view this content at times and places where computer access was not available. Similarly, television show personalities like Oprah Winfrey have found new product development, distribution, and promotion opportunities online through sites like **www.oprah.com** and **www.oxygen.com.**

undifferentiated targeting strategy
A marketing strategy that basically treats everyone as a member of one mass target market.

A second choice for marketers is an **undifferentiated targeting strategy**, which basically treats everyone as a member of one mass target market. The argument made by this strategy is that although individuals have different characteristics, they behave in fundamentally the same way when it comes to the particular product or service. For example, for the most part Internet search engines and directories are designed to be easily manageable and intuitively navigated by a wide range of people seeking information. The hierarchical structure and layout of, say, Yahoo.com is consistent regardless of which branch in its directory the user is scanning. So whether you are looking for fishing lodges in Wisconsin or wedding gifts, the site navigation tools allow you to comfortably explore all of Yahoo!'s lists.

differentiated targeting strategy
A marketing strategy in which more than one identifiable market segment is selected and a unique mix of marketing strategies is tailored to each segment.

A third strategy for selecting market segments is perhaps the most common of the three. A **differentiated targeting strategy** involves the selection of more than one identifiable market segment and the creation of a unique mix of marketing strategies tailored to each segment. Cable News Network (CNN) serves several identifiable market segments such as business, sports, and other specialized news services that are linked to its main website at **www.cnn.com.**

Developing Sales Forecasts

As part of the market selection process, management will need to estimate the market potential of each market segment, or the total amount of sales that might be available to all firms competing in that segment. A segment that has forecasted sales of $10 million annually is going to be more attractive than a smaller niche market that might only provide $1 million. Obviously, the calculated value can vary according to many factors and to the methods used. It should be said that as fundamental as sales estimation is to the entire strategic e-business planning process, it is at best an art, not a science, and is open to wide margins of error. To help them plan, many firms have taken to using customer-driven websites. For example, to satisfy its customers' needs for information, Ford Motor Company has joined up with Microsoft's website (**http://autos.msn.com/**) to help consumers find decision-critical information about Ford's products and dealers from the comfort, convenience, and privacy of their own homes and offices. Ford and Microsoft hope to transform the site into a complete build-to-order system that will link customer orders for options directly into Ford's supplier system. This way, customers get the products they want, and Ford reduces the risks associated with guessing the size of the inventories its dealers should stock.[10]

Some of the key factors that can influence sales forecasts include the e-business model adopted by the firm, the number and types of revenue streams employed, the number and types of customers in the market segment selected, the firm's mix of marketing strategies and its allocation of resources, the reactions by competitors to compete with and counter the firm's marketing effort, and the changes in the economic and other environmental forces that were presented in Chapter 2 of this text.

Popular categories of forecasting methods include the *executive judgment* of experienced or knowledgeable experts whose opinion is trusted; *surveys* of customers' behaviors, which can indicate future sales and responses to the firm's marketing effort; *time series analysis* of historical sales data so the firm or industry can establish sales trends and cycles; *regression analysis* to find the mathematical relationship between historical sales and a predictive factor or factors such as the number of families with high-speed Internet access or changing levels of disposable family income; and *market tests,* in which products and services are actually marketed on a test basis to help assess the overall success of a national market launch. In general, firms are likely to use more than one method of forecasting to help them form an estimate they can have greater confidence in.

Let's use a simple example to illustrate several factors that can influence a sales forecast and the forecasting methods that might be used. Take the case of a firm that wishes to establish an online professional journal for engineers. The firm currently publishes several professional journals in print form, and it believes, based on surveys of current subscribers and focus group discussions, that an opportunity exists to create an online journal that will interest about 30 percent of the subscribers to the firm's current printed journals. The firm believes that it can reach a potential global audience of 100,000 stable subscribers after three years of marketing effort. This figure is derived by looking at other niche publications, both online and in print; at surveys of subscribers to competing professional journals; and at focus group studies of potential subscribers to assess their willingness to subscribe, the price they would be willing to pay, and the content they wish to read. Current economic and competitive conditions suggest that a niche publication could be established with a subscriber base as low as 10,000 readers, and research and opinions expressed by those familiar with the current competitive situation suggest that the trend is clearly toward specialized online publications. If subscribers were to pay $100 annually for access to journal content, as 95 percent of those surveyed indicated they would, then the market potential would conceivably total $10 million. This figure would be modified to reflect any advertising revenues that might be part of the firm's e-business model and any other factors that could affect the initial sales forecast.

e-BUSINESS insight

Marketing Health-Care Information

According to a recent study by AOL and the journal *American Demographics,* the Internet dominates traditional media as the source of information for shoppers before they make any online or traditional bricks-and-mortar purchases. And according to a Harris Interactive study, approximately 100 million Americans now seek medical and health-care advice, treatments, and the latest research information through websites. Whereas in the past people might have consulted their family and friends and sought literature in their local public library or bookstore in addition to their doctor, today the Internet is regarded as a vault of supplementary information, resources, and referrals. These web users tend to be older than the general population and to have a medical condition or have a family member who does.

According to a 2003 study by the Washington research group Pew Internet & American Life Project, 80 percent of American Internet users have searched for a health-related topic online, up from 62 percent of Internet users who said they went online to research health topics in 2001. People mostly searched for information about a specific disease or medical problem (63 percent) or a particular medical treatment or procedure (47 percent). However, they were also interested in diet, nutrition, and vitamins (44 percent); exercise or fitness information (36 percent); prescription or over-the-counter drugs (34 percent); alternative treatments (28 percent); health insurance (25 percent); depression, anxiety, or stress (21 percent); and a particular doctor or hospital (21 percent). The study indicates that looking for health or medical information is the third most popular activity online, behind e-mail at 93 percent of the Internet population and researching a product or service before purchase, at 83 percent.

In response to these developments, pharmaceutical firms like Pfizer and Johnson & Johnson are using their websites to market their prescription drugs directly to potential patients, who they hope will visit their doctors armed with knowledge about their condition and the brand-named treatments available. Customization of websites in support of a firm's marketing activities is likely to expand to other industries as buyers seek the information sites that can improve their ability to make informed decisions about important choices.

Question for discussion: How would you expect a business decision-maker in the health-care industry to respond to this information?[11]

Online Product Development and Thinking

After completing the market selection process and identifying the firm's target market or markets, management will need to develop a full mix of marketing strategies to achieve the sales forecast estimate for each target market. These strategies fall into the four categories familiar to marketing students—product, price, place, and promotion—which are generally referred to as the *4Ps of marketing.* All new strategies should be developed in conjunction with existing plans so as to build a consistent overall business plan for the firm. To begin developing marketing strategies, management should logically first focus its attention on understanding the nature of the product or service to be sold, then make pricing, place, and promotion decisions.

Defining the Scope of Online Products and Services

We define a *product* as anything tangible—or, in the case of a *service,* intangible—that a firm provides to customers in an exchange. What is given in exchange is usually money, but it might also be a customer's time and attention. For example, websites using an advertising e-business model, such as Yahoo!, provide an Internet search facility in exchange for the user's willingness to view advertisements placed on his or her screen. Lack of expertise is not a barrier to firms' using the Internet for marketing activities, as a huge online services industry has developed to help them with those areas where they lack resources. For example, according to research by IDC Inc., industry revenues from hosting firms' websites and providing product information for those firms on hosts' computer systems for a monthly fee were expected to grow from $1.8 billion in 2000 to $18.9 billion in 2004.[12]

To understand the motivation for the exchange process firms must recognize that customers buy products and services because they expect they will satisfy purchasers' wants and needs. High-speed Internet access service that slows noticeably during peak periods of demand will disappoint users. They will identify the service as poor in quality and therefore unsatisfactory because their expectations had been created by the service provider's marketing strategies, which promised fast speed always—not most of the time. Before anything else, then, the firm must be clear about what its product or service—or some combination of the two—actually is and what it is not. It must also learn what its customers believe they are being sold and develop strategies that are consistent with those belief systems.

Before we expand on our general understanding of product strategies, let us first examine several special characteristics of those intangible products that we call services. Services may be sold or they may be provided as part of the purchase of a tangible product. However, the Internet lends itself to the sale of a plethora of services, and so we must give special attention to the unique ways in which customers may perceive the delivery of services online. For instance, because services are intangible customers may have greater difficulty assessing their quality and price-value relationship. What one customer may consider excellent service, another might think is mediocre. Just how fast does an Internet service connection need to be for a home-based customer to consider it *fast?* As with tangible products, experts can offer ratings and opinions to help customers evaluate and rank services, but the very nature of services presents unique issues for marketers to consider.

In addition to being intangible, services cannot be stored for later delivery, which presents problems when business activity is high. Since services can often be delivered only by specially trained employees, as with consulting firms that bill for the time their employees spend on a project, the question facing management is whether the current growth in the demand for services is likely to continue. If it is, then the expense of hiring and training more personnel is justified. However, if the growth in volume is a temporary phenomenon that will ease shortly, then expansion would be a mistake. Employees who are not providing billable services for customers are a drain on a firm and are generally released if they cannot be kept working. It is always preferable to minimize the need to reduce staff, but doing so is often a necessary function of properly managed service-oriented firms.

Services, being delivered by people, are also quite difficult to control. A physical product can be evaluated more readily, machinery can be adjusted, and substandard production can be set aside. However, an employee who delivers a specific service on behalf of his or her firm is unlikely to repetitively provide exactly the same service in every respect. To minimize the variations in quality and other deliverables associated with the services being rendered, firms must carefully train and monitor the performance of service employees. Furthermore, the delivery of the service is inseparable from the employee delivering the service—consulting services provided by one employee cannot simply be transferred to another employee if the original employee should happen to leave the firm. People cannot be substituted for one another as readily as can physical products. The quality of the relationship an employee has developed with a customer is paramount in determining the firm's future ability to maintain a long-term working relationship with that customer.

Product Description and Classification Schemes

There are many other ways to describe, define, and classify products that can give firms useful direction for further strategic market development. For example, we can classify products and services in terms of their intended target markets—*consumer* and *organizational*. This classification can be clarified even further if we examine the segmentation criteria that are used to define the markets. An IBM computer server that is designed to rapidly retrieve files and transfer them on demand to users over the Internet is a product that will probably be of interest only to organizational markets. On the other hand, a laptop computer might have market segments in both consumer and organizational markets and require multiple marketing strategies aimed at each segment individually. IBM, Dell Computer, and other manufacturers commonly advertise in daily newspapers in order to reach both markets, but they will also advertise in business and trade journals to reach specific organizational markets in which large-scale purchases are often common. For consumer markets, these firms will target students with back-to-school specials in the autumn and prepare product models that have features and software that are more appealing to students.

Marketers generally speak about three primary classes of consumer products—*convenience, shopping,* and *specialty*—each of which reflects the consumer's attitude toward and view of the purchase. Consumers generally buy *convenience products* expecting to expend little effort and little cash and to encounter little price differentiation among different retail locations. Newspapers and magazines like the *Wall Street Journal* (**www.wsj.com**) and *Business Week* (**www.businessweek.com**) are good examples of a convenience product that is available online as well as at traditional retail stores. Products and services that might be considered exclusively online convenience products may be difficult to identify today, but the trend is clearly toward the development of more such products as well as the continuing migration of traditional convenience products and services to the Internet. Retailers of office supplies such as Office Depot (**www.officedepot.com**) offer their customers added convenience through websites that provide catalog shopping and delivery service. According to eMarketer's U.S. *eBanking Report,* although only 5 to 10 percent of the customer base now uses online services, consumer banking is expected to grow from 12.2 million users in 2001 to 18.3 million in 2004.[13]

Impulse products are a subcategory of convenience products. As the term suggests, they are bought with little time spent on the decision. Pop-up advertisements and banner advertisements promote impulse purchases such as sending flowers to someone or subscribing to a magazine. Often links lead to other *unsought products,* meaning products that the customer was not originally considering and probably would never have considered purchasing had the advertisement not been placed on the screen.

Shopping products require customers to perform some level of information gathering and investigation before making a purchase decision. Most consumer products that are available online are in this category. They are well served by the capacity of the Internet to provide a storehouse of consumer information or a customer service call center to help close sales online. Everything from computers to automobiles can be bought online as firms seek to reach customers through the Internet. In some cases, consumers may simply use the Internet to gather information and narrow their search before selecting certain bricks-and-mortar retail outlets. For instance, using the Internet to examine fashions, furniture, and automobiles is a sensible first stage in the buying process but is no substitute for sampling the product by trying on clothing, sitting on sofas to see how comfortable they actually are, and test driving a car to see how it feels on the road in your neighborhood.

Traditional retailers need to estimate how much of their current customer base and how many new customers their bricks-and-mortar business currently do not serve can be drawn to an online effort. For example, retailers such as Sears, Roebuck and Borders bookshops hope to increase sales by reaching customers who are unable or unwilling to shop at the firms' physical retail store locations. The question at the heart of a strategy in which a bricks-and-mortar firm migrates to the Web is how many current customers will simply transfer their buying to the website. If sales on the website are simply counterbalanced by reduced sales at physical store locations, then there may not be much economic incentive to mount a retail web presence. The whole idea of going ahead with online retailing is to increase the volume of buying by one's current customers and to add new customers who might never shop at the stores. Otherwise, the venture makes no economic sense.

Finally, the Internet is best recognized as a tool to help vendors reach niche markets of customers anywhere in the world who are interested in buying *specialty products,* such as special-effects digital imaging camera equipment or computer hardware and software. Even hard-to-find books that might be available only at specialty book retailers in major cities are readily available online at specialty book sites like Abebooks.com (**www.abebooks.com**). Online sites such as eBay allow buyers and sellers to market just about anything, and they have opened the door to artists seeking a way to sell their own unique works.

Organizational products classes include *raw materials, major equipment, accessory equipment, component parts, process materials, supplies,* and *services. Raw materials* such as wood, steel, and other commodities are used to manufacture products such as furniture and filing cabinets or components of final products such as door handles. Raw materials are sold by grade and are increasingly being sold through web-based contracting sites where firms can post their needs and suppliers can bid to deliver materials accordingly. Firms are also increasingly making use of the Internet to procure other needed organizational products and to create better links with their customers' inventory and warehousing systems. And, as we've discussed elsewhere in the text, firms are increasingly seeking ways to build better relationships with their customers through the Internet by opening their ordering and inventory control systems to suppliers so that operational activities and costs are somewhat transferred to them, freeing employees to focus on generating revenues.

Major equipment includes large capital purchases such as computer systems or manufacturing machinery, whereas *accessory equipment* is not directly involved in the production of the firm's output but may be used to make that output or may be part of the office work environment. *Component parts* are used to complete production (for example, disk drives that are added to a computer that is assembled at one of Dell Computer's plants), and *process materials,* such as specialized resins and glue, are not readily identifiable as components but are incorporated into the manufacturing process. Finally, *supplies,* from photocopier paper to toner cartridges, are continuously needed for the smooth operation of both the manufacturing and administrative areas of the firm.

Product Mix Issues

product mix
The total number of different products that a firm makes available; the term is used to compare the relative variety of the products available from different companies.

The term **product mix** refers to the total number of different products a firm makes available. The term is used to compare the relative variety of the products available from different companies. For example, IBM has a larger product mix than Dell Computer because it produces several models of large-scale computers and supercomputers that are not part of Dell's product mix.

Given the variety of Internet-based products and services to choose from, it is interesting to note that changes are already well underway in the conventional concept of a wholesaler who bundles together a mix of products for a customer. For example, Redmond, Washington–based InfoSpace Inc. works with providers of all sorts of Internet content, from weather services to news and information sites, to put together specific content mixes for customers' sites.[14]

product line
A group of related products that a firm sells.

The related products that a firm sells can be thought of as a **product line**. Both IBM and Dell Computer produce a line of specialized Internet file servers as well as other product lines of personal computers, laptops, workstations, and so forth. Furthermore, we can describe a firm's product mix in terms of how many lines the firm has (the *product mix width*) as well as the number of individual product items within one line (the *product mix depth*). Companies will expand their product mix when they believe that offering more variety will increase customer satisfaction and the firm's profitability. Likewise, management may choose to reduce its product mix depth and seek economies of scale by concentrating on producing only a few models within a product line, but at lower costs. For example, when Nortel Networks Inc. sold off its DSL high-speed production division in 2001, this decision reflected a change in management's view of the value of putting any further resources into an aging line of technology in contrast to focusing entirely instead on the new frontier defined by fiber optics.

Strategically, a firm may choose to market only certain products online because the selling characteristics of these products lend themselves to an online environment better than do the firm's other products. In some cases, it may make strategic sense to select certain products for sale exclusively online, leaving the firm's existing products for sale only inside the firm's physical retail stores. For example, a jewelry retailer like Zales might choose to sell a diamond bracelet exclusively on its website (**www.zales.com**) if it could only secure a limited quantity of the item, making national distribution through its retail stores impossible. Furthermore, the firm might consider the bracelet an excellent choice for an online, highly discounted, promotional collection of jewelry that drives traffic to the website and helps promote its physical retail stores as well.

e-BUSINESS insight

PatsyPie™.com: Developing Brand Awareness for a Niche Market

Pat and her husband, marketing consultant Michael Libling, launched PatsyPie.com (**www.PatsyPie™.com**) in 2003, only one year after they started their home-based small business. After great success selling Pat's own gluten-free specialty baked products, such as biscotti, cookies, and brownies, online through eBay and in Montreal retail bakeries and restaurants, the entrepreneurial couple decided to commit themselves fully to the task of building brand awareness and sales of their products to the estimated one in 133 people in the population who have celiac disease. People with celiac disease cannot tolerate food products containing gluten. If they eat such products, the lining of their small intestine becomes irritated, possibly resulting in weight loss, chronic diarrhea, abdominal swelling, pain, flatulence, itching, rashes, anemia, and other uncomfortable symptoms. Gluten is the "glue" that makes dough sticky and is found in

wheat, rye, barley and oats and, accordingly, all products made from them. For people intolerant to gluten, foods to avoid may include beer, wheat bran, durum, farina, graham flour, semolina, oat bran, malt, and so on. However, rice, corn, soya, arrowroot, potato flour, cornstarch, tapioca, rice bran, cornmeal, bean flours, and buckwheat are all gluten-free. The "trick" is to prepare baked products that use these substitutes for wheat and that are also as comparably appealing in taste and texture as the regular baked products made with wheat. Unfortunately for those unfamiliar with Pat's delicious family-developed and -tested recipes, common baked products from gluten-free competitors are generally disappointing to the palate.

Pat and two of the Liblings' three daughters have celiac disease. Searching for just the right balance of ingredients to satisfy their demanding tastes was an ongoing activity for years, and favorite family recipes were eventually transformed into gluten-free versions that often tasted the same or better than regular wheat-based products. Eventually, word of mouth led bakeries in the neighborhood to request that Pat supply her lovingly prepared products. The idea for PatsyPie™ was born. The competitive advantages of superior quality and taste, that customers and friends shared, convinced Pat and Michael to transfer full-time production to a dedicated bakery and concentrate their energies building their PatsyPie™ brand and developing a wider selection of products to sell.

Although sales through eBay have been satisfactory, the company's concern is that customers view gluten-free products as a commodity rather than as a product deserving of real brand awareness or preference. According to the Liblings, this is probably due to the limited selection, bland taste, and relatively poor quality typical of gluten-free products on the market. The challenge for PatsyPie™, as it is for any start-up business with little public recognition, is to build their superior brand image directly with individual customers and retailers using their community and distribution-channel e-business model.

Competitors in the specialty foods market can reach targeted audiences by advertising on community support websites such as Celiac.com (**www.celiac.com**) and in magazines such as Living Without (**www.livingwithout.com**). The grocery trade can be reached through sites such as Progressive Grocer (**www.progressivegrocer.com**). Furthermore, the company can buy keywords from search engines such as Google.com so their advertising appears on screen anytime someone enters the search keyword *celiac*. The firm's URL, **www.PatsyPie.com,** is displayed on all company packaging, invoices, and correspondence to further promote brand awareness. Pat Libling has published articles, been a guest speaker on radio, and has presented to

patsypie.com

(*Source:* PatsyPie™ is a registered trademark of PatsyPie™ Gluten-Free Bakery [2622-7033 Quebec Inc.]. Website and logo design by Sychowski Communications Inc., Montreal.)

audiences at conferences concerned with celiac disease. These promotional opportunities now provide her with the chance to build brand awareness for PatsyPie™ as well.

Restaurants, coffee bars, grocery stores, and supermarkets are constantly on the lookout for new specialty products that will appeal to their customers. Often, these newer products can contribute more to profitability through the higher profit margins they command because they enjoy a perceived or real difference in the eyes of customers. A clear-plastic container of PatsyPie's biscotti weighs about 250 grams and sells for about $5. This is competitively priced when compared to the prices asked by other online specialty bakers and distributors

such as Glutenfreemall.com, Dietaryshoppe.com, Missroben.com, and others. Research suggests, however, that consumers' purchase decisions are not about the price as much as the perceived quality and taste of the food product. The problem for firms selling products over the Internet is how to provide a sample and deal with disappointed customers. Because taste is so personal, many people are reluctant to buy food products online. To deal with this issue, PatsyPie™ currently guarantees satisfaction by allowing customers to select a substitute product if they are unhappy with their original purchase.

Question for discussion: How else could PatsyPie.com promote and build brand awareness with individual customers as well as distributors?[15]

Understanding Product Strategy Decisions

Many conceptual models exist that can help marketers understand and frame the strategic decisions before them. In this section of the chapter, we will examine the *product life cycle concept, product differentiation*, and *product positioning*, three important and popular conceptual models. We will also examine their utility to planners in an online strategic environment.

Product Life Cycle

product life cycle

A concept that suggests that the "life" span of products follows a pattern of clearly identifiable stages that coincide with changing sales, profits, and environmental selling conditions.

The **product life cycle** concept suggests that the "life" span of products follows a pattern of clearly identifiable stages that coincide with changing sales, profits, and environmental selling conditions. As a product ages and passes from stage to stage, marketing managers need to adjust their plans to reflect the conditions that the product faces in the marketplace and prepare for its inevitable abandonment and replacement with newer products. For example, semiconductor manufacturers like Intel always have new computer chips waiting to be introduced into the marketplace, but they delay the decision to begin production until management believes it is strategically best to shift resources to the newer technology. Several factors might indicate when it's time to make the shift. For example, sales of the older chip may be declining rapidly, indicating that the market is reaching the limits of demand for the current chip, or perhaps that competitors have introduced a better chip and the firm will lose market share if it does not bring out an equivalent product. Intel might also select the time to launch its next chip so as to maintain its image as a technology leader and not a follower. The product life cycle for Intel's Pentium chips averages about two years, which means that its management and customers anticipate new product introductions about every two years.

The product life cycle, as illustrated in Figure 8.1, has four basic stages: *introduction, growth, maturity,* and *decline.* It is important to note that Figure 8.1 cannot reflect the actual duration of each stage, since this will differ for each and every product. The figure merely helps to illustrate the relative relationship of two critical factors: sales and profits.

In the *introduction stage,* a firm will traditionally experience losses, as it is spending more money than it is receiving in sales revenue. Start-up costs associated with infrastructure investments, switchovers to new production, and the promotional campaigns necessary to inform customers are common strains on the resources of a firm launching a new product. Sales may increase quickly if the product is an instant hit with customers, or the firm may be burdened with a longer, more costly start-up period before the critical mass of customers accumulates. At Amazon.com, it took several years before sales reached a level sufficient to cover the costs of establishing the website and warehouse delivery infrastructure that Amazon.com relies on. Microsoft, like many firms today, gives away free access to a new software program or online service until large numbers of customers have grown familiar with them before bringing in a fee-based arrangement. At the other extreme, sales can increase quickly for, say, new software or for a software update that a firm makes available to an established customer base through its website. For example, software firms like Microsoft depend on quickly selling a large number of software upgrades to a significant portion of their customer base, who will generally respond to improved features that offer additional value. This

FIGURE 8.1   The Four Stages of the Product Life Cycle

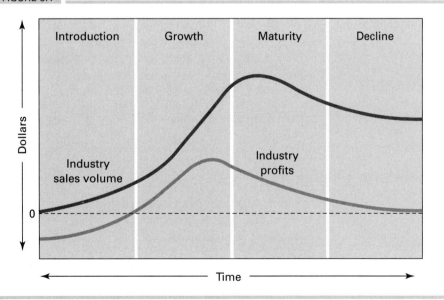

(*Source:* From William M. Pride, Robert J. Hughes, and Jack R. Kapoor, *Business,* Eighth Edition. Copyright © 2005 by Houghton Mifflin Company. Reprinted with permission.)

process is facilitated when the product upgrade can be promoted inexpensively through direct e-mail to the firm's registered customer base and customers can complete the transaction easily by clicking on icons displayed on their screens. The close of the introductory stage is marked by the firm's crossing over from losses to profits.

The Internet is fast becoming an important vehicle for launching new products and is a great equalizer for lesser known brands. For example, Michael Gellert, the author of the philosophical book *The Fate of America—An Inquiry Into National Character,* can be contacted through the book's companion website at **www.the fateofamerica.com.** As well, the site provides sample content for visitors to read and discussion forums that interested readers can use to exchange opinions and arguments about ideas presented in the book.

The *growth stage* is a period of dramatically increasing sales and profits, but also coincides with the entry of new competitors who are drawn by the product's noticeable success during the introductory stage. In addition, during the growth stage there is likely to be more variety in the product mix, and some specialty products that cater to niche markets are likely to emerge. For example, during the growth stage of the wireless communications market, cellular phone makers such as Nokia and Motorola raced to introduce new devices with more features while Research In Motion entered the market with the Blackberry, a smaller and less expensive device that allows mobile users to send and receive e-mail messages. To keep up in an ever more crowded marketplace, manufacturers of cellular phones and hand-held personal digital assistants like Palm have added e-mail communication and camera features to their products, while the Blackberry itself now provides voice as well. Since several products now provide many of the same features, the consumer may determine the best choice based on the service plan that comes with the product and whether he or she plans to use the device mainly for voice or text-based communications.

The *maturity stage* is marked by a steady decline in profits, in which sales reach their peak and then begin to decline. This period can last a long time as customers grapple with the question of how much value continues to be offered by an aging product and firms decide which adjustments need to be made to remain actively involved in this market. Some firms will leave the market to competitors if they feel they have too little to gain in return for the required effort, while others with strong brand recognition may simply cull their product mix and abandon products selectively. Generally speaking, the levels of marketing expenditures and manufacturing costs in the maturity stage will not be as great as in earlier stages, and as a result profits can remain satisfactory for many years. This is also the stage in which mergers or acquisitions among industry competitors is most likely to take place as the industry rationalizes its resources in what is euphemistically termed a *shakeout.*

Finally, the *decline stage* represents a gradual and often extended period of gradual reductions in both sales and revenues as fewer and fewer competitors remain active. By this point, newer technology has made the deficiencies in older technology more obvious, and few buyers are likely to want the product any more even at extremely low prices. For example, when Intel's Pentium IV chips were introduced to the marketplace in the spring of 2001, the Pentium III series was clearly entering the latter part of the maturity stage. The Pentium II series and older versions were already undesirable for the mass market, since they lacked the necessary speed for multimedia software and faster Internet interaction. Similarly, older computers, especially those built before wireless technologies were designed with them in mind, are expected to be replaced in large numbers starting in 2004 according to a study by Gartner Dataquest. Their research suggested that personal computer shipments in the U.S. alone could top 187 million units in 2004, a 13.9 percent increase over 2003, as businesses and individuals trade up to Intel's Centrino chip and other mobile technology.[16]

Short life cycles for hardware can create special problems and lead to creative solutions. According to technology research firm Stanford Resources Inc., about 500 million personal computers will be considered obsolete by 2007. Because of the toxic materials used in computer components, which must be treated as hazardous waste, California no longer allows personal computers to be dumped in landfills, which presents the severe problem of what to do with aging technology components. To help deal with the problem, a recycling plant in Roseville, California, set up by technology manufacturer Hewlett-Packard charges break-even prices ranging from $13 to $34 to handle each item. Whatever cannot be repaired and recycled is mined for usable components or sold to smelters to be blended into other products. Rather than attempting to generate any real revenues, Hewlett-Packard is simply attempting to deflect criticism directed at itself and its industry for manufacturing products that cannot easily be disposed of. Both IBM and Gateway operate similar recycling and disposal programs.[17]

Product Differentiation

product differentiation
Efforts to distinguish a firm's products from those of competitors by its design, color, style, quality, price, brand, and any other element recognized by the customer.

As we discussed in Chapter 5, the firm's overall e-business plan must focus on creating added customer value and a sustainable competitive advantage. Often, this effort begins with the product it sells. **Product differentiation** refers to efforts to distinguish the firm's products from those offered by competitors. A product can be differentiated by design, color, style, quality, price, brand, or any other element recognized by the customer. For example, Intel's Pentium IV chips are faster than its earlier models. Competing chips from other semiconductor producers such as Advanced Micro Devices and Apple Computers are instantly recognizable because of their styling, their clear and candy-flavored colors, as well as their high-quality multimedia technology capability.

According to consultant Patricia Seybold (**www.patriciaseybold.com**), coauthor of *The Customer Revolution,* the Internet has permanently transformed the relationship between buyers and sellers by providing opportunities for firms to distinguish themselves from their competitors by offering *mass-customization* services. This logistical competitive approach is illustrated by the 30,000 commercial-free radio stations available at **www.live365.com** and by manufacturers like Dell Computer (**www.dell.com**) and handbag maker Timbuk2 Designs (**www.timbuk2.com**), which allow customers to construct their purchases online before any order is sent to production. Besides bypassing traditional cost-heavy distribution systems

product position
How customers perceive
the relative value of a
product in comparison to
its competition, by using
important product differentiation criteria.

product positioning
Management activities and
efforts aimed at changing
the product position of
an existing product or
establishing one for a
new product.

perceptual map
A grid that illustrates
the relative position of
competing products as
perceived by customers.

and dealing directly with manufacturers, customers now control this part of the marketing function, which creates new challenges for managers who are trying to compete and satisfy customer needs.[18]

Product Positioning

How customers perceive the relative value of a product in comparison to its competition by using important product differentiation criteria is referred to as the **product position.** Management activities and efforts that are aimed at changing the product position of an existing product or establishing one for a new product are referred to as **product positioning.** The simplest way to understand product positioning is by using a grid called a **perceptual map** that illustrates the relative position of competing products as perceived by customers. Figure 8.2 displays the hypothetical customer's perception of the relative positions of several computer manufacturers with respect to price and quality. We have fabricated this information to illustrate how strategic thinking about product positioning is done. However, in an actual perceptual map, the relative position for each manufacturer would have been generated through survey-style questions. In these questions, customers are asked to use numbers to express their opinion about each manufacturer. For example, the question might be, "On a Likert scale from 1 through 7,

FIGURE 8.2   Hypothetical Perceptual Map Illustrating Product Positions of Major Computer Manufacturers

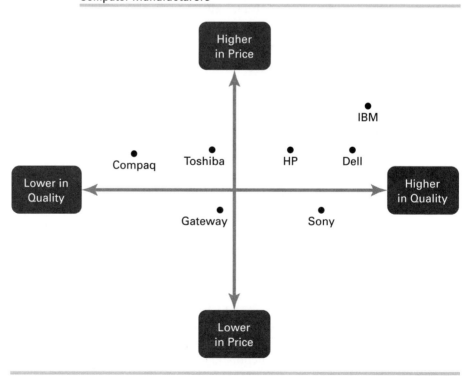

where 1 indicates Very Low, 2 Low, 3 Below Average, 4 Average, 5 Above Average, 6 High, and 7 Very High, what scores would you give IBM for price and quality?" The scores are averaged, and the average scores are used to locate each firm on the perceptual map of the perceived relative differences between them. For example, our hypothetical grid shows that Dell Computer is perceived as less expensive than IBM and a bit lower in quality. If in fact IBM were lower in price than Dell, then IBM management might decide to advertise the incorrectness of this perception and so gain market share. Or perhaps another result of this information might be that Compaq undertakes a major effort to improve the quality of its product and then emphasize this effort as part of a renewed marketing strategy. And finally, suppose another manufacturer recognizes that no firms are selling a high-quality but low-priced product and hence it sees an opportunity to market such a product. Perhaps a new breakthrough production technology can allow this firm to realize what would clearly be a competitive advantage and capture this corner of the market.

Completing the Mix of Marketing Strategies

Although decisions related to product strategies are generally the dominant decisions in most planning situations, the planning process is incomplete unless the other key decision areas of pricing, place, and promotion are also incorporated. In this final segment of the chapter, we will explore issues related to these important components of the marketing mix.

Pricing Strategies

pricing strategies
Strategies for setting and managing prices

Pricing strategies are concerned with both setting and managing prices. The exchange process in a business transaction is facilitated by the customers' ability to pay a given dollar amount for a product or service. High-speed Internet access for home-based customers is worth whatever people are willing to pay, just like telephone service or an airplane flight from New York to Los Angeles. The forces of supply and demand suggest that any product or service that is in high demand and short supply will have higher market prices and that the opposite conditions will result in falling market prices. However, many factors besides these basic market forces influence prices. For example, customers expect new technologies to emerge periodically, and they learn to follow a product life-cycle pattern in which a newer product may be introduced every two years on average. During this period, the older technology will generally fall in price as newer and presumably better technology replaces it. For instance, faster computers and semiconductor chips routinely replace older and slower models. Customers who need or simply want the latest and fastest computer technology are also generally prepared to pay a premium price for the newer technology, whereas those who have delayed their purchases have the added incentive of buying lower priced but slightly older technology.

cost-benefit analysis
A form of analysis that provides the purchaser with an understanding of what benefits can be gained in exchange for the price paid.

For any purchase that is being considered, a **cost-benefit analysis** provides the purchaser with an understanding of what benefits can be gained in exchange for the price paid. Sales representatives can also use cost-benefit analysis to persuade customers that the value they will receive from the purchase is sufficient to justify the price. For example, it might be argued that switching from a lower to a higher Internet access speed can actually save a firm money by saving employees' time and thereby increasing their productivity. Firms have high regard for the use of wireless e-mail devices such as Research In Motion's Blackberry because, among other selling points, it is considerably less expensive for mobile employees to use than laptop computers. Furthermore, it enables users to store and read messages at anytime, providing them with greater control and flexibility compared to cellular phone communications.

shopping agents
Intelligent software tools that will seek out pricing and other product information and report it back to the user.

Buyers can take advantage of **shopping agents**, which are intelligent software tools that will seek out pricing and other product information and report it back. After the buyer fills in a short questionnaire, the agent uses the criteria the buyer indicated to locate websites containing matches. For example, Microsoft's Expedia (**www.expedia.com**) flight reservation system will help users locate airline, hotel, car rental, and other related services online. The use of agents and search engines and the ease with which customers can exchange information among themselves through the Internet have all contributed to a more knowledgeable and price-sensitive customer. Customers who want a clearly identified product can easily retrieve lists of web vendors that are selling the product, ranked according to the offered selling price. To reduce the influence of price on customers' selection of a vendor, the product can be bundled with other products or services to obfuscate the description. However, where customer decision-making is driven by price alone, vendors need to be careful about how they present product descriptions. Furthermore, given the Internet's power to facilitate communication among existing and potential customers, products that consumers perceive to be unsatisfactory in some way or simply not worth the current market price are likely to come under downward price pressure as a result of weakening demand.

The Internet makes comparing prices relatively easy for users. Perhaps not surprisingly, the biggest-selling consumer product on the Internet currently is computer hardware. However, if trends continue, online airline transactions will fly right by it to an estimated $17 billion by 2004, more than $1 billion higher than computer hardware. In 1999 about 5 percent of airline ticket transactions were conducted over the Internet, but this figure is expected to grow to 18 percent by 2004 as customers seek lower prices and convenient shopping for what is fast becoming a commodity item. And according to a report from the Travel Industry Association of America (**www.tia.org**) nearly two-thirds of the 95.8 million global Internet users who travel have consulted online resources for trip planning, and 37 percent have subscribed to travel-related e-marketing promotions or registered with travel websites. Of these, 64 million are Americans who used the Internet in 2003 to get information on destinations or to check prices or schedules. This resulted in 42.2 million actually booking their travel arrangements online—an 8 percent gain over 2002. Furthermore, 29 percent of online bookers made all their travel arrangements online in 2003, compared to 23 percent in 2002, continuing a growing trend toward self-reliance. Besides the industry leader Expedia (**www.expedia.com**), with a 22 percent share of the U.S. market, users also visited Travelocity (**www.travelocity.com**), with a 16 percent share, and Orbitz (**www.orbitz.com**), with a 15 percent share.[19]

Regardless of how much money customers are willing to pay for products and services, over the long run firms must employ pricing strategies that generate revenues high enough to exceed their costs of production and produce a profit. Failure to deliver profits will affect the viability of the organization and undermine management's ability to compete for employees, develop new products and services, and secure access to the external sources of financing necessary to expand the firm. We will explore these topics in greater detail in Chapter 10.

Place Strategies

place (distribution) strategies
Strategies concerned with making the product or service available when and where customers want it.

Place (distribution) strategies are concerned with making a product or service available when and where customers want it. As a distribution tool, nothing beats the Internet in terms of its ability to create *time* and *place utility* by delivering digitized products on demand 24 hours a day, 7 days a week, anywhere in the world where an Internet-ready device is available to the customer. According to a survey by Jupiter Research, consumers cite many advantages of the Internet in crediting what motivates their decision to shop online. Top rank is given to saving time by not going to a store (70%); followed by the ability to shop when stores are closed (69%); the ability to avoid holiday crowds (68%); the belief that they might be able to find better prices (59%), find products more easily (52%), and find products not available in stores (50%); and the ease with which they can compare prices (47%).[20]

Research analysts at International Data Corp. (IDC) estimate that as more and more customers around the world connect to the Internet, any product that can be digitized and thereby delivered on the Internet will contribute to an explosion in e-commerce sales. And according to a report by Jupiter Research, as consumers' level of comfort with online functions such as e-mail and research increases, so too will their participation in e-commerce.[21]

As more devices enter the marketplace, customers will enjoy the flexibility and convenience of receiving many more products online, such as e-books, music, and video programming on demand. According to BiblioMondo Inc. (**www.bibliomondo.com**), whose software allows any private or public library to manage and sell its digital content on the Internet, the world's 712,000 libraries will be joining a growing list of online vendors like netLibrary (**www.netlibrary.com**) and ebrary (**www.ebrary.com**) that are seeking methods for managing their business and earning revenues through online sales. The firm's management suggests that in the future, buyers will see libraries as quality points of purchase that have already screened for the best selections for their clients and have created a brand identity as a source for specific information.[22]

Bricks-and-mortar retailers and firms with highly recognizable brand names such as The Walt Disney Company (**www.disney.com**) continue to expand their reach into global markets by setting up online retail shopping sites. According to research by the Boston Consulting Group, it costs an online retailer about $82 to generate a single customer, whereas it costs an established bricks-and-mortar retailer only $12. This is mostly due to the customer's recognition of the store name and its established associations in the customer's mind.[23]

Furthermore, according to some experts, it costs between $15 and $25 million to build a top-notch website but at least $150 million to build a warehouse and distribution system. The Internet component represents only 10 percent of the investment for online retailing, which gives existing bricks-and-mortar organizations with existing brand recognition, such as The Gap and Radio Shack, a sizable competitive advantage.[24]

Regardless of how great a web presence a firm plans to have, it will also have to ensure it is providing for sufficient online customer support. According to Forrester Research Inc., 37 percent of all online buyers request customer service while shopping online.[25]

Distribution is rarely performed directly from the manufacturer, however. As illustrated in Figure 8.3, *intermediaries* or *middlemen* help to increase exchange

FIGURE 8.3   Efficiency in Exchanges Provided by an Intermediary or Middleman

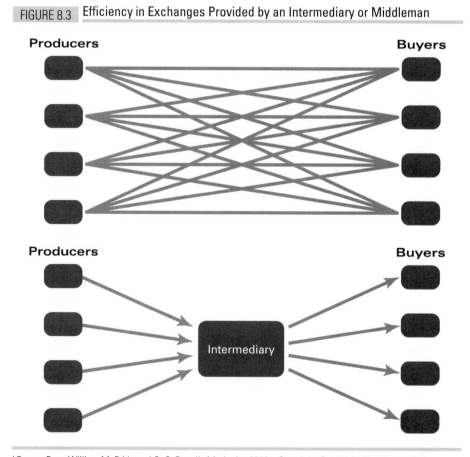

(*Source:* From William M. Pride and O. C. Ferrell, *Marketing* 2000e. Copyright © 2000 by Houghton Mifflin Company. Reprinted with permission.)

efficiencies by reducing the number of contacts that both producers and buyers need to deal with by forming a *marketing distribution channel*. The typical marketing distribution channels are illustrated in Figures 8.4 and 8.5.

In addition, intermediaries facilitate the exchange process by buying and selling, creating assortment, and negotiating prices. Traditional intermediaries (retailers and wholesalers) also operate online, providing physical supply services such as handling, transporting, and storing products and facilitating activities such as consulting services, financing, grading, and providing market information.

The term *supply-chain management,* which was introduced in Chapter 5, refers to a firm's effort to nurture partnerships among its channel members, with its goal being to continuously increase efficiencies in the distribution channel. The Internet provides a variety of solutions that contribute to improvements in supply-chain management such as online buying groups, auctions, reverse auctions, and communications software—ranging from customer relationship management software to simple e-mail—to assist buyers and sellers. Whether through cost

FIGURE 8.4   Typical Channels for Consumer Products

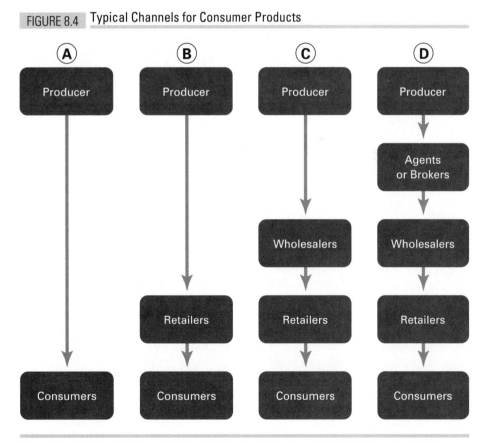

(*Source:* From William M. Pride and O. C. Ferrell, *Marketing* 2000e. Copyright © 2000 by Houghton Mifflin Company. Reprinted with permission.)

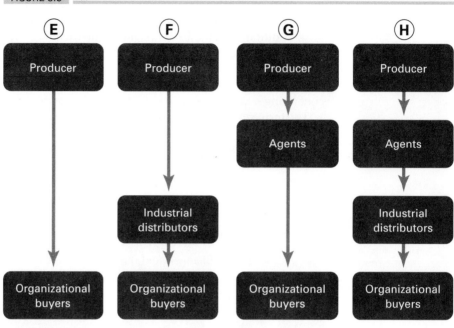

FIGURE 8.5   Typical Channels for Business Products

(*Source:* From William M. Pride and O. C. Ferrell, *Marketing* 2000e. Copyright © 2000 by Houghton Mifflin Company. Reprinted with permission.)

reductions or increased customer satisfaction, the Internet is considered a fundamental tool for improving operations in the supply chain. However, the Internet can also contribute to *channel conflict* since geographic boundaries that would normally set limits on distributors' behaviors are absent. For example, products such as pharmaceuticals and health-related items that would traditionally have been sold through local retail stores can now be bought by customers living anywhere through online vendors. Manufacturers' ability to control prices in different markets is significantly reduced by the power transferred to online buyers. The financial threat the Internet poses to traditional local distributors is real and is likely to grow as more customers seeking lower prices become comfortable with ordering products online. As Dell Computer did, firms may decide to eliminate intermediaries completely and rely on their own direct marketing effort with customers. Other firms that feel they need local bricks-and-mortar representation are likely to require new strategies for tackling the channel conflicts that will increase as customers' use of the Internet grows.

Promotion Strategies

promotion
Any communications activity that is designed to positively influence the buying decision-making behavior of customers; it includes advertising, personal selling, sales promotion, publicity, and public relations.

Promotion is any communications activity that is designed to positively influence the buying decision-making behavior of customers. It includes *advertising,* *personal selling, sales promotion, publicity,* and *public relations.* Coordinated into a single driving force, these activities are collectively referred to as the firm's *integrated marketing communications strategy* or *promotional mix.* For example, according to brand marketing expert Will Novosedlik of San Francisco, California-based Organic Inc., large-scale global firms like Volvo will continue to blend their traditional media with Internet media marketing strategies as they go after technologically comfortable consumers online. Volvo's launch of the S60 model, for instance, was built around a contest that awarded a new S60 to the winner. Consumers could enter the contest by providing data about themselves at a website that offered promotional information about the car. Contestants could use PDAs and wireless devices to monitor developments, which helped the company measure the interest of the users of each group of communication devices. Banner advertising on CBS Sportsline (**www.sportsline.com**) and Volvo's sponsorship of the NCAA basketball March Madness tournament were combined with other online and televised promotions designed to bring audiences to the website.[26]

Many marketers use the Internet to expand their channels of communication with buyers. Research suggests that consumers will not visit a consumer product site unless they have a motivating reason. Understanding why consumers visit websites drives the way marketers design and use them. For example, Unilever Inc., makers of Wisk laundry detergent, has integrated consumer information about stain removal into the product's label and website. Consumers can check the website for the extra information, which is a value-added utility in the marketing mix. [27]

All promotional strategic thinking is guided by the communications and behavioral decision-making models presented in Chapter 7. Here we will expand our understanding of promotion by looking at specific characteristics of each area of the integrated marketing communications strategy.

advertising

Any paid nonpersonal communication that is distributed to a target market through a medium such as television, radio, newspapers, journals, or, of course, the Internet.

Advertising is any paid nonpersonal communication that is distributed to a target market through a medium such as television, radio, newspapers, journals, or, of course, the Internet. According to Forrester Research Inc. of Cambridge, Massachusetts, far from declining in importance, online advertising is expected to rise from an average of 8 percent of advertising budgets in 2000 to 15 percent in 2003 and 25 percent by 2005. However, a switch toward more direct e-mail marketing campaigns is likely to occur that will include contests and other promotional interaction with customers rather than poor-performing banner-style advertising, which is designed to attract attention but has an estimated click (meaning: a click on the banner advertisement) rate of about half a percent. IBM directs about $50 million of its $760 million advertising budget to online advertising, and other traditional, non-dot-com companies like Toyota, MasterCard, and Disney have also begun to develop closer communication ties and information exchanges with current and potential customers by using advertising strategies that engage customers over the Internet.[28]

The Internet is an attractive medium because it allows customers to interact with advertisements. Customers can enter data such as names and phone numbers, and websites can be designed with menu control selections that allow the customer to self-direct their navigation of the site. Instead of mimicking television advertising, which viewers generally regard as an interruption of program entertainment, Internet advertising that attempts to assist motivated shoppers is likely to be more successful. Interestingly, online advertising is also extremely concentrated. Only ten companies received 70 percent of all revenues. Among these firms, the top three, AOL, Microsoft, and Yahoo!, earned more than half of the revenues.[29]

Regardless of the attractiveness and power of Internet advertising, however, the advertising e-business model is generally regarded as a weak one to depend on because viewers often disregard banner advertisements when they visit websites or receive them as e-mail. Furthermore, the increasing use of software that blocks the downloading of advertising makes the whole area of Internet advertising challenging, to say the least. For example, WebWasher (**www.webwasher.com**) and AdSubtract (**www.adsubtract.com**) are programs that are designed to recognize incoming advertisements by analyzing page formats and looking for standard banner advertising shapes. These software programs typically fill the advertising space by restructuring the desirable page content or by simply replacing advertisements with blank spaces. The delays related to the time required for these software programs to filter out advertisements are often worthwhile to users in that they reduce the time spent in downloading unwanted images.

The task facing marketers who are using the Internet is to design advertisements that are likely to engage interested and motivated viewers, such as someone searching for information about digital cameras and photography. According to a study by researchers at NPD Group Inc., building brand awareness by paying search engines to place the advertiser's name among the top positions displayed is three times more effective than a banner advertising strategy.[30]

According to Michele Slack, an analyst at Jupiter Communications Inc., Internet advertising that is placed at an appropriate point in an online presentation, such as at the end of a round of an online game, is more acceptable to the audience. Since such placements resemble the placement of television advertisements, which interrupt programming at regular intervals, this also offers a familiar structured experience for the user. Furthermore, according to Erick Hachenburg, president and CEO of pogo.com, an advertisement-sponsored free Internet multiplayer gaming site, sites like pogo.com draw an audience that regards the placed advertising differently than most Web users do. Instead of wanting to move on as quickly as possible, players welcome advertisements displayed between sets in the game as a respite and do not rush off to another site. Pogo.com players spend an average of 45 minutes at a time playing a variety of Java versions of word puzzles, checkers, and card games like hearts. Pogo.com and other game sites appear to be offering a marketable content site that is interesting to advertisers. As a result, the *cost per thousand (cpm)* exposures to viewers ranges from $15 to $30, and above-average industry click rates on an advertisement of about 1 percent suggest that game sites are likely to find niches of viewers.[31]

According to Forrester Research Inc., online advertising will grow as advertisers move toward a greater degree of integration of online with traditional advertising media.[32] Research by New York–based eMarketer reported a drop in online advertising from $8.2 billion in 2000 to $7.3 billion in 2001. This reflected the fallout from reductions in dot-com advertising as well as the fortunes of those like Yahoo! that relied heavily on online advertising. However, by 2003 online advertising activity had revived the fortunes of firms like Yahoo! as the economic recovery continued to take hold. Advertising levels were still relatively low at $6.3 billion due to lower rates and volumes. Furthermore, although the traditional *display* or *banner* ads are continuing their decline in popularity against other types, they still account for about half of all revenues. The second most popular type of advertising is *keyword* or *paid search*, followed by *classified* advertising.[33]

Furthermore, marketers continue to shift toward what they consider more effective online marketing such as direct e-mail sales promotions, building databases of information online for future communication with potential customers, and e-commerce partnerships.[34] As a result, the cost per thousand (cpm) exposures of banner advertising has fallen dramatically. The cpm can vary from pennies to hundreds of dollars, depending on the size of the banner, the website, the market it can deliver to advertisers, and so forth. A survey by Ad Resource (**www.adresource.com**) suggests that the average cpm is probably about $30 for a typical website that has high-quality content and the ability to deliver an audience for the advertisers.[35] The cpm is the metric that allows advertisers to compare the advertising costs of different media when creating their budgets. Advertisers can expect to pay twice the normal exposure rate for any actual clicks by visitors on the banner advertisement, and many share their revenue from whatever they sell on the Web with the website that presented their advertising. Rather than trying to place their advertising on websites themselves, advertisers can use the services of firms like Doubleclick (**www.doubleclick.com**) and 24/7 Media (**www.247media.com**) to select websites and target specific viewers with sophisticated smart software.

personal selling
Paid communication that relies on personal contact by an individual representing the selling firm with potential customers so as to convey information and persuade them to buy.

Personal selling is also a form of paid communication, but it relies on personal contact by an individual representing the selling firm with potential customers to convey information and persuade them to buy. The equivalent of the sales representative in the bricks-and-mortar world is the online customer service representative who assists customers with pre- and postsale services. The Internet has introduced new challenges to traditional strategic thinking that has worked well for a long time. For example, after being reluctant to move from a face-to-face sales approach to a less personal website approach, Allstate began taking what some consider to be small, catch-up steps by creating an Internet presence to support its established sales force and channels. Firms like eCoverage.com that have exclusively web-based strategies are expected to take a big share of the estimated $4 billion Internet insurance sales market.[36]

sales promotion
Activities and offers that can help motivate positive buyer behavior, including contests, samples, coupons, rebates, and so forth.

Sales promotion refers to activities and offers that can help motivate positive buyer behavior, including contests, samples, coupons, rebates, and so forth.

Go to the Web:
e-Business Online
For tutorials and more on
the topics in this chapter,
visit the student website at
http://business.college
.hmco.com/students and
select "Canzer e-Business."

publicity
Any unpaid nonpersonal
communications activity
designed to generate a
favorable and positive
image for the firm and its
products.

public relations
Paid efforts to manage
the various publics that
the firm deals with, such
as customers, suppliers,
governments, sharehold-
ers, employees, and the
media.

The Internet is especially effective when the sales promotion offer is a digitized item that can be distributed online. The Internet is a cost-effective facilitator, distributing sales promotion offers to customers and potential customers through e-mail campaigns and pop-up and banner advertising on selective websites. However, according to the research firm Brightmail (**www.brightmail.com**), spam now accounts for more than 60 percent of e-mail and poses the greatest risk to legitimate e-mail marketing efforts because it inundates users and crowds out any messages that may be of genuine interest to them. To protect themselves from spam as well as viruses, many users employ screening software. According to a study by Jupiter Research, such programs could cost legitimate e-mail marketers more than $400 million by 2008, double the level in 2003, by preventing the delivery of legitimate marketing e-mails. The study recommends that marketers use confirmed opt-in practices and other methods to confirm the quality of their mailing lists and satisfactory delivery of direct e-mail to intended receivers. However, these measures will likely push up costs to $0.005 per message from the current $0.002, according to the report.[37]

Publicity is any unpaid nonpersonal communications activity that is designed to generate a favorable and positive image for the firm and its products. Publicity includes preparing press releases, participating in press conferences, providing a company representative to be interviewed by news reporters, preparing articles for publication on issues that the firm is considered knowledgeable about, and so forth. Publicity can be thought of as a strategy for getting a positive word out about the firm and its products by using the mass media without having to pay for it. To accomplish this, the firm has to have something of value that reporters will find useful and therefore worth repeating. For example, the release of a new edition of AOL software or Microsoft Windows generally qualifies for freely distributed publicity for these firms. Needless to say, negative publicity about a firm can be a problem, such as a report on a drop in stock value or unhappy shareholders voicing discontent over executives' supposedly excessive compensation packages while stock values fall.

Public relations refers to paid efforts to manage the various publics that the firm deals with, such as customers, suppliers, governments, shareholders, employees, and the media. Public relations activity is concerned with managing the firm's publicity. For example, it might counterbalance negative publicity concerning a dramatic fall in the value of the firm's stock by holding a news conference to announce a new strategic alliance with a partner that is expected to boost sales revenues in the near future. A popular public relations strategy is the preparation and dissemination through the firm's website of white papers and research reports on topics of wide interest to selected target markets. For example, any major firm such as IBM publicizes itself, its industry, and its products to a variety of markets by making freely available the articles and press releases posted on its website. Even small businesses can take advantage of the Internet to generate publicity by posting articles of interest and advice on their websites. Given the relatively low costs involved, Internet-based public relations campaigns can be effective tools for generating good relations on behalf of the firm.

Conclusions

This chapter helped to provide a bridge between conventional marketing theory and practice and strategic e-business planning. Established marketing models such as the marketing management process, market segmentation, and the marketing mix were presented to illustrate how firms should structure marketing strategies to contribute to their e-business plans. In the next chapter we will explore how management theory and practice can be strategically applied to the firm's e-business planning process.

This discussion also helped to provide many possible marketing actions for building a firm's **e-business plan.** A more detailed tutorial on the preparation of the e-business plan is available on the textbook's website.

RETURN TO inside e-business

CASE STUDY

Office Depot's marketing strategy, which incorporates the construction of an online community of buyers for the products it distributes, illustrates the ways in which the Internet can be used simultaneously to build better customer relationships and sell more products. Well-known brands may have less difficulty attracting online shoppers. Lesser-known brand names can take advantage of the implied value-exchange fairness suggested by website distributors like Office Depot.

ASSIGNMENT

1. What other collaborative efforts can a website operator like Office Depot develop with vendors because of its highly recognized and valued brand name?
2. What risks are posed by this collaborative marketing approach for Office Depot? For vendors?

Chapter Review

SUMMARY

ACE Self-Test
For a quick self-test of the content in this chapter, visit the student website at **http://business. college.hmco.com/ students.** Select "Canzer e-Business."

1. **Identify and describe potential markets of online customers.**

Although the marketing management process is by definition a continuous series of activities, new firms or new projects within an established firm must begin somewhere. Logically, a firm needs to first identify potential markets and then select those groups of customers that will be targeted for the firm's marketing effort. A market is characteristically defined as being customers who have a common need or desire to acquire some product and as well as the estimated amount of sales in units and dollars they represent over some period of time. In broad terms, markets are classified by the type of buyer making the purchase decision; they are divided into consumer and organizational markets. These in turn can be segmented into smaller groups of various sizes using descriptive criteria that make it possible to identify large-scale mass markets as well as smaller niche markets.

2. **Examine the process for analyzing and selecting target markets.**

The process that leads to decisions about which market segments a firm will select and which it will pass over requires that management have the ability to weigh risks and rewards and assess the firm's likelihood of succeeding at each available choice. After identifying each of the available market segments and conducting a SWOT analysis, a firm may opt for a *concentrated targeting strategy* and select to focus only on one market; for an *undifferentiated targeting strategy*, which basically treats everyone as a member of one mass target market; or, perhaps the most common of the three, for a *differentiated targeting strategy*, which involves selecting more than one identifiable market segment and creating a unique mix of marketing strategies tailored for each segment. As part of the market selection process, management will need to estimate the market potential of each market segment, or the total amount of sales that might be available to firms competing in that segment.

3. **Discuss topics related to the development of online product strategies.**

To begin developing marketing strategies, management should logically first focus its attention on understanding the nature of the product or service to be sold. At the core of understanding the motivation for the exchange process is the recognition that products and services are bought because purchasers expect that they will satisfy their wants and needs. Before anything else, the firm must be clear about what its product or service (or combination of the two) actually is and what it is not. The firm must also learn what its customers believe they are being sold and develop strategies that are consistent with those belief systems. There are many ways to describe, define, and classify products that can provide useful direction for firms' strategic market development. For example, we can classify products and services in terms of their intended target markets—*consumer* and *organizational.* This classification can be clarified even further if we examine the segmentation criteria that are used to define the markets. Finally, product mix considerations can contribute additional useful information toward the development of online product strategies.

4. **Describe product strategy decision-making using popular conceptual models.**

The product life cycle concept, product differentiation, and product positioning are three important and popular conceptual models that can help planners understand and frame the strategic decisions before them. The product life cycle concept suggests that products follow a life cycle pattern of clearly identifiable stages that coincide with changing sales, profits, and environmental selling conditions. As a product ages and passes from stage to stage, marketing managers need to adjust their plans to reflect the conditions that the product faces in the marketplace and prepare for its inevitable abandonment and replacement with newer products. Product differentiation refers to a firm's efforts to distinguish its products from those offered by competitors. A product can be differentiated by its design, color, style, quality, price, brand, or any other element recognized by the customer. How customers perceive the relative value of a product in comparison to its competition by using important product differentiation criteria is referred to as the product position. Management activities and efforts that are aimed at changing the product position of an existing product or establishing one for a new product are referred to as product positioning.

5. **Explore the development of pricing, place, and promotion strategies.**
   Although decisions related to product strategies are generally the dominant ones in most planning situations, the planning process is incomplete unless it incorporates the other key decision areas: pricing, place, and promotion. Pricing strategies are concerned with both setting and managing prices. Many factors besides basic market forces influence prices. Cost-benefit analysis provides the purchaser with an understanding of what benefits he or she can gain in exchange for the price paid. Sales representatives can also use cost-benefit analysis to persuade customers that the value they will receive from the purchase is sufficient to justify the price. Place (distribution) strategies are concerned with making the product or service available when and where customers want it. As a distribution tool, nothing beats the Internet in terms of its ability to deliver digitized products on demand 24 hours a day, 7 days a week, anywhere in the world where an Internet-ready device is available to the customer. Promotion is any communications activity that is designed to positively influence the buying decision-making behavior of customers; it includes advertising, personal selling, sales promotion, publicity, and public relations. Coordinated into a single driving force, these activities are collectively referred to as the firm's *integrated marketing communications strategy* or *promotional mix.*

REVIEW QUESTIONS

1. Define the marketing management process.
2. Describe what part e-marketing plays in a firm's marketing strategy.
3. Describe the market segmentation variables.
4. What does the term *SWOT* mean to a marketer?
5. What does the term *market potential* mean?
6. What are the key product classifications for consumer products? Provide an example of each one.
7. What are the key product classifications for organizational products? Provide an example of each one.
8. What is the product life cycle?
9. What is product differentiation?
10. Explain what a perceptual map is and the concept of product positioning. Use an example to illustrate your point.
11. What is cost-benefit analysis?

DISCUSSION QUESTIONS

1. List the market segmentation variables that might be used by an Internet-based firm and discuss why you have chosen them.
2. Discuss the key differences between differentiated, undifferentiated, and concentrated targeting strategies.

3. Why might a firm choose a concentrated targeting strategy?
4. Describe how marketing managers might develop some sense of market potential.
5. Describe how firms can use product classifications to market products.
6. Describe how the product life cycle can be used to develop marketing plans.
7. Using an example you have created, discuss which strategies might emerge for a firm as a result of examining a perceptual map.
8. How can cost-benefit analysis be used to set the price for a product?
9. Discuss the advantages and disadvantages of one type of promotional strategy available to a firm.

Building Skills for Career Success

EXPLORING THE INTERNET

Yahoo.com uses an undifferentiated market strategy, whereas Tom's of Maine (**www.toms-of-maine.com**) uses a concentrated niche market strategy to sell all-natural toothpastes and other health products on its website. Many opportunities exist for smaller website operators like Tom's of Maine, who are interested in serving the growing number of Internet users who seek specialized products, services, and information. Many niche markets have also emerged from what were once larger undifferentiated markets. This is especially true when a mass-market website attracts large numbers of viewers and then gradually loses some users to websites that cater to their more narrowly defined niche markets of needs and interests.

ASSIGNMENT

1. Locate, explore, and describe a website that uses a mass-market strategy as well as one that is catering to a specialized niche.
2. Compare the similarities and differences of their respective strategies.

DEVELOPING CRITICAL THINKING SKILLS

The top ten websites dominate the online advertising business. Among these, AOL (**www.aol.com**), MSN (**www.msn.com**), and Yahoo! (**www.yahoo.com**) earn more than half of all advertising revenues. Examine these sites, looking for commonalities that might explain their strengths as compared to their competitors.

ASSIGNMENT

1. Explain why you believe AOL, MSN, and Yahoo! dominate the online advertising industry.
2. How might a competitor attempt to wrest market share from any of these giants?

BUILDING TEAM SKILLS

Building an online presence for an established bricks-and-mortar firm that has a recognized brand name can be facilitated by many factors. First, such a company has an existing customer base that knows about the firm, so the company does not have to create an identity from scratch. Second, the firm has a warehouse and physical infrastructure as well as a supply-chain system already in place that is financially supported by current operations. Select a local firm that has little if any web presence at the moment.

ASSIGNMENT

1. Briefly describe the firm's business, markets, competitors, products, and distribution system.
2. Create a web presence that would be complementary to the firm's current operations without being too disruptive.

RESEARCHING DIFFERENT CAREERS

Designing websites and online advertising requires a blend of creative skills and marketing knowledge about the product and the customer. You can learn a great deal by examining well-designed web content created by others. Select a website or promotional e-mail that you believe represents excellent design and creative work.

ASSIGNMENT

1. What message is being communicated, and to whom?
2. Is the communication effort successful, in your opinion? Explain your answer.

IMPROVING COMMUNICATION SKILLS

Digital photography, in which a camera creates digital images that can be stored and later printed, displayed on websites, sent as attachments with e-mail, and so forth, is a good example of a new technology that is also well suited to marketing on the Internet. Websites such as Megapixel.net (**www.megapixel.net**) and Digital Photography Center (**www.dpreview.com**) provide a buyer's guide to understanding how to select the right camera without the pressure of a retail sales representative. In addition to providing price and the number of megapixels (thousands of dots per square inch) produced by the camera, these sites provide a variety of useful information to help potential buyers. For example, to produce a good-quality 4-inch-by-6-inch color print, the camera should have at least 2.3 megapixels.

ASSIGNMENT

1. Describe the marketing communication strategies on one of these sites.
2. Are the strategies weak in any way?
3. How would you improve the site?

Exploring Useful Websites

These websites provide information related to the topics discussed in the chapter. You can learn more by visiting them online and examining their current data.

1. Most people know that Amazon.com (**www.amazon.com**) is the biggest online retailer, but some might be surprised to learn that Office Depot (**www.officedepot.com**), which generates about $1 billion of sales—at a profit, is the second biggest. Managed in collaboration with Microsoft's bCentral (**www.bcentral.com**), the site offers businesses a rich selection of information through posted articles and links to other useful sites that provide such things as guides for writing business plans, research, and so forth.

2. Television show personalities like Oprah Winfrey have found new product development, distribution, and promotion opportunities online through sites like **www.oprah.com** and **www.oxygen.com**. Cable News Network (CNN) serves several identifiable market segments that are linked to its main website at **www.cnn.com**. MSN's (**http://autos.msn.com/**) sells cars. Hard-to-find books that might be available only at specialty book retailers in major cities are readily available online at specialty book sites like Abebooks.com (**www.abebooks.com**). Competitors in the specialty foods market such as PatsyPie (**www.PatsyPie.com**), Glutenfreemall.com (**www.glutenfreemall.com**), Dietaryshoppe.com (**www.dietaryshoppe.com**), and Missroben.com (**www.missroben.com**), can reach targeted audiences by advertising on community-support websites such as Celiac.com (**www.celiac.com**) and magazines such as Living Without (**www.livingwithout.com**). The grocery trade can be reached through sites such as Progressive Grocer (**www.progressivegrocer.com**).

3. Newspapers and magazines like the *Wall Street Journal* (**www.wsj.com**) and *Business Week* (**www.businessweek.com**) are good examples of a convenience product that is available online as well as at traditional retail stores.

4. According to consultant Patricia Seybold (**www.patriciaseybold.com**), the Internet has permanently transformed the relationship between buyers and sellers by providing opportunities for firms to distinguish themselves from their competitors by offering *mass-customization* services. This is illustrated by the 30,000 commercial-free radio stations available at **www.live365.com** and by manufacturers like Dell Computer (**www.dell.com**) and handbag maker Timbuk2 Designs (**www.timbuk2.com**).

5. Microsoft's Expedia (**www.expedia.com**), Travelocity (**www.travelocity.com**), and Orbitz (**www.orbitz.com**) are the top travel reservation sites, at which users can locate airline, hotel, car rental, and other related services online. The Travel Industry Association of America (**www.tia.org**) provides a variety of research information on the industry.

6. BiblioMondo Inc. (**www.bibliomondo.com**) software allows any private or public library to manage and sell its digital content on the Internet. The

world's 712,000 libraries will be joining a growing list of online vendors like netLibrary (**www.netlibrary.com**) and ebrary (**www.ebrary.com**) that are seeking methods for managing their business and earning revenues through online sales.

7. Bricks-and-mortar retailers and firms with highly recognizable brand names such The Walt Disney Company (**www.disney.com**) continue to expand their reach into global markets by setting up online retail shopping sites.

8. Volvo used banner advertising on CBS Sportsline (**www.sportsline.com**) and its sponsorship of the NCAA basketball March Madness tournament in combination with other online and televised promotions to bring audiences to Volvo's website.

9. WebWasher (**www.webwasher.com**) and AdSubtract (**www.adsubtract.com**) are programs that are designed to recognize incoming advertisements by analyzing page formats and looking for standard banner advertising shapes.

10. Rather than trying to place their advertising on websites themselves, advertisers can use the services of firms like Doubleclick (**www.doubleclick.com**) and 24/7 Media (**www.247media.com**) to select websites and target specific viewers by using sophisticated smart software.

11. Tom's of Maine (**www.toms-of-maine.com**) uses a concentrated niche market strategy to sell all-natural toothpastes and other health products on its website. BackcountryStore.com (**www.backcountrystore.com**) sells specialized gear to outdoors enthusiasts.

12. Websites such as Megapixel.net (**www.megapixel.net**) and Digital Photography Center (**www.dpreview.com**) provide a buyer's guide to understanding how to select the right camera without the pressure of a retail sales representative.

chapter 9

Organizational and Managerial Issues

INSIDE
e-business

Google.com—Small-Business and Entrepreneurial Success Story

Google.com (**www.google.com**) began operations in 1998, shortly after two Stanford University graduate students, Larry Page and Sergey Brin, conceived the search engine algorithm in a school project they had worked on together. Generally considered the third most popular search engine, Google.com serves more than 60 million unique users each month, about half as many as the industry leader Yahoo! and MSN. Users generate an average of 200 million search queries each day through the world's largest indexed database of 3 billion URLs, which Google has categorized and listed.

Today, entrepreneurs Page and Brin still lead an effective, creative, and forward-thinking company in an increasingly competitive and ever-changing environment that forces firms to carefully monitor their managerial resources. There are literally dozens of freely available popular web search engine sites vying for the attention and loyalty of Internet users. Almost all of them base their business model mostly on generating banner-advertising revenues. Many small start-up free-use dot-com sites base their businesses entirely on generating sufficient revenues from advertisers. According to Harvard Business School professor Michael Porter, this approach is a major error in judgment that cannot help a firm sustain a competitive advantage. Fortunately, Page and Brin have managed to avoid this pitfall.

The attraction of advertising revenue for a small start-up site is easy to understand. Given that web searches are the next most popular Internet user activity after e-mail, any site that can attract and keep a loyal audience will be able to generate huge amounts of advertising revenue from vendors that wish to communicate with their users. Success is limited only by the momentous task of attracting users and keeping them at the site in a highly competitive environment with few barriers to entry.

Managing a search engine site is not an easy task. The firm must distinguish itself from its competitors and deal with a variety of psychological factors, such as users' dislike for online advertising and for the delays caused by downloading advertising images along with search data. Many users have even adopted screening software to block the downloading of advertisements, which brings into question the effectiveness of banner advertising. Managers of most sites have expanded their basic search services, attempting to create a personal and preferred Internet portal for users. Free e-mail boxes, file storage, personal webpages, stock market portfolio tracking, and so forth are now common and valuable product strategy additions to sites. The strategic thinking behind these offerings is to make the site an attractive home base for users and thereby increase advertising revenues further.

The use of a business model based on banner advertising is a guiding strategy for many firms, so it may come as a surprise to some people that Google.com distinguishes itself by not selling banner advertising. Nonetheless, the firm has managed to generate sufficient revenues from other forms of advertising and other revenue sources to break even at a time when many competitors struggle just to stay in business. Google.com's core source of revenue is two- and five-line text-based advertising links to sites that are directly related to the search keywords entered by users. For example, someone who is searching for information on cars will be presented with text-based advertising links to car sites. However, because these are text only, the time required to download them is a fraction of that required for graphic advertising. Furthermore, they are less obtrusive for users and less likely to distract them from their search activities. However, because the advertisements are highly targeted and relevant, the click rate on Google's text-based advertisements is four times the industry rate, which allows the firm to charge more than its competitors. Google.com also earns revenues by providing search services to other websites—including Yahoo!.

Google.com distinguishes itself further in the market by providing searchers with superior technology that maintains databases on more than 3 billion ranked webpages. Unlike some search engines, which sell listing positions, Google software analyzes the popularity of pages in terms of how many other pages are linked to them and then delivers the ranked list of webpages. Thus, users know that a website appears at or near the top of the Google results page because it is a popular choice based on the number of links, not because the advertising client paid to have it placed there.[1]

Google.com's strategic efforts to distinguish itself from its competitors and thereby create a sustainable competitive advantage are reflected in the organization's culture, which sees itself as being in close partnership with its users. Google.com is essentially designed the way users wish an ideal free-use search engine to be designed, but it manages to also satisfy the needs of advertisers. Without this compromise between users and advertisers, the site could not generate sufficient revenues to survive. Another entrepreneurial success story uses a somewhat different revenue approach to create a sustainable competitive

advantage. Monster.com (**www.monster.com**) manages more than half of the entire online-recruitment market and earns revenues of more than $679 million by charging employers to search through 30 million job résumés it stores in databases. More than 40 million job seekers search Monster.com regularly—resulting in 46 million unique visitors each month.[2]

Both of these companies exemplify successful e-business strategic thinking and practice, and both have shaped their organizational and managerial plans to reflect their respective operating environments.

In this chapter, the second dealing with micro-level decision-making issues within the firm, we will explore how companies should approach the development of organizational and managerial strategies within an e-business environment. Of course, the entire body of management knowledge applies to all organizations, including those focusing on e-business strategic planning, but within an e-business environment there are nevertheless several important and sometimes unique considerations. We will explore these as we establish a guiding structure for preparing the management component of an e-business plan, beginning with an overview of the principal subject areas of management and their connections to e-business.

An Overview of Management and e-Business

management process
The ongoing planning, organizing, and controlling of the activities that personnel throughout an organization are engaged in, including marketing, finance, production and operations, human resources, and so forth.

The **management process** is the ongoing planning, organizing, and controlling of the activities that personnel throughout an organization are engaged in, including marketing, finance, production and operations, human resources, and so forth. The word *process* suggests that these activities are continuous and never ending. In a simple sense, then, these activities are the work that people do to keep the enterprise moving toward its identified goals with purpose and direction. The management process focuses on the detailed planning issues that need to be addressed within the firm. Much of the terminology we will discuss in this chapter is used to explain how to execute a strategic e-business plan, which organizational structures will be used, how the organization will lead and motivate employees, and so forth.

Planning, Organizing, and Controlling Activities

planning

The setting of goals (longer-term) and objectives (shorter-term) that the personnel at each of the three primary organizational levels of the firm (corporate, divisional/ strategic, and operating/ functional) will strive for and the development of activities to achieve them.

The management process begins with **planning**—the setting of goals (longer-term) and objectives (shorter-term) that the personnel at each of the three primary organizational levels of the firm (corporate, divisional/strategic, and operating/ functional) will strive for and the development of activities to achieve them. You will recall from Chapter 5 that corporate-level planning establishes the framework and, more importantly, the specific goals for the divisional/strategic level of the firm, and that this level, in turn, establishes specific goals for the operating/ functional level.

organizing

The grouping of activities and the marshaling of the resources (*material, human, financial, and informational*) required to achieve specific goals and objectives.

Organizing is the grouping of activities and the marshaling of the resources (material, human, financial and informational) required to achieve specific goals and objectives. After the planning process has established *what* the firm intends to do, organizing answers the questions of *how* it will be done, by *whom*, and with *which resources*. Organizing requires the development of a structure or framework, such as the creation of a new division, and the selection of managers who have the appropriate leadership and motivation skills to accomplish the necessary tasks.

controlling

The monitoring, evaluating, and adjusting of activities to assure the successful achievement of the targeted goals.

Controlling involves the monitoring, evaluating, and adjusting of activities to assure the successful achievement of the targeted goals. For example, suppose planned sales revenues for a new division of a firm were estimated at $10 million for the following year, with incremental growth of 30 percent in each of the following two years. If in fact sales for the first year were disappointing and came in 20 percent lower than was anticipated, managers would have to modify their strategies to take into account this failure to achieve a planned objective. Perhaps a change in advertising strategy is called for or perhaps more specialized human resources should be hired. Identifying all the possible decisions the firm might take is beyond the scope of this short discussion. The important point is that if feedback suggests that longer-term goals are not likely to be achieved unless the firm changes strategy, then managers at each level of the organization will have to adjust their current e-business plans appropriately. We will explore these issues in greater detail in Chapter 11.

Organizational Structures and Issues

Organizational structures define the way in which individuals work together—how they solve problems, make decisions, communicate, and share responsibility, authority, and power with one another. We will describe several types of organizational structure here. It is likely that a firm will employ more than one of these structures over time and that different parts of the firm will use different structures at the same time. So, for instance, a large management-consulting firm like Siebel Systems Inc. might use a bureaucratic organizational structure at its corporate level and organic, matrix, and cross-functional team structures at the divisional and operational levels. According to Eric Schmitt, an analyst at Forrester Research Inc., organizations today are reorganizing themselves and changing the way they do business as they adapt their corporate structure to an online presence that is based on interacting with customers and suppliers over the Internet. For example, Cisco Systems Inc. uses Ariba Inc.'s software to run its online purchasing system, which connects its 20,000 employees with more than 3,000 suppliers. The result has been an estimated 10 to 20 percent savings.[3]

Bureaucratic structures tend to have more rigidly defined structural arrangements, a high degree of job specialization, and formal patterns of communication and relationships among employees. A firm's finance department might be expected to use a bureaucratic structure in which management decisions about which customers will receive credit and how much credit they will receive follow standardized rules. Overriding the set rules would likely require special procedures and multiple approvals from supervisors. For example, an online brokerage firm like E*TRADE would normally follow rigid rules for establishing the margin-trading limits for its online clients. This would be especially important for trading in more speculative instruments such as options, where small changes in price can result in enormous swings in investors' portfolio values.

An *organic structure*, in contrast, would have much more loosely defined structural arrangements among its employees, who would tend to collaborate on work and let informal rules guide their behavior. Authority would tend to be based on an individual's expertise rather than on his or her title in the organization. Organic structures tend to be used in project work, where creative collaboration is needed among employees who bring various types of knowledge and skills to the team. For example, a group that is designing and programming new computer solutions or a webpage for a client is likely to employ an organic structure.

A *matrix structure* is a step up in complexity and combines more than one level of authority within a work project. Matrix structures are common in e-business. When a client commissions a job, a project manager might be assigned responsibility for assuring the successful completion of the entire job, but several specialized teams of employees from different departments would probably be brought together in a matrix structure as they are needed. While working on any given project, employees would report to both their respective team supervisors and the project manager. For example, after a receiving a request from the account manager responsible for maintaining customer relationship management (CRM) software for an existing client, Siebel Systems might initially send in a team of employees to conduct a needs analysis. Next, the details of the project work would be written up in a contract, which would be duly signed, and then several other teams of employees would be scheduled to contribute to the project according to an agreed-upon timetable. First a new hardware installation might be required. Then the software would have to be configured and adapted to ensure there is no conflict with existing software or hardware with which the new installation has to interact—a common problem for new installations. And finally, yet another team of consultants would have to train the client's employees in how to use the new installation. As each group completes its tasks, the group members would be assigned to other projects. Typically, the project manager (leader) would see the project through to its conclusion and act as the liaison between the firm and its client. While the work is being done, employees would report to their supervisor as well as to the project manager. Often, the supervisor would be the channel used to deal with any problems that might arise with the project or the project manager.

An *organizational chart* is a schematic diagram that illustrates the relationships between key positions in the organization and the chain of command or line of authority between individual positions. It gives some insight into the firm's organizational structure. For instance, the chart might show that the organization is using a wide *span of control* (management), in which each manager oversees the work of a large number of employees. This is often the case in organizations that have clearly defined procedures and objectives and competent and self-directing employees. For instance, a call center might have a single supervising manager for dozens of customer service representatives who have been well trained and know how to handle what are generally routine calls. On the other hand, a narrower span of control is likely to be used when the work demands continuous interaction between managers and their subordinates. Furthermore, the organizational chart would illustrate whether the firm's structure is *flat*, in which project managers are likely to be working alongside their staff; or *tall*, which indicates that there are layers of bureaucratic managers who receive progress reports from their subordinates and generally do not participate directly in the work being done.

Production and Operations Management

operations management
The process of coordinating all the activities related to the production of the products and services that an organization provides to its customers.

Operations management involves the coordination of all the activities related to the production of the products and services that an organization provides to its customers. Clearly, in some cases, such as in a CRM consulting firm like Siebel Systems, virtually everything that the firm does can be considered part of operations management. However, in general, the fundamental areas on which operations management focuses are the manufacturing processes, including facilities, capacity, purchasing, inventory, quality control, use of technology, and employees' skills.

The objective of operations management is to deliver the planned production of products and services within set cost limits. Operations management is continually seeking ways to reduce costs and improve the quality of the products and services produced. It accomplishes this primarily by studying how work is organized and done so as to introduce efficiencies and other improvements. For example, a bank's introduction of an automated web-based information distribution system might reduce the number of customers who need to speak to a customer service representative. By simply selecting from a menu on their screens, customers can retrieve, on their own, commonly requested information such as current account balances. As a result, more customer service representatives are freed to deal with people who call a firm's center needing unique information or answers to complex questions. Because automated telephone-based and web-based information retrieval systems are so cost-effective, they are incorporated into the logistics of almost every e-business plan.

The efficiencies derived from online banking systems are prime motivators for management to encourage customers to move online. Research by the firm

Yankee Group Inc. suggests that Internet-based banking transactions are by far the least expensive for banks. They cost 1 cent per transaction, in comparison to 32 cents for automatic teller machines (ATMs), 62 cents for telephone banking, and $1.29 for retail customer service at a local branch. By shifting customers to the Internet, banks may not increase their sales revenues, but they can increase their profits by reducing costs. According to the Yankee Group's North America–wide survey, 46 percent of respondents said they would be switching to Internet-based banking over the next two to three years—doubling the number the banking industry was already serving in this way. The results suggest that the banking industry will continue to expand Internet activity as it answers the demand by technologically comfortable customers for more convenient services. Interestingly, Canadian banking customers, representing 15 percent of all North American customers, are three times more likely to use Internet-based banking services than Americans are. This is attributed to Canadians' greater willingness to adopt technology such as ATMs and debit cards and to the fact that Canada's six largest national banks, which dominate the industry, have historically been heavy promoters of moving their customers to adopt cost-saving technologies by offering incentives and charging higher fees for services provided at bank branches. The trend toward more e-banking is clearly established. Competition for online bill payments and other simple repetitive transactions are likely to become more common within the banking industry, but other organizations such as the postal service are also likely to begin acting as intermediaries for the delivery and storage of statements and the transfer of funds for payments.[4]

Productivity and Efficiency

productivity
The amount of output that an individual worker can produce within a set period of time.

Productivity refers to the amount of output that an individual worker can produce within a set period of time. Productivity is influenced by a variety of factors, including the efficiency and skills of the employees, the tools they have to work with and the training they have received, and the organization's structure and management methods, including leadership and motivation. For example, all of these factors influence how many orders on a firm's website a customer service representative can process. According to Cisco Systems' management, 68 percent of its orders are placed and fulfilled over the Internet, and 70 percent of service calls are resolved online. As a result, the firm has reduced its manufacturing costs by 7 percent, or more than $1.4 billion annually.[5]

Furthermore, a recent survey indicated that there are now about 400 electronic trading communities, including auctions, exchanges, e-procurement hubs, and multisupplier online catalogs, made up of businesses selling to other businesses. According to the investment bank Goldman Sachs, all major industries are expected to begin transforming their processes over the next 5 to 10 years, which will result in increased productivity through reducing inventory, shortening cycle time, and using human effort more efficiently.[6] For this reason, IDC Inc. predicts that B2B online selling will grow about 50 percent each year, reaching a level of more than $2 trillion by 2006.

Productivity improvements are expected to increase dramatically as more economic activity is transferred onto the Internet, which will reduce the costs of servicing customers and handling routine ordering. According to a Jupiter Communications study, the frequency with which human intervention is needed to help online customers rises substantially as the product price increases, from 8 percent at low price levels to nearly 30 percent as the product price crosses the $100 point. If e-commerce efforts are to succeed, authority must be decentralized to the level of the online service representative.[7]

The savings of time and money that productivity improvements make possible allow businesses to increase their profits and turn their efforts to other business opportunities. According to Alan Greenspan, chairman of the Federal Reserve, American labor laws and culture allow unneeded workers to be replaced by those whose skills are more in demand much more quickly than do the labor laws in other countries. As a result, the Internet and high technology in general are contributing to a greater increase in worker productivity in the United States than in Asia and Europe.[8]

However, just as technology can help improve productivity, it can also retard productivity if the volume of communications becomes unmanageable for employees. According to a Gartner Group survey of U.S. businesses, employees reported that 34 percent of the e-mail they received was unnecessary and that they spent 49 minutes each day managing their e-mail; 24 percent of them spent more than an hour.[9]

A firm can increase the productivity of its workers in several ways, such as increasing workers' motivation through financial incentives or introducing improved training methods that help them deal with difficult calls. Questions about operations management and productivity are central to a firm's planning decisions. First, the firm has to decide how to put the e-business plan into operation. Basic questions about how the work will be organized and managed and how employees will be distributed within the firm need to be resolved. In many situations, the firm may decide to outsource certain operations to other organizations that can deal with them more efficiently because they are handling only a limited and very specialized area of work. For example, rather than maintaining a computer system to service their websites, many firms will opt to purchase hosting services from an organization whose only concern is maintaining computer facilities for its clients. In many cases, this choice is motivated not only by cost savings and efficiency but also by the need to keep trained staff on hand to maintain specialized operations, by security concerns, and by the faster access speeds generally provided by hosts, who are often close to a major artery of the Internet. According to the Information Technology Association, an industry shortage of skilled knowledge workers at the peak of e-business activity in 2000 was a driving force behind the trend toward outsourcing computer system needs. By using Internet-based hosts that provide all software and technical services for a monthly fee, firms avoided the need to fill many highly specialized jobs. The association estimated that there were about 850,000 unfilled technology jobs, and that the shortage of workers was exacerbated by the strong growth in e-business activities.[10]

Interestingly, although the shortage of skilled workers eased considerably during the industry downturn that began in 2000–2001, many firms continue to outsource rather than hire their own staff to meet their needs. Similarly, to improve their purchasing system, aerospace giants Boeing, BAE Systems, Lockheed Martin, and Raytheon jointly developed an online exchange that links more than 37,000 suppliers, hundreds of airlines, and national governments into a single web-based marketplace for an estimated annual sales of $400 billion in parts. The exchange also reduces administrative costs and speeds the procurement process for private and government aerospace and defense concerns worldwide.[11]

e-BUSINESS insight

Yahoo!—The First Internet Search Engine Grows Through Global Partnerships

Yahoo! was started up in 1994 by David Filo and Jerry Yang while they were Ph.D. candidates in Electrical Engineering at Stanford University. Like many Internet success stories, what started as a personal tool for organizing records was quickly recognized as a breakthrough opportunity for generating wealth on the Internet. The Yahoo! business model helped establish the basic e-business recipe for success: First, create content that can continuously attract an audience, and then sell advertising space to businesses that are interested in reaching this audience. In the case of Yahoo!, whose 2003 revenues exceeded $1.6 billion, success was built on an early lead over competitors in providing users with an Internet search engine that would help them to find sites in a complex and rapidly expanding universe of websites. Since then, hundreds of search engine firms have entered the market using variations on the algorithm for locating websites. In order to continue to differentiate itself in the marketplace and capitalize on the enormous value of its widely recognized brand name, Yahoo! grows through strategic partnerships with other firms.

For example, most websites provide a search engine to serve their audiences as they search within the site or beyond onto the web. They can either develop their own; create a link to an outside website that provides the search service, like Yahoo!; or buy the software and give it their own brand identification. Given the choice, efficiency arguments suggest that firms should concentrate on creating the content they are best suited to produce and acquire those other services specified by their e-business plan through purchases, licensing agreements, or other partnership arrangements. In most cases, the search engine brand is not visible to the user but is likely to be one of the major brands like Yahoo!.

Through a strategic alliance with Rogers Cable, Canada's largest cable operator, Yahoo! subscribers receive high-speed Internet access bundled with a combination of customized Yahoo! products and services, optimized for broadband. This enhanced service includes Yahoo!'s leading tools and services, such as a powerful customized browsing environment; a personalized homepage; enhanced e-mail, including spam control and additional storage; security and parental controls; premium pop-up advertising blocking; enhanced instant messaging capabilities; digital photo tools and storage; and online music and game services.

In another strategic partnership, Philips and Yahoo! are jointly developing and delivering Yahoo! content and broadband Internet services through Philips' Streamium Internet-enabled Home Entertainment devices that consumers can experience anywhere in their homes, such as on their television sets and home entertainment systems. Royal Philips

Electronics of the Netherlands is one of the world's biggest electronics companies and Europe's largest, with sales of €31.8 billion in 2002.

And finally, Yahoo! and SINA Corporation, a leading Chinese portal, have established a joint venture that will provide a new auctions-based e-commerce service for small- and medium-sized businesses and buyers and sellers in China. The new service will combine SINA's leading brand and valuable audience in China with Yahoo!'s global brand strength and proven e-commerce expertise from its top-ranked auctions services in Japan, Taiwan, and Hong Kong.

Question for discussion: What other types of partnership agreements might Yahoo! pursue with other organizations?[12]

Leadership, Motivation, and the Corporate Culture

Businesses that are operating in the fast-changing environment of the Internet need a corporate leadership approach that can motivate employees and support employee trust and risk taking. Creating a culture of trust can lead to increases in growth, profit, productivity, and job satisfaction. A culture of trust can help a firm retain the best people, inspire customer loyalty, develop new markets, and increase its creativity. Critics suggest that IBM inadvertently developed a culture that punished those who took reasonable risks and then failed. As a result, up until the early 1990s, the organization became overly bureaucratic, and people gradually stopped taking competitive risks in order to avoid failure. Today, IBM's leadership approach is vastly different, reflecting the new age of creative thinking about managing organizations.[13]

Corporate Leadership and Influence

Arguably more than any other factor, the leadership a firm's management exhibits can have a dramatic influence on whether the firm achieves its goals. Success for both the firm and individual employees is generally acknowledged to be highly determined by strong leadership qualities that filter down throughout the organization so everyone is unified in purpose and direction. Microsoft, GE, IBM, Dell Computer, Sun Microsystems, and Oracle are only a few of the celebrated firms that are led by dynamic and charismatic leaders who built their empires by uniting everyone from highly ranked executives to lower-level employees, as well as bankers, investors, suppliers, and other players. In each of these great e-business success stories, an outstanding leadership figure and an overall leadership style that emanated from the top contributed importantly to the firm's success. For instance, Larry Ellison, chairman and CEO of Oracle Corporation of Redwood Shores, California, built the firm's annual revenues up from a mere $282 million in 1988 to an estimated $9.7 billion today—an incredible increase of more than 3,350 percent. Much of that growth has taken place since 1994 as Oracle capitalized on its global leadership in Internet software in addition to its base in information management software. As a measure of its growth, Oracle now has more than 23,000 employees in 144 countries aside from the 21,000 working in the United States.[14]

In general, e-business activities require a large number of self-motivated individuals, and such people will not flourish in a working atmosphere led by someone with an authoritarian leadership style. Besides knowing that highly skilled personnel can readily leave and find work at other firms that will treat them better, such employers recognize the need for a free-thinking, creative work environment where new ideas can more readily emerge. Since much of the work e-business workers do is measurable, such as number of lines of computer programming code written, webpages created, or new sales contracts closed, both management and employees know whether employees can reach targets. Furthermore, employees can help management adjust current strategies, since they are the closest to the action and can shed the greatest light on possible reasons and solutions for failures.

Motivation, Recognition, and Compensation Issues

motivation

In a business environment, the drive that individuals feel to perform their assigned tasks.

Motivation in a business environment refers to the drive that individuals feel to perform their assigned tasks. Research suggests that employees are likely to be more motivated in their work when the firm has clearly defined goals and realistic objectives for them to strive for. These expectations can be communicated through meetings with supervisors and by giving employees edited portions of the business plan or the full plan. People who are directly involved in decision-making and in preparing those business plans will feel a greater sense of ownership and a greater drive to realize them.

Needless to say, compensation and recognition of achievement are important motivational factors. Employees expect fair monetary compensation and might be more motivated by bonus payments for successfully reaching targeted individual and group objectives that are part of the e-business plan. Higher-level managers traditionally seek performance bonuses for leading a division or project successfully. Stock options (which we will discuss in greater detail in Chapter 10) and revenue- or profit-sharing plans are also common motivational tools. To motivate top executives and, increasingly, middle-ranking managers who work long hours for what they consider poor salaries, many Internet-related firms provide *stock options* as part of the employee compensation package. A stock option is simply the right to buy shares of the firm within a prescribed time at a set price. If the firm does well, and its stock price rises past the set price (presumably at least in part because of all the work being done by the employee), the employee can exercise the option and immediately sell the stock to cash in on the company's success. For example, Joseph Galli was lured away from Black & Decker to take the president's post at Amazon.com. Along with an annual salary of $200,000, Galli was given 3.9 million options on Amazon.com stock. When Amazon's stock soared, those options rose to a theoretical value of more than $200 million, but they fell to no value as the stock market turned on Amazon. Time will tell whether Galli's options turn out to be worthless or make him a fabulously rich man.[15]

After the industry shakeout in 2000, the perceived value of an equity stake in an e-business fell dramatically as employees came to view stock options as mere promises of corporate riches that might not ever be achievable. Therefore, demands for higher salaries today are likely to increase as stock option plans fall from favor. Looking at the successes of celebrated industry leaders, we can easily understand the strength of the financial incentives. Even after the huge fall in technology share values in 2000–1, Bill Gates, the chairman of Microsoft Corporation, was still the richest man in the world for the seventh year in a row, with an estimated $60 billion of assets. Paul Allen, Microsoft's cofounder with Bill Gates, was third at $30 billion; Larry Ellison of Oracle Corporation was fourth at $26 billion; and Michael Dell of Dell Computer was twenty-seventh.[16]

Recognition through public acknowledgement, especially among peers, can produce great motivation, and, more importantly, the absence of proper acknowledgement or acknowledging the wrong people can be counterproductive. Organizations can promote their successes and the people that made them happen by giving them awards and publicizing their achievements. Sometimes a very small expenditure, such as for a photo and an article in the firm's newsletter, can boost the ego-sensitive motivation that is lying dormant in most of us. Maslow's hierarchy of needs theory, which suggests that people rank and arrange their needs in an order of importance and subsequently act to satisfy them in order of importance, provides a useful way of viewing employee motivation. Maslow's theory suggests that most employees are primarily motivated by social and ego needs. A firm with an unfriendly work environment or one that does not support these needs will have difficulty finding and retaining highly motivated individuals. Senior management may be driven by their personal desire to contribute to building an enterprise from scratch. Given the widespread publicity and accolades conferred on individuals and firms like Microsoft and Yahoo!, many individuals came to see e-business as a new frontier, without the barriers or limits that were traditionally found in older, more established industries. Many saw this work environment as a once-in-a-lifetime chance to create a business monument they could be forever associated with and simultaneously be rewarded with huge salaries, stock options, bonuses, and so forth.

All of us want to feel that we matter and that our work is recognized and properly rewarded. Of the major motivational theories experts employ to understand the e-business working environment, equity and expectancy theories are quite useful. *Equity theory* suggests that people are motivated by their personal *sense of equity* or ownership in a situation. In brief, this means that if an individual perceives that he or she is well treated and rewarded, then that individual will complement this belief with an appropriate level of motivation and effort in his or her work. By contrast, if someone perceives that he or she is not being treated and rewarded well, the theory suggests that that person will adjust his or her motivation and perform accordingly. Somewhat similarly, *expectancy theory* (also discussed in Chapter 7 to explain buyer behavior) suggests that motivation is associated with how much an individual wants to achieve a given objective and how much she or he believes it can be achieved. The message of expectancy theory is that management must be sure to make the accomplishment of employees' assigned tasks both important to the individual employees and achievable in their minds. Weaknesses in either one of these factors will undermine the individual's motivation to complete the set tasks successfully.

In deciding how best to motivate employees, the developers of the firm's e-business plan must be confident that they are not compensating employees beyond the true worth of their contribution and what the firm can realistically afford to pay. Criticism of excessive compensation packages for high-tech executives was not common when stock market prices were soaring but poured into the press as disgruntled stockholders saw their investments collapse in value. For example, when retiring Nortel Networks Inc. CEO John Roth stepped down in the spring of 2001, he did so after having exercised stock options that earned him $135 million. This was during a year in which the firm's stock value had fallen more than 80 percent from the previous year's high.[17]

Corporate Culture and the Informal Organization

The term *corporate culture* refers to the general values and behaviors that are considered normal within a firm. As we discussed in Chapter 3, corporate culture sets the tone for ethical behavior. In addition, corporate culture sets the tone for leadership, decision-making, risk taking, and the communication behaviors that are generally used within a particular group of employees and across the entire firm.

Part of the corporate culture is the *informal* organization that exists within its formal organizational structure and often explains how the organization really functions. For instance, although decisions may be made formally at committee meetings called expressly for that purpose, people may meet informally in smaller groups and exchange e-mail messages to discuss their decisions before the meetings take place. Informal communication can take place outside the organization as well. For example, in response to their personal experiences of burnout, Steve Baldwin and Bill Lessard launched a New York–based website and wrote a book aptly called *Netslaves* (**www.disobey.com/netslaves**). The two are driven by the goal of demythologizing the media image of work in the Internet industry and providing a forum where other managers can exchange stories about the difficulties of working in a dot-com world.[18]

The use of communication technologies is generally associated with positive outcomes, but research suggests that there may be a growing negative impact on corporate culture as well. According to research, the use of technological tools such as e-mail can contribute to dysfunctional work-related problems, including stress, loneliness, anger, and even depression. Because e-mail is convenient and ubiquitous, it may reduce the amount of face-to-face human interaction to a level below that which people have come to accept as normal. Communicating through e-mail can frustrate both the receiver and the sender because it does not allow individuals to communicate in subtle human ways, such as through eye contact, gestures, body language, and voice tones. And e-mail creates the expectation that questions will be answered instantly, which leads to the feeling that work never seems to have an end.[19]

Ironically, the same technology that may contribute to dysfunctional behaviors and work-related problems may also provide solutions. One of North America's largest employee-assistance program providers, the Warren Shepell Company (**www. warrenshepell.com**) of Toronto, Ontario, has over 1,000 e-counselors who use e-mail to help more than 3 million employees at 1,300 corporate clients. They rely on e-therapy as a method for dealing with employees' personal problems in addition to using conventional face-to-face and telephone-based sessions. However, research has shown that, in addition to saving client firms money and providing faster service to employees, asynchronous e-mail, which refers to e-mail that may be sent at any time of day suitable for the sender, benefits clients by giving them the time they need to contemplate their exchanges with counselors before they formulate a response.[20]

The Internet presents new challenges for firms whose employees can use convenient high-speed connections at work to enjoy easy access to sites. An employee's behavior online can be viewed as offensive to coworkers and can possibly be illegal. Research by Websense and the Center for Internet Studies revealed that nearly two out of three companies nationwide have disciplined employees and nearly one out of three have fired employees for Internet misuse in the workplace.[21]

Interestingly, today's high-technology and Internet-based firms rank relatively high when it comes to environmental issues, working conditions, the representation of minorities and women in upper management, animal testing, and charitable donations. The New York watchdog group the Council on Economic Priorities examines more than 700 of the country's largest companies annually. According to them, the cultures of new-economy firms tend to be rated better than average, but they are not immune from criticism either.[22]

e-BUSINESS insight

Yahoo! as a Marketing Research Firm

In 2003, in partnership with ACNielsen, Yahoo! Consumer Direct launched a research service aimed at the consumer packaged goods (CPG) industry. These firms, which market a wide variety of products from snack foods to floor cleaners, are interested in learning how to reach consumers more effectively online and how to directly measure the sales impact of these efforts. In almost all cases, sales are transacted inside retail stores and not online. The research challenge is to better understand how online marketing strategies can influence those sales. To do so, researchers need to be able to track and record a variety of information, including the sites consumers visited and their response to online promotions.

Members of ACNielsen's 61,500-household Homescan® consumer panel allow their offline purchasing to be analyzed in conjunction with their activity on the Yahoo! network. Yahoo! and ACNielsen then use the information derived from the Homescan panelists to find groups with similar demonstrated interest trends among Yahoo!'s millions of monthly visitors. The Consumer Direct team then works with CPG clients to communicate with those consumers via customized online media campaigns, using a range of solutions from Yahoo!'s media and promotion suite. Lastly, the ACNielsen Homescan panel is used to evaluate the campaigns' return on investment, including gathering metrics on the campaign's impact on retail sales, brand loyalty, and more.

Question for discussion: What other research-related partnerships would be desirable for Yahoo! to form with other firms or organizations?[23]

Topics in Management

In this final section of the chapter, we will explore three important topics in management: human resources management, small-business management and entrepreneurial issues, and management consulting services. Although a large body of knowledge exists on each topic, we will introduce these topics only briefly and then highlight several important connections they have to e-business planning.

Human Resources Management

human resources management
All of the activities related to acquiring, maintaining, and developing the people who do the work in the firm.

Human resources management is concerned with all of the activities related to acquiring, maintaining, and developing the people who do the work in the firm—the firm's *human capital.* Acquiring the employees needed to do the tasks entailed in running the firm requires planning for future human resources needs, creating descriptions and analyses of the jobs that will need to be done, finding and hiring employees for those jobs, and integrating the employees into the firm.

Evaluating Skills and Knowledge

In evaluating the true value of an applicant's or employee's skills and knowledge, continuous assessment and certification will likely grow in importance, since the assessment of the firm's human resources is so strongly related to the speed with which knowledge ages. For example, ten years of experience in programming old and outdated software is of little value if a firm requires programmers who are knowledgeable about the Internet and e-commerce software programs in use today.[24]

Finding Specialized Employees

Finding qualified specialized employees can require a firm to use a number of strategies, many of which are rather traditional. According to Michael Boyd, senior HR analyst at IDC, Internet-based sites such as Monster (**www.monster.com**) and CareerBuilder (**www.careerbuilder.com**), which hold millions of résumés that employers can choose from, are not the primary connections for successful high-tech job hunters. In fact, only 8.1 percent of those hired were recruited through web-based employment services. Boyd's studies suggest that the complex social networks of human interaction, such as word of mouth and employee referrals, still account for more than a third of all high-tech recruiting. Even job fairs, print and TV ads, and old-fashioned headhunters are better than online agencies.[25]

Employee Dissatisfaction on the Job

The high level of dissatisfaction at high-tech firms, especially among employees at dot-com start-ups, is a growing reality. Many people who are working long hours, often without much social contact outside of the workplace, have decided that career advancement does not make up for the absence of a personal life.[26]

Once employees have become part of a firm's human resource infrastructure, they represent a valuable investment in terms of the time and money the firm has spent to get them there. Replacing them is an additional cost that does not contribute to profitability. Internet software solutions firms like SAS Institute Inc. of Cary, North Carolina, work hard to find and keep good high-technology workers. Interestingly, by promoting a normal workweek that takes into consideration the importance that employees place on spending time with their families, relaxing, and participating in other aspects of life has helped to create a more content and motivated workforce. As a result, employee turnover is an astonishingly low 4 percent, compared to a 20 percent industry rate.[27]

For some jobs, however, such as the customer service representatives employed in a call center, the turnover is high. Employees may not last more than a few months, and those that suffer from burnout and cannot be promoted to other tasks are lost. Firms can attempt to maintain employees through good treatment, good working conditions, fair compensation, and other benefits.

Developing Skills and Knowledge

Developing employees' skills and knowledge is recognized as both a factor in determining whether they stay or quit and is an important means of producing employees who have the skills needed at higher organizational levels within the firm. A by-product of the boom in Internet and information technology employment is the high demand for highly skilled workers. Interestingly, many high-technology workers fear losing their jobs and, with them, access to the ability to learn about new knowledge and skills, which provides something of a counterbalance to employees' demands for higher salary and wage in this sector of the economy.[28] In addition to these dynamics influencing highly skilled employees and employers, the industry slowdown that began in 2000–2001 also had an impact.

Since many jobs require cumulative skills and knowledge, it would be logical for a firm to build on its existing employee base rather than hire from outside as it generates new jobs requiring more advanced skills. Not only is this motivational for the firm's employees, but the firm also benefits by being in a position to mold the knowledge and skills each employee accumulates over time. Thus, the firm's human resources planning can be directed toward internal training and development.

A recent report prepared by the American Society for Training and Development (ASTD), an industry association that monitors and also promotes employee-learning strategies, revealed the value of employee education programs. The report found that for every $600 investment the firms it surveyed made in the education of each employee, the firms experienced a 57 percent increase in sales per employee and a 37 percent increase in gross profit. In dollar terms, this means that for every $100,000 in sales per employee and gross profit per employee, the added investment returned $157,000 in net sales and $137,000 in gross profit.[29]

Online Learning Systems

Driven by savings in cost, travel, and time, online learning, either pursued alone or in face-to-face learning situations, is a strong alternative strategy. The costs of training and development are inflated by the fact that employees are not working when they are away at training seminars or conferences or using

Internet-distributed courseware. Nevertheless, Internet-distributed courseware is growing in popularity for many reasons, particularly because of its flexibility and its adaptability to the learning style and needs of the learner. Courseware is generally divided into small modules, each of which may take only 10 or 15 minutes to complete. Employees can therefore explore several modules in sequence if they have time. And while they are traveling on business, employees can pass long evenings in their hotel rooms more productively by completing many modules at one sitting. Often, learners can even retrieve courseware modules from directories for *just-in-time learning*, enabling the user to call up a module or two to help with a particular learning situation. This is common in information technology (IT) training, where the knowledge required for software tasks generally emerges over time as the user's expertise increases. Therefore, it makes more sense to train employees to *find* the information they need than to expect them to learn everything and retain that knowledge indefinitely.

Online learning systems are a cost-effective way to initiate new employees into company procedures, regulations, and policies. Popular and repeated questions can be combined to create a self-service listing of frequently asked questions (FAQ) or "what to do if . . ." or "who to speak to when . . ." knowledge bases. Furthermore, online learning systems can work well to familiarize employees with the firm's executives and with one another. These systems can take the form of personal webpages that typically contain biographical information and photographs of the people in the organization.

According to research by International Data Inc., the corporate market for e-learning in the United States is expected to grow more than 500 percent— from $2.2 billion in 2000 to more than $11 billion in 2007. The reasons are well established by now: convenience, lower costs of delivery, reduced need for travel, immediate delivery of learning to large numbers of employees at the same time, flexibility in design to accommodate different learning styles, and so forth. For example, since Circuit City moved its sales training course online, 90 percent of its 55,000 plus staff have taken more than 400,000 courses, each lasting about 30 minutes to an hour. Not only are these courses popular with employees, but the firm is able to measure learning progress through online tests and then compare the scores with changes in sales performance and employee turnover. American Airlines' flight attendants are now able to take part of their annual certification training online as an alternative to classroom-based instruction. The courses review emergency, security, and other procedures and are approved by the Federal Aviation Administration. Finally, after taking part in a pilot program, 94 percent of MasterCard International's employees responded positively to online training, indicating that they would prefer that all or part of their training be provided online. Given that it costs MasterCard $10 to have each learner take a sexual harassment course online in comparison to the $150 cost of classroom-based delivery, it is highly likely that all MasterCard employees will be seeing more continuing education and training services delivered online.[30]

Once a company decides to adopt online learning as part of its overall training and development effort, it faces the still complicated task of selecting the best learning management system for its needs. The term *learning management system* refers to the software that contains the learning content. Such software may allow sophisticated authoring of online course content, testing, tracking of employee development, and analysis of employee skills along with providing advice on individual training needs and courses. There are more than 100 competing learning management systems, each with various strengths and weaknesses. They are not all compatible with one another; content developed on one may not be readily transferable to another. Vendors may also host learning systems and charge clients according to the number of employees, number of courses, or hours spent by employees accessing the system. According to consultant and e-learning expert Brandon Hall, firms are well advised to look for a good fit between the system and the firm's business processes. Furthermore, the firm should be sure to properly organize learning groups and facilitate continuous communication among all participants.[31]

In addition to setting up internal organizational learning systems for employees, many firms have established formal online learning courses that meet at scheduled times and are organized into work and study groups. Some organizations have developed working relationships with academic institutions in which these institutions provide online courses that allow the organizations' employees to earn academic credits. Hybrid courses can involve some classroom lecture time in combination with an online learning component. The majority of colleges and universities around the world are competing in this growing market segment, even offering fully accredited undergraduate and graduate degrees. In all of these cases, the learning system must prove itself worthwhile through measurable results. Such results can include test scores upon completion of a module or entire course, appraisal feedback by the learners, and assessments of the learners by their supervisors when they return to work and apply their newly acquired skills and knowledge.

Small-Business Management and Entrepreneurial Issues

According to a recent report by American Express, 66 percent of the small businesses it surveyed had already integrated the Internet as a tool in helping them run their businesses. Among the applications were making travel plans and purchasing office supplies, equipment, or other business services (tied at 36 percent); conducting industry or market research (34 percent); marketing or advertising (29 percent); networking with other entrepreneurs (24 percent); purchasing goods from wholesalers (22 percent); and managing accounts and making payments (16 percent). Furthermore, 51 percent viewed the Internet as more cost-effective than other marketing methods, and 29 percent stated that the Internet is the most cost-effective method. Considerably fewer respondents considered direct mail, newspapers and magazines, or Yellow Pages advertising to be the most cost-effective marketing strategy. Finally, growth in small-business Internet-based solutions is likely, given that 77 percent of these businesses agree that a website is a "must have" for small business; 60 percent said that they wish they had built a website for their business sooner; and 85 percent would also advise other small-business owners to have a website.[32]

For thousands of people around the world, the Internet has been a boon to small-business and entrepreneurial efforts. The reasons are simple: The traditional barriers to entry that exist for most businesses are far lower for small e-business start-ups. e-Business start-ups do not require large amounts of capital, many employees, and established distribution relationships with suppliers and customers. They can be, have been, and continue to be launched on a shoestring budget, sometimes by one person using a home office. The only critical tool is a computer with access to the Internet.

Recognizing an opportunity to capitalize on the needs of small businesses that have limited cash, firms like BigStep (**www.bigstep.com**) provide small businesses with the opportunity to create their own website for a small monthly fee, a service that generally would cost about $250 a month and more from other website service firms. Backed by partnerships with Sun Microsystems, Washingtonpost.com, and Newsweek Interactive, BigStep makes its money from sponsorships and fees for optional services.[33]

What Can Small Businesses Do?

Small e-businesses often thrive because they provide services to larger firms on a contractual basis. Once the work is completed, they are free to pursue other contracts with other firms. The larger firms save money by doing this because they need not hire permanent personnel for what might be a short-term project and are not obliged to pay a variety of employee taxes and benefit costs, such as insurance and pension programs.

Common services provided by small e-businesses include designing and setting up webpages, writing simple applications in a computer software program code like Lotus Notes, training employees (particularly on the use of software), researching new products and markets, and preparing business plans for internal use as well as for external parties such as lenders and investors. Often, an innovation made by a small business contributes a valuable service to an established industry as demonstrated by San Mateo, California–based MakeOverStudio (**www.makeoverstudio.com**) founded by Lori Von Rueden. The free Internet service allowed users to upload a digital photo of themselves and then experiment with the latest makeup products and hair colors offered by cosmetics vendors who licensed the product. Customers could change their hair and lipstick color a thousand different ways with just a click of their mouse. When customers at the vendors' sites purchased the products that delivered their online look, MakeOverStudio earned a percentage of the online sales. Although Makeoverstudio.com had quickly registered 400,000 users, it fell victim to a lack of funding when the dot-com crash hit in 2000, proving that although the concept was good, building a successful e-business requires significant funding until revenues are strong enough to cover expenses.[34]

Formula for Success

According to entrepreneur Bill Tatham, the founder of Janna Systems of Toronto, Ontario, the most important advice start-up firms must follow is to focus on those strategies that will generate revenue soonest and to target a market that has at least $1 billion in annual sales. After Janna Systems' sales doubled each year for six years in a row, its biggest rival, Siebel Systems, acquired it for $1.76 billion in 2000. Janna Systems' CRM software was particularly popular with Wall Street firms and fit well within the Siebel organizational structure. Tatham acknowledges that the firm made mistakes in the beginning by chasing after the wrong customers. It was only after it changed the focus of its plan to seeking profitability that business began to really change for the better. Tatham suggests that after the competitive shakeout of 2000–1, e-business strategy will have to be different. To raise capital, a firm will need to rely much more heavily on a proven management team, a distinct product, and profitability.[35]

Web Threatens Small Business

Although the Internet has given rise to many new opportunities for small businesses, it has created many challenges as well. For example, according to the American Society of Travel Agents (ASTA), the industry shift to Internet-based operations has been nothing short of catastrophic for small-business travel operators. The number of member agents in 140 countries around the world fell from 33,000 in 1994 to 24,000 in 2002—a drop of more than 27 percent. Motivated by customers and industry vendors seeking ways to cut their costs, online operations are being transformed by firms like **www.travelocity.com** and **www.expedia.com**.[36]

However, the number of ASTA member agents has stabilized at about 20,000, and interestingly, the Internet has also changed the way in which firms operate. According an ASTA survey in 2003, 89 percent of agencies now provide Internet access for every staff member at their own workstations, up from 74 percent in 2002; 59 percent have a website and of those agencies with websites, 35 percent provide some kind of online booking capabilities; booking online is increasingly popular at agencies, with more than 76 percent reporting that they have booked directly on supplier's websites; and finally, 94 percent of agents now use e-mail for business communications.[37]

Management Consulting Services

The Internet has been a boon to the management consulting industry, since the services that e-businesses need can be provided by consultants—both large and small. Creating a website and setting up an online retail service for a client that only needs a few hundred hours of services from a knowledgeable consultant might be a simple enough task for a small business. However, considering all the complexities entailed when a large retailer like Sears or the Home Depot decides to establish an online presence and how work processes would have to be changed to accommodate the new e-business structure, it is safe to say that the management of such corporations need a variety of services to work through the process and launch their sites. In most cases, large-scale organizations roll out an e-business effort without enlisting the coordinating and research help provided by consulting firms that have the talented and knowledgeable employees needed to manage such projects. Complex projects can run on for years as various divisions of the organization are gradually brought on-stream according to a planned schedule. Even installing popular programs such as CRM software from firms like Siebel Systems, which is modular in design and can be built in stages as the client firm grows, is a complex affair that requires a variety of corporate resources, some that only larger management consulting firms can provide.

Today, e-business management consulting services have attracted many seemingly unrelated companies whose clients are demanding e-business services. Rather than see revenues and possibly clients lost to competitors, large-scale enterprises have established management consulting divisions or entirely new independent businesses to go after the growing market for e-business management consulting services. Accounting firms (Ernst & Young), computer hardware vendors (IBM), telecommunications firms (AT&T), and established management consulting firms (Accenture) are all competing for what appears to be a great growth opportunity. Accenture Corp. (**www.accenture.com**) is the world's leading provider of management and technology consulting services and solutions, employing more than 80,000 people in 46 countries who deliver a wide range of specialized capabilities and solutions to clients across all industries. Accenture operates globally and has built a network of businesses that can meet the full range of any organization's needs for consulting, technology, outsourcing, alliances, and venture capital. The company generated revenues of $11.8 billion for the fiscal year 2003.[38]

**Go to the Web:
e-Business Online**
For tutorials and more on the topics in this chapter, visit the student website at **http://business.college. hmco.com/students** and select "Canzer e-Business."

Conclusions

In this chapter, we explored the ways in which firms can approach the organizational and managerial issues surrounding strategic planning in an e-business environment. Several important subject areas were examined, including the components of the management process, organizational structures, production and operations, and productivity and efficiency issues. We saw how leadership and corporate culture play an important role in operations and in motivating employees, and, finally, we examined e-business issues related to several key areas of management decision-making, including human resources management, small-business management, and consulting.

This discussion also helped provide a guiding structure for preparing the management component of an **e-business plan**. A more detailed tutorial on preparing the e-business plan is available on the textbook's website.

In the next chapter, we will examine financial planning and investment in an e-business environment.

RETURN TO
inside e-business

Google.com's management and its more than 200 employees have carved out a niche for their firm in a highly competitive market. Google.com simplifies interaction with its users, rather than offering more choices and complexity, as many competitors continue to do. One search on the Google.com site illustrates just how different Google is from Yahoo! and other competitors. Examine the websites of several search engines, including Google, Yahoo!, and Alta Vista.

ASSIGNMENT

1. Compare the strategic choices that Google.com's management has made on the Google site (**www.google.com**), which make it stand out from competing sites such as Yahoo! (**www.yahoo.com**) or Alta Vista (**www.altavista.com**).

2. What strategy for future growth would you recommend to Google.com that is consistent with creating a sustainable competitive advantage?

Chapter Review

SUMMARY

ACE Self-Test
For a quick self-test of the content in this chapter, visit the student website at **http://business.college. hmco.com/students.** Select "Canzer e-Business."

1. **Examine the connections between management and e-business planning.**

The management process is the ongoing planning, organizing, and controlling of all the activities that personnel throughout the organization are engaged in, including marketing, finance, production and operations, human resources, and so forth. The word *process* suggests that these activities are continuous and never ending. In a simple sense, then, these activities are the work that people do to keep the enterprise moving toward identified goals with purpose and direction. Organizational structures define the way in which individuals work together; how they solve problems; make decisions; communicate; and share responsibility, authority, and power with one another. Common structures are the bureaucratic, organic, and matrix structures. Operations management involves the coordination of all the activities related to the production of the products and services that the organization provides to its customers; its focus is on the manufacturing processes, including facilities, capacity, purchasing, inventory, quality control, use of technology, and employees' skills. The objective of operations management is to deliver the planned production of products and services within set cost limits. Operations management is continuously seeking ways to reduce costs and improve the quality of the products and services produced. This is accomplished primarily by studying how work is organized and done so that efficiencies and other improvements can be introduced.

2. **Describe the e-business issues related to leadership, motivation, and corporate culture.**

Businesses that are operating in the fast-changing environment of the Internet need a corporate leadership approach that can motivate employees and support trust and risk taking. The leadership a firm's management exhibits can have a dramatic influence on whether the firm achieves its goals. In general, e-business activities require a large number of self-motivated individuals who will not flourish in a working atmosphere led by someone with an authoritarian leadership style. Motivation in a business environment refers to the drive that individuals feel to perform their assigned tasks. Research suggests that employees are likely to be more motivated in their work when the firm has clearly defined goals and realistic objectives for them to strive for. The term *corporate culture* refers to the general values and behaviors that are considered normal within the firm. Corporate culture sets the tone for ethical behavior, leadership, decision-making, risk taking, and the communication behaviors that are used within a particular group of employees and across the entire firm.

3. **Explore human resources management, small-business management and entrepreneurial issues, and the role of management consulting in the world of e-business.**

   Human resources management is concerned with all of the activities related to acquiring, maintaining, and developing the people who do the work in the firm. Acquiring the employees needed to do the tasks entailed in running the firm requires planning for future human resources needs, creating descriptions and analyses of the jobs that will need to be done, finding and hiring employees for these jobs, and integrating the employees into the firm. The Internet has been a boon to small-business and entrepreneurial efforts for tens of thousands of people around the world. The reasons are simple: The traditional barriers to entry that exist for most businesses are far lower for small e-business start-ups. e-Business start-ups do not require large amounts of capital, many employees, or established distribution relationships with suppliers and customers. They can be, have been, and continue to be launched on a shoestring budget, sometimes by one person using a home office; the only critical tool is a computer with access to the Internet. The Internet has also been a boon to the management consulting industry. Today, e-business management consulting services have attracted a range of seemingly unrelated companies whose clients are demanding e-business services. Rather than see revenues and possibly clients lost to competitors, a variety of large-scale enterprises have established management consulting divisions or entirely new independent businesses to go after the growing market for e-business consulting services.

REVIEW QUESTIONS

1. Define the management process.
2. Explain the meaning of each of the components that make up the management process.
3. What is an organizational chart and how is it used?
4. Define span of control.
5. What are bureaucratic, organic, and matrix structures?

6. Define operations management.
7. What is meant by corporate culture?
8. What are some special human resources management issues related to e-business planning?
9. What are the advantages and disadvantages of being a small e-business?
10. How can management consulting services help the organization?

DISCUSSION QUESTIONS

1. Discuss the management process, using an example to illustrate your answer.
2. Discuss the importance of using the management process.
3. Why is span of control so important in management planning?
4. Discuss the importance of leadership and motivation in management planning.
5. How can e-business increase productivity?
6. Discuss why outsourcing is a good idea for an e-business.
7. Discuss why opportunities exist for both large and small e-businesses.

Building Skills for Career Success

EXPLORING THE INTERNET

Accenture Corp. is an example of a large-scale management consulting firm that specializes in providing e-business services to clients. Located on the Web at **www.accenture.com**, Accenture is the world's leading provider of management and technology consulting services and solutions, with more than 80,000 people in 46 countries delivering a wide range of specialized capabilities and solutions to clients across all industries. Accenture's website provides many case study examples to illustrate how the firm has helped its clients with a variety of e-business applications.

ASSIGNMENT

1. Describe one case study example in which Accenture saved a client money.
2. What e-learning applications does Accenture offer?

DEVELOPING CRITICAL THINKING SKILLS

Equity and expectancy theories are popular models for gaining insight into motivation. Consider the case of a thirty-year-old executive who, after three years, left a large international consulting firm similar to Accenture. The young executive was earning in excess of $100,000 per year in salary and was making excellent progress along the training and development path set out by the firm. He had learned much about customer relationships and the company's products and selling methods during his time at the firm. While he had been involved with more than thirty projects, he had also gained some specialized expertise that he felt made him very valuable to his clients and his employer.

ASSIGNMENT

1. Using equity and expectancy theories as the basis for your analysis, write a report that explains the possible motivations for the executive's decision to leave the firm.
2. Given the reasons that you have identified, what can the firm do to reduce the chances that other executives will follow the same route out of the firm?

BUILDING TEAM SKILLS

Successful organizations are often outstanding because of the leadership of key individual managers who have a strong vision about where they want to lead their team. Many of these individuals, like Bill Gates of Microsoft, have written articles and books explaining their passion to those interested in gaining insight into their managerial methods.

ASSIGNMENT

1. Assign each member of your team to search the Internet for material written by a successful e-business executive and prepare a summary report that highlights that executive's vision and reasons for success.
2. Compare the similarities and differences between each report's findings and submit a summary analysis.

RESEARCHING DIFFERENT CAREERS

Management consulting firms like Accenture (**www.accenture.com**) are popular choices for students seeking jobs after graduation. These firms generally offer a wide variety of opportunities and provide a track for training and development in specialized fields such as software, systems installations, and customer support. Examine the employment opportunities available at Accenture or some other large management consulting firm.

ASSIGNMENT

1. Write a brief report describing one job opportunity that you uncovered online.
2. What qualifications are required?
3. Explain why you would or would not be motivated to do the job.

IMPROVING COMMUNICATION SKILLS

The SmartDraw Organization Resource Center (**www.smartdraw.com**) is one of many websites that provide visitors with opportunities to learn more about communicating organizational structure through the use of charts. The site provides visitors with access to sample software that is useful for illustrating relationships between people, methods of communication, and workflows.

ASSIGNMENT

1. Describe the basic tools (lines and geometric shapes) that are used in an organizational chart.
2. Create an organizational chart and write a short description to explain what it is communicating.

Exploring Useful Websites

These websites provide information related to the topics discussed in the chapter. You can learn more by visiting them online and examining their current data.

1. Google.com (**www.google.com**), Yahoo! (**www.yahoo.com**), and Alta Vista (**www.altavista.com**) are competing search engine sites.

2. Monster.com (**www.monster.com**) manages half of the online-recruitment market. Careerbuilder (**www.careerbuilder.com**) is another major career site.

3. Netslaves (**www.disobey.com/netslaves**) provides a forum where managers can exchange stories about the difficulties of working in a dot-com world.

4. The Warren Shepell Company (**www.warrenshepell.com**) has over 1,000 e-counselors who use e-mail to help more than 3 million employees at 1,300 corporate clients.

5. BigStep (**www.bigstep.com**) provides small businesses with the opportunity to create their own website.

6. Individual travel customers and travel industry vendors who are seeking ways to cut their costs are targeted online by firms like **www.travelocity.com** and **www.expedia.com**. The American Society of Travel Agents (**www.astanet.com**) represents 20,000 agents in 140 countries.

7. Accenture Corp. (**www.accenture.com**) is the world's leading provider of management and technology consulting services and solutions.

8. The SmartDraw Organization Resource Center (**www.smartdraw.com**) is one of many websites that provide visitors with opportunities to learn more about communicating organizational structure through the use of charts.

chapter 10

Financial Planning and Working with Investors

INSIDE
e-business

Nortel Networks Inc.—A Financial Microcosm of the 2000–1 Crash

At its peak market value of 124 Canadian dollars (C$124) a share in July 2000, the Brampton, Ontario–based telecommunications equipment manufacturer Nortel Networks Inc. (**www.nortelnetworks.com**) represented 36 percent of the entire Toronto Stock Exchange index of 300 firms. At that time, the firm had achieved spectacular sales growth, with sales reaching nearly C$45 billion, and it had become the top Canadian business organization, with a market capitalization of C$300 billion. Just as Lucent Technologies (**www.lucent.com**) was a spin-off from AT&T, so Nortel had emerged from Bell Canada Enterprises as an independent firm to build the fiber-optic and wireless technology infrastructure of the Internet. As telecommunications firms expanded to accommodate the growth in Internet and other telecommunications demand, firms like Nortel quickly moved ahead by providing customers around the world with the computers, cables, and connectors that make up this infrastructure.

From only C$30 a share in the summer of 1999, Nortel's stock had skyrocketed, reaching new highs daily as the world investment community rushed to put money into all sorts of e-business firms. Like all the firms that were building the Internet infrastructure of the day and for the future, Nortel required massive capital inflows, and investment capital gravitated to the firm as its management presented convincing arguments that the new economy was only getting started and the best was yet to come. Comparisons to the inventions of the telegraph and the automobile a hundred years earlier convinced many investors that e-businesses could deliver increasingly greater returns through growth in revenues without end. This optimism eventually created a bubble of stock market overvaluation that was destined to burst at some point. The only real question was when that would happen and whether an individual investor would be able to sell his or her shares before everyone else started selling en masse.

Unfortunately, hindsight is always 20/20. By the time it became clear that sales revenues at Nortel, Cisco Systems, Lucent, and others had reached at least a temporary limit, corporate commitments to major capital expenditures were already done deals. Nortel's acquisitions of other firms were facilitated by the inflated value of Nortel's shares. Nortel management bought firms that had developed new technologies that it believed would eventually prove worthwhile to the Nortel product line. Between 1998 and 2001, using Nortel shares as currency, the firm acquired Bay Networks for US$9 billion, Qtera Corp. for US$3 billion, Clarify Inc. for US$2 billion, CoreTek Inc. for US$1 billion, Xros Inc. for US$3 billion, Alteon WebSystem Inc. for US$7 billion, and the Zurich plants of JDS Uniphase Inc. for US$3 billion. By the summer of 2001, Nortel was obliged to write down the value of those acquisitions on its financial statements by 70 percent. What looked like a quick strategy for acquiring new technologies and growing revenues for the company turned out to be overly optimistic when the industry downturn hit in 2001.

By the winter of 2001, the falloff in sales was clear, and a widespread perception of industry overcapacity set in. To help deal with the sudden change in revenues, which had created a record-setting $19 billion second-quarter loss, Nortel laid off more than 30,000 employees—about a third of its global workforce. With less and less revenue coming in and no immediate turnaround in sight, investors sold the stock of Nortel and other Internet-related firms heavily. A year later, the panic selling was over, and some sense emerged of how dramatic the fall had been emerged. Nortel shares had fallen to about C$14 (US$9), meaning they had lost more than 88 percent of their value of a year earlier and now represented only 8 percent of the Toronto Stock Exchange index. Nortel had lost C$300 billion in market capitalization within a year! Nortel stock continued to fall, trading in the C$6 range before turning up in the autumn of 2001 when the appointment of veteran manager Frank Dunn as the new CEO and president was announced. However, the firm's stock value then resumed its fall and reached new lows in 2002, trading in the C$2 range as investors lost patience waiting for the promised turnaround in industry and company fortunes.

Then in the fall of 2002, as Nortel's cash flow crisis grew and the threat of de-listing from the New York Stock Exchange had investors running for the exits, the stock value fell to its lowest point of only 67 cents. Nortel's new management had already begun the task of radically changing the firm's financial structure and orientation away from manufacturing and toward what management felt was its greatest competitive advantage—research and development. As Canada's largest spender on R&D, Nortel spent more than $2 billion in 2003, representing 20 percent of its revenues. By early 2004, Nortel was no longer manufacturing any of its own products, having sold off all the facilities it owned, and was now outsourcing production work in order to concentrate its resources on developing the next generation of wireless technology. As a result of these financial and managerial changes, Nortel returned to profitability, and its share value climbed to the $12 range.[1]

Nortel was hit with heavy investor selling, as were all e-businesses affected by the sudden freeze in purchasing by customers who could no longer find the financing to continue their expansion into more Internet-related technology. This was because there was no longer any clear indication of what the company's future revenues and earnings would be. Added to this problem were the announcements of the retirement of Nortel's chief executive officer,

John Roth, and chief operating officer, Clarence Chandran, with no clear successors until Frank Dunn emerged with a successful turnaround plan for revitalizing the firm and investors' interest in it. Because of the firm's lack of leadership and direction in 2002, investors punished Nortel's share value. Rumors about mergers with other technology firms circulated, but in the absence of a new management team and recovering sales, investor confidence remained weak until 2003. With its new management team in place, and a recovery in earnings, share values once again reflected the firm's great technological expertise until 2004 when questions about earlier financial reporting forced the resignation of Frank Dunn and his replacement with William Owens as President and CEO. Interestingly, although some clarification concerns remain, investors appear to have confidence that Nortel shares have found a foundation from which to build long-term value. The volitility of Nortel share values reflect investors' changing perception of the risk and long tern prospects for owning the firm.

Financial planning is the last of the three micro-level decision-making areas of the e-business planning process that we need to consider. In this chapter, we will first explore financial planning from the firm's point of view. We'll look at financial tools that are useful for illustrating and explaining strategies in the business plan, such as pro forma income statements, balance sheets, and cash flow statements. We will also examine financial matters from the perspective of investors who own shares of publicly traded companies; **venture capital** firms, which help entrepreneurs launch new businesses by providing them with the funding they need to get started; and institutions like banks and insurance companies, which are the major lenders to established businesses.

An Overview of Financial Planning and e-Business

venture capital

Investment funds provided by firms that help entrepreneurs launch new businesses.

financial planning

Determining how each of the marketing and management decisions that firms have made during the planning process will be paid for.

budgets

Financial statements that detail the firm's planned expenditures and revenues for some stated period.

Functionally speaking, **financial planning** is concerned with determining how each of the marketing and management decisions that firms have made during the planning process will be paid for. In a very simple business plan, the work that needs to be done is itemized, and the various costs associated with these tasks are totaled. At the operational level of the firm, local **budgets**, which detail the firm's planned expenditures and revenues for some stated period, are prepared. All budgetary information from across the firm is then collected and reorganized to show consolidated information, such as sales or expenses by product line or division of the firm. The business plan arranges these data in whatever way is deemed appropriate to provide information about the firm's expected future course of action. This can include breakeven analysis and the use of charts, graphs, and other displays of financial information. Figure 10.1 shows the sales budget and several graphic displays of the data for Hypothetical Technologies Inc, an imaginary firm that we will use to illustrate the form and structure of financial documentation in an e-business plan.

Pro Forma Financial Statements in the e-Business Plan

income statements

Financial statements that list revenues and expenses for a period of time and display the net profit or loss.

balance sheets

Financial statements that list assets, liabilities, and the owner's equity in the firm as of a specific date.

cash flow statements

Financial statements that show the flow of money into and out of the firm.

Business plans generally provide *pro forma* income statements, balance sheets, and statements of cash flows for the coming three to five years. **Income statements** list revenues and expenses for a period of time and display the firm's net profit or loss for that period. **Balance sheets** list assets, liabilities, and the owner's equity in the firm as of a specific date. **Cash flow statements** show the flow of money into and out of the firm. Cash flow statements generally have sections covering the firm's *operating activities*, which generate the revenues and expenses that appear on the firm's income statement; *investing activities*, such as large capital purchases or the disposal of items that are no longer needed; and *financing activities*, which involve changes in equity and debt. The firm's investing and financing activities are also reflected in the changes in the firm's balance sheet from year to year. The firm's e-business plan should contain information at the appropriate level for the audience the plan is intended for. Outsiders are not likely to be given the detailed statements that the firm uses at the operational level, for instance.

Although a detailed exploration of the financial statements is beyond the scope of this textbook, students are encouraged to prepare them at whatever level reflects their degree of familiarity and capability with such statements. What is important when preparing an e-business plan is to demonstrate an appreciation for the financial implications of the marketing and management decisions that you have presented. The financial part of your plan forces you to evaluate the costs and returns of doing what you have proposed and thus provides a reality check on the scale and feasibility of your plan. In the real business world, should a firm need formal documentation to make a presentation to, say, potential investors, it would

FIGURE 10.1   Sales Budget for Hypothetical Technologies Inc. and Graphic Display of Sales Data

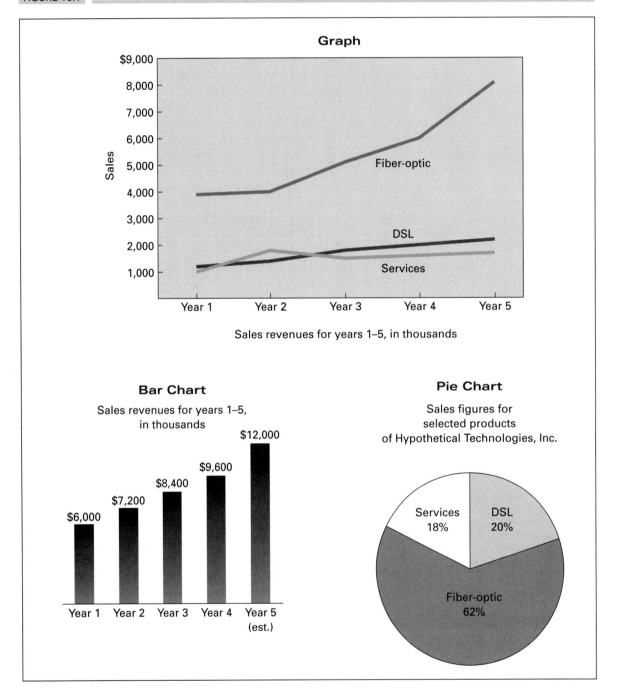

probably hire financial professionals who are familiar with the proper format and terminology. However, these professionals would still need to know the information that you outlined in your e-business plan in order to complete the task.

Figures 10.2 to 10.4 display simplified financial statements that you should be able to use to build the documentation for your plan. If your financial knowledge permits you to produce more sophisticated documentation, then by all means do so.

Understanding Financial Information

A common and realistic assumption often made about new firms is that they will not produce profits or even positive cash flows until the third year of operation or even later. For example, for a long time Internet-based retailer Amazon.com was spending over $115 million each month to keep the company on track toward the day when it would eventually sell enough merchandise to generate profits for its shareholders. Amazon's operating losses over a period of six years totaled more than $1.2 billion, scaring away some who feared that the firm would never reach the promised profit goals set by visionary founder Jeff Bezos.[2] Amazon finally turned a profit in the last quarter of 2001.

FIGURE 10.2 Consolidated Pro Forma Income Statements for Hypothetical Technologies Inc.

Hypothetical Technologies Inc.
Consolidated Pro Forma Statements of Income
(thousands of U.S. dollars)

	Year 1	Year 2	Year 3	Year 4	Year 5
Revenues	6,000	7,200	8,400	9,600	12,000
Cost of revenues	4,000	4,800	5,600	6,400	8,000
Gross profit	**2,000**	**2,400**	**2,800**	**3,200**	**4,000**
Marketing and administrative expense	750	900	1,050	1,200	1,500
Amortization and depreciation expense	100	120	140	160	200
Research and development expense	55	66	77	88	110
	1,095	**1,314**	**1,533**	**1,752**	**2,190**
Interest expense	10	12	14	16	20
Earnings (loss) before taxes	**1,085**	**1,302**	**1,519**	**1,736**	**2,170**
Income tax provision	50	60	70	80	100
Net income available to stockholders	**1,035**	**1,242**	**1,449**	**1,656**	**2,070**

FIGURE 10.3   Consolidated Pro Forma Balance Sheets for Hypothetical Technologies Inc.

Hypothetical Technologies Inc.
Consolidated Pro Forma Balance Sheets
(thousands of U.S. dollars)

	Year 1	Year 2	Year 3	Year 4	Year 5
ASSETS					
Cash	1,625	1,685	2,569	3,666	3,797
Accounts receivable	1,500	1,630	2,282	2,651	3,292
Inventories	750	900	950	1,520	1,701
Other assets	6,450	7,740	8,431	9,134	11,253
Total assets	10,325	11,955	14,232	16,971	20,043
LIABILITIES					
Accounts payable	1,600	1,920	2,688	4,301	4,670
Long-term debt	500	1,790	2,481	3,184	5,303
Other liabilities	100	120	168	269	538
Total liabilities	2,200	3,830	5,337	7,754	10,511
SHAREHOLDERS' EQUITY					
Common shares	8,125	8,125	8,125	8,125	8,125
Retained earnings	0	0	770	1,092	1,407
Total shareholders' equity	8,125	8,125	8,895	9,217	9,532
Total liabilities and shareholders' equity	10,325	11,955	14,232	16,971	20,043

Concern can turn to worry, however, if the preliminary negative cash flows expected during the initial period in which the firm's products are introduced in the marketplace show no sign of the hoped-for turn toward positive levels. If a company runs out of funding and there is no infusion of cash from sales, new investors, partners, or some other source, the firm is effectively bankrupt. Whatever money, time, and effort has been invested in it is lost. In worst-case scenarios, firms may be forced to sell off entire divisions of their business, as Nortel did, in order to acquire cash. This is why the statement of cash flows is considered such an important document within the e-business plan. For example, Pets.com was an example of a dot-com start-up that lost control of its finances. Backed by Disney and Amazon.com, the firm spent $27 million in 1999 on television and other media advertising to generate awareness and sales. The funny advertisements featuring the famous talking dog sock puppet could not create a critical mass of buyers

FIGURE 10.4   Consolidated Pro Forma Statements of Cash Flows for Hypothetical Technologies

Hypothetical Technologies Inc.
Consolidated Pro Forma Statements of Cash Flows
(thousands of U.S. dollars)

	Year 1	Year 2	Year 3	Year 4	Year 5
Cash flows from operating activities					
Net profit (loss) and other cash inflows	6,000	7,200	8,400	9,600	12,000
Net expenditures and other cash outflows	4,865	5,838	6,811	7,784	9,730
Net cash from operating activities	1,135	1,362	1,589	1,816	2,270
Cash flows from investing activities					
Net cash inflows from investing activities	0	0	0	0	0
Net cash outflows from investing activities	500	1,290	691	703	2,119
Net cash from investing activities	−500	−1,290	−691	−703	−2,119
Cash flow from financing activities					
Net cash inflows from financing activities	0	0	0	0	0
Net cash outflows from financing activities	−10	−12	−14	−16	−20
Net cash from financing activities	−10	−12	−14	−16	−20
Net increase (decrease) in cash	625	60	884	1,097	131
Cash at beginning of period	1,000	1,625	1,685	2,569	3,666
Cash at end of period	1,625	1,685	2,569	3,666	3,797

quickly enough to offset the advertising and other operational costs. As a result, for every dollar of pet supplies revenue received, the firm lost five dollars, quickly creating a cash crisis.[3]

In 2001, such concerns prompted Amazon.com to modify its planning to prove to impatient and critical investors that the company's business would eventually be profitable, despite suffering operating losses for its first six years. Staffing was reduced to cut expenses, and planned expansion was trimmed to help meet investor expectations and at least halt the negative cash flow that was draining the firm of funds. In June 2001, after the stock prices of Amazon and other technology companies fell, and at a time when ten-year U.S. Treasury bills were yielding about 6 percent, Amazon's convertible bonds due February 2009 had an effective yield of 14 percent. Given Amazon's six years of losses and $1.5 billion of unsecured debt, that bond yield reflected investors' very real concerns and their perception that Amazon.com could default on its payments.[4] Higher interest rates cost firms more when they must borrow money to operate their businesses, which further exacerbates the obstacles to achieving profitability. Should Amazon need to issue new bonds or other forms of debt, interest costs would be higher, reflecting the riskier financial conditions for lenders.

Budgets become progressively more comprehensive as the budget planning process moves from the operational level of the firm, where departments estimate their funding requirements in anticipation of the work they will be expected to perform, to the divisional level, and ultimately to the corporate level. The firm's **master budget** is a compilation of all the budgetary decisions at all levels of the organization. For example, the **sales budget** details the sources of the revenues that the company expects to receive in order to pay its expenses and generate profits. At the operational level, the department responsible for a product line will develop a sales budget that itemizes the revenues it expects from each product in the line and perhaps organizes information in several ways, such as according to sales territories and customers. The sales budget helps the department to set performance targets, which we will examine in more detail in Chapter 11.

Besides identifying the sources of the funds that the firm will need for planned activities, the financial planning process also attempts to show the broader impact that implementing the plan will have on the firm's overall financial condition through pro forma income statements and balance sheets. Without adequate sources of funds and proper financial management, the firm cannot hope to accomplish the goals and objectives stated in its e-business plan. All of these issues are also important to the firm's investors and lenders, who need to consider whether the risk of involvement through equity or debt is worthwhile. The financing activities segment of the pro forma cash flow statement indicates the participation expected of investors and lenders over the planned time period. Failure to receive infusions of cash at planned times will undermine management's ability to succeed with the overall plan.

Developing the Financial Plan to Avoid Failure

People who are preparing a strategic plan for a new business are generally going to be seeking equity from investors, which will allow them to launch the first phase of their business plan. If the first phase turns out satisfactorily for investors, the same participants, or possibly others, are likely to consider a second and often a third round of funding. This was the pattern followed by the hundreds of so-called dot-com or e-business start-ups that were created in the rush to take advantage of the first commercial development phase of the Internet, leading up to the year 2000. Petopia.com and eToys.com, two online retailing (e-tailing) firms created to market well-established brand-name products over the Internet, are good examples of firms that ran out of capital before they could establish a sufficient cash flow to carry the firm to its next phase of development. According to research by Softbank Venture Capital Inc., one of the biggest venture capital firms investing in Internet companies, it costs about $15 to $25 million to build a high-profile commercial website but ten times this amount to set up the warehousing and distribution (fulfillment) system to go along with it.[5]

master budget
A compilation of all the budgetary decisions at all levels of the organization.

sales budget
A budget that details the sources of the revenue that the company expects to receive.

The many early dot-com failures were a result of many factors, including the high costs of establishing logistical warehousing and distribution systems, excessive number of competitors selling the same products and services, customers who were slow to switch their buying from traditional bricks-and-mortar local retailers to the Internet, the high promotional costs of informing potential customers of the firm's existence, poor managerial decision-making, and the absence of enough partnerships or alliances to help establish brand awareness and customer acceptance. Failure to meet financial backers' expectations often led those backers to decide quickly to deny the firm a second wave of investment dollars so it could continue its drive to achieve profitability. For example, in one month alone, Digital Entertainment Network shut its video streaming site, clothing distributor boo.com closed after spending more than $100 million in only six months of business, and healthshop.com shut its doors completely after failing to meet its investors' expectations.[6]

Sources of Funds

In this section we will examine two prominent sources of funding that are commonly associated with e-business ventures: venture capital firms and funds from within the organization.

Venture Capital Investors

Venture capital investors perceive a start-up e-business to be a high risk, and so they demand terms and conditions to compensate for their involvement. In most situations, venture capitalists will not want to take more than a 40 percent stake in a start-up firm so the owner/management team they are backing still has sufficient entrepreneurial incentive. Also, the thinking is that the less money a firm's management has at stake, the less concerned it will be with the firm's performance and achievement of the goals stated in the business plan.

Venture capital investors are generally not interested in long-term working relationships with start-up firms. Instead, they prefer to support and nurture a management team that they believe can bring the firm to a viable and functioning position in the market, then sell their ownership to others who are interested in a more established investment. They prefer to invest in start-up situations, where the higher risk often goes along with a higher payback if the start-up is successful, and then move on to other firms with good ideas that need capital and perhaps help in creating a network of contacts involving potential customers, strategic alliances, suppliers, and so forth. Often, these are the vital resources that boost the chances of success for a start-up management team that has a good idea but lacks sufficient capital and knowledge of networks to make the firm a success.

A venture capital firm will generally place one or more of its representatives on the board of directors of the firms it has invested in so they can monitor management's activities more closely and help with its decision-making. These directors often sit on several boards and look for ways to facilitate business activities, especially among the firms they have funds invested in. Directors will usually receive regular briefings and reports that describe in detail how well management is doing at realizing the goals and objectives set forth in the firm's business plan. In essence, the business plan is considered a contractual agreement between venture capital investors and the owner/management team. Both groups want the stated goals and objectives to be achieved as scheduled.

Venture capital firms are major players in the financial gamble of building e-businesses. According to the Corporate Venturing Report, more than 200 corporations make investments in Internet-related start-ups. An estimated $10 billion was invested in 1999, five times the amount invested in 1998. A second-round investment of $10 million in a start-up can easily turn into $100 million if and when the firm goes public through an initial public offering (IPO) of its stock. For example, Oracle Venture Fund was up some 504 percent in its first year of operation after successful IPOs by both C-bridge Internet Solutions and Red Hat.[7]

The heady early days of aggressive venture capitalism ended with the industry shakeout that began in 2000, when, according to Venturewire Inc, investment in start-ups peaked at more than $90 billion. More than 823 Internet companies went bankrupt between 2000 and 2002, but, according to researchers at Webmergers.com, an estimated 7,000 to 10,000 remain. Furthermore, estimates that $100 billion in venture capital wait to be deployed suggest that activity will once again become robust when investors who were once burned by losses resume funding new technology and online start-ups.[8]

Conventional Sources of Funds

An e-business venture may be either a completely new business, that has had no previously existing plan, or a new addition to a firm's current business plan. In the first case, investors and lenders will need a complete set of financial plans detailing how the entire enterprise will be expected to perform before they will be convinced that they should become involved.

In the second situation, however, the firm will need to document how the e-business activities will contribute to its existing revenue streams or create new ones and what changes in existing budgets will be required. Planners will need to seek approval to allocate internal sources of funding and resources to the current or future master business budget and overall plan. They might argue that the e-business venture is really a new promotional strategy that should replace an existing program or be added to the current promotional effort. For instance, to create a website, funds that had previously been budgeted for advertising or some other promotional activities might simply be redirected. Senior management might be more easily persuaded of the value of experimenting with a web presence if the first step is a relatively lower-risk and lower-cost project. A cost-benefit analysis might be prepared that justified funding the construction of a website.

This website might be dedicated to distributing many types of corporate information to interested publics for the purpose of showing the short- and longer-term benefits that are expected. Should the venture fail to live up to expectations, its advocates can argue that the firm can always return to the current budgetary allocations for promotional expenditures.

Unconventional Sources of Funds

Alternatives to accelerating the expansion of businesses by using cash to pay salaries or to acquire other firms have gained a great deal of public attention because of the fantastic gains made by some individuals. In this section we will take a closer look at this phenomenon and some of the implications of this financial strategy.

Using Stock Options as a Substitute for Salaries

One of the funding trends that emerged as new-economy share prices soared was the use of stock options as a substitute for salaries. A **stock option** is the right to purchase a share at a set price, or *strike price*, between two dates in the future. If the price of the shares rises above the strike price, holders of the options can exercise their right to buy the stock at the strike price and then quickly sell it at the higher market price, keeping the difference.

stock option
The right to purchase a share at a set price, or strike price, between two dates in the future.

The use of stock options was initially popular as an incentive for senior management, but it quickly spread to middle-ranking managers when it was recognized as a means for deferring payment to individuals who otherwise would have demanded higher salaries. The expected future value of those stock options motivated individual employees to perform better and work overtime and weekends more willingly, while also allowing the firm to save its limited cash reserves. In many cases, Internet start-ups even provided stock options for all employees as a motivational and financial planning tool.

However, stock options are controversial because they allow the firm to avoid charging what would otherwise be tax-deductible salary expenses against current earned income and instead dilute the value of shares owned by regular investors. This occurs because if and when options are exercised, the firm must honor the set purchase price, which is generally well below the market value of the stock. In addition, some executives have made what some regular shareholders consider to be unconscionable gains as part of their executive compensation packages. For instance, John Roth, CEO of Nortel Networks, earned $135 million in 2001 as a result of exercising stock options before Nortel shares tumbled in value later that year.[9]

According to a survey conducted by the brokerage house Merrill Lynch, thirty-six of the world's biggest technology companies overstated their true 2000 earnings by an average of 25 percent, typically by ignoring the impact of stock option plans. Since these plans would have reduced earnings, the firms' shares may be overpriced because investors are valuing them on the basis of reported earnings. If the fair value of stock option grants had been included in the calculations, 61 percent of the corporate profits would have vanished. The worst offender was Yahoo!, whose $1.3 billion stock option costs would have obliterated its $71 million reported income. Besides failing to report stock option costs, the other common accounting deficiencies include reporting one-time financial gains from the disposal of assets and nonoperating sources of revenue such as pension fund income. Merrill Lynch suggests that the real earnings of Ericsson AB were 94 percent below what the company reported because of a one-time $25 billion gain in earnings and that Lucent Technologies overstated earnings by 110 percent by including $3.6 billion in pension plan income as part of operations. Furthermore, of the earnings reported by the thirty-six surveyed firms, 48 percent were derived from tax breaks on stock options, which will not be available in the following year. Finally, the Merrill Lynch report is also very critical of the earnings reduction strategies used by Nortel Networks and JDS Uniphase. Merrill Lynch claims that these firms use creative accounting methods to make their long-term growth rates look better than they really are by immediately writing off costs associated with the acquisitions of other firms. The message to investors is clear enough: Read the details in firms' financial statements and take the banner messages of higher revenues and earnings with caution until all of the information that explains how these numbers are derived is known.[10]

Using Shares as Currency to Grow by Acquisition

Another phenomenon soared in popularity with the rapid rise in the share values of new-economy businesses. This was the use of a firm's shares as currency when it acquired other firms. In essence, instead of having to borrow more cash, generate cash through operations, or sell more shares, a firm with high share values could merge with or acquire another firm by exchanging its stock for the other firm's. Often the owners who were surrendering control of their firm were given some portion of the purchase price in cash, but the amount of cash that large firms with high stock prices required if they wanted to grow their businesses by acquiring other businesses was reduced by the high value of their firms' shares. For example, in the race to gain technological expertise in the highly specialized optical networking field, the Microelectronics Group of Lucent Technologies acquired Herrmann Technology, Inc., a privately held company based in Dallas, Texas, in 2000 for approximately $450 million of Lucent stock and about $10 million in actual cash for Herrmann's owners. Larger firms like Lucent will commonly make this type of acquisition to fill gaps in technology or manufacturing capacity in their own operations. On the reverse side of this strategic coin, many small businesses that can be easily integrated into a large firm like Lucent are more than happy to become an operational division and thereby grow at a rate that they would not otherwise enjoy if they remained independent. In exchange, their owners receive shares in the larger corporation, and generally some cash as well.[11] In retrospect, like many other technology acquisitions by large firms, this acquisition by Lucent might appear to suffer from poor timing, as the industry downturn began soon after.

e-BUSINESS insight

eBay Share Value Reflects Revenue Growth

San Jose, California-based eBay (**www.ebay.com**) is today the most popular e-commerce shopping destination on the Internet for individuals as well as businesses. Launched during the boom times of the mid-1990s, the NASDAQ-traded firm (symbol: EBAY) is clearly among the most recognized brands that operate exclusively online.

The eBay community includes more than 85 million registered members worldwide who are looking to buy and sell a seemingly endless array of new and used products, ranging from automobiles to collectible tea sets. Members, who spend more time on eBay than users of any other online site, can search through millions of items listed under more than 27,000 categories. These categories include antiques and art, books, business & industrial, cars & other vehicles, clothing & accessories, coins, collectibles, crafts, dolls & bears, electronics & computers, home furnishings, jewelry & watches, movies & DVDs, music, musical instruments, pottery & glass, real estate, sporting goods & memorabilia, stamps, tickets, toys & hobbies and travel.

eBay members can participate in auctions, which end at a time displayed next to the item, or they can buy immediately and bypass the auction process. Payments can be made directly to the vendor privately or by using eBay's payment system, called PayPal. Using PayPal allows buyers to avoid sending confidential credit card and banking information to sellers. eBay primarily earns revenues from sellers through commissions on sales and listing fees as well as fees for using PayPal. Unlike Amazon.com or other e-commerce operations that must deal with fulfillment costs, eBay has no inventory or warehousing costs—which represented a major competitive advantage for the firm as it built its brand name in the marketplace.

Annualized gross merchandise sales of goods sold on eBay was $14.87 billion in 2002, earning the firm $1.2 billion net revenues and a remarkable 80 percent margin or $1 billion gross profit. Net profit grew consistently from $7 million in 1998 to $90 million in 2001 and then more than doubled to $249 in 2002. Estimates indicate that eBay's records will be pushed higher still, to more than $2.1 billion in 2003, almost doubling 2002 net revenues, and $2.9 billion in 2004. For the firm's more than 5,000 employees and its satellite operations around the world, limits to growth appear nowhere in sight.

Although eBay is clearly among the more volatile stocks in the marketplace, those public eBay investors who first bought shares at $1.50 in 1998 have been financially well rewarded—if they held on for the ride. In 2003, shares traded as low as $33 and as high as $61. This is especially sobering for investors when compared to other firms that also began about the same time with untested e-business models—many of whom are no longer in business.

The e-business model developed by eBay has become the de facto standard for many other exchange sites. Although eBay clearly dominates the broad market, many sites have chosen to differentiate themselves by focusing on more narrowly defined categories such as antiques. By offering more specialized services and perhaps a selection of products not likely to be found on a widely used site like eBay, these firms can successfully compete by catering to specialized niche markets of buyers and sellers.

Question for discussion: Do you believe eBay's stock value properly reflects current and future financial conditions?[12]

Evaluating e-Business Risks and Investments

Evaluating whether an e-business activity is worthwhile is typically done by using cost-benefit analysis. After comparing the financial and other costs required to undertake the venture with the financial and other benefits gained, management can make an effective assessment of the value that the project represents to them.

Perceived Risks and Expected Earnings

From an outside investor's point of view, the decision to purchase equity in a firm or to lend the firm funds is made based on the perceived risk of the investment and the projected returns it offers on invested capital. Many factors might affect these two items, including changes in technology, interest rates, general economic activity, and so forth. Many (now embarrassed) individuals once argued that the so-called new economy was immune to the ravages of the business cycle that regularly afflicted the traditional industries of the old economy. However, the drastic fall in the stock market prices of new-economy leaders like Dell Computer, Oracle, Nortel Networks, Cisco Systems, and all the others during the 2000–3 industry slowdown clearly put that argument on the junk heap.

The factors that caused these industry giants to gain and then lose fantastic amounts of value in such a relatively short time can be explained in simple terms. Values rose because investors believed that the future growth in these firms' revenues would continue to outpace that of firms in the traditional economy, and they were willing to pay for the opportunity to grow their investments faster. Whereas 5 to 10 percent annual growth in earnings might be considered exceptional for an old-economy business, many of the new-economy firms were growing at annual rates of 40 to 100 percent and more. Investors lost any sense of what normal growth for this sector of the economy was likely to be. So they bid up prices to levels that reflected their confidence that these firms' future revenue growth would be so great that today's purchase price would seem cheap. Unfortunately, for many of these firms, profit growth did not keep pace with revenue growth; often, in fact, profit never materialized. These disappointing trends eventually led to a failure in confidence and the financial collapse of many firms as investors sold their shares.

expected earnings
The difference between a firm's expected revenues and its expected expenses.

price-earnings (P/E) ratio
The current price of one share of a firm's stock divided by the firm's earnings per share for the past year.

Needless to say, however, new-economy businesses should be evaluated in the same way and on the same basis as any other business. The primary factor that determines a firm's future share value is its **expected earnings**—that is, the difference between its expected revenues and its expected expenses. The **price-earnings (P/E) ratio** for any firm is the current price of one share of the firm's stock divided by the firm's earnings per share for the past year. So a P/E of 30 would mean that investors were willing to pay $30 for $1 of current earnings. The expectation, of course, is that the earnings will continue to grow. If the ratio remains the same, then the share value will rise proportionately. If earnings decline, however, the share value will decline proportionately as well.

price-earnings-growth (PEG) ratio

A ratio that combines a firm's growth expectations with its P/E ratio; it is calculated by dividing the P/E ratio by the growth rate.

To factor a firm's growth expectations into the analysis of a firm's value, some analysts use the **price-earnings-growth (PEG) ratio**, which is calculated by dividing the P/E ratio by the growth rate. So, if the firm with a share price of $30 and $1 of earnings per share has a projected growth rate of 50 percent, it would have a PEG ratio of 0.6, as illustrated below.

Price per Share / Earnings per Share = P/E Ratio / Growth Rate = PEG Ratio

$30   / $1   = 30   / 50   = 0.6

Although what exactly constitutes attractive PEG and P/E ratios is hotly debated by investment analysts, as a general rule, a technology firm that has a P/E ratio below 30 and a PEG ratio under 1.0 would deserve further investigation to better assess its value as an investment. This is especially true if the historical ratios for the firm have been higher; thus, the company may currently be undervalued.

Historically, the average P/E ratio of the companies that make up the Standard & Poor's 500 index has varied from 5.9 in 1944 to 35 in 1999.[13] Before the speculative bubble burst in 2000, many new-economy firms were trading at P/E ratios of 100 or higher. Some firms could not even calculate a P/E ratio, since they had not yet generated any earnings from their revenues. Clearly, the investors who bought these stocks had high growth expectations for the products the firms produced. When that growth failed to reach the expected levels and eventually became unpredictable, investors began to question the value of the shares. Many investors sold at whatever price they could, and the stock markets on which these shares were heavily represented, such as the NASDAQ, tumbled. From its peak at 5,048 on March 3, 2000, the NASDAQ fell 67 percent to 1,619 on April 4, 2001; it later dipped below 1,114 in October 2002.[14] Since then, many high-tech firms have begun to recover in value, but many others have continued their freefall—for example, by 2002 Nortel Networks was selling at less than 2 percent of its peak price in 2000. Technology firms in general, as represented by the NASDAQ, were down nearly 80 percent from their peak.

In contrast to most e-business stocks' dramatic fall in value during the 2000–1 downturn, NASDAQ-listed eBay (**www.ebay.com**) managed to recover quickly to $68 a share and to outperform other well-known Internet players like Amazon and Yahoo!. The reasons can be found in the superior numbers that investors look for when selecting and evaluating shares, such as eBay's 2001 first-quarter profit per share of 11 cents versus the expected 8 cents (a 592 percent year-over-year increase), a 79 percent increase in revenues, and the addition of 7 million new users to the 23 million who already were using eBay's services in the fast-growing peer-to-peer market. In the summer of 2001, eBay traded at a P/E ratio of 185 times 2001 earnings and 105 times estimated 2002 earnings, reflecting eBay's long-term growth rate of 50 to 75 percent. The resulting PEG ratio of 3 was virtually unheard of and suggested either overvaluation, which would at some point be corrected, or in fact the beginning of new revenue growth through expansion of operations.[15]

However, as the NASDAQ spiraled downward to below 1,400 in the summer of 2002, eBay continued to trade near $60, reflecting investors' confidence in eBay's 50 to 60 percent growth rates going into 2003.[16]

But perhaps another viewpoint should be included here. According to Baruch Lev, professor of accounting and finance at New York University's Stern School of Management and a director of the Project for Research on Intangibles, the accounting methods currently used to evaluate and measure Internet-related firms are inadequate. He suggests that we need new accounting and finance principles that are better equipped to communicate value in a world of intangibles. We are failing to properly value the most valuable corporate assets, intangibles such as brand, market power, business processes, and research and development. Instead, we are focusing on hard assets and current revenues as though online businesses are no different from any other businesses.[17]

Critics of current accounting practice also point to the way firms measure their earnings. Given that investors in stocks are willing to pay a certain amount of money for every dollar of earnings that a firm generates, it is misleading, these critics say, to fail to distinguish between the different sources of total earnings provided in company reports. Real performance, they argue, is best reflected by the business's cash flows from operations. For example, critics suggest that International Business Machines Corporation's (IBM) reported earnings are inflated because they are affected by changes in pension-fund accounts, which in turn are linked to the firm's stock market value.[18]

Several recent financial scandals at major firms, including industry giant WorldCom Inc. and Nortel, suggest that closer scrutiny of accounting and financial reporting is needed as well as better governance of the financial institutions that audit business practices.

The Credit Crunch of 2000

The rapid and in some cases fatal financial collapse of Internet-dependent firms in 2000 was a clear illustration that although the Internet was originally funded by the military and later by educational institutions, it is now very much subject to the same economic laws as any other industry. The phase of the traditional boom-and-bust business cycle in which sales slow and firms must clear excessively large inventories arrived suddenly, rudely awakening firms like WorldCom, Lucent Technologies, Nortel Networks, Cisco Systems, Celestica, and countless others whose fortunes were all heavily tied to the rate at which their customers bought Internet infrastructure technology.

The rapid collapse in e-business sales can be better explained by understanding how customers often finance their purchases. It is common in most industries for sellers to provide financing to their customers, especially when the terms of the sale can heavily influence the buyer's decision which supplier to buy from. For example, IBM is the largest computer maker in terms of sales, and, not surprisingly, its financing unit, with $35 billion in assets and 125,000 customers in more than 40 countries, is the largest financer of information technology purchases, according to researchers at Bloomberg.[19]

What caused the sudden slowdown of 2000 was an old-fashioned *credit crunch*—the inability of buyers to raise funds on their own or through vendor financing to purchase more new equipment. This took place because the investors who had made these funds available in the past were becoming increasingly unsure about some firms' ability to generate enough revenue to pay back loans or to earn sufficient profits from the deployment of these newly acquired technologies. While explaining to Nortel shareholders why the company's stock market value had dropped 80 percent, CEO John Roth said that "the lesson we've learned is we need to stay very, very close to the financial component of our customer, as well, because even though the network engineers want to do it and the marketing people have the ambitious plans, if the capital markets are cutting off our customers, we need to be aware of that."[20]

Many people had viewed the high-tech industry as lacking growth limits because its customers were deriving productivity improvements by transferring more work to the Internet and because of the continuing convergence of technologies. Such optimistic certitudes fell suddenly to earth and the industry became like any other—albeit one with greater potential growth than most.

Who Will Survive the Shakeout?

According to veteran financial analyst and former stockbroker Hugh Anderson (**www.unclehughie.com**), the 2000–1 crash in the stocks of highly overrated technology firms marked the moment when the public finally became aware of just how poor was the quality of analysis and advice emanating from major brokerage firms. This decline in quality can be attributed mostly to the gradual change in the traditional roles played by analysts and in the shift in brokerage firms' earnings

e-BUSINESS
insight

eBay Motors—Problems with Growth

According to a survey conducted by financial analysts Smith Barney in October 2003, eBay Motors, the auction firm's automotive site, may experience future challenges competing with other online auction sites. The survey of 150 U.S. used-car dealers found that 40 percent had discontinued listing cars on eBay Motors or had decided against using the site after evaluating the complexity and costs. At the time, eBay Motors accounted for more than $6 billion, or 20 percent, of eBay's total sales and 11 percent of its revenue. The stock fell 2.4 percent on the day the report was made public as investors weighed its implications for the future earnings growth of the division and the firm as a whole.

Question for discussion: Do you agree with the report that suggested that eBay Motors will have trouble attracting and keeping used-car dealers in the future?[21]

**Go to the Web:
e-Business Online**
For tutorials and more on
the topics in this chapter,
visit the student website
at **http://business
.college.hmco.com/
students** and select
"Canzer e-Business."

away from traditional commissions and toward greater reliance on the underwriting and financing of new issues. Rather than investigating and reporting on the firms they were assigned, analysts became trusting reporters of the information they were fed by the management of these same firms. Furthermore, instead of acting as a counterbalance to the brokerage firms' sales teams, they effectively joined in and became promoters of the companies as well.[22]

As is normally the case after a shakeout, the strongest firms survive because of the competencies they possess, which provided them with their competitive advantage in the first place. These firms will likely re-organize and revise their e-business plans to reflect the new reality of the competitive landscape. In some cases, this may involve acquiring the valuable assets, made available at bankruptcy sale prices, of those failed firms and perhaps even merging with other surviving firms. This will go hand-in-hand with an overall consolidation of effort in the industry.

Conclusions

This chapter examined the importance of finance to a firm's overall planning process, the sources of funding, the role of venture capitalists, the stock market's valuations of firms, and other investment- and finance-related topics. The discussions presented here should help learners grasp the relationship between business plans and the funding that is required to actually bring them to fruition. Finally, the chapter presented steps for creating the financial component of the overall **e-business plan.** A more detailed tutorial on the preparation of the e-business plan is available on the textbook's website.

In the following chapter, we will conclude our discussion of the strategic e-business planning process by examining issues related to implementation and control of the plan.

RETURN TO
inside e-business

CASE STUDY

The experience of Nortel Networks and other e-businesses during the 2000–1 run-up and crash landing focused attention on several basic points related to the way in which investors evaluate corporations. These involve the stability of the firm's business plan, the basic business models it uses, and the related major components, which include the firm's revenue streams, cash flows from operations, product lines, and management. The saga of Nortel and other such firms will continue to unfold as events under management's control, and those that are not, become evident. You can follow these events on the firm's website, at **www.nortelnetworks.com.**

ASSIGNMENT

1. What has happened to Nortel's share value since the winter of 2004?
2. What reasons can you offer, such as new products and management, changes in customer buying patterns, and so forth, to explain Nortel's changes in share values?

Chapter Review

SUMMARY

ACE Self-Test
For a quick self-test of
the content in this chapter,
visit the student website
at **http://business.
college.hmco.com/
students.** Select
"Canzer e-Business."

1. **Examine the connections between financial planning and e-business planning.**

Financial planning is concerned with determining how each of the marketing and management decisions that a firm has made during the planning process will be paid for. In a very simple business plan, the work that needs to be done under the plan is itemized, and the various costs associated with these tasks are totaled. At the operational level of the firm, local budgets, which detail the firm's planned expenditures and revenues for some stated period, are prepared. All budgetary information from across the firm is then collected and reorganized to show consolidated information, such as sales or expenses by product lines or divisions of the firm. The business plan arranges these data in whatever way is deemed appropriate to provide information about the firm's expected future course of action. This can include breakeven analysis and charts, graphs, and other displays of financial information. Business plans generally provide pro forma income statements, balance sheets, and statements of cash flows for the next three to five years. A common and realistic assumption is that new firms will not produce profits or even positive cash flows until the third year of operation or even later. Investors' concern can turn to worry, however, if the expected preliminary negative cash flows show no sign of the hoped-for turn toward positive levels after the initial period in which the firm introduces its products into the marketplace.

2. **Explore the sources of funds employed by e-businesses.**

Venture capital investors perceive a start-up e-business to be a high-risk situation and demand terms and conditions that compensate them for their involvement. In most situations, venture capitalists will not want to take more than a 40 percent stake in a start-up firm so the owner/management team they are backing will have sufficient entrepreneurial incentive. Also, the thinking is that the less money a firm's management has at stake, the less concerned it will be with the firm's performance and its ability to successfully achieve the goals stated in its business plan. Venture capital investors are generally not interested in long-term working relationships with start-up firms. Instead, they prefer to support and nurture a management team that they believe can bring the firm to a viable and functioning position in the market. They then sell their ownership to others who are interested in a more established investment. One of the funding trends that emerged as new-economy share values soared was the use of stock options as a substitute for salaries. The expected future value of those stock options drove individual employees to perform better and work overtime and weekends more willingly, while also allowing the firm to save its limited cash reserves. Another phenomenon that soared in popularity was the use of a firm's shares as currency for acquiring other firms. In essence, instead of having to borrow more cash, generate it through operations, or sell more shares, a firm with high share values could merge with or acquire another firm by exchanging its stock for the other firm's.

3. **Examine strategies for evaluating e-business risks and investments.**
   Evaluating whether an e-business activity is worthwhile is typically done by using cost-benefit analysis. After comparing the financial and other costs required to undertake the venture with the financial and other benefits gained by doing so, management can make an effective assessment of the value that the project represents to them. From an outside investor's point of view, the decision to purchase equity in a firm or to lend the firm funds is based on the perceived risk of the investment and the projected returns on invested capital. Many factors might affect these two items, including changes in technology, interest rates, general economic activity, and so forth. Many (now embarrassed) individuals once argued that the so-called new economy was immune to the ravages of the business cycle that regularly afflicted the traditional industries of the old economy. But the drastic fall in the stock prices of new-economy industry leaders like Dell Computer, Oracle, Nortel Networks, Cisco Systems, and many others during the 2000 industry slowdown clearly put that argument on the junk heap. The factors that caused these industry giants to gain and then lose fantastic amounts of value in such a relatively short time can be explained in simple terms. Values rose because investors believed that the future growth of these firms' revenues would continue to outpace that of firms in the traditional economy, and they were willing to pay for the opportunity to grow their investments faster.

REVIEW QUESTIONS

1. Explain how budgets are used in the financial planning process.
2. What is venture capital?
3. What does the term *price-earnings ratio* mean?
4. What does the term *price-earnings-growth ratio* mean?
5. How are stock options used to motivate a firm's management?
6. How should the value of shares be evaluated?

DISCUSSION QUESTIONS

1. Discuss the financial planning process.
2. Why do many e-business ventures fail?
3. Describe how venture capital investors work with the management of a firm.
4. Discuss the investing strategy followed by a venture capital firm.
5. What criticisms are made against the use of stock options as a substitute for paying salaries?
6. Explain how a firm can grow faster by using its high share value.

Building Skills for Career Success

EXPLORING THE INTERNET

Financial information is widely available on the Internet. Perhaps a good place to explore e-businesses and growth-oriented technology businesses that focus on the Internet is at the NASDAQ website, **www.nasdaq.com**. Here you can view graphic illustrations of the NASDAQ stock indexes and of individual stocks. In addition, the NASDAQ site presents informative articles on technology breakthroughs and provides links to individual firms and other sources.

ASSIGNMENT

1. Summarize the current direction of the stocks listed on NASDAQ.
2. What reasons does the NASDAQ site give to explain why share values have been moving in this direction?

DEVELOPING CRITICAL THINKING SKILLS

The Internet provides easy access to a variety of financial information about firms whose stock is publicly traded. The public firm's management is motivated to publicize positive developments that will contribute directly to revenue growth and tries to counteract any negative information that might be circulating. A public firm's website will generally provide financial statements, prognostications by senior management, press releases highlighting positive financial news, and so forth. Select a well-known firm that you are interested in, such as Microsoft or IBM, and examine its corporate website for disclosures of its current financial information. Then explore news sites like CNET (**www.cnet.com**) or Bloomberg (**www.bloomberg.com**).

ASSIGNMENT

1. What financial information stood out on the corporate website you visited?
2. What was the interpretation of that information by independent news services?

BUILDING TEAM SKILLS

Developing an e-business plan requires a firm's partners to prepare estimated future financial statements that contain data everyone can agree with. There is little to be gained, for example, by setting sales estimates well beyond management's realistic expectations. After all, any shortfalls that occur will only aggravate working relationships when solutions are needed for the problems caused by the firm's failure to achieve targeted goals. Discuss an e-business idea that your group considers viable, such as establishing an e-commerce site to distribute a specialized product. Estimate the people and resources you will need to set up the firm and operate it for the next five years.

ASSIGNMENT

1. Briefly describe the e-business idea you are considering.
2. Using Figures 10.2, 10.3, and 10.4 as guides, develop your own set of pro forma financial documents.
3. Explain the meaning of your pro forma financial documents.

RESEARCHING DIFFERENT CAREERS

The American Institute of Certified Public Accountants (AICPA) website (**www.aicpa.org**) provides a variety of information that is useful to accountants. Of particular relevance is information on business practices over the Internet, such as taxation issues, security for payments, and relationships with suppliers and customers.

ASSIGNMENT

1. Explore the AICPA website and summarize the content presented there.
2. Prepare a report on one item that accountants currently consider important as presented in an article on the AICPA site.

IMPROVING COMMUNICATION SKILLS

Electronic data interchange (EDI) is a precursor of Internet-based communication between large-scale users that is still in use today. In simple terms, EDI uses standardized forms for exchanging information between two computer systems. Among the financial information typically exchanged using EDI is that found on invoices, order forms, bills, shipping documents, and so forth. Major suppliers use EDI to reduce their order-processing costs and better serve their customers. For example, a major supplier like Procter & Gamble uses EDI to service Wal-Mart stores. Rather than using the network software and hardware protocols available on the Internet, EDI is proprietary. This means that the system used by Wal-Mart and Procter & Gamble may not be compatible with another system used to serve another supplier or vendor. However, the security of the EDI system and other features might be superior to those alternatives available on the Internet.

ASSIGNMENT

1. Using a search engine, research EDI and prepare a report on its use today.
2. What do you think is the likely long-term future use of EDI?

Exploring Useful Websites

These websites provide information on the topics discussed in the chapter. You can learn more by visiting them online and examining their current data.

1. Nortel Networks (**www.nortelnetworks.com**) is a leading telecommunication equipment manufacturer that competes with Lucent Technologies (**www.lucent.com**) and other firms to build the fiber-optic and wireless technology infrastructure of the Internet.

2. Hugh Anderson (**www.unclehughie.com**) is a veteran financial analyst and former stockbroker.

3. Siebel Systems (**www.siebel.com**), PeopleSoft (**www.peoplesoft.com**), and Oracle (**www.oracle.com**) are some of the larger vendors of software services.

4. A good place to explore e-businesses and growth-oriented technology businesses that focus on the Internet is the NASDAQ website, located at **www.nasdaq.com**. News sites like CNET (**www.cnet.com**) and Bloomberg (**www.bloomberg.com**) provide financial information about firms.

5. The American Institute of Certified Public Accountants (AICPA) website (**www.aicpa.org/index.htm**) provides a wide range of financial information that is useful to accountants.

chapter 11

Implementation and Control of the e-Business Plan

INSIDE e-business

FitMoves.com—Building an Online Community for Fitness Professionals from Scratch

Interest in personal fitness and exercise has grown tremendously, along with the popularity of the professional instructors who help guide and motivate individuals in both private and group settings. Aerobic, cardiovascular, weight & strength training, step, yoga, cycling, dance, kick-boxing, and Pilates classes are only a few of the specialized areas in the fitness marketplace that professional trainers serve in local gyms, in corporate work environments, and in the homes of clients. The fitness instruction marketplace is highly fragmented and globally dispersed, which perhaps helps to explain why professionals have gravitated to the Internet and the many online communities frequented by their peers for guidance. Several professional associations provide instructors with training, certification, and ongoing education in the fitness specialties.

Rozel Gonzales, a Montreal, Quebec-based personal trainer and corporate wellness consultant, believed that the marketing efforts of instructors like herself, who were always on the lookout for new ideas and information on choreography, training, and exercise techniques to use in their own routines, were not well served by what was available on the Internet. So, with an aim to promoting her consulting business and sharing knowledge with other exercise enthusiasts at the same time, Gonzales designed and built an online community to better serve instructors like herself. She began by posting her own creative workout contributions and solicited content from other like-minded instructors who also saw the self-promotional value of volunteering articles, photographs, and commentary on how to build their businesses. Today, after just a few years of development and growth, FitMoves.com (**www.fitmoves.com**) provides professional instructors and exercise enthusiasts with a sophisticated center where they can exchange highly valued photographs, video clips, music, and other products that instructors find particularly useful.

Gonzales is in friendly competition with other peer-developed communities like her own who have built their brands and traffic by freely exchanging content with and links to each other's sites. This strategy makes good sense because these website operators are typically motivated more by the desire to exchange useful information with their peers, and thereby develop their professional skills, than to profit financially directly from their e-commerce activity.

FitMoves.com also benefits from friendly collaboration with the many for-profit and professional associations, such as Can-Fit-Pro (**www.canfitpro.com**), a division of Canadian Fitness Professionals Inc.; IDEAfit (**www.ideafit.com**); the International Fitness Association (IFA) (**www.ifafitness.com**); FitnessTEC (**www.fitnesstec.com**); the Aerobics and Fitness Association of America (AFAA) (**www.afaa.com**); the American College of Sports Medicine (**www.acsm.org**); the American Council on Exercise (ACE) (**www.acefitness.org**); and the American Fitness Professionals & Associates (AFPA) (**www.afpafitness.com**). Far from being "cut-throat," the competition among these organizations and professionals is highly collaborative as they help each other build their industry.

Most of these sites, such as Can-Fit-Pro (**www.canfitpro.com**), promote their own certified training and sponsor training events and conferences. At these events, they sell products such as books, music, DVDs, clothes, equipment and other products of interest to trainers in collaboration with vendors to the narrowly defined target market of training professionals. For example, Can-Fit-Pro sells yoga bags and videos distributed by Gonzales.

Fitness professionals may advertise through trade shows, magazines, and the websites of organizations like Can-Fit-Pro. Furthermore, some organization's websites may distribute video clips or complete DVDs produced by individual trainers as well as host their professional page. These sites offer products and services similar to those illustrated by IDEAfit (**www.ideafit.com**), which is a leading organization of health and fitness professionals that has more than 19,000 members in over 80 countries. IDEAfit member benefits include access to the organization's publications, a comprehensive insurance program, continuing education opportunities, and career development programs. It serves six membership categories: *Business Membership*, for owners and managers of health clubs, fitness centers, gyms and studios, as well as for entrepreneurs, consultants, and those who own their own businesses; *Program Director Membership*, for fitness/aerobics directors, program supervisors, and other fitness professionals in a management/supervisory role; *Personal Trainer Membership*, for practicing personal trainers, sports conditioning professionals, coaches, and athletic trainers; *Health Professional Membership*, for exercise physiologists, nutritionists, health/wellness educators, registered nurses, medical doctors, dietitians, and holistic health professionals; and *Student Membership*, for full-time students who have an interest in the health and fitness industry.[1]

Although Rozel Gonzales launched FitMoves ostensibly to help promote her fitness-training career, it soon became clear that her website, which was peaking at 5,000 users per day, had the potential to become a more commercially viable operation. The question was how? After completing her MBA at McGill University in 2003, Gonzales began to examine more closely what she had managed to create on a student's shoestring budget and identify features with the potential for future development. This chapter provides an insider's view of the way the FitMoves e-business plan was realized, managed, and developed during its startup phase. We will focus a spotlight on how Gonzales implemented and controlled her e-business plan for Fit-Moves in the chapter's two *e-Business Insight* vignettes. Finally, in the *Return to Inside e-Business* case study, we will present a brief SWOT analysis (strengths, weaknesses, opportunities, threats) to illustrate how Gonzales might assess her current situation and determine the next phase of development.

In addition, this final chapter of the textbook also concludes our general discussion of the e-business planning process by looking at how e-business plans are *implemented* and then *controlled* by a firm.

Fitmoves.com

(*Source:* Copyright 2003 FitMoves. Reprinted with permission.)

Implementation of the e-Business Plan

implementation

Carrying out the actual tasks that must be performed to realize the objectives established in the e-business plan.

Implementation refers to carrying out the actual tasks that must be performed to realize the objectives established in the e-business plan. Implementation requires coordinated managerial action using all of the organization's resources—informational, financial, material, and human—as well as the procedural systems that direct how work is done within the firm. The implementation stage of the plan specifies who will perform each task; what special skills, training, supervision, or motivation each person should have; when the work will be scheduled within the firm's overall timetable; the costs associated with the work; how communication between employees will be established; and so forth.

According to research by the Gartner Group, half of all customer relationship management (CRM) projects fail because management does not properly implement a transition to the new system. Key departments may be left out of the decision-making process, and customer expectations may not be incorporated into the plan. Companies need to take a realistic approach to the complex demands of rolling out a system if such systems are to have a chance of succeeding. Firms must consider the expectations of users and the difficulties that may ensue from switching procedures.[2]

Project Management Scheduling Tools

Firms can schedule the work that needs to be completed and identify who will be responsible for each task by using a variety of tools, such as Gantt charts and Program Evaluation and Review Technique (PERT) diagrams, as illustrated in Figures 11.1 and 11.2, respectively. Gantt charts and PERT diagrams provide project managers with a visual understanding of the sequence of activities and the time required to complete all of the planned activities. Some work may be able to be done simultaneously, which is indicated by parallel time lines. In other cases, certain tasks will need to be completed before the next stage in the plan can be started. For instance, installing computer software and integrating it with the firm's back-office system cannot begin until any new computer hardware that is required has been installed.

PERT diagrams also provide a clearer understanding of the project's *critical path*, which is the series of events from start to finish that will take the longest amount of time. In other words, the critical path not only measures the minimum amount of time required to complete the project but also highlights those activities that can delay the entire project if they are not completed as scheduled. Experienced management consultants can often predict within a reasonable margin of error how long it will take to roll out a new installation for their clients. Often, however, problems can arise that will cause delays and cause expected task completion dates to be missed.

Implementation timetables encompass timetables at the corporate, divisional, and operational levels of the firm. Each timetable includes the level of detail appropriate for the managers who are responsible for seeing that the work is carried out successfully. At the operational level, the timetable could include the names of individual employees and of others who could replace them if necessary when the tasks are scheduled. This could facilitate implementation and reduce the

FIGURE 11.1 Gantt Chart of CRM Software and Computer Installation

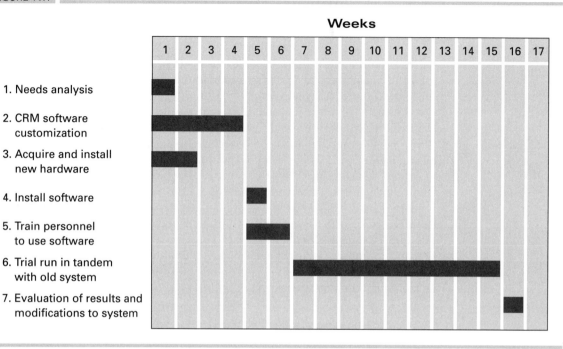

risk of problems caused by a lack of available skilled employees. Furthermore, detailed planning schedules can help management estimate the time and resources required for future work of a similar nature. By comparing the actual results with the detailed original estimates, management can learn how to estimate the complexities of the process and make more accurate assessments of the work still to be done. This is especially important for management consulting firms, as they must prepare bids for services they will be expected to deliver to their customers. By examining historical data, management can learn from past errors in judgment and develop more accurate forecasts of the problems that can arise when complex projects are implemented.

Problems and Solutions

According to recent research, as many as two-thirds of all software-related projects, such as the customization and installation of a CRM system, fail to meet their planned delivery dates and budgets. Furthermore, about half of major projects are eventually cancelled as a result of a loss of project control.[3] These failures to properly plan, implement, and control projects contribute to managers' unwillingness to undertake the risk of major spending projects, especially those projects whose contributions to profitability or productivity might be questionable. To avoid problems and disappointments as much as possible, a well-thought-out

FIGURE 11.2 PERT Diagram of CRM Software and Computer Installation

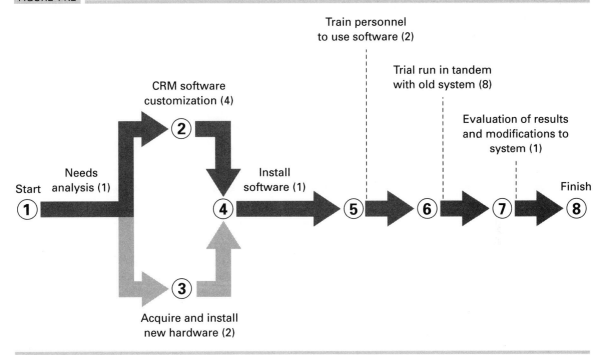

implementation strategy will consider the real time and costs required to deliver the project as well as the expected benefits. If customer satisfaction ratings are expected to improve after implementing a CRM installation, then levels of customer satisfaction should be measured before and after the work is done in order to methodically document the project's effectiveness.

Problems with the implementation of plans are normal. Planning should be flexible so as to accommodate circumstances that might arise when the time comes to put the plan into action. Since the environmental forces that can influence strategic planning are assumed to be continuously changing, the firm should expect that any plan will have to be modified somewhat once it is removed from the discussion table and put into practice in the real world. Sometimes environmental changes can be extreme and happen quickly, as was the case during the sudden fall in demand for telecommunications equipment in 2001. Few analysts—experts included—predicted the dramatic halt in new orders experienced by firms like Cisco Systems, Lucent Technologies, and Nortel Networks. As a result of the chain reaction that ensued, business plans had to be drastically adjusted at all of these firms as well as firms that were to a greater or lesser degree affected by the sudden fall in technology equipment buying.

Problems also typically arise during the implementation of a business plan if the responsibilities for planning and implementation have been separated. Planning is often limited to the corporate and division levels of the firm, and operational-level employees, who generally are the ones expected to carry out the assigned tasks, are left out of the loop. In some instances, higher-level planners might call for some activity that operational staff, if they knew about it, would quickly dismiss for good reasons. However, the planners do not learn of the problems posed by these activities until the plan is implemented. To avoid delays and budget overspending, planners need to include operational-level people in the planning process.

e-BUSINESS insight

FitMoves.com—Implementation of the e-Business Plan

Goals and Objectives

Rozel Gonzales launched FitMoves.com to help promote herself as a fitness instructor to individuals and as a consultant to corporations that are interested in designing and setting up wellness programs and exercise facilities for their employees. (To distinguish between these two endeavors, she set up a separate business called Energie EnCorps [**www.energieencorps.com/index.html**] in partnership with another fitness professional.) She had no other clearly defined objectives other than to learn from others and build her reputation as an expert in a field where word of mouth is the still the least expensive and most effective marketing tactic. As a result, the website's content grew organically as visitors added items and sent letters to Gonzales detailing what they wanted to know and answering the questions she posted online.

Creating the Site

Although based in Montreal, Canada, Gonzales chose to register the domain name FitMoves with an American-based company called GoDaddy.com (**www.godaddy.com**) because at $10, it was the cheapest price she could find for the service. It did not matter which company actually conducted the registration process, as long as it was done properly and allowed her to relocate the site to any hosting service without restriction. Gonzales was therefore guided by endorsements she received from others.

Gonzales then looked for an inexpensive host that offered customer support and chose Wisconsin-based ReadyHosting.com (**www.readyhosting. com**). For $75 per year, Gonzales receives what she rates as excellent customer support for very little cost.

The FitMoves.com site has been a work in progress from the start. Gonzales and her husband designed and set up the main template for the site using Microsoft FrontPage together with interactive databases that collect user-supplied information such as song suggestions, choreography, and the like. Once the template was done, Gonzales spent approximately 50 hours populating the site with articles, pictures, video clips, and other content. She then invests 2-3 hours each week adding more content.

Marketing

FitMoves' early online marketing effort involved listing the URL (**www.fitmoves.com**) at all of the major search engines by using key words (metatags) that cause the search engine algorithms to properly categorize the site in their directories. These keywords included *choreography, aerobics, fitness, instructor, videos, spinning, Canada, Montreal, presenter, Rozel Gonzales, gyms, yoga, step,* and *video clips* and are embedded in the HTML code of the FitMoves webpage. Though not displayed on the user's screen, they play an important role in communicating information about the site to any automated search software that comes by the site in search of new listings to update its directories. Although she could eventually opt to have FitMoves.com displayed whenever a particular keyword is entered, for now Gonzales is content to build her brand without spending funds in this way. As a result, depending on the specifics of each search engine's algorithm, FitMoves.com's rank is based fundamentally on its popularity. This is typically measured by the number of other sites that have links to it and by how much traffic it receives.

Gonzales also began spreading the word about FitMoves by joining *web-rings,* which are groups of websites who swap links and collaborate with other site owners to help each other build traffic. Later, Gonzales found other owners like herself who were willing to swap articles and content, which would allow her to both build the content of her site and promote the FitMoves brand name without any cash outlay. The strategy was a great success. FitMoves received hits from all over the world, and visitors enthusiastically responded to the site's content. The trading links strategy even allowed Gonzales to negotiate a deal with a firm to create a logo design for FitMoves in exchange for posting a link to the design firm on her webpage. Later, Gonzales negotiated the exchange of links placed on her website for indexing FitMoves.com with Montreal-based search engines in their fitness and personal training categories—all without any cash outlays.

Many of the fitness professionals who visited the FitMoves site asked if they could post a link on it. Some were internationally renowned, such as Gin Miller—the creator of STEP choreography (**www. ginmiller.com/gmf04/linksAssoc/instlinks.htm**). Gonzales also found that many local organizations, like Monster Gym (**www.monstergym.net/en/ bio_rozel.shtml**), were willing to post her bio and those of other popular trainers free of charge because they believed that it reflected well on them to be affiliated with leading fitness professionals in the community.

Gonzales continued building brand awareness for FitMoves by adding references to her site in any literature she prepared for distribution to participants at the numerous fitness conventions she presented at. In this way, all of her workshop participants, who typically were members of the professional fitness community, would learn about her website. Gonzales also began writing articles for several sites that serve fitness professional, such as Fitforces (**www.fitforces.com**), TimeForFitness (**www.timeforfitness.com/aerobic/spinning. htm**), and TeachFitness (**www.teachfitness.com/ articles13.htm**). Writing articles allowed her to generate more awareness of FitMoves by placing links at the end of the articles and by using **viral marketing** tactics that encouraged readers to e-mail the article to a friend. Viral marketing refers to a strategy whereby marketing information is voluntarily spread from one individual to another. She also made use of services offered free of charge from Bravenet.com (**www.bravenet.com**) that allowed her to send e-mail to lists of registered users, surveys, guest maps, chat boards, and so forth.

Gonzales recognized the importance of keeping the content on her site fresh so as to maintain current users and attract new ones. She often used royalty-free content that many sites make available so as to build their traffic. She then began offering fitness professionals the opportunity to post their bios on FitMoves. This tactic brought more life to the site and made it more personalized since real people and their photos were displayed along with their promotional bios.

Finally, Gonzales experimented with e-commerce by selling yoga bags on the FitMoves site. Although the results were nominal, the learning experience she gained by using the Paypal's free software to create a simple online store justified her effort in her mind, especially if she eventually decides to develop her site's e-commerce profile in the future.

Question for discussion: Discuss the strategies that Gonzales and others have used that might be used to build brand recognition for the FitMoves website.[4]

Control of the e-Business Plan

viral marketing
A strategy whereby marketing information is voluntarily spread from one individual to another.

control
Management's efforts to monitor, measure, evaluate, and modify the e-business project as needed while it is being implemented so as to ensure that the project is delivered as planned.

Control refers to management's efforts to monitor, measure, evaluate, and modify the e-business project as needed while it is being implemented so as to ensure that the project is delivered as planned. To accomplish this, management must establish performance objectives and standards for the project's activities. As the plan is implemented, comparisons made against these performance standards will indicate whether the plan is still under management's control. Management will then have to adjust the plan and take corrective action to close any gap between what was planned and the actual events unfolding.

If planning was done well in the first place, management can expect to make adjustments, but radical changes will not be necessary. If radical changes are called for, then management should initiate a full audit to establish whether the planning process was flawed because of poor research, poor communications, poor information, poor decision-making and judgment on the part of management, or for some other reason, such as radical changes in the environment that are beyond managers' control. Certainly, the rapid collapse of e-business activity in 2000–1 qualifies as a reason why many business plans failed to meet managers' and shareholders' expectations. Everyone in the organization should learn from the experience with the goal of returning to the planning process better prepared.

Setting Performance Objectives and Standards

performance objectives
The targeted results of activity that the firm seeks to achieve by implementing the e-business plan.

performance standards
More specific performance reference points, which might be set by the firm or by the industry of which it is a part.

Performance objectives are the targeted results of activity that the firm seeks to achieve by implementing the e-business plan. In contrast, **performance standards** are more specific performance reference points that might be set by the firm or by the industry it belongs to. For example, a performance objective for the installation of a customer relationship management (CRM) system might include improving customer service by reducing the wait times for placing orders with customer service representatives, whereas a performance standard might be expressed as reducing customer wait time to no more than 2 minutes. According to a recent J. D. Powers study, automobile dealers' websites are getting better and better at achieving their primary objectives: selling cars online and allowing customers to be more informed and better prepared when they visit dealerships so the dealers can close sales. Sales online have increased steadily, and data indicate that automobile dealers have a higher close ratio when customers are referred to them by manufacturers' websites. Independent automobile website operators like Autobytel (**www.autobytel.com**) and Microsoft's MSN Autos (**http://autos.msn.com/**) enjoyed early leads in developing online customer relationships and brand recognition. However, the trend is clearly favoring manufacturers as car customers learn to use the manufacturers' websites to better understand the potential purchase and even—in growing numbers—to make that purchase online. Furthermore, the study suggests that the Internet is an efficient way to keep in touch with customers and is also a hit with dealers, whose level of satisfaction with manufacturers' websites continues to increase.[5]

Measuring and Evaluating Performance Results

Performance objectives and performance standards are critical if a firm is to have any possibility of evaluating performance results and thereby learning from the planning experience. **Metrics** are measurements used to gauge performance and evaluate how well the firm is achieving its objectives as defined in the e-business plan.

Financial metrics—such as increases in return on investment (ROI), profitability, sales revenue, profit margins, operating income, earnings per share, cash flow, and market share and reductions in expenses—are readily measured outcomes that are particularly important to shareholders. A study by the Framingham, Massachusetts, research group IDC (**www.idc.com**) revealed that 80 percent of potential buyers planned to use ROI to evaluate their application service provider (ASP) installations. Furthermore, a study of fifty-four ASP installations of CRM, supply chain management (SCM), and other software solutions showed that the five-year ROI was 404 percent. Interestingly, IDC found that more than 56 percent of the firms surveyed reported an ROI greater than 100 percent and that 12 percent experienced an ROI of more than 1000 percent. The average reported initial investment by firms was $399,000, and their average total expenditure for ASP installations reached $4.2 million. However, the average payback period was only 1.33 years.[6]

Meanwhile, according to a study conducted by Cap Gemini Ernst & Young, 42 percent of North American companies have no idea what the return on their investment in CRM software actually is. The reasons cited for this include the complexity of costing at the divisional levels, where costs are often transferred from other divisions, and the general weakness in understanding and defining metrics for the proper monitoring and evaluation of CRM installations.

The firm advises clients to develop metrics in three companywide areas—marketing, sales, and service—and, more importantly, to do so before considering the acquisition of a CRM installation. Only when they do this can the returns for adopting CRM solutions be readily evaluated in terms of the benefits they are expected to provide, such as reductions in costs, increased efficiencies, improved customer relations, and so forth. Following this approach, Marriott Hotels (**www.marriott.com**) used *marketing metrics* (sales levels before and after implementation of the CRM system), *sales metrics* (the time required to close a sale), and *service metrics* (the cost of servicing an order [a customer] after the sale was completed) to evaluate whether its installation was a success and to provide a basis for control.

Canada Post (**www.canadapost.ca**) selected the cost to serve a single customer, wait times in its call center, the number of times a customer went to the website, and invoice adjustment costs as important criteria for deciding to adopt an SAP Inc. (**www.sap.com**) CRM system and as metrics for evaluating that system's contributions

---

metrics

Measurements used to gauge performance and evaluate how well the firm is achieving its objectives as defined in the e-business plan.

financial metrics

Readily measured outcomes that are particularly important to shareholders, such as increases in return on investment (ROI), profitability, sales revenue, profit margins, operating income, earnings per share, cash flow, and market share and reductions in expenses.

balanced scorecard
An approach to strategic
control that calls for
recognizing the contribu-
tions that improved
efficiency, quality,
innovation, and respon-
siveness to customers
make to building a
competitive advantage
in the marketplace.

efficiency metrics
Measurements that focus
on the firm's internal
operations, such as
reducing the time spent
entering a customer's
order online as well as
costs associated with
the order.

quality metrics
Metrics that measure
improvements in the firm's
products and services,
such as a reduction in the
number of complaints the
firm receives from unhappy
customers.

innovation metrics
Metrics that measure how
quickly the firm can
introduce new products
based on changing
customer needs.

**responsiveness-to-
customers metrics**
Metrics that measure how
well the firm is responding
to its customers' needs;
these metrics include
customer retention rates
and measures of customer
loyalty and satisfaction
with the firm's services in
general, as determined by
periodic surveys.

to operations. Setting a target reduction of 50 percent of its annual 48,000 invoice adjustments, the profit-oriented organization expects to cut costs and move customers to more cost-effective self-servicing on its website. Given that the cost for a sales representative to visit a client is about $200 to $300 and the cost of a website transaction is about 5 cents, the advantages of building revenues through the website—once the sales staff has established the client relationship—become crystal clear.

And finally, Wynne Powell, the president of London Drugs Ltd. (**www.londondrugs .com**), is confident that his western Canadian retail chain will be able to measure the effectiveness of its CRM system solution by comparing the customer satisfaction metrics it has gathered for the past 22 years with its future results. And rather than looking for fast returns on its investment in terms of improved profitability, London Drugs' management is confident that the CRM solution will produce noticeable results gradually over the years.[7]

R. S. Kaplan and D. P. Norton's **balanced scorecard** approach to strategic control calls for recognizing the contributions that improved efficiency, quality, innovation, and responsiveness to customers make to building a competitive advantage in the marketplace.[8] **Efficiency metrics** focus on the firm's internal operations, such as reducing the time spent entering a customer's order online as well as costs associated with the order. If orders are entered 20 percent faster, then the same number of service representatives can handle more orders each hour or the company can lower its costs by reducing the number of representatives it employs. **Quality metrics** measure improvements in the firm's products and services, such as the actual download and upload speeds that an Internet service provider makes available during peak demand periods. A quality metric for service improvements could be to reduce the number of complaints the firm receives from unhappy customers. **Innovation metrics** measure how quickly the firm can introduce new products based on changing customer needs. And finally, **responsiveness–to–customers metrics** measure how well the firm is responding to its customers' needs. These metrics include customer retention rates and measures of customer loyalty and satisfaction with the firm's services in general, as determined by periodic surveys. Metrics like these help define the degree of success of e-business projects. For example, a recent study showed that fewer than 1 percent of the more than $1 trillion in transactions made by all levels of American government take place over the Internet. IBM put Arizona's vehicle-registration program online and reduced the average wait time from 45 minutes to only 3. Furthermore, the cost to the state of registering a vehicle fell from $6.60 to $1.60, saving the motor bureau about $1.25 million each year. In exchange, IBM earned $1 on each transaction. Clearly, these metrics suggest that more government services will be moving onto the Internet in the future.[9]

Taking Corrective Actions

Firms need performance measurements to know whether their planned strategies are being implemented as expected. If the gap between planned and actual

e-BUSINESS insight

FitMoves.com—Control of the e-Business Plan

The early feedback from FitMoves' users, which took the form of e-mail messages and other sites' interest in exchanging links, gradually became too limited to help Gonzales understand whether FitMoves was evolving into the sort of online community she wanted it to be. Furthermore, she needed to know how users were responding to specific actions she took online such as posting a new article or link. As the volume of traffic on the site grew to 5,000 hits per day, Gonzales needed a more sophisticated analytical tool that would report a variety of statistics about who was using the site and how they were navigating through it. As part of its service package, ReadyHosting (**www.readyhosting. com**), the firm that hosts FitMoves, provides a plethora of useful statistics to web owners such as tracking who's on at any moment; usage statistics (hits, hits per session, page views, session time, pages viewed, time spent per visit, users' entry and exit point to any page); and how users arrived at the site (through a search engine referral; if so, which keyword they used; and so forth).

Gonzales reviews these statistics daily, which allows her to see which sections of FitMoves are the most popular and whether new material has caused a spike in hits and sessions. Furthermore, the data provides her with insight into where in the world visitors come from and how long they spend on each page. She can even see users' IP addresses, so she is able to know who are repeat users and which sites are referring users to FitMoves. For example, she knows that although most users come to FitMoves via Google, Yahoo!, and the other major search engines, many smaller independent sites are also sending her traffic.

Question for discussion: Discuss the strategies that Gonzales uses to measure online activity and other strategies that she might use to measure activity.[10]

---

results is sufficiently wide, then managers should take the necessary corrective action to close the gap, or even consider reexamining the entire planning process if the strategy is no longer realistic or desirable. In this way, the firm can document its progress toward the successful delivery of the plan and direct information that might be useful to the development of newly emerging plans to those who can incorporate these findings into the ongoing planning process (Figure 11.3).

According to venture capitalist William Gurley of Benchmark Capital Inc. (**www. benchmark.com**), the most important and comprehensive website performance metric is the **conversion rate**, or a percentage that reflects the number of visitors to a website who respond to the offers and activities presented on their screens. If, for example, the conversion rate of visitors to a retailing site like Amazon.com increased from 2 to 3 percent, this would translate into a 50 percent increase in sales revenues. Gurley argues that no other comprehensive metric measures as effectively the attractiveness or user-friendliness of the interface design, the performance

conversion rate
A percentage that reflects the number of visitors to a website who respond to the offers and activities presented on their screens.

FIGURE 11.3   The Strategic Planning Process

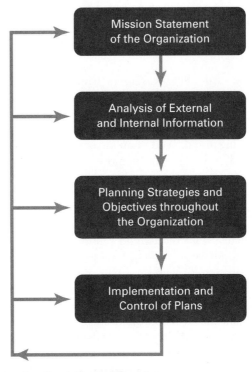

Feedback Flow of Results

After the organization has established its mission statement, an analysis of relevant information leads the firm to develop strategic plans and subsequently implement them. Feedback links assure the continuous incorporation of new information at all steps of the process.

Go to the Web:
e-Business Online
For tutorials and more on the topics in this chapter, visit the student website at **http://business .college.hmco.com/ students** and select "Canzer e-Business."

of the site, its convenience of use, the effectiveness of advertising and targeting customers, the site's overall popularity, and the number of visitors who tell others about their satisfaction with the site. According to Gurley, 10 percent or more would be a high conversion rate, while an average might be closer to 3 to 5 percent. Below 2 percent would be considered poor overall performance.[11]

Conclusions

Implementation and controlling activities complete the strategic planning process cycle, as illustrated in Figure 11.3. After creating and implementing their e-business plan for the first time, managers must continually weigh ongoing research and results and then integrate this information into a revised plan for the future.

Now that you have completed an examination of the principal concepts of the e-business strategic planning process, you are in a much better position to begin analyzing and reporting on current business strategies. Perhaps you even feel confident enough to begin the process of researching and preparing a plan of your own. Whether the plan involves adding an e-business dimension to an existing business operation or starting up an entirely new business, you can feel confident that the critical concepts and procedures have been covered—the rest lies in the details and having the right idea.

To help you get started, the Appendix and companion website present several valuable items to further your understanding of strategic planning. The Appendix provides a longer and more complex comprehensive case study than the shorter ones included in each chapter that you can analyze and discuss in your class. To help you, the textbook website presents a tutorial for preparing case study reports and additional case studies. The website also presents a model e-business plan that was actually used to launch a small firm so you can see how a real e-business plan might look. In addition, a detailed tutorial is available to help guide you toward the preparation of your own **e-business plan**—just as many of the entrepreneurs we have discussed in this textbook have done. Ideally, the many examples and case studies we have examined have helped to prepare you for this step.

 # RETURN TO
inside e-business

CASE STUDY

Entrepreneurs like Rozel Gonzales have demonstrated how a firm can successfully develop an online presence from scratch with limited start-up capital and operating budget. The fundamental question facing Gonzales at this early stage is whether she should continue with her present strategic plan and further develop the site so as to earn revenues from the professional services she provides to individuals and organizations. Alternatively, she could launch a new phase of development for FitMoves that might include converting her growing volume of traffic into new sources of revenue. To help her scope out the possibilities for her planning, we will focus our attention on the key elements that describe FitMoves' current situation and then frame the alternatives Gonzales can realistically consider. First, we will examine the competitive advantage that FitMoves has established thus far, and then we will conduct a brief SWOT analysis.

COMPETITIVE ADVANTAGE

The personal and professionally recognized competencies that Rozel Gonzales possesses are directly associated with FitMoves and therefore contribute to the major competitive advantage her site enjoys— it is Rozel Gonzales's personal site. As a result of her growing reputation, Gonzales can take advantage of her status in the fitness industry to promote traffic to the site and provide a superior-quality image and endorsement of her service. Unlike obviously commercial sites, FitMoves enjoys a peer-to-peer sharing image that is not heavily motivated by e-commerce activity. Because the site offers free access to users and has not attempted to commercialize in an obvious or aggressive way, it has benefited from a "viral" marketing campaign whereby individuals freely promote the site to their friends and associates. Furthermore, a general willingness to cooperate, share content, and exchange links with other like-minded sites as well as with clearly established commercial sites has helped promote the Fitmoves .com brand at very little cost. However, the cooperative good nature of these commercial sites may not continue if they perceive a real competitive threat to their business model from a more commercialized FitMoves.

STRENGTHS

FitMoves is a growing community website that provides free access to a range of high-quality information such as fitness articles, photos, video clips, links, and insightful personal stories describing fitness instructors' solutions to the challenges they face as they build their businesses. The site has grown because it offers user-friendly interactive capabilities that allow instructors to contribute their comments, questions, ideas, choreography, and so forth. The site enjoys high traffic volume of about 5,000 hits per day, an international audience of mainly American and European readers, and perhaps a unique feature for spinning instructors—a spinning database, one of the most popular sections on the site.

WEAKNESSES

Gonzales recognizes that FitMoves' limited server capabilities result in slow video streaming to users. If she is going to continue to make video an important content item, then some investment is going to be necessary to speed up downloading time. Gonzales admits she has limited time available for this and for other efforts to improve the site. Besides performing daily maintenance of the site, which includes answering e-mail, posting new articles and video clips, Gonzales recognizes that the site will also need a major design update every few years if it is to remain attractive to users. Although she is satisfied with the work done thus far with very limited funds, Gonzales considers the website's design somewhat amateurish, outdated, and poorly organized. A major overhaul will require her to invest time and money as well as hire people who can provide professional design services that are beyond the skill set Gonzales and her husband can bring to the site.

Furthermore, she is unclear what her objectives should be for the site. Should she just continue operating the site as a limited extension of her fitness consulting business or should she instead attempt to capitalize on the growing traffic and brand recognition she has developed so far and turn serious attention to building a successful e-business? Although Gonzales's only e-commerce effort—to sell yoga bags online—was poorly received, the effort convinced her that any future e-commerce venture would require her to make a greater investment in the necessary e-business resources.

OPPORTUNITIES

FitMoves became the online community that it is today primarily because Gonzales responded to the feedback of users who requested information, new choreography video clips, and other information. In general, users want Gonzales to recommend DVDs, books, certification conferences and organizations, equipment, and accessories, and they trust her non-commercially motivated answers. How users would respond to advice that involved a commercial endorsement is an unanswerable question without some research. However, one could reasonably hypothesize that commercializing on the reputation she enjoys among current and possible future users is something Gonzales should consider.

Gonzales's research suggests that few sites on the Web sell choreography clips and DVDs, which provides Gonzales with a possible niche market opportunity that fits well with her synergistic competencies in producing and distributing not only her own video clips but those of other instructors as well. Furthermore, Gonzales believes that her site has grown in popularity because it provides short video clips of routines rather than the traditional long videotape of a 20- or 30-minute workout. Users can quickly select only the clips of routines that they are interested in and can catalog them on their computers using names they assign. Gonzales believes that expanding the choreography video-clip section offers great potential. She could try to charge a monthly membership for viewing the choreography video clips, charge on a per-clip basis, or provide sample clips free of charge to motivate users to purchase DVDs containing a collection of clips.

Gonzales has also considered marketing FitMoves as a site where other presenters could advertise themselves and post their workshops, bios, and video clips. However, many other sites provide the same service and do not charge any fees, so how successful such an effort might be is open to question.

THREATS

FitMoves faces no serious threats—with the exception of a growing marketplace of competitors, many of whom are spending significant e-business resources to build up their brand recognition both online and off. FitMoves' true commercial competitors occupy a niche in the marketplace that may involve selling products and services, training, certification, conferences, and so forth. If they ever consider FitMoves to be a real competitor to their revenue-generation efforts, they might curtail the collaborative free exchange of links and other friendly relations. Other than these obviously commercially motivated organizations, FitMoves will face increasing competitive pressures from a growing number of other websites established by fitness professionals that may have devoted the effort and resources to offer better

services than she can. For instance, a small group of five fitness instructors who pool their time and other resources would have an easier time competing with other free sole-proprietor sites like FitMoves.

ASSIGNMENT

1. Should the site focus only on promoting the training and consulting services provided by Rozel Gonzales? Explain your arguments.
2. What else would you recommend to help build traffic on FitMoves?
3. How else could FitMoves generate revenues from its traffic?
4. What products could FitMoves sell online?
5. What are the drawbacks to fully converting Fit-Moves into a true commercial website? Explain your thinking.

Chapter Review

SUMMARY

ACE Self-Test
For a quick self-test of the content in this chapter, visit the student website at **http://business. college.hmco.com/ students.** Select "Canzer e-Business."

1. **Examine how the e-business plan is implemented within a firm's organizational structure and integrated into that structure.**

   Implementation refers to carrying out the actual tasks required to realize the goals and objectives established in the e-business plan. Implementation requires coordinated managerial action using all of the organization's resources—informational, financial, material, and human—as well as the procedural systems that direct how work is done within the firm. The plan's implementation specifies who will perform each task; what special skills, training, supervision, or motivation each person should have; when the work will be scheduled within the firm's overall timetable; the costs associated with this work; how communication between employees will be established; and so forth. Encountering problems when implementing plans is normal. Planning should be flexible so as to accommodate circumstances that might arise when the time comes to put the plan into action. Since the environmental forces that can influence strategic planning are assumed to be continuously changing, it is to be expected that any plan will require some modification once it is removed from the discussion table and put into practice in the real world.

2. **Describe how management controls the e-business plan by setting performance objectives and standards, measuring and evaluating results, and directing future actions and decisions.**

Control refers to management's efforts to monitor, measure, evaluate, and modify the e-business project while it is being implemented to ensure that the project is delivered as planned. To accomplish this, the firm must establish performance objectives and standards for the implementation activities. As the plan is implemented, comparisons with performance standards will indicate whether or not the plan is under control. Management will then have to adjust the plan and take corrective action to close any gap between what was planned and the actual events that are unfolding. Performance objectives are the targeted results that management hopes are achieved by implementing the e-business plan, whereas performance standards are more specific performance reference points that might be set by the firm or by the industry it belongs to. Performance objectives and performance standards are critical if the firm is to have any real possibility of evaluating performance results and thereby learning from the planning experience. Financial results—such as increases in return on investment, profitability, sales revenue, profit margins, cash flow, and market share and reductions in expenses—are readily measured outcomes. However, R. S. Kaplan and D. P. Norton's so-called balanced scorecard approach to strategic control calls for recognizing the contribution that improved efficiency, quality, innovation, and responsiveness to customers make to building a competitive advantage in the marketplace.

REVIEW QUESTIONS

1. What does the implementation of an e-business plan involve?
2. What is a Gantt chart?
3. How is a Gantt chart used to implement the e-business plan?
4. What is a PERT diagram?
5. How is a PERT diagram used to implement the e-business plan?
6. What does control of the e-business plan involve?
7. What is meant by performance objectives and performance standards?
8. What are metrics?

DISCUSSION QUESTIONS

1. What are some of the difficulties associated with implementing an e-business plan?
2. Explain why implementing the e-business plan requires the involvement of the entire organization.
3. Describe the steps in the control process.
4. What might explain a gap between planned performance and actual results?

**Building
Skills
for Career
Success**

EXPLORING THE INTERNET

The need to make radical changes in a firm's existing e-business plans is perhaps most obvious when the core of the firm's current strategy is failing. For instance, after implementing its plan, Napster was sued in the U.S. courts over copyright violations. In many respects, Napster management's ability to control future events quickly evaporated as the courts ordered Napster to modify its e-business plan to comply with international copyright law. Similarly, websites like Yahoo! that based their strategies on increasing web-advertising revenues have also been forced to radically rethink many of their core assumptions. Examine the website of a firm that has recently undergone a fundamental revision of its e-business thinking. You can find one by researching one of the many online journals and information gateways, such as CNET (**www.cnet.com**).

ASSIGNMENT

1. Describe the reasons why changes to the e-business plan of the company you selected are needed.
2. How is the firm planning to change its current e-business plan?

DEVELOPING CRITICAL THINKING SKILLS

Some analysts have suggested that where advertising expenditures are concerned, the definition of ROI needs to be expanded beyond simple sales and profits. For instance, Internet advertising might be evaluated as part of a firm's overall integrated media campaign to build brand awareness, identity, and loyalty. To measure these effects properly, the firm needs to collect data on changes and monitor them over a longer period of time by using databases of customer information. The Internet is an ideal tool for this, because it provides a two-way channel for communicating with customers.

ASSIGNMENT

1. Select one of the e-commerce websites you are familiar with, such as Yahoo!, and develop five online survey questions that could be asked of visitors to that site to help measure the changes in its brand equity.
2. As a manager of that firm, what other changes would you want to measure over time?

BUILDING TEAM SKILLS

According to a Jupiter Media Metrix (**www.jmm.com**) survey, 36 percent of Internet users would visit a content site more often if it featured a customized layout that allowed the user to select and personalize the content displayed on his or her screen. Users were particularly interested in customizing financial and news content. Furthermore, according to Datamonitor (**www.datamonitor.com**), global investment in personalization technologies will grow from $500 million in 2001 to $2.1 billion in 2006.[12]

Suppose your group were asked to help design a menu for a website that would allow it to be customized to target the students attending your school. Explore a variety of websites that enable users to customize selections such as local news and weather.

ASSIGNMENT

1. Select a website and identify why you have chosen it.
2. Create at least three categories of menu choices that would provide users of the site with personalization. Explain why they would make the site more attractive to users.

RESEARCHING DIFFERENT CAREERS

A variety of careers are available in the IT industry. Software development firms like PeopleSoft (**www.peoplesoft.com**), Siebel Systems (**www.siebel.com**), and SAP (**www.sap.com**) will post descriptions for positions that they are looking to fill on their website. These positions can include everything from direct selling of large-scale software systems to providing customer support online. These different positions require specialized training, skills, personality, and ambition. This is especially true for positions involving the writing of customized software code or the design of user-friendly input and output screens. Some people might be well suited for one type of job and not another. Aside from the technical side of design, the content experts who prepare the specialized content that appears online and the experts who understand how users are likely to interact with the different screen designs and information flows are also important roles. Select a firm you are familiar with and explore the job opportunities available there. Select one job that interests you.

ASSIGNMENT

1. Write a short cover letter to the firm, identifying the position that you want to be considered for.
2. Prepare a resumé or curriculum vitae that includes details supporting your claim to be a good candidate for this job.

IMPROVING COMMUNICATION SKILLS

Implementing and controlling IT solutions is a complex process. For example, the launch of a CRM solution requires understanding and commitment by many people across all levels of the firm. Gantt charts and PERT diagrams can help communicate the plan and the set the schedule. Choose an IT project for a firm and consider the implementation issues involved in it.

ASSIGNMENT

1. Create a Gantt chart and a PERT diagram to explain the implementation of the solution.
2. Write a descriptive letter to one group of employees that explains why the firm is adopting the solution and how it will help them in their jobs.

Exploring Useful Websites

These websites provide information related to the topics discussed in the chapter. You can learn more by visiting them online and examining their current data.

1. FitMoves.com (**www.fitmoves.com**) provides professional instructors and exercise enthusiasts with a sophisticated center where they can exchange highly valued photographs, video clips, music, and other products that are particularly useful to instructors. To distinguish between her effort to serve the professional fitness market and her corporate consulting, Rozel Gonzales also set up a separate business called Energie EnCorps (**www.energieencorps.com/index.html**). She chose to register the domain name FitMoves with GoDaddy.com (**www.godaddy.com**), and the site is hosted by ReadyHosting.com (**www.readyhosting.com**). She made use of services available free of charge from Bravenet.com (**www.bravenet.com**) that allowed her to send e-mail to lists of registered users, conduct surveys, and offer guest maps, chat boards, and so forth. FitMoves.com benefits from friendly collaboration with many for-profit and professional associations such as **www.canfitpro.com**, **www.ideafit.com**, **www.ifafitness.com**, **www.fitnesstec.com**, **www.afaa.com**, **www.acsm.org**, **www.acefitness.org**, and **www.afpafitness.com**. Gonzales also began writing articles for several sites, such as Fitforces (**www.fitforces.com**), TimeForFitness (**www.timeforfitness.com/aerobic/spinning.htm**), and TeachFitness (**www.teachfitness.com/articles13.htm**).

2. Marriott Hotels (**www.marriott.com**), Canada Post (**www.canadapost.ca**), and London Drugs Ltd. (**www.londondrugs.com**) have all successfully implemented CRM solutions. The experience of Sobeys Inc. (**www.sobeys.com**), Canada's second-largest food retailer, should serve as a warning of how bad results can be even when management is fully behind a project, top-level consultants are engaged, and top-quality software is deployed. The project was scrapped after a year of technical difficulties, system crashes that resulted in inventory outages, and repeated failures on the part of SAP Inc. (**www.sap.com**), Europe's largest software solution provider. Competing software development firms are PeopleSoft (**www.peoplesoft.com**) and Siebel Systems (**www.siebel.com**).

3. IDC (**www.idc.com**), Jupiter Media Metrix (**www.jmm.com**), and Datamonitor (**www.datamonitor.com**) are IT research firms. CNET (**www.cnet.com**) is a research and information gateway for the IT industry.

4. According to venture capitalist William Gurley of Benchmark Capital Inc. (**www.benchmark.com**), the most important and comprehensive website performance metric is the conversion rate of visitors to a site into respondents to the offers and activities presented on the site's screen.

appendix

U-Swap.com:
A Comprehensive Case Study

Comprehensive Case Study

and

Model e-Business Plan

adapted from information provided by

Introduction

U-Swap (**www.u-swap.com**) provides an online classified advertising website through which college and university students can buy, sell, or exchange (swap) their articles and services—typically with fellow students attending the same school. Students logging on to U-Swap.com are presented with a list of virtual communities identified by individual school names. By selecting the school they attend from the list of participating institutions, students can find products and services offered for sale by other students who they can readily meet up with on their campus.

The original U-Swap website was launched in September 1999. U-Swap was an instant success, capturing the attention of approximately 10 percent of the student population of its original two campus test sites after only one month of operation. These early results prompted the development of a plan to roll out the model to more campuses. The firm rapidly expanded to 31 schools in North America and Europe before cutting back on its initial expansion plans.

Available in English, French, and Spanish, U-Swap was custom designed to meet the needs of college and university students. The site features categories that are not found in traditional classifieds, such as textbooks, as well as advanced features such as key-word search, comparative shopping, auto-notify agents, and multimedia capabilities. At its peak, the site reached over 10 percent of the total student population on the campuses it served.

The company was conceived of by two McGill University MBA graduates and began operations through the efforts of only four university graduates, Internet investment company VC Inc.,[1] a seasoned board of advisors, and a network of more than 30 local campus representatives and chapter affiliates. It has alliances with student portals and other websites.

Business Concept

Students represent a very lucrative market. According to Jupiter Research, the 16 million students in America spend approximately $35 billion each year. Over 85 percent of these cost-conscious individuals buy and sell secondhand goods on a regular basis. Students seek a fast, effective way of completing these transactions with someone in their community. U-Swap meets this need.

U-Swap's strength lies in its local, school-by-school approach. The company's team of campus representatives and chapter affiliates promotes the local chapters of the site in two ways: with smart, local on-campus advertising and via alliances with clubs and associations. U-Swap's local team ensures that it can become an integral part of the community, which results in a highly populated database of local ads. This unique community approach creates significant barriers of entry for new potential competitors and is easily implemented on a global basis.

Surprisingly, U-Swap faced very little direct competition at the outset. Even competitors such as student portals College Club.com or Campus Access.com had only a fraction of the database that U-Swap had created. Moreover, they had neither a local, on-campus presence nor were their websites tailored to the specific needs of each student community.

Competitive Advantages of U-Swap
Website tailored to the local community
Highly populated database
Smart, cost-effective on-campus marketing
Team of representatives and affiliates
Lower customer acquisition costs
Strong management team and board of advisors

Financial Overview

U-Swap was designed to have several revenue sources, including service fees from featured classifieds and banner advertising at both a local and a national level. Additional potential sources of revenue included auction fees, referral sales, and marketing for third parties. U-Swap anticipated revenues of approximately $5 million in four years, to be generated from banner advertising, auction and classified fees, e-commerce partnerships, and special service fees, resulting in earnings before taxes of approximately $2 million. The company anticipated breaking even during the

---

[1] Other investments of VC Inc. include Mamma.com (meta-search engine) and Bam Solutions (online media).

second year of the plan. However, the plan failed to produce the desired growth after the initial capital to launch the enterprise was consumed. By 2003, only the Canadian campus sites remained operational along with a database of 60,000 users.

The Business Model

U-Swap is based on a C2C community e-business model incorporating several revenue streams and services. Unlike geographically wide-reaching classified sites such as eBay, U-Swap is focused on serving the local student community associated with a single campus. U-Swap has a separate database for each university that is customized on a school-by-school basis. In doing so, U-Swap effectively tailors the system to the needs of each community, thereby providing a superior product for its users and competitive advantage.

U-Swap attracts students to the website by offering free student classifieds and by using novel cost-effective advertising on campus. U-Swap has developed a comprehensive marketing campaign that is implemented and controlled by its team of campus representatives and chapter affiliates. These local students have in-depth knowledge specific to their campus and help U-Swap tailor the promotional approach needed to succeed.

Alliances with student portals, clubs, and associations further aid U-Swap's acceptance on and off campus. Various student societies promote U-Swap on their private websites. As a result of these links and advertising, students are made more aware of U-Swap and recognize it as part of their community.

Users are attracted to their campus website through eye-catching campus posters, campus newspaper advertising, the support of key influencing parties such as student clubs and associations, and by providing a superior product to any alternative choices. As illustrated in the following figure, traffic is an essential part of U-Swap's business model as a generator of revenues.

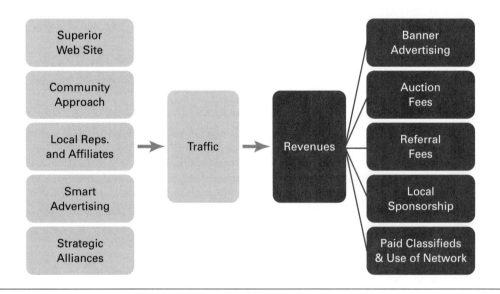

Current and Potential Revenue Streams

Several revenue streams support U-Swap's business model. In the long run, banner advertising, local sponsorships, and auction fees are expected to remain the principal sources of revenue for the company, followed by classified fees and commissions from sales referred from the site.

Distributions of U-Swap's potential revenue from banner advertising, auction fees, local sponsorships, and paid classified and referral fees are illustrated in the following graph. These proportions are expected to remain about the same over the life of the plan.

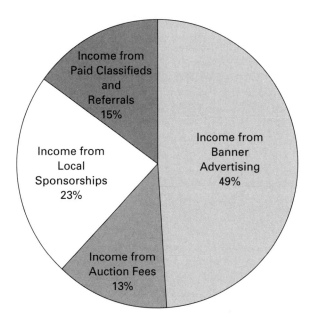

a) **Banner Advertising:** Given the targeted nature of the site, advertisers were eager to purchase banner space on U-Swap at first. At its peak, U-Swap's banner inventory was sold at an average cost per thousand impressions (CPM) of $25. Large advertising and media agencies such as Cossette Communications and BBDO regularly purchased U-Swap's banner inventory on behalf of clients such as Visa, General Motors, and Bell Canada before the dramatic general fall in online advertising after the tech crash in 2000.

b) **Auction Fees:** After the introduction of its auction module in January 2001, U-Swap began collecting user fees for successful transactions conducted over the site with a fee structure similar to that of eBay. Fees vary according to the type of item and category sections selected and were expected to yield an average of $3 per item sold. However, the appeal of an auction site is determined by the inventory of the selection available. Somewhat like the proverbial "chicken-and-egg" problem, users will only frequent a site that rewards them with a satisfactory selection of items for sale. Likewise, vendors will only post items for sale on auction sites that can draw a large and willing market of buyers. U-Swap's inventory of auction items (besides textbooks) as well as regular for-sale inventories of products, experienced difficulty attracting the volumes of both buyers and sellers that were expected after the formative stages of development.

c) **Local Sponsorships:** U-Swap's local campus approach and product category divisions into sections (i.e., computer hardware and software, sports equipment, etc.) attract the attention of local advertisers that wish to sponsor specific sections of the site. Sponsorships can take the form of banners on the right navigation bar of the website, direct e-mails when a user registers or places an ad, coupon pages, or any other type of co-branding activities. While U-Swap's management team sells national sponsorships, local sponsorships can be pursued by U-Swap's local network of campus representatives and chapter affiliates, providing an additional local incentive to generate revenues.

d) **Referral Sales:** Students using U-Swap are generally seeking used articles to purchase or specific services like tutoring and language instruction. By offering visitors direct links to vendors who sell the same type of items that are new, U-Swap can generate additional revenue through collaboration with retailers and other online sellers.

e) **Classified Fees:** As a means to increase the exposure and impact of users' advertising, U-Swap provides for the additional purchase of visibility options such as bolded ads, featured ads at the top of the results page, and so forth. Prices range between $3 and $5 depending on the section where the ad is posted and the type of visibility feature selected. U-Swap also earns posting fees from advertisers wishing to reach the student market through either the jobs or apartments-for-rent sections, where a $20 fee applies to these categories.

The Website

The results of in-depth market research conducted at McGill University in June of 1999 helped define U-Swap's look and service offerings. The figure below provides an overview of the site's main sections (taken from U-Swap's website). Sections such as "Textbooks" or "Tutors and Lessons," which are not found on traditional websites, are the backbone of U-Swap. Research shows that users appreciate the custom design of the site and repeatedly praise U-Swap for being a "well-developed, clear, and easy-to-use website."

As extremely discriminating consumers, students seek out sites that incorporate cutting-edge technology and design. U-Swap has successfully done this by incorporating a number of added-value features into the website. These include:

> ▶ **Multimedia Features:** upload photographs, sounds, or video.
> ▶ **Quick Search:** search the entire website by using keywords.
> ▶ **Auto Notify:** be notified when a new ad matches your criteria.
> ▶ **Shopping List:** select items of interest for later review.

Target Market

University and college students constitute a large and untapped niche market. In the United States and Canada, January 2000 enrollment figures were estimated to have reached 16 million and 1.4 million, respectively. The age range for these North American students is between 17 and 26 years. They are generally considered to be trendsetters and have a higher-than-average percentage of disposable income. Additionally, they are characterized as brand-sensitive consumers, tend to purchase higher-priced trendy items, and are heavily influenced by advertising. Jupiter Communications estimates that they constitute a market potential of over $35 billion annually. Furthermore, the research suggests that 85 percent of students buy and sell used items at least three or four times a year.

Positioning

To illustrate U-Swap's positioning strategy in the student-classified market, we can compare the company to potential competitors using two factors: degree of regional presence and database population (number of ads published). As can be seen from the positioning grid, U-Swap is the only website that has both a local presence and a relatively large database of ads.

Competitors' Grid

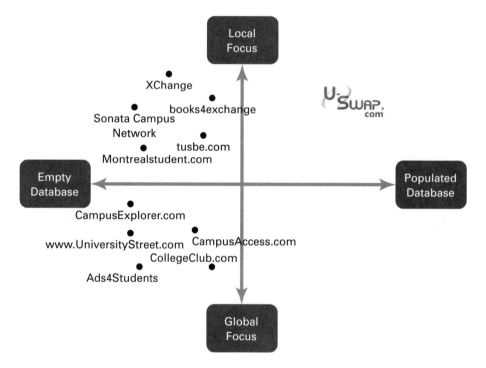

Competitive Analysis

U-Swap faces indirect competition from a variety of old and new forms of classified providers. Local newspapers and campus reviews often contain a classified section that could substitute for the services of U-Swap. Two types of websites can also be considered indirect competitors: Student portals that sometimes offer classifieds as an extra feature (Campus Access) and local web projects developed by students (University Street).

Local Newspapers

Local or campus newspapers present students with an alternative method of buying and selling goods. These indirect competitors are slowly beginning to offer both print classifieds and online classifieds. Fees are charged by word or by line, and range from $10 to $30 per day for a small ad. Placing an ad can be done via phone or fax and generally must be requested at least 24 hours in advance. The categories available are generally not customized to the students' needs.

Student Portals

Student portals are websites that strive to be the home page of all university students. These sites are generally content-driven and offer member benefits such as free Internet access or free e-mail access. Examples of large student portals that offer classifieds as a subcategory of their site include CollegeClub.com and campusaccess.com.

Local Web Projects

Local web projects are small websites that a student, or group of students, develops as a school project. Generally, these sites are developed on limited budgets and are not promoted outside of their campus. Several of these local initiatives have recently popped up in different cities but have a very limited user base. Examples of these include tradinggrounds.com, University Street.com, and xchange.ca. Although U-Swap's competitors fail to match U-Swap's offering in several ways, for completeness, an in-depth analysis of each, as well as other smaller, less popular sites, is presented in the following table.

Table: Competitive Analysis

Competitor	Key Advantages	Key Disadvantages
Village Auction, Inc.	• Dedicated to auctions • Limited success in some U.S. schools • Decent site	• Unappealing site • Unpopulated database • Relatively new • Site often out of order
College Club	• Leading portal for college students in the U.S. • Has substantial financial backing (+$40 million) • The site has excellent content • Offers many advanced features such as e-mail and voice messaging • Established since 1993 • Large network of students using the site • Offers an auction and classifieds sections	• Their classified and auction sections are not populated and have declined in popularity in past months • Major promotional initiatives limited to United States • Site hasn't been popular in Canada • Only in English • Company founder has recently resigned • Company is said to be in financial difficulties due to burn rate—cash flows
College HQ	• U.S. classified site for students that is linked with geek.com and surfer.com • Based in Texas, created by IT/IS students • Site allows users to browse by university	• Site is unpopulated • Has had no promotion • Uses only one global database for all ads, although allows users to browse by university • Only in English • Is a secondary business of founders

(continued)

Table: Competitive Analysis (*Continued*)

Competitor	Key Advantages	Key Disadvantages
Campus Access	• Well-developed U.S. and Canadian portal for university students • Smaller version of College Club.com (see above) • Esthetically pleasing and has good content	• Almost nonexistent classified database (has been stagnant for the past 8 months) • Young team with limited number of support staff • Only available in English
University Street	• Young, attractive-looking site tailored to university students • Run by two Concordia Commerce students • Strong presence at Concordia University	• Very limited number of users and ads • Very limited marketing • Functionality of site is questionable • Only available in English
Sonata Campus Network	• Portal for specific universities in Canada: University of Toronto and University of British Columbia • Very pleasing for users	• Classified database is unpopulated • Fair content • Available at two universities only
tusbe	• Large database of books • Focused on exchange of books • Good search engine	• Limited to Toronto area with minimal success • Restricted to offering book exchange forum • Only available in English
XChange	• Bilingual site • Facilitates exchange of textbooks for university and college students • Fair database of books • Appealing site • Brand-name sponsorship	• Charges users a fee by semester or by year • Limited to textbooks • Very limited promotion and access to site
Ads4Students	• Ontario-based classified site • Used good software to build site (same as U-Swap) • Unique database for each school	• Unappealing design and color scheme of site • Time to load site lengthy • Very new team • Much is unpopulated
books4exchange	• Targeted university students in Canada • Great name, easy to remember • Good site functionality • Large database of books (only at McGill) • Offers an easy-to-use user interface	• Facilitates the exchange of textbooks only • Is limited by design and name • Has shown very limited growth • Lacks infrastructure • Site not in French

Marketing Strategy

A large part of U-Swap's success can be attributed to the firm's ability to develop innovative, eye-catching, and cost-effective advertising campaigns that leverage word-of-mouth advertising. U-Swap was careful to identify key hot spots on campus and then develop specific promotional material and events to leverage the local traffic of these areas and attract attention to the site.

Examples of marketing initiatives used by U-Swap include the following:

<u>Offline:</u>
- Newspaper print editions of online classified
- Handout style flyers
- Bulletin-board posters
- Customized U-Swap Post-it notes
- U-Swap car covered with ads
- Direct calls by U-Swap team
- PR with local newspapers

<u>Online:</u>
- Links with key student associations and clubs
- Banner advertising on relevant local sites
- Alliances with portals to replace/become their classified section
- Direct e-mail messages

Strategic Development Plan

In 2003, U-Swap was acquired by LivingOnline Group Inc. (www.livingonline.ca) and other investors to complement the community website mix of online products and services such as news, magazine articles, discussion forums, and various e-commerce activities aimed at the postsecondary student market. The strategic question now facing U-Swap.com and Livingonline.ca is how to capitalize on the synergies of each firm and thereby promote growth for both sites independently and collectively. Some strategic planning ideas to consider are presented here.

Improve Product and Service Offerings

Online classifieds and auctions are quickly becoming the standard for buying and selling products or services at virtual community sites. U-Swap will offer users the option of auctioning their products providing significant added value for students selling items such as vehicles, sports equipment, and computer equipment, where bidding might bring higher prices and quicker sales of items.

Pursue More Partnerships

U-Swap can continue creating partnerships with key retailers that are particularly interested in reaching the student market such as consumer electronics vendor Future Shop and Ikea furniture outlets. Each partner could have a smart-banner that dynamically modifies according to users' search requests. U-Swap clients would benefit by having easy access to information on new articles identical to those being offered in the U-Swap classified databases. The company would benefit from these alliances through a negotiated shared percentage of sales generated through the site. Partnerships represent a mutually beneficial relationship for all parties and represent an important source of revenue growth and co-branding opportunities in the future.

Continue Implementing the Chapter Affiliate Program

U-Swap can continue the Chapter Affiliate Program (CAP) to help fuel strategic growth. U-Swap's organization can continue to be built around a local campus representatives or chapter affiliates at each school campus. These individuals are generally students or groups of students that work with the team of marketing coordinators at the corporate level of the firm. Chapter affiliates have exclusive rights to promote their campus site and share in the revenues generated from banner advertising and local sponsorship. This equity-based approach promotes motivation by local stakeholders. In contrast, campus representatives are paid an hourly wage and are responsible for implementing the marketing campaign activities at their campus, such as placing posters, distributing flyers, sending e-mails to clubs and associations, and so forth. Both parties provide valuable information to the corporate level regarding local market specifics such as competitors, vendors, and upcoming important events.

Students are advised to follow the "Tutorial for Preparing a Case Study Report," available on the textbook website, to help guide them through the recommended structure and steps necessary for preparing a report for this case.

Chapter 1

Note: This chapter was originally written in 2001 by the author, Brahm Canzer, for an introductory business textbook. The chapter was later edited by William M. Pride, Robert J. Hughes, and Jack R. Kapoor, retitled "Navigating the World of e-Business," and published in the Seventh Edition of their textbook, *Business,* Copyright © 2002 by Houghton Mifflin Company. It subsequently appeared in the Eighth Edition of *Business* as well, Copyright © 2005. Reprinted with permission.

1. Based on information from AOL online press releases. MSN Money website report on AOL, **http://moneycentral.msn.com/investor/home.asp**, September 21, 2003; David Wise, "AOL appeals to kids with new service," *The Gazette,* September 17, 2003, p. B1; Lisa Singhania, "AOL Time shakeup," *The Gazette,* January 14, 2003, p. B2; Jim Krane, "America Online clings to outmoded dial-up base," *The Gazette,* January 14, 2003, p. B2; "America Online and Time Warner Announce New Content & Promotional Agreements," February 16, 2000, and "AOL & Time Warner Will Merge to Create World's First Internet-Age Media & Communications Company," January 10, 2000; **http://media.web.aol.com/media/search.cfm**.

2. ClickZ Staff, "Population Explosion!" May 10, 2004, **http://www.clickz.com/stats/big_picture/geographics/article.php/5911_151151**.

3. For more information about e-business definitions, terminology, and strategies see IBM's website, **www.ibm.com/ebusiness**.

4. Forrester Research, Inc., online glossary; **www.forrester.com**.

5. Robyn Greenspan, "Autosales Drives Consumers to the Web," *CyberAtlas,* August 19, 2003, **http://cyberatlas.internet.com/big_picture/traffic_patterns/article/0,,5931_3065321,00.html3**.

6. Lyman, Peter, and Hal R. Varian, "How Much Information," 2003. Retrieved from **http://www.sims.berkeley.edu/research/projects/how-much-info-2003/** on June 8, 2004.

7. Michael Pastore, "Search Engines, Browsers Still Confusing Many Web Users," February 14, 2001, *CyberAtlas,* **http://cyberatlas.internet.com/big_picture/applications/article/0,,1301_588851,00.html**.

8. Stacy Perman, "Automate or Die," eCompany Now, July 2001, pp. 60–67.

9. "U.S. Q4 e-Commerce Sales at $5.3B," *USA Today online,* March 2, 2000; **www.usatoday.com/money/economy/econ0059.htm**.

10. *CyberAtlas* Staff, "Global Usage, August 2003," September 30, 2003, **http://cyberatlas.internet.com/big_picture/traffic_patterns/article/0,,5931_3084761,00.html**.

11. **http://cyberatlas.internet.com/big_picture/traffic_patterns/article/0,,5931_2237901,00.html**.

12. Michael Pastore, "Why the Offline Are Offline," *CyberAtlas,* July 14, 2001; **http://cyberatlas.internet.com/big_picture/demographics/article/0,,5901_784691,00.html#table**.

13. "Small Businesses Buy, but Shy to Sell, Online," May 17, 2000; **http://cyberatlas.internet.com/markets/professional/article/0,1323,5971_365281,00.htm**.

14. Robyn Greenspan, "Small Biz Benefits from Internet Tools," March 28, 2002; **http://cyberatlas.internet.com/markets/smallbiz/article/0,,10098_1000171,00.html**.

15. Lyman, Peter, and Hal R. Varian, "How Much Information," 2000. Retrieved from **http://www.sims.berkeley.edu/how-much-info** on October 31, 2003; "IP Communications—Get Ideas Now," Cisco Systems Inc. Retrieved from **http://www.cisco.com/offer/powernow/ca/tree.taf-asset_idkbk93067.htm?sid=123902_1** on November 2, 2003.

16. Special supplement in *Business Week,* February 28, 2000, p. 74.

17. Don Tapscott, "Online Parts Exchange Herald New Era," *Financial Post,* May 5, 2000, p. C7.

18. Spencer E. Ante, Amy Borrus, and Robert D. Hof, "In Search of the Net's Next Big Thing," *Business Week,* March 26, 2001, p. 141.

Chapter 2

1. Based on these sources of information: Frank Ahrens, "A Major Change in Their Tunes,"*Washington Post,* May 28, 2004, p. E01 and online at **http://www.washingtonpost.com/wp-dyn/articles/A61771-2004May27.html**; Holly M. Sanders, "Wal-Mart to offer music downloads," Bloomberg News in *The Montreal Gazette,* November 7, 2003, p. B1; Amy Braunschweiger, "Roxio's Napster to join chorus of digital music services,"*Financial Post,* September 10, 2003, p. IN1; Bernard Warner, "Virgin joins digital music gold rush," *Financial Post,* September 9, 2003, p. FP4; Tim Burt and Alison Beard, "Music majors try to bridge digital divide,"*Financial Post,* September 9, 2003, p. FP4; Peter Foster, "Music theft is not 'sharing,'" *Financial Post,* October 3, 2003, p. FP11; James Harding, "Desperate Napster to Charge Fees," *Financial Post,* February 21, 2001, p. A1; David Akin, "Peer to Peer Seen as the Next Big Wave," *Financial Post,* January 16, 2001, p. C7; James Harding, "Bertelsmann Sees Napster IPO in Future," *Financial Post,* November 6, 2000, p. C11; Paul Schiff Berman, "Danger or Opportunity? Internet's Impact on the Music Business Need Not Be What Some Fear," *Montreal Gazette,* September 18, 2000, p. B3; Spencer E. Ante, "Inside Napster," *Business Week,* August 14, 2000, pp. 113–121; David Akin, "Don't Shoot the MP3 Player," *Financial Post,* May 13, 2000, p. D11; Don Tapscott, "Napster Secured Page in Internet History," *Financial Post,* May 12, 2000, p. C9; Jon Healy, "Robin Williams Braces for Laughter, Tears, Applause, Heckles . . . by Email," *Financial Post,* April 20, 2000, p. C7; Sue Zeidler, "Napster Lands Deal with MusicNet," *Financial Post,* June 7, 2001, p. C3; Robert Thompson, "Music Industry Out of Tune on Digital Future," *Financial Post,* July 24, 2001, p. C3; **www.napster.com, www.mp3.com, www.liquidaudio.com, www.realaudio.com.**
2. Ibid.
3. Thomas L. Friedman, *Lexus and the Olive Tree: Understanding Globalization,* (New York: Farrar, Straus & Giroux, 2000); Christopher Caldwell, "The Lexus and the Olive Tree (Review)," *Commentary Magazine,* October 1999, located at **www.findarticles.com/cf_0/m1061/3_108/56744998/p1/article.jhtml?term5.**
4. Mark Evans, "A high-tech mecca fights to stay on top," *National Post,* October 20, 2003, p. FP1; Peter Brieger, "Cold calling, Bangalore Style," *National Post,* July 16, 2003, p. FP1 & FP9.
5. Ibid. *CyberAtlas* Staff, "More Than Half of U.S., Canada Online," May 2, 2003, **http://cyberatlas.internet.com/big_picture/geographics/article/0,,5911_2200601,00.html#table.**
6. Ibid.
7. Brian Caulfield, "HP defines merger," *National Post,* May 26, 2003. p. BE4.
8. Mark Evans, "Yahoo enjoys surge in second quarter," *National Post,* July 10, 2003, p. FP1 & FP7.
9. Brian Bremmer and Hiroko Tashiro, "Is Japan Back?" *BusinessWeek Online,* June 14, 2004, **http://www.businessweek.com/magazine/content/04_24/b3887002.htm.**
10. Photo Marketing Association International, "Photo Industry 2004: Review and Forecast," **http://www.pmai.org/**; Jason Chow, "Old-school Kodak hit by switch to digital cameras," *National Post,* July 24, 2003, p. FP1 & FP9; Photo Marketing Association International, "Photo Industry 2003: Review and Forecast," **http://www.pmai.org/.**
11. Peter Foster, "Music theft is not 'sharing,'" *Financial Post,* October 3, 2003, p. FP11.

Chapter 3

1. Based on information available from the Zero-Knowledge corporate website, accessed June 16, 2004, **www.zeroknowledge.com.**
2. Brian Krebs, "U.S. Internet Gambling Crackdown Sparks WTO Complaint," *Washington Post,* July 21, 2003, **http://www.washingtonpost.com/wp-dyn/articles/A24490-2003Jul21.html**; Roy Mark, "House Passes Internet Anti-Gambling Bill," *Internet News,* June 11, 2003, **http://dc.internet.com/news/article.php/2220141**; Michael J. Weiss, "Online America," *American Demographics,* March 2001; **www.americandemographics.com.**
3. Associated Press, "Bosses Say They Know Who's Surfing," *Montreal Gazette,* July 16, 2001, p. E2.
4. Techweb News Staff, "Security Pays Off As Cybercrime Costs Fall," Information Week, June 11, 2004, **http://www.informationweek.com/story/showArticle.jhtml?articleID=21700472**; Paul Lima, "Internet Fights the Fear Factor," *Financial Post,* August 20, 2001, p. E1.
5. *BBC News World Edition,* "Identity theft explodes in U.S.," July 21, 2003, **http://news.bbc.co.uk/2/hi/business/3085277.stm.**
6. Katherine Reynolds Lewis, "Internet Fraud Focus of Probe," *Financial Post,* June 27, 2001, p. C11.

7. TechWeb Staff, "User's, IT Disagree on Spam's Impact," *TechWeb,* June 16, 2004, **http://www.techweb.com/wire/story/TWB20040616S0006**; Robyn Greenspan, "Spam Threatens Revenue, Kids," *Internet News,* June 9, 2003, **http://www.internetnews.com/bus-news/article.php/2219211**.

8. Wojteck Dabrowski, "The Hidden Economic Cost of Spam,"*The National Post,* July 14, 2003, p. FP1.

9. Robyn Greenspan, "Spam Threatens Revenue, Kids," *Internet News,* June 9, 2003, **http://www.internetnews.com/bus-news/article.php/2219211**.

10. *Washington Post,* June 3, 2003, **http://www.washingtonpost.com/wp-dyn/articles/A6236-2003Jun3.html**.

11. "Online Music Sales Will Grow 520% to $6.2 Billion in 2006," Jupiter Media Metrix Press Release, New York, July 23, 2001; **www.jmm.com/xp/jmm/press/2001/pr_072301.xml**.

12. Susan Decker, "Spacey Fights for Web Domain," *Montreal Gazette,* May 7, 2001, p. A13.

13. Jeffrey Birnbaum, "The Taxman Cometh," *Business 2.0,* August 2000; **www.business2.com/articles/mag/0,1640,6846,FF.html**.

14. Amy Harmon, "Whose Net Is It?" *Montreal Gazette,* July 11, 2001, p. C2.

15. David Akin, "Noose Tightens on Right, Net Expert Warns," *Financial Post,* March 27, 2001, p. C9.

16. David Akin, "Ottawa Helps Open e-Commerce Door for Small Business," *Financial Post,* June 28, 2001, p. C9.

17. Nate Hendley, "Of Mice and Women," *Financial Post,* March 19, 2001, p. E8.

18. Austin Macdonald, "Out of Court, Online," *Financial Post,* June 4, 2001, p. E3.

Chapter 4

1. Based on these sources of information: Stephanie Olson, "Amazon gets into shopping search," *CNET News.com,* September 25, 2003, **http://news.com.com/2100-1024-5082594.html?tag=nl**; "Jeff Bezos," *Business Week,* September 29, 2003, i3851, p. 118; Monica Roman, "Caution at Amazon," *Business Week,* November 3, 2003, i3856, p. 44; Robert D. Hof, "Amazon.com. free e-commerce for merchants," *Business Week,* November 24, 2003, i3859, p. 104; Chip Bayers, "The Last Laugh," *Business 2.0,* September 2002, pp. 86–93.

2. Based on information from websites located at **www.amr.com**, **www.retailexchange.com**, and

www.overstock.com; Carol Pickering, "Web as Surplus e-Store," *Financial Post,* March 5, 2001, p. E1.

3. Based on information available at **www.etrade.com**.

4. Based on information available at **www.yahoo.com**.

5. Based on information available from various documentation posted on the IBM e-business website, located at **www.ibm.com/e-business**, as well as IBM Global Services article entitled "Fostering Customer Loyalty in the Electronic Marketplace."

6. Ken Mark, "Airline Supply Chain System Takes Flight," *Financial Post,* June 18, 2001, p. E11.

Chapter 5

1. Based on information available on the Home Depot website, accessed June 5, 2004; **www.homedepot.com**.

2. Based on mission statements available on websites located at **www.aoltimewarner.com/about/mission.html**, accessed January 1, 2002, and **www.corp.aol.com**, accessed January 15, 2004.

3. Damien McElroy, "AOL Time Warner Gains Hold in China," *Financial Post,* June 12, 2001, p. C14.

4. Burke Campbell and Murray Conron, "Race to Restructure," *Financial Post,* June 18, 2001, p. E1.

5. Michael E. Porter, "Strategy and the Internet," *Harvard Business Review,* March 2001, pp. 63–78.

6. Robyn Greenspan, "Moderate, Steady CRM Growth Through 2006," *CyberAtlas,* July 3, 2003, **http://cyberatlas.internet.com/big_picture/applications/article/0,,1301_2230361,00.html**.

Chapter 6

1. Based on information available from the Forrester Research Inc. website, **http://www.forrester.com/**, accessed on January 16, 2004; Forrester Research Inc. investor information site, **http://www.forrester.com/ER/Investor/PR/0,1309,431,00.html**; and Forrester Research Inc. press release site, **http://www.forrester.com/ER/Press/Release/0,1769,684,00.html**; and Tony Schwartz, "If You Work 20 Hours a Day, Your Product Will Be Crap," *Fast Company,* December 2000, p. 324, **http://www.fastcompany.com/online/41/tschwartz.html**.

2. Jeanine Lee Siew Ming, "High-Flying Aptitude," *Montreal Gazette,* June 18, 2001, p. F1.

3. "Kodak Gets into Digital Films," *Financial Post,* March 5, 2002, p. FP9.

4. Based on information from Andrew Bartels, "ISM/Forrester Report on Technology in Supply Management: Q3 2003," October 27, 2003, **http://www.forrester.com/ER/Research/Brief/ 0,1317,33008,FF.html**; "NAPM/Forrester Research Announce Results of First Report on eBusiness," press release, January 22, 2001; **http://www.forrester.com/ ER/Press/Release/0,1769,479,FF.html**.

5. Robyn Greenspan, "Net No Threat to Newspapers," *CyberAtlas*, January 16, 2004, **http://cyberatlas. internet.com/big_picture/traffic_patterns/article/ 0,,5931_3300281,00.html**; "Internet Exceeds All Other Media in Growth of Heavy User Groups; Surpass Newspapers," news release from The Media Audit, January 13, 2004, **http://www.themediaaudit.com/ markets.htm**.

Chapter 7

1. Based on information available on the ComScore Media Metrix Inc. website **www.comscore.com**; press release, "comScore Media Metrix Announces Top 50 U.S. Internet Property Rankings for December 2003," ComScore Media Metrix, January 14, 2004, **http://www.comscore.com/press/ release.asp?press=402**; press release, "Online Consumers Spent $18.5 Billion During 2003 Holiday Season, According to the Goldman Sachs, Harris Interactive and Nielsen/NetRatings Holiday eSpending Report," Nielsen/NetRatings, January 5, 2004 **http://www.nielsen-netratings.com/pr/ pr_040105_us.pdf**; press release, "Weekly Online Retail Sales Break Through $2 Billion Mark, comScore Reports," ComScore Media Metrix, December 18, 2003 **http://www.comscore.com/ press/release.asp?press=388**.

2. "Online Polls Are a Cheap and Easy Way to Be Interactive," *Financial Post*, June 12, 2001, p. C8.

3. Michael J. Mandel and Robert D. Hof, with Linda Himelstein, Dean Foust, and Joann Muller, "Rethinking the Internet," *Business Week*, March 26, 2001, p. 127.

4. Martin Stone, "Survey Shows College Student Shopping Habits," *Newsbytes*, March 6, 2001; **http://www.newsbytes.com/news/01/162742.html**; Kevin Featherly, "Note to Marketers: Teens Use Web to Buy Offline—Jupiter," *Newsbytes*, September 13, 2000; **http://www.newsbytes.com/ news/00/155147.html**.

5. "How the Internet Has Changed Our Lives," Nielsen/NetRatings press release, December 29, 2003, **http://www.nielsen-netratings.com/pr/ pr_031229_uk.pdf**.

6. I. M. Rosenstock, "The Health Belief Model: Explaining Health Behaviour Through Expectancies," in *Health Behaviour and Health Education: Theory, Research, and Practice*, ed. K. Glanz, F. M. Lewis, and B. K. Rimer (San Francisco: Jossey-Bass, 1990); W. B. Carter, "Health Behaviour as a Rational Process: Theory of Reasoned Action and Multiattribute Utility Theory," in *Health Behaviour and Health Education: Theory, Research, and Practice*, ed. K. Glanz, F. M. Lewis, and B. K. Rimer (San Francisco: Jossey-Bass, 1990).

7. I. Ajzen and M. Fishbein, *Understanding Attitudes and Predicting Behaviour* (Englewood Cliffs, NJ: Prentice-Hall, 1980); I. Ajzen and T. J. Madden, "Prediction of Goal-Directed Behaviour: Attitudes, Intentions and Perceived Behavioral Control," *Journal of Experimental Social Psychology* 22 (1986): 453–474.

8. J. Kuhl, "A Theory of Self Regulation: Action vs. State Orientation, Self-discrimination and Some Application," *Applied Psychology: An International Review* 41, no. 2 (1992): 97–129; J. Kuhl, "Volitional Mediators of Cognition-Behaviour Consistency: Self-Regulatory Processes and Action Versus State Orientation," in *Action Control: From Cognition to Behaviour*, ed. J. Kuhl and J. Beckmann (New York: Springer-Verlag, 1985); J. Kuhl and J. Beckmann, "Historical Perspectives in the Study of Action Control," in *Action Control: From Cognition to Behaviour*, ed. J. Kuhl and J. Beckmann (New York: Springer-Verlag, 1985).

9. D. O. Sears, L. Peplau, and S. Taylor, *Social Psychology*, 7th ed. (Englewood Cliffs, NJ: Prentice-Hall, 1991).

10. R. P. Abelson, "Script Processing in Attitude Formation and Decision Making," in *Cognition and Social Behaviour*, ed. J. S. Caroll and J. W. Payne (Hillsdale, NJ: Erlbaum, 1976).

11. L. Festinger, *A Theory of Cognitive Dissonance* (Stanford, CA: Stanford University Press, 1957).

12. D. J. Bem, "Self-Perception: An Alternative Interpretation of Cognitive Dissonance Phenomena," *Psychological Review* 74 (1967): 183–200.

13. M. W. Eysenck, *A Handbook of Cognitive Psychology* (London: Lawrence Erlbaum Associates, 1984).

14. I. Ajzen, "From Intentions to Actions: A Theory of Planned Action," in *Action Control: From Cognition to Behaviour,* ed. J. Kuhl and J. Beckman (New York: Springer-Verlag, 1985).

15. Kuhl and Beckmann, "Historical Perspectives in the Study of Action Control."

16. Kuhl, "Volitional Mediators of Cognition-Behaviour Consistency."

17. Kuhl, "A Theory of Self-Regulation."

18. Kuhl, "Volitional Mediators of Cognition-Behaviour Consistency."

Chapter 8

1. Based on information available at the Office Depot Inc. website; **www.officedepot.com**.

2. Ron Miller, "Broadband Poised for Takeoff," *CyberAtlas,* January 30, 2004, **http://cyberatlas. internet.com/markets/broadband/article/0,,10099_3306361,00.html**.

3. Anne Marie Owens, "Mad About Harry," *National Post,* July 10, 2000, p. D1.

4. Caroline Humer, "Dell plans big consumer electronics push," *National Post,* September 26, 2003, p. FP4.

5. "Forrester Research Segments B2B Technology Behavior in the Launch of Business Technographics," press release, January 9, 2001; **http://www.forrester.com/ER/Press/Release/0,1769,474,00.html**.

6. Duff McDonald, "A website as big (and cheap) as the Great Outdoors," *Financial Post,* September 29, 2003, p. FE6.

7. Laura Rush, "E-Commerce Growth Spurred by Maturation," *CyberAtlas,* January 23, 2004, **http://cyberatlas.internet.com/markets/retailing/article/0,,6061_3303311,00.html**.

8. "Active Internet Users by Country, December 2003," *CyberAtlas,* January 29, 2004, **http://cyberatlas. internet.com/big_picture/geographics/article/0,,5911_3305941,00.html**; Jim Wagner, "China's Internet Use Surges," *CyberAtlas,* January 16, 2004, **http://cyberatlas.internet.com/big_picture/geographics/article/0,,5911_3300411,00.html**; Robyn Greenspan, "Western European E-Com to Reach Nearly €100B," *CyberAtlas,* December 5, 2003, **http://cyberatlas.internet.com/markets/retailing/article/0,1323,6061_3285861,00.html**; "E-Commerce Numbers Add Up in December," *CyberAtlas,* December 17,
2001; **http://cyberatlas.internet.com/markets/retailing/article/0,,6061_941461,00.html#table**.

9. Donna Fuscaldo, "Outsiders are biggest bulls on SanDisk," *Financial Post,* September 17, 2003, p. IN3; Photo Marketing Association International, "Photo Industry 2003: Review and Forecast," **http://www.pmai.org/**; Eric Hellweg, "A Photo Finish for Digital Imaging," June 26, 2001; **http://www.business2.cSom/articles/ web/0,1653,41720,00.html**.

10. Julie Landry, "Ford's Internet Efforts Encounter Roadblocks," December 14, 1999; **http://www.redherring.com/insider/1999/1214/news-ford.html**.

11. Jane Weaver, "More people search for health online," MSNBC, July 16, 2003, **http://www.msnbc.com/news/939723.asp**; Michael J. Weiss, "Online America," *American Demographics,* March 2001, located online at **www.americandemographics.com/**.

12. Peter Burrows, "Technology on Tap," *Business Week,* June 19, 2000, p. 80.

13. "Online Banking Continues to Disappoint," *CyberAtlas,* September 10, 2001; **http://cyberatlas.internet.com/markets/finance/article/0,,5961_881271,00.html**.

14. Jay Greene, "The Man Behind All Those E-Ads," *Business Week,* June 26, 2000, p. 76.

15. Based on information provided by Pat and Michael Libling and the PatsyPie (**www.PatsyPie.com**) website.

16. Ron Miller, "PC Sales Expected to Soar in 2004," *CyberAtlas,* February 13, 2004, **http://cyberatlas.internet.com/big_picture/hardware/article/0,,5921_3312731,00.html**.

17. Colleen Valles, "Computer-Makers Are Slow to Embrace Recycling Plans," *Montreal Gazette,* May 23, 2001, p. D3.

18. Patricia Seybold, with Roni T. Marshak and Jeffrey M. Lewis, *The Customer Revolution: How to Thrive When Customers Are in Control,* (New York: Crown Business, 2001).

19. Robyn Greenspan, "Internet High on Travel Destinations," January 28, 2004, *CyberAtlas,* **http://cyberatlas.internet.com/markets/travel/article/0,,6071_3304691,00.html**; David Provost, "Up, Up, and Away," *Business 2.0,* June 1, 2000; **http://www.business2.com/content/magazine/numbers/2000/06/01/10982**.

20. Robyn Greenspan, "E-tailers Will See Green," *Clickz Network,* November 6, 2003, **http://www.clickz.com/stats/markets/retailing/article.php/6061_3105491**.

21. Laura Rush, "E-Commerce Growth Spurred by Maturation," *CyberAtlas*, January 23, 2004, **http://cyberatlas.internet.com/markets/retailing/article/0,,6061_3303311,00.html**; Burrows, "Technology on Tap"; Michael Pastore, "U.S. E-Commerce Spikes in Q4 2001," *CyberAtlas*, February 20, 2002; **http://cyberatlas.internet.com/markets/retailing/article/0,,6061_977751,00.html#table**.

22. Andy Riga, "The Global E-library," *Montreal Gazette*, June 20, 2001, p. D1.

23. Donalee Moulton, "e-Tailer Hits the Bricks," *Financial Post*, June 18, 2001, p. E4.

24. Michael J. Mandel and Robert D. Hof, with Linda Himelstein, Dean Foust, and Joann Muller, "Rethinking the Internet," *Business Week*, March 26, 2001, p. 120.

25. Zhenya Gene Senyak, "Talk Shops," *Business 2.0*, June 1, 2000; **http://www.business2.com/content/magazine/marketing/2000/06/01/12980**.

26. Will Novosedlik, "Teaming Up for the Wallets of Tech-Savvy Consumers," *Financial Post*, March 22, 2001, p. C9.

27. Kay Parker, "Old-Line Goes Online," *Business 2.0*, June 1, 2000; **http://www.business2.com/content/magazine/marketing/2000/06/01/12979**.

28. Susan Heinrich, "It Finally Clicks: Web Ads Can Work," *Financial Post*, July 9, 2001, p. C4.

29. Brahm Eiley, "Online Ads Far from Dead," *Financial Post*, June 7, 2001, p. C15.

30. Mandel et al., "Rethinking the Internet."

31. Susan Kuchinskas, "Fair Gamers," *Business 2.0*, June 1, 2000; **http://www.business2.com/content/magazine/marketing/2000/06/01/12914**.

32. Diana Janssen, "Online Advertising Picks Up Again," Forrester Research Report press release, May 2002; **http://www.forrester.com/ER/Research/Report/Summary/0,1338,14576,FF.html**.

33. Janis Mara, "Display Ads Back from the Dead," *CyberAtlas*, December 31, 2003, **http://cyberatlas.internet.com/markets/advertising/article/0,,5941_3293451,00.html**; John Gaffney, "The Online Advertising Comeback," *Business 2.0*, June 2002, pp. 118–120.

34. Andy Riga, "Internet Firms Finding New Marketing Tools," *Montreal Gazette*, May 30, 2001, p. D1.

35. Based on data provided online at **http://adres.internet.com/adrates/article/0,1401,,00.html**.

36. Kevin Hogan, "Not the Agents of Change," *Business 2.0*, June 1, 2000; **http://www.business2.com/content/magazine/indepth/2000/06/01/11008**.

37. Robyn Greenspan, "The Deadly Duo: Spam and Viruses," *Clickz Network*, February 4, 2004, **http://**

www.clickz.com/stats/big_picture/applications/article.php/3308091; Janis Mara, "Costs of Blocking Legit E-Mail To Soar," *Clickz Network*, January 28, 2004, **http://www.clickz.com/stats/markets/advertising/article.php/5941_3305011**; Jean Eaglesham, "Junk E-mail Remedy Worries Marketers," *National Post*, April 16, 2001, p. E6.

Chapter 9

1. Based on information from the Google.com website **www.google.com**, accessed January 25, 2004; Andy Riga, "The Search Engine That Could," *Montreal Gazette*, July 4, 2001, p. F1; Michael Porter, "Strategy and the Internet," *Harvard Business Review*, March 2001, pp. 63–78.

2. Based on data available on the MonsterWorldWide website (**www.monsterworldwide.com**), accessed on February 27, 2004; Michael J. Mandel and Robert D. Hof, with Linda Himelstein, Dean Foust, and Joann Muller, "Rethinking the Internet," *Business Week*, March 26, 2001, p. 132.

3. Peter Burrows, "The Second Coming of Software," *Business Week*, June 19, 2000, p. 88.

4. Andy Riga, "Canadians Taking the E-banking Plunge," *Montreal Gazette*, May 23, 2001, p. D1.

5. Mandel et al., "Rethinking the Internet," p. 120.

6. Werner Antweiller, "The Power of e-Business," *Financial Post*, July 2, 2002, p. FP11.

7. Zhenya Gene Senyak, "Talk Shops," *Business 2.0*, June 1, 2000; **www.business2.com/content/magazine/marketing/2000/06/01/12980**.

8. David Morgan, "Tech Boom Still Driving the Economy," *Financial Post*, July 12, 2000, p. C11.

9. "Context: Extraneous Email Reported," *eCompany Now*, July 2001, p. 42.

10. Peter Burrows, "Technology on Tap," *Business Week*, June 19, 2000, p. 82.

11. Steve Bennett, "Wings and a Prayer," *Business 2.0*, June 1, 2000; **http://www.business2.com/content/magazine/indepth/2000/06/01/13040**.

12. Based on press releases at **www.yahoo.com**; "Rogers Cable and Yahoo! Announce Alliance to Deliver Innovative Co-branded High-speed Internet Service," January 20, 2004, **http://docs.yahoo.com/docs/pr/release1141.html**; "Philips and Yahoo! Enter Global Partnering Deal to Move Internet Content Beyond the PC and into Consumers' Living Rooms," January 7, 2004, **http://docs.yahoo.com/docs/pr/release1138.html**; "Yahoo! and Sina Announce Auctions Joint Venture," January 13, 2004, **http://docs.yahoo.com/docs/pr/release1139.html**.

13. Arthur Ciancutti and Thomas Steding, "Trust Fund," *Business 2.0*, June 1, 2000; **http://www.business2.com/content/magazine/ebusiness/2000/06/01/12910**.

14. Based on information at Oracle Corporation's corporate information website; **http://www.oracle.com/corporate/**.

15. Shawn Tully, "The Party's Over," *Fortune*, June 26, 2000, p. 156.

16. Kyle Foster, "Gates Still Richest Man," *Montreal Gazette*, June 22, 2001, p. D1.

17. Rod McQueen, "If It Makes You Feel Better, Call Nortel Deal a 'Recall,'" *Financial Post*, June 6, 2001, p. C9.

18. Michael Petrou, "Striking a Nerve," *Financial Post*, July 8, 2000, p. D7.

19. Sheila McGovern, "Forget E-mail; Let's Do Lunch," *Montreal Gazette*, March 19, 2001, p. F1.

20. Nate Hendley, "A Shrink's Couch on Your Desk: Online Counselling," *Financial Post*, March 5, 2001, p. E4.

21. James Underwood, "Should You Watch Them on the Web," *CIO*, May 15, 2000; **http://www.cio.com/archive/051500_face.html**.

22. Ilan Greenberg, "The PC Crowd," *Red Herring*, May 18, 2000; **http://www.redherring.com/mag/issue51/rd.html**.

23. Press Release, "ACNielsen AND Yahoo! Introduce Measurable Online Marketing Service for Consumer Packaged Goods Industry," July 21, 2003, **http://docs.yahoo.com/docs/pr/release1126.html**.

24. Michael Schrage, "You're Nuts If You're Not Certifiable," *Fortune*, June 26, 2000, p. 338.

25. "Plus a Change: Job Boards Search for Work," *Business 2.0*, June 1, 2001; **http://www.business2.com/content/magazine/filter/2000/06/01/12973**.

26. Petrou, "Striking a Nerve."

27. Michelle Conlin and Kathy Moore, "Dr. Goodnight's Company Town," *Business Week*, June 19, 2000, p. 192.

28. Morgan, "Tech Boom Still Driving the Economy."

29. Sandra Dillich, "Training or Learning," *Computing Canada*, June 23, 2000, p. 25.

30. Alison Diana, "Online Learning and the ROI of Training High-Tech Wizards," *Tech News World*, December 8, 2003, **http://www.technewsworld.com/perl/story/32325.html**; Susan Stellin, "Online Courses Effective, Cheaper," *Financial Post*, May 11, 2001, p. C2.

31. Sandra Mingail, "Sift Gold from the Software Pile: How to Choose a Package," *Financial Post*, March 5, 2001, p. E4.

32. Robyn Greenspan, "Small Biz Benefits from Internet Tools," March 28, 2002; (**http://cyberatlas.internet.com/markets/smallbiz/article/0,,10098_1000171,00.htm**).

33. Alan Joch, "E-Business Without the E-Cost," *Fortune's Small Business Online Magazine*, July 16, 1999; **http://www.fsb.com/fortunesb/articles/0,2227,320,00.html**.

34. Carlye Adler et al., "The FSB 25," *Fortune's Small Business Online Magazine*, February 8, 2000; **http://fortunesb.com/articles/0,2227,565,00.html**.

35. Kim Hanson, "Angels May Be a Startup's Best Bet in Tough Times," *Financial Post*, March 22, 2001, p. C9.

36. Tyler Maroney, "An Air Battle Comes to the Web," *Fortune*, June 26, 2000, p. 315.

37. ASTA Press Release, "2003 Ends on Brighter Note for Travel Agents," American Society of Travel Agents website, December 23, 2003, **www.astanet.com**.

38. Based on information available on the firm's website, **www.accenture.com**.

Chapter 10

1. Andrew Wahl, "Nortel's next big thing," *Canadian Business*, February 2, 2004, **http://www.canadianbusiness.com/features/article.jsp;jsessionid=BFPIEHOHKMDB?content=20040202_58359_58359**; Wayne Lilley, "Widowed and Orphaned," *National Post Business*, July 2001, pp. 55–60; "FP500 Canada's Largest Corporations: And the Winner Is. . .," *National Post Business*, June 2001, p. 96; Donald MacDonald, "Nortel Investors in Nightmare," *Montreal Gazette*, June 16, 2001, p. C1; Mary Lamey, "We Overpaid for Firm: Nortel," *Montreal Gazette*, June 16, 2001, p. C1; information available on the Nortel website, **www.nortelnetworks.com**.

2. David Akin, "Amazon.com Plummets on Talk of Cash Crunch," *Financial Post*, June 24, 2000, pp. C1, C2.

3. Susanne Koudsi, "Why Is This Sock Puppet Still Smiling?" *Fortune*, June 26, 2000, p. 54.

4. Larry MacDonald, "Time for Tech Bonds," *Montreal Gazette*, June 13, 2001, p. D3.

5. Michael J. Mandel et al., "Rethinking the Internet," *Business Week*, March 26, 2001, p. 120.

6. Kim Girard and Sean Donahue, "Crash and Learn: A Field Manual for Ebusiness Survival," *Business 2.0*, June 11, 2000; **http://www.business2.com/content/magazine/indepth/2000/06/28/13700**.

7. Brenon Daly, "Venture Forth," *Business 2.0,* June 1, 2000; **http://www.business2.com/content/magazine/ investing/2000/06/01/12932**.

8. Staff writers, "Numbers: A Bright Future for Technology Startups," *Business 2.0,* June 2002, pp. 32–33.

9. Rod McQueen, "If It Makes You Feel Better, Call Nortel Deal a 'Recall,'" *Financial Post,* June 6, 2001, p. C9.

10. Steve Maich, "Tech Profits Overstated," *Financial Post,* June 20, 2001, p. D1.

11. Based on "Lucent Technologies Acquires Herrmann Technology, a Leading Supplier of Optical Devices for Next-Generation DWDM Networks," Lucent Technologies press release, June 19, 2000; **http:// www.lucent.com/press/0600/000619.coa.html**.

12. Based on eBay information available at **www.ebay.com**, accessed March 1, 2004; 2002 Annual Report, **http://investor.ebay.com/annual.cfm**; **http://investor.ebay.com/faq.cfm**.

13. Paul Kedrosky, "The Meaning of Cheap," *Financial Post,* March 17, 2001, p. D11.

14. NASDAQ website statistics; **www.nasdaqnews.com**.

15. Robert Farzad, "Ebay's Price Leaves No Room for Error," *Financial Post,* June 28, 2001, p. D3.

16. Based on estimates calculated by Zacks Investment Research and presented on MSN.com. July 5, 2002.

17. Jim Griffin, "Rethinking Internet Valuation," *Business 2.0,* June 1, 2000; **http://www.business2.com/ content/magazine/vision/2000/06/01/10989**.

18. Bethany McLean, "Hocus-Pocus: How IBM Grew 27% a Year," *Fortune,* June 26, 2000, pp. 165–168.

19. Bloomberg News, "IBM offers lower financing to boost sales," *National Post,* July 25, 2003, p. FP3.

20. Andy Riga, "Lowdown a Shock: Roth, Nortel Chief Takes Heat from Investors at Annual Meeting," *Montreal Gazette,* April 27, 2001, pp. C1, C3.

21. Greg Wiles, "Ebay Motors stall; sell rating helps knock stock down 2.4%," Bloomberg News, in *Montreal Gazette,* October 14, 2003, p. B5.

22. Hugh Anderson, "Research Credibility Hits Bottom," *Financial Post,* February 21, 2001, p. D4.

Chapter 11

1. Based on information provided by Rozel Gonzales and presented on the websites referred to in the text.

2. Shane Shick, "Why CRM Projects Fail," *eBusiness Journal,* October 2001, p. 16.

3. Michael MacMillan, "Enterprise Computing— Hidden Problems," *Computing Canada,* June 15, 2001, p. 21.

4. Based on information provided by Rozel Gonzales and presented on the FitMoves.com website as well as on the other websites referred to in the text.

5. Thomas Watson, "Automakers Hit Back in Online Battle," *Financial Post,* June 25, 2001, p. C3.

6. Based on "PeopleSoft eCenter Measures Up to the Test of ROI," PeopleSoft article, November 2001; **http://www.peoplesoft.com/corp/en/ent_strat/ articles/ecenter_roi.asp**.

7. Geoffrey Downey, "CRM: What's It Worth?" *eBusiness Journal,* July 2001, pp. 14–15.

8. R. S. Kaplan and D. P. Norton, "The Balanced Scorecard—Measures That Drive Performance," *Harvard Business Review,* January–February 1992, pp. 71–79.

9. Jeffrey H. Birnbaum, "Death to Bureaucrats, Good News for the Rest of Us," *Fortune,* June 26, 2000, pp. 241–242.

10. Based on information provided by Rozel Gonzales and presented on the FitMoves.com website.

11. J. William Gurley, "The Most Powerful Internet Metric of All," *CNET News.com,* February 21, 2000; **http://news.cnet.com/news/0-1270-210-3287257-1 .html**.

12. Michael Pastore, "Consumers Turn Backs on Bells and Whistles," *CyberAtlas,* September 11, 2001; available online at **www.cyberatlas.intern et.com/big_picture/applications/article/0,,1301_ 881121,00.html**.

glossary/index

*Key terms, which appear in **boldface**, are followed by their definitions.*

Acquisition A larger firm buying a smaller operation and taking it into its organizational structure, 124

Action control theory, 197–200

Advanced Research Projects Agency (ARPA) An agency of the U.S. Department of Defense that was responsible for the forerunner of the Internet, **Webpage 4**

Advantages and disadvantages of e-business practices, 10

Advertising Any paid nonpersonal communication that is distributed to a target market through a medium such as television, radio, newspapers, journals, or, of course, the Internet, **237**

Advertising e-business model An e-business model based on earning revenues in exchange for the display of advertisements on a firm's website, **24, 97**

Affiliation e-business model An e-business model that involves payments to website operators for customers who find their way to a company's site and either buy merchandise or services or perform some other action, such as registering and providing certain information, **25, 99**

Agent Software code that will automatically seek out information on the Internet, **77**

Analog signal The type of signal that is used on conventional twisted-pair telephone wires, **Webpage 12**

Analysis The study and evaluation of both external and internal factors to the firm that are considered important environmental forces acting upon customers, current

strategies, and new plans still under development, **121**

Application service providers (ASPs) Firms that sell software access over the Internet to customers for a monthly fee rather than for a one-time purchase price, **Webpage 20**

ARPAnet The forerunner of today's Internet, **Webpage 4**

Backbones The mainline telecommunications channels of the Internet, built with high-capacity fiber-optic cables that move data at the speed of light, **Webpage 10**

Balance sheets Financial statements that list assets, liabilities, and the owner's equity in the firm as of a specific date, **277, 280**

Balanced scorecard An approach to strategic control that calls for also recognizing the contributions to building a competitive advantage in the marketplace that are made by improved efficiency, quality, innovation, and responsiveness to customers, **308**

Bandwidth The capacity of Internet lines to carry data, **Webpage 11**

Benchmarking A firm's comparing itself to performance standards established by other firms inside or outside of its industry, 134

Bits The individual digits (either 0 or 1) in a string of digital code, **Webpage 5**

Broadband service A term referring collectively to higher-speed cable television and telephone connections, **Webpage 13**

Brokerage e-business model An e-business model that covers online

marketplaces in which buyers and sellers are brought together in an organized environment to facilitate the exchange of goods, **23, 94**–96

Budgets Financial statements that detail the planned expenditures and revenues for some stated period of time, **277**

Business model A group of shared or common characteristics, behaviors, and methods of doing business in order to generate profits by increasing revenues and reducing costs, **20, 92**

Business plan A document containing detailed descriptions of the fundamental structure of the firm and the activities within it, including sources of revenue, the identity of target customers, pricing, promotion, and other strategies, **27**

Business-to-business (B2B) model A business model in which firms use the Internet mainly to conduct business with other businesses, **20**

Business-to-consumer (B2C) model A business model in which firms use the Internet mainly to conduct business with consumers, **22**

Buying processes, consumer and organizational, 182–186

Cash flow statements Financial statements that show the flow of money into and out of the firm, **277**, 281

Causal research Research that attempts to determine whether there is a causal relationship between two variable items, **158**

CERN and Tim Berners-Lee, Webpages 8–9

Channels of distribution, 233–236

339

network of communication devices such as desktop and laptop computers, interactive television, and wireless telephones that use the Internet, **180**

Membership e-business model An e-business model in which access to a site is controlled by membership fees, **24, 98**

Merger The combining of two more or less equal firms into a new firm, **124**

Metrics Measurements used to gauge performance and evaluate how well the firm is achieving its set objectives as defined in the e-business plan, **307**

Mission statement A basic description detailing the fundamental purpose for the organization's existence, **121**

Mode The group or class of data with the most entries, **159**

Model A representation of an actual device, **92**

Moore's Law, Webpage 13

Mosaic One of the first Internet browsers; it was distributed to the public without charge, **Webpage 9**

Motivation In a business environment, the drive that individuals feel to perform their assigned tasks, **258,** 258–260

Multidomestic strategy A strategy that recognizes the need to customize the firm's operations to reflect selected local conditions, **139**

Niche market A market that is smaller in size and more specialized in character than a mass market, **213**

Nodes Connecting points of Internet backbones, **Webpage 11**

Noise Any disturbance in the environment that prevents the receiver from fully receiving the intended message, **181**

Online behavior, moment-to-moment, 190–200

Online communication process A sequence of steps that successfully transfers multimedia content and information from one person to another through the Internet, **177**

Online communities Groups of individuals or firms with a shared interest who generally use a website to exchange information, products, or services over the Internet, 28

Online learning systems, 263–265

Online sellers and content providers, 14–15

Open standards A term used to refer to the fact that a protocol or other coded information is not owned by any individual organization, whereas proprietary standards refers to those that are, **Webpage 7**

Operating- (functional-) level planning Planning that occurs within specific departments of the organization, **122**, 127–128

Operations management The process of coordinating all the activities related to the production of the products and services that the organization provides to its customers, **253**

Organizational markets Markets composed of businesses, governments, the military, nonprofit groups, and any other group where purchasing is done by an individual or a committee on behalf of the entire organization, **211**

Organizational structures, 251–253

Organizing The grouping of activities and the marshaling of the necessary resources (material, human, financial, and informational) in order to achieve specific goals and objectives, **251**

Packet switching A technology for sending data on the Internet in which messages are broken into packets or parts and reassembled into the correct order at the destination point, **Webpage 5**

Partnership An arrangement that is viewed as a more permanent and longer-term commitment between firms than a strategic alliance, **123**

Pay-per-view e-business model An e-business model in which access to a site is controlled by a charge to view single items, **24, 98**

Peer-to-peer (P2P) software Software that allows individuals to exchange data directly with one another over the Internet without the use of an intermediary central computer, 23

Perceptual map A grid that illustrates the relative position of competing products as perceived by customers, **230**

Performance measurement and evaluation, 306–310

Performance objectives The targeted results of activity, to be achieved through implementation of the e-business plan, **306**

Performance standards More specific points than performance objectives, that might be set by the firm or by the industry of which it is a part, **306**

Personal digital assistants (PDAs) Small electronic communication devices, such as Palm Pilots, cell phones, notebook-sized computers, e-book readers, and personal organizers, that generally take advantage of Internet technology, **Webpage 15**

Personal factors Those general characteristics that are closely associated with the individual buyer; they can be categorized as demographic, lifestyle, and situational, **187**

Personal selling Paid communication that relies on personal contact with an individual representing the firm to convey information and persuade customers, **239**

PERT diagram, 303

Place (distribution) strategies Strategies concerned with making the product or service available when and where customers want it, **233**

Planning Organizing and detailing all of the strategies that will be undertaken throughout the firm and their expected or targeted objectives and results, **122, 251**

Point of presence (POP) The name of a special switch that connects smaller-scale users, such as individuals and small businesses, to their ISP using a dial-up modem, ISDN, and DSL telephone lines, **Webpage 11**

Political and legal forces, 53–54